ISBN 978-1-332-75810-4
PIBN 10433123

# 1 MONTH OF
# FREE
# READING

## at
## www.ForgottenBooks.com

By purchasing this book you are eligible for one month membership to ForgottenBooks.com, giving you unlimited access to our entire collection of over 700,000 titles via our web site and mobile apps.

To claim your free month visit:
www.forgottenbooks.com/free433123

AN

# ELEMENTARY GRAMMAR

OF THE

# GERMAN LANGUAGE

COMBINED WITH

EXERCISES, READINGS AND CONVERSATIONS

BY

## Dr. EMIL OTTO

*Late Professor of Modern Languages and Lecturer
at the University of Heidelberg*

*WITH A VOCABULARY*

BY

GEORGE MORITZ WAHL

NEW YORK

## HENRY HOLT AND COMPANY

F. W. CHRISTERN

BOSTON: CARL SCHOENHOF

Henry Holt & Co having regularly volunteered
honorarium for their American adaptations of
works, their publication of them has my full
sanction.

Heidelberg March 17th 1876.

D. Emil Otto.

# NOTE TO THE AMERICAN EDITION.

Having used in my classes the Fourth German Edition of Otto's Elementary German Grammar, I have felt the lack of a general vocabulary and of an alphabetic list of the irregular verbs. Moreover, the body of the work has needed some corrections of slight oversights. I have therefore succeeded in inducing DR. OTTO's American publishers to issue an edition with corrections of such oversights as I have detected in using it, and the addition of the apparatus of which I felt the lack.

GEORGE MORITZ WAHL, M. A. .

SOUTH BRAINTREE, MASS.,
*June,* 1890.

# AUTHOR'S PREFACE.

An experience of many years has convinced me that in teaching younger pupils German, better success is obtained by choosing at first the most important parts of each lesson in my *German Grammar*, and by taking at a later stage in the pupil's progress those parts which were previously omitted, together with a repetition of what has already been learned.

It being a somewhat difficult matter for even the most competent teacher to select exactly those parts which should first claim the learner's attention, it appeared to me much better to arrange them separately in a smaller book, and this gave rise to the idea of publishing this *Elementary German Grammar.* As a mastery of the German Grammar requires in the ordinary school-course at least two or more years, this smaller Grammar may be profitably placed in the hands of *beginners* for the first year, and the larger Grammar should follow in a later or higher class.

In this *"Elementary Grammar"* exactly the same method is followed as in the larger one, and it combines in the same manner the grammatical rules with their constant application to *writing* and *speaking German*.

The book is likewise divided into *"Lessons,"* each of which contains a part of the Grammar concisely stating its leading principles, a Reading Exercise, an Exercise for translating into German, an easy Conversation re-embodying the matter introduced in the previous exercises, and occasionly an easy little Reading-lesson. From its nature, however, it comprises only the *Etymology*, the *Syntax* being reserved for the larger Grammar. Special attention is also devoted to the chapter on *Pronunciation*, which should be mastered above all in learning a foreign language.

In respect to the mode of employing this Grammar, the author begs that he may be allowed to offer teachers and pupils a few suggestions. The rules with their examples and "Words" should be first learned by heart, and the German "Reading Exercise" read and translated into English. This done, the "*Conversation*" should be read, then the Exercise for *translation* (Aufgabe) put into German, and when corrected, written out fairly and studied over again. Finally, the "*Conversation*" should be repeated and committed to memory. The pupil may commence learning the easy conversational expressions on pages 240, etc., as soon as the teacher considers him sufficiently advanced.

The advantage of *conversational* exercises is evident. Whoever has occupied himself with the study of modern languages, is aware that by far the most difficult thing is to comprehend the foreign idiom. Accustomed from the very beginning to understand the easy questions the teacher addresses to him in German, and to answer in the same language on easy subjects already known to him from the foregoing Reading Exercise and translation, the learner exercises equally his *ear* and *tongue,* and will in a short time be enabled to express his thoughts fluently and correctly in the foreign language.

As to the method of presenting the etymological part of the Grammar in small *fragments,* so frequently adopted in elementary books, I cannot approve of it, as a long experience in teaching modern languages has taught me that a *correct* and *systematic* knowledge of German cannot be acquired by that method, but only by a grammatical system, which must, of course, be gradual and based on the pupil's intellectual development, and supported by practical exercises as will be found in this "*Elementary Grammar.*"

I am convinced that any one who thoroughly masters this little book will lay a solid foundation for his further study of the German language.

Dr. EMIL OTTO.

# CONTENTS.

| A a | B b | C c | D d | E e |
|-----|-----|-----|-----|-----|

| F f | G g | H h | I i | J j | K k |
|-----|-----|-----|-----|-----|-----|

| L l | M m | N n | O o | P p |
|-----|-----|-----|-----|-----|

| Q q | R r | S s s | T t | U u |
|-----|-----|-------|-----|-----|

| V v | W w | X x | Y y | Z z |
|-----|-----|-----|-----|-----|

### COMPOUND CONSONANTS.

| ch | ck | ss | sz | sch | sp | st | th | tz |
|----|----|----|----|-----|----|----|----|----|

Amt, Bild, Christ,

Damm, Eis, Frau, Gold,

Haus, Igel, Jagd, Rohr,

Laub, Mann, Nacht,

Ort, Pferd, Qual, Ring,

Sand, Wein, Tisch, Uhr,

Volk, Welt, Zeit, Aller

Anfang ist schwer.

Reden ist Silber,

Schweigen oft Gold.

# ON PRONUNCIATION.

## Letters of the Alphabet.

1) The German Alphabet consists of 26 letters, which are represented as follows:

| CHARACTERS. | | NAME. | CHARACTERS. | | NAME. |
|---|---|---|---|---|---|
| 𝔄, 𝔞 = a | | ah. | 𝔑, 𝔫 = n | | enn. |
| 𝔅, 𝔟 = b | | bey. | 𝔒, 𝔬 = o | | o. |
| ℭ, 𝔠 = c | | tsey. | 𝔓, 𝔭 = p | | pey. |
| 𝔇, 𝔡 = d | | dey. | 𝔔, 𝔮 = q | | koo. |
| 𝔈, 𝔢 = e | | ey. | 𝔑, 𝔯 = r | | airr. |
| 𝔉, 𝔣 = f | | eff. | 𝔖, ſ, 𝔰 = s | | ess. |
| 𝔊, 𝔤 = g | | gay. | 𝔗, 𝔱 = t | | tey. |
| 𝔥, 𝔥 = h | | hah. | 𝔘, 𝔲 = u | | oo. |
| 𝔍, 𝔦 = i | | ee. | 𝔙, 𝔳 = v | | fow (fou). |
| 𝔍, 𝔧 = j | | yot. | 𝔚, 𝔴 = w | | vey. |
| 𝔎, 𝔨 = k | | kah. | 𝔛, 𝔵 = x | | iks. |
| 𝔏, 𝔩 = l | | ell. | 𝔜, 𝔶 = y | | ipsilon. |
| 𝔐, 𝔪 = m | | em. | 𝔷, 𝔷 = z | | tset. |

Of these, 𝔞, 𝔢, 𝔦, 𝔬, 𝔲, 𝔶 are simple vowels, the others are s i m p l e consonants.

2) Besides these, there are in German *double vowels*, *modified vowels*, *diphthongs* and *compound consonants*:

### Double Vowels.

𝔄𝔞, 𝔞𝔞.          — 𝔢𝔢.          — 𝔬𝔬.

### Modified Vowels.

𝔄̈ [𝔄𝔢], ä.      𝔒̈ [𝔒𝔢], ö.      𝔘̈ [𝔘𝔢], ü.

## Diphthongs.

| | | |
|---|---|---|
| **Ai, ai.** | **Ei, ei.** | **Ey, ey.** |
| **Au, au.** | **Äu, äu.** | **Eu, eu.** |

### Double and compound Consonants.

**Ch, ch,** ch. — **chs** = x. **Sp, sp,** sp. **Th, th** = t.
**Sch, sch,** sh. — **ck** = ck. **St, st,** st. — **tz** = tz.
**Qu, qu,** qu. — **ng** = ng. — **ss, ss,** ss.

Several of the letters being almost similar, we must recommend them to the special attention of beginners, as they may easily be confounded with each other. To prevent such mistakes, we give them here:

**B** and **V**; **C** and **E**; **N, N** and **K**; **O** and **Q**;
**b** and **h**; **s** and **f**; **v, p** and **h**; **r** and **x**.

## PRONUNCIATION OF THE VOWELS.

### 1. Simple and double Vowels.

### A, a.

**A, a** has always the same sound, and is pronounced like *a* in the English words: *farthing, father, are;* never like *a* in *ball, name* or *hat.* Ex.:

ab, an, all, gar, a-ber, ha-be, la-ben, Mann.

**Aa, aa** is pronounced in the same manner, but longer:

Aas, Haar, Saal.

### E, e.

**E, e** has three different sounds:

1) the *broad* one, like *a* in the English word *hare,* as:

er, der, wer, es, ge-ben, le-ben, Mehl;

*short,* as in the word *shell:*

> heſſ, wenn, fett, En-de, lebt, Feld.

*NB.* When the e is followed by two consonants or a double one, it is considered to be *short.*

2) the *acute* sound like the French é in été, as:

> Reh, weh, eben, geht, lehrt, rede.

This is also the sound of the double **ee,** as:

> Heer, Meer, See, Kaffee.

3) e at the end of a word or in an unaccented final syllable, is very short, and has nearly the same sound as the final *-er* in the English word *manner:*

> ha-be, be-te, ſa-ge, Elle,, ſtel-len, lob-te, See-le.

## J, i.

**J, i** has only one sound, the same as in *sin, milk;* never like *i* in *wise,* as:

in, im, bis, im-mer, mir, Lippe, mild, Tiſch, Kind.

*NB.* This vowel appears in some words lengthened by e *mute* after it, as in *field:* die = *dee.* Ex.:

hier (*here*), vier = *feer,* Lie-be, Wien, Dieb, die-ſer.

*Note.* In some words, however, the letter i belongs to the first syllable, and e to the following; in this case i and e are of course both pronounced: **Spanien** = Spa-ni-en, **Lilie** = Li-li-e (three syllables). This does not take place in the final syllable of foreign words, where the accent falls on the last syllable, as: Melodi'e = m e l o d e e; Harmon i'e.

**J, i** is also made long by the insertion of h mute, but only in some personal and possessive pronouns with their derivatives, as: pers. **ihm, ihr, ihn, ihnen, Ihnen**; poss. **ihr, ihre, ihr, der, die, das ihrige, Ihrige.**

## O, o.

**O, o** when long, is like the English *o* in *no*, but without the final short *u* of the English pronunciation as:

**Ofen, Hof, Bo-den, Rohr, Rose, los, oder, so.**

When followed by two consonants, **o** is short, and sounds nearly like the English *o* in *off*, *loss*, as:

**Gott, kom-men, soll, oft, of-fen, Korn.**

Double **o** (**oo**) is always long ò as: **Moos, Boot.**

## U, u.

**U, u** sounds in long syllables like the English *u* in *rule, soup,* or the *oo* in *root,* as:

**du, nun, gut, Blut, Ruhe, Uhr, ru-fen;**

a little shorter, when followed by two consonants, like *full:*

**Null, Mund, Butte, Brunnen, murren.**

Double **u** does not occur.

## Y, y.

**Y, y** appears only in foreign words, where its sound does not differ from that of the **i,** as: **Ly-si-as, &c.** Preceded by **e,** it will be mentioned with the diphthongs. The German **y** is never used as a consonant.

## 2. Modified Vowels.

# Ä [Ae], ä.

The sound of this vowel, when long, is nearly the same as in *fair* (the French è), as: Kä-se, grämen, Bäder, wählen. — When short, the sound becomes rather slender, almost as in *crept*, as: Fäl-le, Käl-te, Bälde, Hände, Fässer, kämmen.

# Ö [Oe], ö.

Long ö, written ö or öh has the sound of French *eu* in *feu*, and is produced by the combination of the mouth position for *o* and the tongue position for *e*, as: ö-de, Köh-ler, Höh-le, Rö-mer, 2c.

Short ö is more open than the preceding sound and must be pronounced like *eu* in French *peuple*, as: Höl-le, öf-ter, kön-nen, 2c.

# Ü [Ue], ü.

The English have nothing corresponding to this sound. It is exactly the French *u* in *ruse*, *sur* etc., as: für, über, Übel [Uebel], Hüte, Brüder, füllen.

### READING-LESSON I.

Da, das, dann; als, alt, kalt; er, wer, her; hin, mit, in, im, bin; oft, offen, soll, Gott; so, los, ob, oben, Ton; du, gut, nur, um, uns, dumm, Kuh; haben, Rabe, hatte, lassen, fassen, Saft, Glas, Gras; Rahm, lahm, Aal, Haar. — Essen, besser, Feder, Ende, Betten. See, Seele, Reh, Klee, heben. Sinn, sinnen, binnen, bitten, immer;

nie, sieben, Biene, diese, fiel, fielen, ihn, ihnen. — Oben,
loben, Ofen, Dose; wollen, kommen, kosten, hoffen; Moor,
Boot. — Hufe, rufen, Butte, unter, Mutter. — Hände,
hätte; hören, Föhre, können; für, rühren, Hütte, Mütter.

---

### 8. Diphthongs.

## Ai, ai.  Au, au.  Äu, äu.

**Ai,** which occurs only in a few substantives, is pronounced like *i* or *y* in *fire, sky,* as: Mai = *my,* Kai-ser,
Waise, Hain, Main.

**Au,** like the *ou* in *house, sound,* as: aus, Haus, Baum,
Raum, glau-ben, faul.

**Äu, äu** has the same pronunciation as English *oy* in
*boy,* as: Häu-ser, Bäume, träumen (as if spelled Höiser,
Böime).

## Ei, ei (ey).  Eu, eu.

**Ei** has always the sound of the English *i* in *mind,*
as: mein, Bein, klein, weinen, Reim, heilen, Eier, sein.

**Eu, eu** has the same sound as **äu.**  Ex.: Leute, heute,
treu.

*NB.* **ie** is not a diphthong, only a long **i:** fiel, hier; see
under **J, i.** *NB.* pag. 3.

---

## PRONUNCIATION OF THE CONSONANTS.

### 1. Simple Consonants.

**B, b** and **D, d,** as in English; but when they end a
word or even a syllable followed by another consonant,
they have the sound of **p** and **t,** as: Ball, Birne, breit, ab,
Grab, El-be, Damm, der, wild, Tad-ler, Abend.

**C, c.** This letter by itself, appears only in foreign words, and is pronounced, 1) before ä, ö, e, i, and y like *ts* (the same as z), as: Cäsar, Ceder, Citrone, Cypern, Certifikat, Citat; 2) before the other vowels and consonants, hard like k, as in: Casino = Kasino, Cato, Cuba, Colonel, Claudius.

**F, f; L, l; M, m; N, n; P, p; T, t** and **X, x** are quite the same as in English, as: Fall, finden, auf, Affe, frei; Liebe, loben, fallen, fiel; Mann, mir, im, Hammer, nimmt; Tafel, Traum, Bett, be-treffen; Xaver, Axe, Exempel.

**T** in words ending in **ion'**, which are taken from the Latin, sounds like z (*ts*), as: Lektion' = Lek-zion', Portion = Por-zion, Nation, &c.

**G** has various sounds.

1) Like English *g* in *garden*, at the beginning of a syllable; as gut, "good"; groß, "great."

2) Like Scotch *ch* in *loch* after a, o, u; as: Tag, "day"; bog, "bent," etc.

3) Like palatal German *ch* in ich (see below): Sieg, "victory"; trägt, "carries," etc.

In the unaccentuated final syllable **ig**, especially, it sounds like ich, as: Kö-nig (= Könich), billig, gütig, wenig; likewise in their derivatives, as: Königin, &c.

**G** before **n** is always pronounced separately with the hard sound above mentioned. Ex.: Gnade.

**H, h** at the beginning of words is more aspirated than in English: haben, Held, Haus, hören, Hut, hundert, Krank-heit.

Between two vowels the aspiration is so slight as to be scarcely heard: sehen, Schuhe, Höhe, ziehen.

Before a consonant and at the end of words it is mute: it serves only to make the preceding vowel long, as: Ohr, Hahn, roh, Ehre, Mohr, Stroh, Uhr, wohnen.

𝕵, 𝖏 (yot) corresponds to *y* (consonant) in *you*, as. Jahr, ja, jeder, jung, Jude, be-jahrt.

𝕶, 𝖐 is like the English *k*, as: kahl, kalt, Kreuz, Klee, Balken; it is never mute before 𝖓, as: Knie, Knabe.

𝖖 see page 9.

𝕽, 𝖗 is pronounced shriller than in English. Ex.: Rad, Ruhm, Erde, bergen, Burg, her, Haar, Flur, Führer.

𝕾, 𝖋, 𝖘 has the hard sound, like the English *s*, in *son:* 1) at the beginning of words: satt, sein; 2) in the inner part of words, when following the letters b, p, d, t, ch, k und ck: Erbse, Lotse; 3) before a consonant: fasten, Wespe; 4) likewise at the end of words, and in the inner part of words, when the syllable it ends constitutes a root; in which latter cases it is written s: es, Haus, Bosheit, ausgehen, Hausthür. — It sounds like the English soft *s* in *rose:* in the centre of words between two vowels, and before e after n, m, r: lesen, Rose, Riese, Linse, Hirse, Gemse.

𝖁, 𝖛 is now mostly pronounced completely like the German f, except in foreign words where it retains the sound of *v*, as: von, Vater, vier, viel, voll, verloren, Vetter, Frevel, Sklave.

𝖂, 𝖜 answers to the English and French *v*, as: Wein, wer, wann, wo, Wille, ewig, gewohnt.

𝖜 is never used at the end of words.

𝖅, 𝖟 is pronounced like *ts* in *gets* or *wits*, as: zehn, zu, dazu, Zeit, Zoll, Tanz, an-ziehen.

The sounds of the English *j*, *w* or *wh* and *th* do not occur in German.

### READING-LESSON II.

Auf, Bau, aus, Lauf, Maus, Auge, Mai, ein, mein, kein, sein, klein, klar, gar, Gans, ganz, Bart, Ball,

Baum, für, vor, von, vom, hin, her, hier; nie, nun, jetzt,
Reis, lau, blau, bloß. Heu, heute, Freund, Räume,
Bälle, Band, Bänder, Bund, Bündel, Dorf, Dörfer, Ton,
Töne, Tau, Tag; Frei-heit, Frau, Vater, Vetter; Haus,
Häuser, Baum, Bäume, Kind, Abend, Glas, König,
Lärm; lesen, gehen, reiten, er-finden, befehlen, bezahlen,
erlassen.

---

### 2. Double and compound Consonants.

**Ch, ch** has three different sounds:

1) When placed after **a, o, u** and **au,** its sound is a
guttural one and resembles the Scotch *ch* in *loch.* It
is impossible to define it more clearly. The pupil must
therefore refer to his teacher for its correct pronunciation, as: Bach, lachen, Loch, kochen, Kuchen, Buch, auch,
Rauch.

2) The other sound, which occurs after **e, i, ei, ä, ö,
äu, eu** and **ü** and after a consonant, is a *palatal sound*,
as: recht, ich, Licht, reich, Bäche, Lö-cher, räu-chern, heu-cheln,
Bü-cher, wel-che, Händ-chen, Gläs-chen.

3) At the beginning of words **Ch** is pronounced like
**K,** as: Charakter, Chor, Christian, Christ = Krist; except
before **e** and **i,** as: Chemie, Chili (see 2).

**chs** is like *ks* or *x,* as: Wachs = Waks or Wax; thus:
Ochs, Ochsen, Fuchs, Füchse, Achsel, wachsen.

*NB.* This, however, cannot be so in compound words,
when *ch* and *s* belong to different syllables, as: wachsam =
wach-sam, nachsuchen = nach-suchen, nach-setzen, durch-sehen, or
when the **s** is abridged from **es,** especially in the Genitive
case, as: des Buchs, for Buches; des Dachs, for Daches.

**ck** appears at the end or in the middle of a word,
after a vowel with the sound of a double **k,** as in Eng-

lish, thus: Stock, Pack, strecken, Glocke, Nacken, drücken; — ck is never allowed after a consonant.

**ng** sounds like the English *ng* in *long*, as: lang, Ring, Gesang. — The same pronunciation is retained, when **ng** is followed by a vowel, as in *singer:* lange = lang-e (not lan-ge), hangen, Fing-er, bringen, singen, gelung-en.

In compound words, when the first part ends in **n** and the other begins with **g**, each is pronounced separately, as: an-genehm, an-gesang-en, Un-geduld.

**Qu, qu** is like *kv*, and not like the *qu* in English *queen*. In German it is found in few words only, as: Quarz, quer, Quirl, Qual, Quelle.

**ss, ß***); the former is used as double *s* in the middle of a word after a short vowel, the latter in the middle of a word after a long vowel, and as final double *ss* (not *sz*) at the end of words and syllables, as: lassen, besser, müssen; — grüßen, fließen, daß (= dass), Haß, Spaß, Schloß, muß-te.

**Ph, ph** has the same sound as **f**, as: Epheu, Philo= sophie, Geographie, Photograph.

**Pf, pf.** Here the two letters **p** and **f** are united in one sound, as: Pfahl, Pfeil, Apfel, Pferd.

**Sch, sch** like the English *sh* in *ship*, as: Schiff, schaf= fen, Asche, wischen, kindisch.

**Sp, sp** and **St, st** in most parts of Germany not quite as in English; the difference is, that **sp** and **st**, chiefly at the beginning of words, approach somewhat *sht* and *shp*, as: Spreu, Sparren, Spieß, Spule, sprechen, spielen; Stall, Stein, Stroh, ꝛc.).

---

*) This letter is not compounded, as it appears in print, of **f** and **z**, but of **f** and **s** (final *s*) = **fs**; it sounds like *ss*, not *sz*.

𝔗𝔥, 𝔱𝔥 must not be pronounced otherwise than a simple 𝔱; it never has the sound of the English *th*, thus 𝔗𝔥at, 𝔗𝔥or, 𝔱𝔥un, 𝔗𝔥eater sound like 𝔗at, 𝔗or, tun, 𝔗eater.

𝔷 is equivalent to 𝔷 = *ts*, as: 𝔗a𝔷e, 𝔅li𝔷, 𝔐ü𝔷e.

---

## HANDWRITING.

As the characters for German *handwriting* differ greatly from the printed letters, they have been annexed in two tables, and should be carefully copied and practised.

The *signs of punctuation* being the same as in English, need no further explanation.

## ACCENT.

All that the beginner requires to enable him to read correctly, may be simply reduced to the following rules:

1) *Simple* words have one accent, *compound* ones have (generally) two or more.

2) *Simple* words are either *monosyllabic roots*, as: gut, 𝔐ann; or *derivative words*, of two or more syllables, as: lef'en, 𝔎in'der, hat'te.

3) When a simple word is not monosyllabic, it consists of a *chief syllable* and of one or more *accessory syllables*, and is called a *derivative*. Those syllables are partly *prefixes*, partly *suffixes*, which are never used by themselves, and appear only in connection with root-words. They are all unaccented.

4) Hence the two principal rules.:

a) *All derivative German words have their accent on their root or chief syllable, but never on either of the accessory syllables.*

### EXAMPLES WITH UNACCENTED PREFIXES.

Bĕ-rúf, Ĕmp-fáng, ĕnt-gíng, ĕr-fúhr, Gĕ-braúch, Vĕr-núnft. ĕr-laubt′, zĕr-ſtört′, bĕ-fand′.

### EXAMPLES WITH UNACCENTED SUFFIXES.

Liebĕ, Mítt-el, lóbĕn, Túgĕnd, Bílbĕr, ſtein-ĕrn, Gútĕs, rédĕſt, bíttĕt, ártĭg, hólzĭcht, Löw-ĭn, hérrlĭch, kíndĭſch, Bäum= chĕn, Wóhnŭng, Wóhnŭngĕn.

### EXAMPLES WITH BOTH.

Bĕ-rúf-ĕn, Ĕmpfängĕr, Ĕrfáhrŭng, Ĕrfáhrŭngĕn, gĕbräuch= lĭch, vĕrlórĕn, ĕntſpréchĕn, Zĕrlégŭng, Vĕrwünſchŭngĕn.

b) *Compound words have an accent on each of the components.* **Ex.:**

Óſtwind (Óſt-wind), Múnd-koch, Aúfträg, geíſtreich, Mítleid, Nót-durſt [Nóthdurſt], Úmgáng, Männlein, Freúndſcháft, Aus= fúhr, Zúkunft, frúchtbár, Freíheit, Júngling, Lábſál, Állmácht.

### PROMISCUOUS EXAMPLES.

Fínſtĕr, mítleidĭg, aúfhörĕn, bĕmítleidĕn, hĭnaúffahrĕn, hĕreínkómmĕn, úm-gänglĭch, aus-gefúhrt, zúkünftĭg, Júnglings= áltĕr, Reíchtum [Reíchthum], Reíchtümĕr, baufällĭg, Abĕndbrót [Abendbrod], líebkóſĕn, Abĕrglaubĕ, tódĕsmútĭg [todesmuthig]. — Räubereí, Sónnĕn-ſchein, Úhrſchlüſſĕl, Féldméſſĕr, Féld= zúg, Féldzeug-meíſtĕr, Kriegs-záhlámt, Ún-übĕr-tréfflĭchkeit, Líebĕns-würdĭgkeit, Maúlbeer-bäumĕ, zúſammĕn-kómmĕn, ún= gĕrécht, zúrück-kehrĕn, dázwiſchĕn-légĕn.

### Foreign Words.

Words taken from foreign languages have their peculiar accent; all those *nouns*, however, which assume a German termination, have the accent on the last syllable, as Soldat', Student', Metall', Offizier', General', Portion', Chemie'; all *such verbs* have it on the last but one, as: ſtudie'ren [ſtudiren], pro'bieren [probiren], ꝛc.

## READING-LESSON III.

### Rom.

Rom iſt eine ſehr alte Stadt. Sie wurde von Romulus und Remus auf einem Hügel erbaut. Aber im Lauf der Zeit vergrößerte ſie ſich immer und erſtreckte ſich zuletzt über ſieben Hügel. Ihre Bewohner nannten ſich Römer; ſie waren ein ſehr tapferes Volk und führten viele Kriege mit andern Völkern.

Anfangs wurde Rom von Königen regiert; ſpäter war es eine Republik, und zuletzt ein Kaiſer-reich.

---

PRELIMINARY NOTES. PARTS OF SPEECH.

There are in the German language *ten* parts of speech.

1) The Article, der Artikel or das Geſchlechtswort.

2) The Noun *or* Substantive, das Hauptwort.

3) The determinative Adjective *or* Adjective Pronoun, das Beſtimmungswort; (including the indefinite and definite numerals, das unbeſtimmte und beſtimmte Zahlwort).

4) The (qualifying) Adjective, das Eigenſchaftswort.

5) The Pronoun, das Fürwort.

6) The Verb, ba§ 3eitwort.

7) The Adverb, ba§ Umftanb§wort.

8) The Preposition, ba§ Borwort.

9) The Conjunction, ba§ Binbewort.

10) The Interjection, ba§ 2lu§rufung§wort.

The first six are variable, the last four invariable.

The change which the first five undergo by means of *terminations*, is called *declension* (Deflination); it refers to *gender*, *number* and *case*.

There are in German three *genders*: the *masculine*, the *feminine* and the *neuter* gender.

There are also two *numbers*: *Singular* (Sinjahl) and *Plural* (Mehrjahl), and four *cases*, expressing the different relations of words to each other, namely: the *nominative*, *genitive* or *possessive*, *dative* and *accusative case*.

---

# LESSON I.

### The definite Article.

1) There are two articles in German as in English: the *definite* and the *indefinite.*

2) The *definite article* answers to the English *the;* but with the important difference that for each gender in the singular it has a particular form, viz.:

> *masc.* **ber,** *fem.* **bie,** *neut.* **ba§,** the, as:

> **ber** Mann    the man.
> **bie** Frau    the woman.
> **ba§** Kinb    the child.

3) The following words, also used with nouns to determinate them, have the same termination as above:

| masc. | fem. | neuter. | |
|---|---|---|---|
| **dieser,** | d i e f e, | d i e f e s, | this. |
| **jener,** | j e n e, | j e n e s, | that. |
| **welcher,** | w e l ch e, | w e l ch e s? | which? |
| **jeder,** | j e d e, | j e d e s, | every. |

### Examples.

Dieser Mann  this man.                Jener Baum  that tree.

Diese Frau  this woman.            Jede Mutter  every mother.

Welcher Baum?  which tree?    Jedes Kind  every child.

### Words.

**der** Mann  the man.               **das** Haus  the house.

der Vater  the father.              das Kind  the child.

der Sohn  the son.                   das Brot [Brod]  (the) bread.

der Garten  the garden.          das Wasser  (the) water.

der Wein  the wine.                 das Buch  the book.

der Stock  the cane, stick.

der Hund  the dog.

#### fem.

                                               groß  large, tall.

                                               klein  small, little.

**die** Frau  the woman.            jung  young.

die Mutter  the mother.           gut  good.

die Tochter  the daughter.       alt  old.

die Feder  the pen.                  ja  yes; nein  no.

die Stadt  the town.                ist  is.  und  and.

die Katze  the cat.                   wie?  how?

die Rose  the rose.                  wer?  who?

### Exercise (Übung) 1.

1. Der Mann und die Frau.  2. Der Garten und das Haus.  3. Die Mutter und das Kind.  4. Welche Mutter?  5. Diese Mutter.  6. Welches Kind?  7. Jenes Kind.  8. Dieser Garten.  9. Jener Garten.  10. Welcher Sohn?  11. Der Vater ist alt.  12. Die Mutter ist gut.*)  13. Dieser Hund ist groß.  14. Jene Katze ist klein.  15. Wie ist dieser

---

*) Adjectives, used predicatively, are invariable, see page 95.

Wein? 16. Dieſer Wein iſt gut. 17. Wie iſt das Kind? 18. Das Kind iſt klein. 19. Die Tochter iſt jung. 20. Jener Mann iſt alt. 21. Dieſes Buch iſt groß. 22. Welches Brot [Brod] iſt gut? 23. Dieſes Brot iſt gut.

### Conversation.

| Questions. | Answers. |
|---|---|
| **Wer** iſt alt? | Der Vater iſt alt. |
| Wer iſt gut? | Die Mutter iſt gut. |
| **Wie** iſt die Stadt? | Die Stadt iſt groß. |
| Wer iſt klein? | Das Kind iſt klein. |
| Wie iſt der Garten? | Der Garten iſt klein. |
| Wie iſt dieſe Feder? | Dieſe Feder iſt gut. |

# LESSON II.

## The indefinite Article.

The indefinite article is *masc.* **ein**, *fem.* **eine**, *neut.* **ein**; it is equivalent to the English *a* or *an*, and has also three genders; but in the nominative, the masculine and neuter are alike, viz.:

| | |
|---|---|
| **ein** Vater | a father. |
| **eine** Mutter | a mother. |
| **ein** Kind | a child. |

The following determinative words have the same endings:

| masc. | fem. | neuter. | |
|---|---|---|---|
| kein, | keine, | kein, | no. |
| mein, | meine, | mein, | my. |
| dein, | deine, | dein, | thy. |
| ſein, | ſeine, | ſein, | his. |
| ihr, | ihre, | ihr, | her. |
| unſer, | unſ(e)re, | unſer, | our. |
| euer, | eu(e)re, | euer, | your. |
| Ihr, | Ihre, | Ihr, | your. |
| ihr, | ihre, | ihr, | their. |

## Examples.

| | |
|---|---|
| kein Brot [Brod]  no bread. | meine Tochter  my daughter. |
| mein Vater  my father. | Ihr Freund  your friend. |
| unser Garten  our garden. | keine Feder  no pen. |
| Ihre Mutter  your mother. | sein Bruder  his brother. |

## Words.

| | |
|---|---|
| der Freund  the friend. | das Haus  the house. |
| ein Freund  a friend. | ein Haus  a house. |
| die Schwester  the sister. | das Papier  the paper. |
| die Blume  the flower. | das Buch  the book. |

| | |
|---|---|
| die Freundin (female) the friend. | schön  fine, beautiful. |
| eine Freundin (female) a friend. | neu  new. |
| der Bruder  the brother. | krank  ill, sick.    auch  also. |
| der Hut  the hat. | wo?  where?  was?  what? |

## Exercise 2.

1. Ein Vater.  2. Eine Tochter.  3. Eine Mutter.  4. Ein Sohn.  5. Kein Buch.  6. Deine Schwester ist jung.  7. Unser Freund ist alt.  8. Dein Hut ist neu.  9. Ihr Kind ist krank. 10. Eine Blume ist schön.  11. Uns(e)re Mutter ist gut.  12. Die Rose ist eine Blume.  13. Mein Vater ist Ihr Freund.  14. Ihr Bruder ist mein Freund.  15. Seine Schwester ist meine Freundin.  16. Wer ist krank?  17. Meine Mutter ist krank. 18. Mein Buch ist neu.  19. Ihr Buch ist alt.  20. Mein Freund ist gut.  21. Meine Freundin ist auch gut.  22. Wo ist mein Hut?

## Conversation.

| | |
|---|---|
| Wer ist gut? | Mein Vater ist gut. |
| Was ist neu? | Dein Hut ist neu. |
| Wie ist Ihre Mutter? | Uns(e)re Mutter ist krank. |
| Was ist die Rose? | Die Rose ist eine Blume. |
| Wie ist diese Blume? | Diese Blume ist schön. |
| Wer ist alt? | Mein Freund ist alt. |
| Wie ist Ihr Buch? | Mein Buch ist schö |

# LESSON III.

## Declension of the Article.

They are varied in the four cases: the *nominative, genitive, dative* and *accusative*. It will be observed that the *accusative singular* of the feminine and neuter gender, and the *accusative plural* are always like the *nominative*.

### 1. Declension of the definite Article.

|  | masc. | fem. | neuter. |  | Plural for all genders. | |
|------|------|------|------|--------|------|--------|
| *Nom.* | der | die | das | the | die | the |
| *Gen.* | des | der | des | of the | der | of the |
| *Dat.* | dem | der | dem | to the | den | to the |
| *Acc.* | den | die | das | the. | die | the. |

### Declension of dieser.

|  | masc. | fem. | neuter. |  | Plural for all genders. | |
|------|------|------|------|--------|------|--------|
| *N.* | dieser | diese | dieses | this | diese | these |
| *G.* | dieses | dieser | dieses | of this | dieser | of these |
| *D.* | diesem | dieser | diesem | to this | diesen | to these |
| *A.* | diesen | diese | dieses | this. | diese | these. |

Thus too are declined: jener, welcher and jeder.

---

### 2. Declension of the indefinite Article.

|  | masc. | fem. | neuter. |  |
|------|------|------|------|--------|
| *Nom.* | ein | eine | ein | a, an |
| *Gen.* | eines | einer | eines | of a, an |
| *Dat.* | einem | einer | einem | to a, an |
| *Acc.* | einen | eine | ein | a, an. |

The indefinite article has no Plural.

### 3. Declension of a Possessive Adjective.

| | | | | | | | |
|---|---|---|---|---|---|---|---|
| *Nom.* | mein | meine | mein | my | *Pl.* | meine | my |
| *Gen.* | meines | meiner | meines | of my | | meiner | of my |
| *Dat.* | meinem | meiner | meinem | to my | | meinen | to my |
| *Acc.* | **meinen** | meine | mein | my. | | meine | my. |

### Words.

ich liebe  I like, I love.
das Pferd  the horse.
die Birne  the pear.
der Apfel  the apple.
die Frucht  the fruit.
das Tier [Thier]  the animal.
geben Sie mir  give me.

die Gabel  the fork.
das Messer  the knife.
der Löffel  the spoon.
lieben Sie?  do you like, love?
hier  here; hier ist  here is.
aber  but.

### Singular.

ich habe  I have
du hast  thou hast
er hat  he has
sie hat  she has
es hat  it has.

habe ich?  have I?
hast du?  hast thou?
hat er?  has he?
hat sie?  has she?
hat es?  has it?

### Plural.

wir haben  we have
ihr habet }
Sie haben } you have
sie haben  they have.

haben wir?  have we?
habet ihr? }
haben Sie? } have you?
haben sie?  have they.

---

### Exercise 3.

1. Ich habe einen Freund.   2. Mein Bruder hat auch
einen Freund.   3. Ich liebe meinen Freund.   4. Haben
Sie einen Garten?   5. Wir haben keinen Garten.   6. Dieser
Mann hat mein Pferd.   7. Lieben Sie diesen Mann?
8. Welchen Mann?   9. Ihren Vater.   10. Mein Kind hat

eine Birne. 11. Diese Birne ist gut. 12. Der Sohn hat
einen Apfel. 13. Die Katze ist ein Tier [Thier]. 14. Ich
liebe dieses Tier. 15. Die Tochter hat eine Blume. 16.
Geben Sie mir dieses Buch. 17. Unser Freund hat ein
Pferd. 18. Meine Schwester hat eine Gabel, aber ich habe
keine Gabel. 19. Wo ist mein Löffel? 20. Hier ist Ihr
Löffel.

### Conversation.

| | |
|---|---|
| Was haben Sie? | Ich habe eine Blume. |
| Haben Sie eine Rose? | Ja, ich habe eine Rose, |
| Hast du ein Pferd? | Nein, ich habe kein Pferd. |
| Hat das Kind eine Gabel? | Ja, das Kind hat eine Gabel. |
| Wer hat mein Buch? | Deine Schwester hat dein Buch. |
| Hat der Mann ein Pferd? | Ja, er hat ein Pferd. |
| Wo ist meine Feder? | Hier ist Ihre Feder. |
| Hat Ihr Vater einen Bruder? | Mein Vater hat einen Bruder und eine Schwester. |

# LESSON IV.

## Declension of Nouns.

There are *five* declensions, the three first of which
comprise the *masculine*, the fourth the *feminine*, the
fifth the *neuter* nouns, a few exceptions not included.

1) The first declension comprehends all *masculine*
and *neuter* nouns ending in **el, en, er,** and all diminutives
ending in **chen** and **lein.**

2) The second comprehends all *masculine* nouns
ending in **e,** and most foreign masculine substantives
having the accent on the last syllable.

3) The third contains, *a)* all *monosyllabic masculine*
nouns, *b)* those of two syllables ending in ich, ig and
ling, and *c)* a few words of foreign origin.

4) To the fourth belong *all the feminine nouns.*

5) To the fifth all *neuter* substantives not ending in
el, en, er, chen and lein (see 1).

### REMARKS.

Before we present the declensions themselves, we
think it proper to give the following general hints,
which may facilitate their study.

1) The genitive case in the Singular of all *masculine* nouns (except those of the 2d decl.), and of all
*neuter* nouns, without any exception, ends in $ (or e$).

2) The *accusative* Singular of feminine and neuter
words is always like the nominative.

3) The accusative Singular of all masculine nouns
not belonging to the 2d decl., is also like the nominative.

4) The *vocative* case, in either number, is always
understood to be the nominative without the article;
it will therefore not be mentioned.

5) In the Plural the *nominative, genitive* and *accusative cases* are always alike.

6) The *dative* plural of all declinable words term-
inates in n.

7) All root-nouns (*i. e.* without the prefix Ge=) ending
in e form their Plural in en, without modifying their
vowel.

8) All *feminine* substantives remain unchanged in
the singular.

9) Most *monosyllables* having a, o, u or au in
their root, modify in the plural this vowel into ä, ö,
ü or äu.

10) In all *compound nouns* only the last component is declined according to the declension it belongs to.

TABLE OF THE ENDINGS OF THE FIVE DECLENSIONS.

### Singular.

| | *Masculine.* | | | *Feminine.* | *Neuter.* |
|---|---|---|---|---|---|
| | I. | II. | III. | IV. | V. |
| N. | — - | — e | — | — - | — (-) |
| G. | — -s | — en | — es (s) | — - | — es (s) |
| D. | — - | — en | — (e) | — - | — (e) |
| A. | — - | — en | — | — - | — - |

For IV. (Feminine): singular / no / change / at all.

### Plural.

| | I. | II. | III. | IV. a) | IV. b) | V. a) | V. b) |
|---|---|---|---|---|---|---|---|
| N. | ″ -*) | — en | ″ e | — en (n) | ″ e | — e | ″ er |
| G. | ″ - | — en | ″ e | — en (n) | ″ e | — e | ″ er |
| D. | ″ -n | — en | ″ en | — en (n) | ″ en | — en | ″ ern |
| A. | ″ - | — en | ″ e | — en (n) | ″ e | — e | ″ er†) |

## First Declension.

1) The first declension contains all *masculine* and *neuter nouns* ending in el, en and er, besides all diminutives in chen and lein, which are all of the neuter gender.

---

*) These marks ″ indicate the *modified* vowels, ä, ö or ü.

†) Under that system the declensions may also be classified as only two, the strong and the weak. Declensions II. and IV a. above correspond to each other, and are termed the *weak declension*, not subject to any modification of the vowels. All the other declensions likewise correspond, and are called the *strong declension*. Thus we have the following two systems of endings:

| WEAK DECLENSION. | | | STRONG DECLENSION. | | |
|---|---|---|---|---|---|
| | *Sing.* | *Plur.* | | *Sing.* | *Plur.* |
| *Nom.* | —— | -en | *Nom.* | —— | -(e)   or   -er |
| *Gen.* | (-en) | -en | *Gen.* | -(e)s | -(e)    -er |
| *Dat.* | (-en) | -en | *Dat.* | -(e) | -(e)n    -ern |
| *Acc.* | (-en) | -en | *Acc.* | —— | -(e)    -er. |

By learning the smaller class of words which belong to the *weak declension*, the pupil will be enabled to classify all the rest with the *strong,* as a matter of course.

2) They take ß in the genitive singular, and n in the dative plural. In the plural, most words belonging to the 1st declension modify the three vowels a, o, u into ä, ö, ü. Nouns with other vowels or diphthongs remain unchanged.

### a) MASCULINE.

#### Example in el.

| Singular. | Plural. |
|---|---|
| N. der Apfel the apple | die Äpfel [Aepfel] the apples |
| G. des Apfels of the apple | der Äpfel of the apples |
| D. dem Apfel to the apple | den Äpfeln to the apples |
| A. den Apfel the apple | die Äpfel the apples. |

Thus are to be declined :

| | |
|---|---|
| der Stiefel the boot. | der Mantel the cloak. |
| der Flügel the wing | der Vogel the bird. |
| der Löffel the spoon. | der Schlüssel the key. |
| der Spiegel the looking-glass. | der Esel the ass, donkey. |
| der Beutel the purse. | der Onkel the uncle. |

*Plur.* die Stiefel, die Beutel, die Mäntel, die Vögel ꝛc.

---

#### Example in er.

| Singular. | Plural. |
|---|---|
| N. der Bruder the brother | die Brüder the brothers |
| G. des Bruders of the brother | der Brüder of the brothers |
| D. dem Bruder to the brother | den Brüdern to the brothers |
| A. den Bruder the brother. | die Brüder the brothers. |

Thus too :

| | |
|---|---|
| der Vater the father. | der Schneider the tailor. |
| der Teller the plate. | der Lehrer the teacher, master. |
| der Engländer the Englishman. | |
| | der Schüler the pupil. |
| der Diener the (man-)servant. | der Gärtner the gardener. |

*Gen.* des Vaters, des Engländers, des Dieners, des Lehrers
*Plur.* die Väter, die Engländer, die Lehrer, die Schüler ꝛc.

### Example in en.

| Singular. | | Plural. | |
|---|---|---|---|
| N. der Garten | the garden | die Gärten | the gardens |
| G. des Gartens | of the garden | der Gärten | of the gardens |
| D. dem Garten | to the garden | den Gärten*) | to the gardens |
| A. den Garten | to the garden. | die Gärten | the gardens. |

Thus:

der Regen   the rain.      der Ofen   the stove.
der Wagen   the carriage.     der Kuchen   the cake.

Plur. die Wagen*), die Öfen [Oefen], die Kuchen†) 2c.

---

### b) Neuter Nouns.

### Example.

| Singular. | | Plural. | |
|---|---|---|---|
| N. das Fenster | the window | die Fenster | the windows |
| G. des Fensters | of the window | der Fenster | of the windows |
| D. dem Fenster | to the window | den Fenstern | to the windows |
| A. das Fenster | the window. | die Fenster | the windows. |

Thus too:

das Zimmer   the room.     das Federmesser the penknife.
das Wasser   the water.      das Wetter   the weather.
das Messer   the knife.      das Silber   the silver.

Plur. die Zimmer, die Messer, die Federmesser.

---

### c) Diminutives.

| Singular. | | Plural. | |
|---|---|---|---|
| N. das Mädchen | the girl | die Mädchen | the girls |
| G. des Mädchens | of the girl | der Mädchen | of the girls |
| D. dem Mädchen | to the girl | den Mädchen | of the girls |
| A. das Mädchen | the girl. | die Mädchen | the girls. |

---

*) Nouns ending in n take no second n in the dative plural.

†) Kuchen is not modified in the plural.

Thus likewise:

das Hündchen the little dog.
das Bäumchen the little tree.
das Häuschen the little house.

das Büchlein the little book.
das Vög(e)lein the little bird.

## Words.

der Kaiser the emperor.
der Vetter the cousin.
der Spanier the Spaniard.
die Thüre the door, gate.
der Italiener the Italian.

er ist he is. sie ist she is.
hier ist here is; gesehen seen.
hier sind here are; sehr very.
zwei two; drei three.
das Federmesser the penknife.

## Exercise 4.

1. Der Bruder des Vaters. 2. Die Brüder des Vaters.
3. Das Haus des Lehrers. 4. Der Garten des Kaisers.
5. Mein Vater hat einen Esel, und der Gärtner hat zwei Esel.
6. Dem Schüler. 7. Ich liebe den Schüler. 8. Der Beutel
des Italieners. 9. Das Zimmer deines Lehrers. 10. Ich
habe den Schlüssel meines Zimmers. 11. Die Schlüssel dieser
Zimmer sind neu. 12. Der Sohn hat den Wagen seines
Vaters. 13. Der Mantel des Spaniers ist alt. 14. Wo ist
das Buch des Schülers? 15. Hier ist das Buch des Schülers.
16. Das Mädchen hat keinen Spiegel. 17. Die Mädchen
haben keine Spiegel.

## Exercise 5.

1. The friend of the father. 2. The hat of the brother.
3. The house of the Spaniard. 4. The son of the father.
5. The penknife of the pupil. 6. The book of my
teacher. 7. Where is the knife? 8. Which knife?
9. The knife of the servant. 10. I have not the knife
of the servant. 11. Who has the key of my room?
12. Here is the key of your room. 13. The door of the

garden is very large. 14. The daughter of my teacher is ill. 15. The girl has the stick of the father. 16. Have you a bird? 17. Yes, I have two birds. 18. I have 'seen 'the 'house 'of 'the 'tailor*). 19. Have you also seen the garden of the Englishman? 20. No, I have not seen it (ihn).

### Conversation.

| | |
|---|---|
| Wer ist dieser Mann? | Er ist ein Italiener. |
| Wer ist dieses Mädchen? | Sie ist die Tochter meines Bruders. |
| Haben Sie den Garten des Engländers gesehen? | Ja, ich habe den Garten eines Engländers gesehen. |
| Wer ist dieser Schüler? | Er ist der Sohn meines Lehrers. |
| Kennen Sie (do you know) den Bruder meines Vaters? | Ja, ich kenne ihn (I know him); er ist sehr alt. |
| Ist dieser Mann ein Schneider? | Nein, er ist ein Gärtner. |
| Wo ist der Schlüssel dieses Zimmers? | Hier ist der Schlüssel. |
| Was hat der Schüler? | Er hat ein Messer. |

---

# LESSON V.

## Second Declension.

This declension contains another series of *masculine* words, viz.:

1) all those ending in e. Here all the cases, both of the singular and plural, are formed by adding n, without altering the vowel in the plural:

---

*) The figures put before the words indicate the order in which they are to be placed in German. In this language the past participles are at the end of principal clauses.

**Example:**

| *Singular.* | *Plural.* |
|---|---|
| *N.* der Knabe  the boy | die Knaben  the boys |
| *G.* des Knaben  of the boy | der Knaben  of the boys |
| *D.* dem Knaben  to the boy | den Knaben  to the boys |
| *A.* den Knaben  the boy. | die Knaben  the boys. |

Thus are declined:

| | |
|---|---|
| der Neffe  the nephew. | der Bediente  the (man)-servant. |
| der Ochse (Ochs)  the ox. | der Russe  the Russian. |
| der Löwe  the lion. | der Preuße  the Prussian. |
| der Hase  the hare. | der Franzose  the Frenchman. |
| der Rabe  the raven. | der Deutsche  the German. |

*Plur.* die Neffen, die Ochsen, die Löwen, die Hasen, die Raben, die Russen, die Franzosen, die Deutschen ꝛc.

2) A few words, though now monosyllabic, are also subject to this mode of inflexion, because they were originally dissyllabic.

| | |
|---|---|
| der Graf  the count. | der Herr  the gentleman, master. |
| der Fürst  the prince. | der Mensch  man, mankind. |
| der Bär  the bear. | der Prinz  the prince. |

*N.* der Graf, *G.* des Grafen, *D.* dem Grafen ꝛc.  *Plur.* Die Grafen.

*Plur.* die Bären, die Fürsten, die Herren, die Menschen ꝛc.

3) Further all masculine nouns derived from other languages, not ending in l, n, r or en*), and having the accent on the last syllable, are declined in the same manner:

---

*) These belong to the third declension; see page 30.

| *Singular.* | *Plural.* |
|---|---|
| N. der **Student'** the student | **die Studen'ten** the students |
| G. des Studenten of the student | der Studenten of the students |
| D. dem Studenten to the student | den Studenten to the students |
| A. den Studenten the student. | die Studenten the students. |

### Such are:

der Elefant' [Elephant] the elephant.

der Diamant' the diamond.

der Soldat' the soldier.

der Kamerad the companion.

der Philosoph' the philosopher.

der Präsident' the president.

der Advokat' [Advocat] the lawyer.

der Christ the Christian.

*Plur.* die Elefanten, die Soldaten, die Christen 2c.

### Words.

der Hut the hat.

der Kopf the head.

viel much. viele many.

wie? how?

wie viele? how many?

der Name(n) the name.

jung young.

der Affe the monkey.

groß large.

vier four; fünf five; sechs six.

gesehen seen; sind are.

aber but; in in.

### Exercise 6.

1. Der Neffe des Kaisers. 2. Der Hut des Knaben. 3. Ich habe zwei Neffen. 4. Die Elefanten [Elephanten] sind groß. 5. Der Kopf des Ochsen und des Löwen. 6. Der Lehrer meines Neffen ist jung. 7. Das Haus eines Advokaten [Advocaten]. 8. Die Franzosen und die Russen. 9. Die Knaben sind klein. 10. Ich habe 'einen ²Affen 'gesehen. 11. Meine Brüder haben zwei Raben. 12. Wir haben keine

Ochsen gesehen. 13. Haben Sie zwei Hasen? 14. Nein, wir haben drei Hasen. 15. Der Mantel des Studenten ist neu. 16. Wo sind die Mäntel der Studenten? 17. Die Bedienten des Prinzen. 18. Hier ist der Garten des Präsidenten. 19. Der Kaiser hat viele Soldaten.

### Exercise 7.

1. The knife of the boy. 2. These boys are my nephews. 3. The ravens are birds. 4. My mother has a diamond. 5. The name of the student. 6. The elephants are very large. 7. The house of the prince. 8. I have seen the garden of the president. 9. My brother is a lawyer. 10. Where is the Frenchman? 11. Where are the Frenchmen? 12. The Germans are here, but the Frenchmen are not here. 13. Have you 'seen 'the 'soldiers?*) 14. I have seen many soldiers. 15. These boys are Russians.

### Conversation.

| | |
|---|---|
| Wo ist der Hut des Knaben? | Hier ist sein Hut. |
| Hat der Schüler einen Raben? | Nein, er hat einen Hasen. |
| Sind die Schüler Studenten? | Ja, sie sind Studenten. |
| Hat der Kaiser Soldaten? | Ja, der Kaiser hat viele Soldaten. |
| Haben Sie den Grafen gesehen? | Ja, er ist in dem Garten. |
| Kennen Sie diese zwei Studenten? | Ja, ich kenne sie (them), sie sind meine Neffen. |
| Haben Sie einen Elefanten [Elephanten] gesehen? | Ich habe einen Löwen und einen Elefanten gesehen. |
| Wie viele Neffen haben Sie? | Ich habe zwei Neffen. |

*) See the Note page 26.

# LESSON VI.

## Third Declension.

1) This declension contains the *monosyllabic masculine* substantives. In the *singular*, the genitive is formed by adding **es** or **s** to the nominative; in the dative, the word remains either unchanged or takes an **e**; the accusative is like the nominative. All the plural cases take **e** and in the dative **en**. Moreover, most of those which have **a, o, u** or **au** in the root, modify it into **ä, ö, ü** or **äu**.

### Examples.

| *Singular.* | *Plural.* |
|---|---|
| N. **der** Freund  the friend | **die Freunde**  the friends |
| G. des Freundes  of the friend | der Freunde  of the friends |
| D. dem Freund(e)  to the friend | den Freunden  to the friends |
| A. den Freund  the friend. | die Freunde  the friends. |
| **der** Stock  the cane or stick | **die Stöcke**  the canes |
| des Stockes  of the cane | der Stöcke  of the canes |
| dem Stock(e)  to the cane | den Stöcken  to the canes |
| den Stock  the cane. | die Stöcke  the canes. |
| **der** Baum  the tree | **die Bäume**  the trees |
| des Baumes  of the tree | der Bäume  of the trees |
| dem Baum(e)  to the tree | den Bäumen  to the trees |
| den Baum  the tree. | die Bäume  the trees. |

Thus are to be declined:

| | |
|---|---|
| der Sohn  the son. | der Fisch  the fish. |
| der Tisch  the table. | der Platz  the place. |
| der Stuhl  the chair. | der Rock  the coat. |
| der Hahn  the cock. | der Brief  the letter. |
| der Ast  the branch.. | der Kopf  the head. |
| der Hut  the hat, bonnet. | der Fuchs  the fox. |
| der Fuß  the foot. | der Wolf  the wolf. |

*Plur.* die Tische, die Stühle, die Äste [Aeste], die Füße, die Röcke ꝛc.

*Remarks.* The following words do not modify their vowel in the plural:

| Singular. | Plural. |
| --- | --- |
| der Arm  the arm | die Arme. |
| der Hund  the dog | die Hunde. |
| der Tag  the day | die Tage. |
| der Schuh  the shoe | die Schuhe. |
| der Punkt  the point | die Punkte. |

2) The third declension contains further the *masculine derivatives* ending in **ich, ig, al, aſt, at, ier, on** and **ling**, as:

| Singular. | Plural. |
| --- | --- |
| N. der König  the king | die Könige  the kings |
| G. des Königs  of the king | der Könige  of the kings |
| D. dem König(e)  to the king | den Königen  to the kings |
| A. den König  the king. | die Könige  the kings. |

Such are:

| | |
| --- | --- |
| der Teppich  the carpet. | der General'  the general. |
| der Honig  the honey. | der Admiral'  the admiral. |
| der Monat  the month. | der Palaſt'  the palace. |
| der Offizier' [Officier]  the officer. | der Baron'  the baron, baronet. |

*Gen.* des Teppichs, des Monats, des Offiziers, des Generals ꝛc.

*Plur.* die Teppiche, die Monate, die Generäle, die Paläſte ꝛc.

### Words.

| | |
| --- | --- |
| der Name(n)  the name. | der Nachbar  the neighbor. |
| der Wald  the wood. | ich kenne  I know; in  in. |
| der Fluß  the river. | hoch  high; reich  rich. |
| der Onkel  the uncle. | ſchön  beautiful; oder  or. |

### Exercise 8.

1. Der Name des Freundes.  2. Meine Freunde ſind gut.
3. Die Söhne des Vaters.  4. Die Bäume des Waldes.
5. Ich habe den Stock des Bruders.  6. Haben Sie den Hut des Knaben?  7. Die Hüte des Franzoſen.  8. Wo ſind die Fiſche?  9. Die Fiſche ſind in den Flüſſen.  10. Die Äſte

[Äfte] des Baumes find hoch.  11. Die Schuhe des Mädchens find klein.  12. Die Füße des Elefanten [Elephanten] find fehr groß.  13. Wir haben zwei Füchfe und drei Wölfe gefehen.  14. Die Köpfe diefer Fifche find fehr klein.  15. Die Teppiche des Engländers find fehr fchön.  16. Die Zimmer des Palaftes find hoch.  17. In den Paläften der Könige.  18. Die Tage des Monats.  19. Ich kenne die Söhne des Generals.

### Exercise 9.

1. The. letter of the friend.  2. The letters of my friend.  3. The hats of the boys.  4. The chairs of the room.  5. A branch of a tree.  6. The branches of the trees.  7. I have no cane (stick).  8. We have no sticks.  9. The foxes are in the (dem) wood (*dat.*).,  10. The fish(es) are in the water.  11. Has your uncle a dog?  12. My uncle has two dogs.  13. The kings are rich.  14. The carpets of the king are very large.  15. Where are my shoes?  16. Your shoes are in the (dem) room.  17. The fish(es) have no feet.  18. In three or four days (*dat.*).

### Conversation.

| | |
|---|---|
| Haben Sie einen Freund? | Ich habe zwei Freunde. |
| Wer hat meinen Stock? | Ich habe Ihren Stock. |
| Wo find die Söhne des Prinzen? | Sie find in dem Palafte. |
| Wo find die Teppiche? | Sie find in den Zimmern. |
| Haben die Fifche Füße? | Nein, die Fifche haben keine Füße. |
| Wo find die Bäume? | Die Bäume find in dem Wald. |
| Wer hat den Hund gefehen? | Mein Freund hat den Hund gefehen. |
| Sind die Schuhe alt? | Nein, die Schuhe find neu. |
| Sind jene Bäume hoch? | Jene Bäume find fehr hoch. |
| Wie viele Monate? | Fünf Monate. |
| Wie viele Tage? | Drei Tage. |

# LESSON VII.

## Fourth Declension.

The fourth declension comprises all the substantives of the *feminine* gender.

In the singular feminine words remain *unchanged* in all the cases. The plural depends on the number of syllables.

### I. Feminine Monosyllabic Nouns.

The *real monosyllables* take **e** in the *plural*, at the same time modifying their vowel.

**Declension.**

| *Singular.* | | *Plural.* | |
|---|---|---|---|
| N. die Hand | the hand | die **Hände** | the hands |
| G. der Hand | of the hand | der Hände | of the hands |
| D. der Hand | to the hand | den Händen | to the hands |
| A. die Hand | the hand. | die Hände | the hands. |

Such are:

| | |
|---|---|
| die Bank  the bench; bank. | die Magd  the (fem.) servant. |
| die Frucht  the fruit. | die Maus  the mouse. |
| die Gans  the goose. | die Nacht  the night. |
| die Kuh  the cow. | die Nuß  the walnut. |
| die Kunst  the art. | die Stadt  the town, city. |

*Plur.* die Bänke, die Früchte, die Gänse, die Kühe, die Künste, die Mäuse, die Nächte, die Nüsse, die Städte.

---

### II. Feminine Polysyllabic Nouns.

The dissyllabic and polysyllabic feminine nouns take **n** or **en** in the plural of all cases, *without modifying the vowel*\*). Words ending in **l** or **r** have no **e** before **n**.

---

\*) Except the two words: die Mutter and die Tochter which form their plural: die **Mütter** and die **Töchter.**

### Examples.

| Singular. | | Plural. | |
|---|---|---|---|
| N. die Blume | the flower | die Blumen | the flowers |
| G. der Blume | of the flower | der Blumen | of the flowers |
| D. der Blume | to the flower | den Blumen | to the flowers |
| A. die Blume | the flower. | die Blumen | the flower. |

| | | | |
|---|---|---|---|
| die Feder | the pen, feather | die Federn | the pens |
| der Feder | of the pen | der Federn | of the pens |
| der Feder | to the pen | den Federn | to the pens |
| die Feder | the pen. | die Federn | the pens. |

### Such are:

| | | | |
|---|---|---|---|
| die Aufgabe | the exercise. | die Mauer | the wall. |
| die Farbe | the color. | die Gabel | the fork. |
| die Birne | the pear. | die Nadel | the needle. |
| die Kirsche | the cherry. | die Stecknadel | the pin. |
| die Kirche | the church. | die Arbeit | the work. |
| die Schule | the school. | die Krankheit | the illness. |
| die Pflanze | the plant. | die Wissenschaft | the science. |
| die Rose | the rose. | die Grammatik | the grammar. |
| die Stunde | the hour. | die Hoffnung | the hope. |
| die Straße | the street. | die Freundin*) | (female) the friend. |
| die Tante | the aunt. | die Königin*) | the queen. |
| die Schwester | the sister. | die Prinzessin*) | the princess. |

*NB.* Observe that all derivative nouns ending in ei (ey), heit, keit, schaft, ung and in are feminine and take in the plural en. Ex.: die Arbeiten, die Krankheiten, die Hoffnungen ꝛc.

*Remark.* A small number of feminine *monosyllabic* nouns, likewise take en in the plural. Such are:

---

*) Feminine nouns in in double their n in the plural, as: die Königinnen, die Prinzessinnen or Fürstinnen (the princesses) etc.

| *Singular.* | *Plural.* |
|---|---|
| die Frau  the woman, wife | die Frauen. |
| die Pflicht  the duty | die Pflichten. |
| die Schlacht  the battle | die Schlachten. |
| die Schuld  the debt; guilt | die Schulden. |
| die That  the action | die Thaten. |
| die Uhr  the watch, clock | die Uhren. |
| die Welt  the world | die Welten. |
| die Zahl  the number | die Zahlen. |
| die Zeit  the time | die Zeiten. |

## Words.

die Schülerin  the pupil (fem.).
die Nichte  the niece.
die Milch  the milk.
die Wurzel  the root.
gekauft  bought.
ich gebe  I give.
der Einwohner  the inhabitant.
die Thür  the door.
die Ente  the duck.

der Nußbaum  the walnut-tree.
reif  ripe.
geschlafen  slept.
rot [roth]  red.
ich liebe  I like.
lang  long; so  so; als  as.
schlecht  bad; besser  better.
war  was; waren  were.
die Stahlfeder  the steel-pen.

## Exercise 10.

1.  (Monosyllabic.) 1. Die Hand des Kindes ist klein.
2. Die Hände der Königin sind klein. 3. Die Früchte der
Bäume. 4. Die Federn der Gänse. 5. Wir haben drei
Kühe. 6. Die Mäuse sind in den Zimmern. 7. Die
Städte sind groß. 8. Ich liebe die Nüsse. 9. Meine
Mutter hat viele Nüsse gekauft. 10. Lieben Sie die Künste?

2.  (Polysyllabic.) 11. Die Blumen sind schön. 12.
Die Farbe der Rose. 13. Die Farben der Blumen. 14. Die
Feder der Königin. 15. Die Federn meiner Schwestern.
16. Ich habe die Aufgaben der Schülerinnen gesehen. 17. Die
Wurzeln der Pflanzen. 18. Ich gebe diese Blumen der
Königin. 19. Die Hoffnungen der Menschen. 20. Das Kind

hat viele Kirſchen.  21. Die Mauern der Stadt ſind hoch.
22. Die Pflichten des Soldaten.  23. Die Stunden des Tages
ſind lang.  24. Die Prinzeſſinnen ſind die Schweſtern der
Prinzen.  25. Die Arbeiten dieſes Schülers waren ſehr ſchlecht.
26. Lieben Sie die Kirſchen?

### Exercise 11.

*Monosyllables.*  1. I have two hands.  2. What have
you in your hands?  3. I have cherries.  4. Are they
ripe?  5. Yes, they are ripe.  6. (The) geese have
feathers (Federn).  7. I like (the) geese.  8. The milk of
the cows is good.  9. The fruits of the trees are ripe.
10. (The) walnuts are very good.  11. (The) cows are
not so big (groß) as (the) oxen.  12. My neighbor has five
cows.  13. The inhabitants of (the) towns have not
many ducks and geese.  14. (The) walnuts are the
fruit(s) of the walnut-tree.

### Exercise 12.

1) *Polysyllabic.*  1. I like (the) flowers.  2. Which
flowers do you like best (am meiſten)?  3. I like the
roses best.  4. The colors of the roses are beautiful.
5. The walls of the town are high.  6. How many doors
has that house?  7. It has four rooms and six doors.
8. I have slept five hours.  9. How long has your
brother slept?  10. He has slept six hours.  11. To
whom (Wem) do you give these steel-pens?  12. I give
them (ſie) to my (female) friends.

2)  13. Where are your sisters?  14. They are here;
they are writing (write) (ſchreiben) their exercises and
their letters.  15. I love my aunts; they are very kind
(gütig).  16. These pens are not very good; Robert's
pens are much better.  17. The pupil has bought two

grammars. 18. Do you know my two nieces? 19. Yes, Sir, I know them very well (gut). 20. The streets of this town are very wide (breit).

### Conversation.

| | |
|---|---|
| Haſt du meine Federn? | Deine Schweſter hat ſie (them). |
| Haben Sie Kirſchen gekauft? | Nein, ich habe Birnen gekauft. |
| Sind die Nadeln Ihrer Schwe=ſtern gut? | Ja, ſie ſind ſehr gut. |
| Wo iſt die Königin? | Die Königin iſt in der Kirche. |
| Wo ſind die Schweſtern dieſes Mädchens? | Sie ſind in der Schule. |
| Wo ſind die Kirſchen? | Die Kirſchen ſind hier. |
| Lieben Sie die Roſen? | Ja, ich liebe die Roſen. |
| Sind die Arbeiten gut? | Nein, ſie ſind ſehr ſchlecht. |
| Haben Sie eine Uhr? | Ich habe zwei Uhren. |
| Wie lange haben Sie ge=ſchlafen? | Ich habe fünf Stunden ge=ſchlafen. |

# LESSON VIII.

## Fifth Declension.

It includes merely the nouns of the *neuter* gender except those ending in el, en, er, chen and lein, which belong to the 1st declension.

In the singular, they have the mode of inflexion of the *third* declension, viz.: the genitive is formed by adding es or s, the dative by adding e, which may, how-ever, be omitted in ordinary conversation.

In the plural, most *monosyllabic neuter* nouns take er and modify the vowel.

## I. Declension of *monosyllabic* neuter Nouns.

*Singular.*

N. bas Kind  the child
G. des Kindes  of the child
D. dem Kind(e)  to the child
A. bas Kind  the child.

*Singular.*

N. bas Buch  the book
G. des Buch(e)s  of the book
D. dem Buch(e)  to the book
A. bas Buch  the book.

*Plural.*

N.&A. die Kinder the children
G. der Kinder  of the children
D. den Kindern to the children.

*Plural.*

die Bücher  the books
ber Bücher  of the books
ben Büchern  to the books.

Thus are to be declined:

bas Blatt  the leaf.
bas Band  the ribbon.
bas Bild  the picture.
bas Dorf  the village.
bas Huhn  the hen.
bas Schloß  the castle.
bas Kleib  the dress.
bas Land  the country.
bas Geld  the money.

bas Ei  the egg.
bas Feld  the field.
bas Haus  the house.
bas Kalb  the calf.
bas Glas  the glass.
bas Wort  the word.
bas Lied  the song.
bas Nest  the nest.

*Plur.* die Blätter, die Bänder, die Eier, die Dörfer, die Kleider, die Lieber, die Häuser, die Länder, die Nester zc.

---

## II. *Dissyllabic* and *trisyllabic* neuter nouns follow the *third* declension, having s in the genitive singular, and e in the plural.

*Declension of a dissyllabic neuter Noun.*

*Singular.*

N.&A. bas Geschäft the business
G. des Geschäfts  of the business
D. dem Geschäft(e) to the business.

*Plural.*

die Geschäfte
ber Geschäfte
ben Geschäften.

**Such are:**

das Geschenk  the present, gift.
das Gewehr  the musket.
das Gespräch  the conversation.
das Gebirge  the mountain.
das Gesetz  the law.
das Gebäude  the building.

das Kamel' [Kameel]  the camel.
das Metall'  the metal.
das Papier'  the paper.
das Konzert'. [Concert]  the concert.
das Billet'  the ticket.
das Kompliment [Compliment]  the compliment.

*Plur.* die Geschenke, die Gewehre, die Gebirge, die Gesetze, die Kamele, die Metal'le, die Billet'te.

### Words.

das Gemälde  the painting.
der Amerikaner  the American.
grün  green.
neu  new.

das Land  the country.
verloren  lost.
gebrochen  broken.
zu Hause or zu Haus  at home.

### Exercise 13.

1. (Monosyllabic.) 1. Das Kind hat ein Buch. 2. Ich habe zwei Bücher. 3. Die Straße des Dorfes. 4. In dem Dorf. 5. Die Blätter des Baumes. 6. Die Thüre des Hauses. 7. Die Häuser der Stadt sind hoch. 8. Die Kinder sind in dem Felde. 9. Die Länder der Könige sind sehr groß. 10. Ich gebe das Buch den Kindern des Lehrers. 11. Meine Schwester singt (sings) Lieder. 12. Die Bücher meiner Nichte sind neu. 13. Wo haben Sie diese Kleider gekauft. 14. Sie sind sehr schön. 15. Ich liebe die Eier der Hühner.

2. (Polysyllabic.) 16. Die Geschäfte des Vaters. 17. Die Geschenke der Königin waren reich. 18. Ich habe drei Billete für das Konzert [Concert] gekauft. 19. Jene Gebäude sind sehr alt. 20. Die Gesetze der Amerikaner. 21. Das Gold und das Silber sind Metalle. 22. Hier sind die Gewehre der Soldaten. 23. Machen (make) Sie keine Komplimente [Complimente].

### Exercise 14.

1. *Monosyllables.* 1. The child is small. 2. I have seen a village. 3. These villages are not large. 4. The servant has broken the glasses. 5. How many glasses has he broken? 6. He has broken three glasses. 7. Do you like (the)*) eggs? 8. The ribbons of my niece are green, your ribbons are red. √9. Have you seen the pictures? 10. Yes, I have seen them (fie). 11. These two boys have lost their books. 12. Which books? 13. Their grammars. 14. (The) hens lay (legen) eggs. 15. The eggs of the birds lie (liegen) in the nests (*dat.*). 16. How are the dresses of the children? 17. The dresses of those children are very old.

2. *Dissyllables.* 18. The presents of the king. 19. The business of the father. 20. Gold and silver are metals. 21. The laws of the Americans. 22. I have bought two tickets for the theatre (für bas Theater). 23. The mountains of this country are very high.

### Conversation.

| | |
|---|---|
| Welches Buch haben Sie gelesen (read)? | Ich habe dieses Buch ge= lesen. |
| Wo wohnen (live) Sie? | Ich wohne in einem Dorfe. |
| Hat die Frau viele Kinder? | Sie hat drei Kinder. |
| Was hat das Kind gekauft? | Es hat Bilder gekauft. |
| Lieben Sie die Eier? | Ja, die Eier der Hühner. |
| Was haben die Vögel? | Die Vögel haben Nester. |
| Wo sind die Eier der Vögel? | Sie sind in den Nestern. |
| Wie sind die Blätter der Bäume? | Die Blätter der Bäume sind grün. |
| Wie sind die Metalle? | Die Metalle sind schwer (heavy). |

*) Observe that words in round parenthesis ( . . ) are to be translated; whereas those enclosed in brackets [ . . ] are to be *left out.*

# LESSON IX.

## The Partitive Sense.

1) The idea conveyed by *some* or *any* before a noun
employed in the partitive sense, is expressed in German
by the *mere* word, without any article, both in the
singular and plural.

### Examples in Singular.

Brot [Brod]  bread or some
  bread.
Gold  gold or some gold.
Silber  silver.  Eisen  iron.
Mehl  flour (meal).
Kaffee [Caffee]  (some) coffee.

Zucker  (some) sugar.
Tinte [Dinte]  (some) ink.
Tuch  (some) cloth.
Bier  (some) beer.
Wasser  (some) water.

### Examples in Plural.

Kinder  children.
Federn  pens.
Bleistifte  pencils.
Blumen  flowers.
Schafe  sheep.
Schweine  pigs.

Kühe  cows.
Pferde  horses.
Kleider  clothes.
Schuhe  shoes.
Hunde  dogs.

2) This form (without article) is also employed after
nouns denoting *measure, quantity* and *weight;* nor is
the English preposition *of* then translated in German.

### Examples.

Ein Glas Wasser  a glass of water.
Eine Flasche Wein  a bottle of wine.
Ein Stück Brot [Brod]  a piece of bread.
Ein Pfund Kirschen  a pound of cherries.
Ein Paar Strümpfe  a pair of stockings.
Ein Dutzend Bleistifte  a dozen pencils.

## Words.

| | |
|---|---|
| die Butter  butter. | die Handschuhe  the gloves. |
| ein Stück  a piece. | der Kaufmann  the merchant. |
| der Schinken  ham. | wollen Sie? { will you have? / do you wish? } |
| das Salz  salt. | |
| der Pfeffer  pepper. | der Bleistift  the pencil. |
| der Käse  cheese. | gekauft  bought. |

### Exercise 15.

1. Ich habe Brot [Brod] und Butter; Sie haben Brot und Käse.  2. Die Frau hat Butter und Eier gekauft.  3. Wollen Sie Brot und Schinken?  4. Geben Sie mir ein Stück Brot und ein Stück Schinken!  5. Geben Sie mir auch Salz und Pfeffer!  6. Wollen Sie Wein?  7. Ja, geben Sie mir Wein oder Bier!  8. Hier ist eine Flasche Wasser.  9. Ich habe Birnen und Äpfel [Aepfel] gekauft; ich gebe sie (them) den Kindern meines Lehrers.  10. Haben Sie Tinte [Dinte]?  11. Hier sind Federn, Papier und Tinte.  12. Hat der Schüler Bleistifte?  13. Er hat ein Dutzend Bleistifte und drei oder vier Federn.

### Exercise 16.

1. We have sugar and coffee.  2. Have you also bread?  3. Yes, we have bread and butter.  4. Our mother has flour and salt.  5. My neighbor has horses, cows, sheep and pigs.  6. Will you have beer or wine? 7. Give me some beer.  8. I have bought clothes and shoes.  9. Give me a piece of bread and a piece of ham. 10. Here is a glass of wine and a bottle of water. 11. What have you bought?  12. I have bought a pound of cherries and a dozen pencils.

### Conversation.

| | |
|---|---|
| Was hat der Kaufman? | Er hat Salz, Öl [Del] und Pfeffer. |
| Hat er auch Kaffee [Caffee]? | Ja, er hat Kaffee und Zucker. |

Was haben Sie auf dem Markte (at the market) gekauft?

Wie viel Paar Schuhe haben Sie?

Was hat der Knabe?

Hat er auch Bücher?

Wollen Sie Bier oder Wein?

Ich habe Butter und Eier gekauft.

Ich habe zwei Paar Schuhe und ein Paar Stiefel.

Er hat Federn, Bleistifte, Papier und Tinte [Dinte].

Ja, er hat viele Bücher.

Geben Sie mir eine Flasche Wein?

# LESSON X.

## Irregular Plurals.

The following nouns form their plurals as follows:

### 1. *Belonging to the First Declension.*

| Singular. | Plural. |
| --- | --- |
| der Bauer the peasant | die Bauern. |
| der Vetter the cousin | die Vettern. |
| der Nachbar the neighbor | die Nachbarn. |
| der Namen or Name the name | die Namen. |

### 2. *Of the Third Declension.*

| Singular. | Plural. |
| --- | --- |
| der Staat the state | die Staaten. |
| der Strahl the ray, beam | die Strahlen. |
| der See the lake | die See[e]n. |
| der Mann the man | die Männer. |
| der Gott the god | die Götter. |
| der Wurm the worm | die Würmer. |
| der Wald the forest | die Wälder. |

### 3. Of the Fourth Declension.

| Singular. | Plural. |
|---|---|
| die Mutter  the mother | die **Mütter.** |
| die Tochter  the daughter | die **Töchter.** |

(See also the "Remark" page 33.)

### 4. Of the Fifth Declension.

| Singular. | Plural. |
|---|---|
| das Herz  the heart | die Herzen. |
| das Ohr  the ear | die Ohren. |
| das Auge  the eye | die Augen. |
| das Jahr  the year | die Jahre. |
| das Haar  the hair | die Haare. |
| das Tier [Thier]  the animal | die Tiere. |
| das Schaf  the sheep | die Schafe. |
| das Schiff  the ship | die Schiffe. |
| das Spiel  the play | die Spiele. |
| das Heft  the copy-book, writing-book | die Hefte. |
| das Pferd  the horse | die Pferde. |
| das Schwein  the pig, swine | die Schweine. |
| das Werk  the work | die Werke. |

### Words.

| | |
|---|---|
| die Erde  the earth. | ich kenne  I know. |
| warm  warm. | mehr als  more than. |
| Deutsche *Pl.* Germans. | der Römer  the Roman. |
| kennen Sie?  do you know? | die Sonne  the sun. |
| blau  blue. | die Gräfin  the countess. |

### Exercise 17.

1. Die Bauern sind in den Dörfern.  2. Ich habe zwei Vettern.  3. Die Strahlen der Sonne sind warm.  4. Diese Männer sind Deutsche.  5. Die Würmer sind in der Erde. 6. Die Römer hatten viele Götter.  7. Die Mütter lieben (love) ihre Töchter.  8. Ich kenne die Herzen der Kinder.

9. Die Ohren des Esels sind lang. 10. Die Augen dieses Mädchens sind blau. 11. Drei oder vier Jahre. 12. Die Schafe und Schweine sind kleiner (smaller) als die Pferde. 13. Der Schüler hat zwei Hefte gekauft. 14. Ich habe die Schiffe der Amerikaner gesehen. 15. Ich liebe die Spiele der Kinder.

### Exercise 18.

1. The peasants are not rich. 2. I have no cousins. 3. I like the beams of the sun. 4. Who are these men? 5. These men are Frenchmen. 6. How many daughters has the countess? 7. She has three daughters. 8. Has she no sons? 9. Yes, she has also two sons, but the sons are younger than the daughters. 10. The hearts of the children. 11. How are the ears of the donkey. 12. They are long. 13. Your eyes are blue. 14. The child is five years old. 15. How many copy-books have you bought? 16. The peasants have sheep and pigs; they have also horses and oxen (see page 27).

### Conversation.

| | |
|---|---|
| Was haben die Bauern? | Die Bauern haben Pferde, Kühe, Schafe und Schweine. |
| Wie viele Töchter hat Ihre Tante? | Sie hat drei Töchter. |
| Wo sind die Mütter dieser Kinder? | Sie sind in der Kirche. |
| Wie sind die Ohren eines Esels? | Seine Ohren sind sehr lang. |
| Was haben die Schüler gekauft? | Sie haben Hefte gekauft. |
| Hat Ihr Onkel Pferde? | Ja, er hat vier Pferde. |
| Wie sind die Schiffe der Engländer? | Sie sind groß und schön. |
| Wo sind Ihre Vettern? | Sie sind in England. |
| Wie sind die Strahlen der Sonne? | Die Strahlen der Sonne sind warm. |

# LESSON XI.

## Prepositions.

German prepositions govern either the dative or the accusative, or both of these, or also the genitive case. For the present, we only give such as are most used:

**1. Prepositions governing the *accusative*:**

| | |
|---|---|
| **burdj** through, by. | **ohne** without. |
| **für** for. | **um** round, about, at (*time*). |
| **gegen** against, towards. | |

### Examples.

Durdj b e n Garten (*acc. masc.*) through the garden.
Durdj b i e Straße (*acc. fem.*) through the street.
Durdj b a 8 Waſſer (*acc. neut.*) through the water.
Für mein e Schweſter (*acc. fem.*) for my sister.
Gegen mein e n Bruder (*acc. masc.*) against my brother.
Ohne ein e n Freund without a friend etc.

**2. Prepositions with the *dative*:**

| | |
|---|---|
| **aus** out of, of, from. | **ſeit** since. |
| **bei** near, at, by (with). | **von** of, from, by. |
| **mit** with. | **zu** to. at. |
| **nach** after, to (*a place*). | **gegenüber** opposite (to). |

### Examples.

Aus b e m Haus (*dat. neut.*) from (out of) the house.
Aus b e r Stadt (*dat. fem.*) out of (the) town.
Mit ein e m Stock (*dat. masc.*) with a stick.
Mit ein e r Feder (*dat. fem.*) with a pen.
Nach b e m Eſſen (*dat. neut.*) after (the) dinner.
Nach b e m Walde (*dat. masc.*) to the forest.
Von b e m Nachbar from (by) the neighbor etc.

3. Prepositions which govern the *genitive:*

| | |
|---|---|
| ſtatt or ⎫ instead of.<br>anſtatt ⎰ | während during.<br>wegen on account of. |

### Words.

der Hof  the court, yard.
das Bad  the bath.
die Erlaubnis [Erlaubniß]  the permission.
das Schloß  the castle.
der Bediente  the (man-)servant.

die Brücke  the bridge.
der Monat  the month.
der Winter  the winter.
gehen Sie?  do you go?
ich gehe  I go.
ausgegangen  gone out.
der Regen  the rain.

### Exercise 19.

1)  1. Gehen Sie durch den Garten? Nein, ich gehe durch den Hof.  2. Dieſer Hut iſt für den Sohn des Grafen. 3. Ich habe Geſchenke für die Kinder meines Lehrers gekauft. 4. Gegen die Thüre.  5. Die Schüler ſind ohne meine Er= laubnis [Erlaubniß] ausgegangen.  6. Gehen Sie um die Kirche? Nein, ich gehe um das Dorf.

2)  7. Ich komme (I come) aus der Stadt.  8. Die Poſt iſt bei der Kirche.  9. Ich habe den Vater mit ſeinem Sohne geſehen.  10. Nach dem Regen.  11. Der Franzoſe wohnt (lives) bei dem Schloſſe.  12. Ich bin ſeit drei Tagen hier.  13. Ich ſpreche von dem Vater und der Mutter meiner Schülerin. 14. Wegen des Regens. 15. Während des Winters.

### Exercise 20.

1)  1. Through the window.  2. This book is for my brother, and that pen is for my mother.  3. Against the bridge.  4. Without a stick.  5. Round the table.  6. I go through the yard and through the garden.

2)  7. Do you go *out of* the house?  8. Yes, I go out of the house.  9. Near the bridge.  10. I go with my

master (Herrn).   11. After the rain.   12. Since a month.
13. Since three days.   14. The servant goes (geht) to (zu)
his master.   15. I go to my uncle(s).   16. From my
teacher.   17. Opposite the castle.

3)   18. Instead of a letter.   19. Instead of a pen.
20. During the rain.   21. On account of the winter.
22. Instead of a horse.

---

4) Prepositions which govern both the *dative* and
*accusative*.   The following *nine* take the *dative* in
answer to the question "*where*"? indicating a state of
rest, or sometimes an action within a certain place.
They require, however, the *accusative* after the question
"*whither? or to what place?*" with a verb denoting a
direction or motion from one place to another:

| | | |
|---|---|---|
| **an** (*w. dat.*) at. | **in***) (*dat.*) in, at. | **über** over, across. |
| an (*w. acc.*) to. | in (*w. acc.*) into. | **unter** (*place*) under. |
| **auf** on, upon. | **neben** beside, near. | unter (*number*) among. |
| **hinter** behind. | **vor***) before, ago. | **zwischen** between. |

### Examples with the dative (rest).

An dem Fenster (*dat. neut.*) at the window.
Auf dem Tisch(e) (*dat. masc.*) on the table.

In dem Hof(e) (*dat. masc.*) in the (court-)yard.
In der Stadt (*dat. fem.*) in (the) town.

Über [Ueber] dem Fluß (=ffe) over the river.
Unter dem Tisch(e) under the table.

5) Several of the above-cited prepositions may be
contracted with the definite article, in which form they
are in very general use.

---

*) **in** and **vor**, when denoting *time*, always take the dative, as:
In zwei Tagen in two days.   Vor einem Jahr a year ago.

am for an dem.
beim for bei dem.
im for in dem.
vom for von dem 2c.

ans [an's] for an das.
durchs [durch's] for durch das.
ins [in's] for in das.
übers [über's] for über das.

Ex.: am Fenster; im Garten; ins Wasser 2c.

## Words.

der Arm  the arm.
die Thüre  the door.
das Thor  the gate.
der Boden  the floor.
der Stall  the stable.
wohnt lives.  wohnen live.
das Schaf  the sheep.
spielt plays.  geht goes.

der Berg  the mountain.
der Storch  the stork.
das Bett  the bed.
das Theater  the theatre.
gehen Sie (imperat.) go!
kommen to come.  so so, thus.
zu Hause at home.
nach Hause home.

## Exercise 21.

1) 1. An dem (am) Arm. 2. An der Thüre. 3. Auf dem Boden. 4. Hinter dem Thor(e). 5. Neben der Brücke. 6. Auf den Bäumen. 7. Ich bin in dem Hause. 8. Ich gehe in das Haus. 9. Die Kinder sind in der Schule. 10. Sie gehen (they go) in die Schule. 11. Die Pferde sind in dem Stall. 12. Die Kühe sind in dem (or im) Hof. 13. Die Schafe sind auf den Feldern.

2) 14. Das Bett steht (stands) zwischen der Thüre und dem Fenster. 15. Der Hund liegt (lies) unter dem Stuhle. 16. Wir wohnen in der Stadt. 17. Unser Freund wohnt in einem Dorfe. 18. Die Fische sind im Wasser. 19. Die Frauen sind in der Kirche. 20. Gehen Sie auf das Schloß? 21. Nein, wir gehen auf die Brücke. 22. Das Messer liegt auf dem Tisch. 23. Die Katze spielt unter dem Tische.

### Exercise 22.

1. At the window.   2. On the floor.   3. Under the tree.   4. Before the castle.   5. The boy stands (steht) at the door.   6. They go on (*acc.*) the mountain.   7. What is on the (*dat.*) mountain?   8. The stork sits (sitzt) on our house.   9. Where is your stick?   10. It lies (er liegt) in the water.   11. The fish(es) are in the river. 12. The girl stands behind the door.   13. My book lies on the table.   14. The dog goes under the table. 15. The cat lies under my chair.   16. My neighbor lives (wohnt) close to (neben) my house.   17. The house stands in the garden.

### Conversation.

| | |
|---|---|
| Wo ist Ihr Lehrer? | Er ist im (or in dem) Zimmer. |
| Wo sind die Schüler? | Sie sind in dem (im) Hof. |
| Wo wohnt Herr Moll? | Er wohnt in der Stadt, neben der Brücke. |
| Hast du meine Feder gefunden? | Ja, sie war unter dem Stuhl. |
| Wo war der Knabe? | Er war an (bei) dem Flusse. |
| Wohin (where) geht diese Frau? | Sie geht in den Wald. |
| Haben Sie meine Nichte gesehen? | Ja, sie ist in dem (im) Garten. |
| Woher (whence) kommen Sie? | Ich komme aus dem Bad (bath). |
| Wo waren Sie, mein Freund? | Ich war im Theater. |
| Wo sind Ihre Pferde? | Sie sind in dem (im) Stall. |
| Gehen Sie heute ins [in's] Theater? | Nein, ich gehe ins Konzert [Concert]. |
| Sind Ihre Neffen zu Hause? | Nein, sie sind nicht zu Hause; sie sind ausgegangen (gone out). |

# LESSON XII.

## (Personal) Proper Names.

### (Eigennamen).

1) The inflexion of Proper Names of *persons* is very simple; the genitive takes $, and the other cases remain unchanged. Christian names, however, may take the article.

### Declension.

#### 1. Family Names.

| | | | |
|---|---|---|---|
| N. | Byron Byron | Schiller Schiller |
| G. | Byrons of B. or B.'s | Schillers of Sch. or Sch.'s |
| D. | Byron to Byron | Schiller to Schiller |
| A. | Byron Byron. | Schiller Schiller. |

#### 2. Male Christian Names.

| | | | |
|---|---|---|---|
| N. | Wilhelm William | Friedrich Frederick |
| G. | Wilhelms William's, of W. | Friedrichs Frederick's, of F. |
| D. | Wilhelm to William | Friedrich to Frederick |
| A. | Wilhelm William. | Friedrich Frederick. |

Or also: *N.* der Wilhelm, *G.* des Wilhelm, *D.* dem Wilhelm, *A.* den Wilhelm.

Such names are:

| | | |
|---|---|---|
| Ludwig Lewis. | Georg George. | Heinrich Henry. |
| Eduard Edward. | Karl [Carl] Charles. | Johann John. |

### Special Rules.

2) When a name is accompanied by an adjective, it must take the article. Ex.:

*N.* der arme Heinrich poor Henry. *G.* des armen Heinrich. *D.* dem armen Heinrich. *A.* den armen Heinrich.

3) Proper names of persons terminating in a hissing consonant (ß, ß, ſch, x or z) replace the ß of the genitive by the article des, some also by the termination ens. Ex.:

Auguſtus Augustus. — *Gen.* des Auguſtus of Augustus.
Der Bruder des Thomas Thomas's brother.
Die Bücher Moritzens the books of Maurice.

### 3. Female Christian Names.

Most of these form their genitive in ens or ns, as: Mariens, and the dative in en. But when no ſ precedes the e, they can simply take ß in the genitive as: Maries, Fannys ꝛc.; or they may take the feminine article, in which case they remain unchanged, as: Marie, *G.* der Marie ꝛc.

### Declension.

*Nom.* Luiſe [Louiſe] Louisa
*Gen.* Luiſens [Louiſens] or der Luiſe [Louiſe]
*Dat.* Luiſen [Louiſen] or der Luiſe [Louiſe]
*Acc.* Luiſe [Louiſe] or die Luiſe [Louiſe].

| | | |
|---|---|---|
| *Nom.* Marie Mary | | Eliſe Eliza |
| *Gen.* Mariens or der Marie | | Eliſens or der Eliſe |
| *Dat.* Marien or der Marie | | Eliſen or der Eliſe |
| *Acc.* Marie or die Marie. | | Eliſe or die Eliſe. |

Such are:

Amalie Amelia.    Sophie Sophia, —y.    Karoline [Caroline] Caroline.

Julie Juliet.    Eliſabeth Elizabeth.    Emi'lie Emily.

*Note.* Feminine names in a and y take only ß in the genitive, and remain unchanged in the two other cases, as:

*Gen.* Emmas, Saras [Sarahs], Annas, Roſas, Lauras, Fannys.
*Dat.* Emma (or der Emma), (der) Fanny. — *Acc.* Emma.

### Remarks.

1) As in English, the proper name, when in the genitive without the article, and marking the possessor, often precedes the other noun:

Karls [Carls] Bücher (for die Bücher Karls) Charles's books.
Elisens und Rosas Handschuhe Elisa's and Rosa's gloves.
Byrons Werke Byron's works.

2) If a proper name is preceded by a common name such as: (der) Herr **Mr.**; Frau or Madame **Mrs.**; Fräulein **Miss**; or der König, die Königin, der General ꝛc., the latter is declined, whereas the proper name remains unchanged, as:

Der Kaiser Wilhelm, *Gen.* des Kaisers Wilhelm.
Die Königin Viktoria [Victoria], *Gen. & Dat.* der Königin Viktoria.

### Declension.

*N.* (der)*) Herr Müller      (die)*) Frau Braun
*G.* des Herrn Müller      der Frau Braun
*D.* dem Herrn Müller      der Frau Braun
*A.* (den) Herrn Müller.      (die) Frau Braun.

**Ex.:** Der Sohn des Herrn Bill the son of Mr. Bill.
       Der Hof des Königs Ludwig the court of king Lewis.

### Words.

bie Kappe (die Mütze) the cap.    der Handschuh the glove.
das Gedicht (*pl.* -e) the poem.    gelesen read.   da there.
der Oheim er Onkel the uncle.    heißt is called.
bie Tante the aunt.    ausgegangen gone out.

### Exercise 23.

1. Ludwig ist jung. 2. Die Kappe Heinrichs. 3. Die Bücher Wilhelms or Wilhelms Bücher. 4. Rousseaus Name.

---

*) In the *nom. sing.* the article is generally omitted; sometimes also in the accusative case.

5. Ich liebe Berangers Gedichte. 6. Haben Sie Schillers Werke gelesen? 7. Ich habe Schillers Gedichte gelesen. 8. Hier sind Napoleons Werke. 9. Emmas Mutter ist krank. 10. Friedrich Wilhelms Söhne. 11. Byron, Milton und Shakespeare waren berühmte Dichter (renowned poets). 12. Mein Sohn heißt Karl [Carl], meine Tochter heißt Luise [Louise]. 13. Der Oheim Johanns ist mein Bruder. 14. Luisens [Louisens] Tante heißt Fanny. 15. Wo sind Friedrichs Bücher? 16. Sie sind auf dem Tische. 17. Die Kaiserin von Österreich [Oesterreich] (Austria) heißt Elisabeth.

### Exercise 24.

1. Charles is my brother; Emily is my sister. 2. I have Sophy's gloves. 3. Where is Mr. Peter? 4. He is not here. 5. Where is the aunt of Miss Louisa (or Miss Louisa's aunt)? 6. She is in Paris. 7. Have you seen Mr. and Mrs. Müller? 8. No, Sir. 9. Here is Mary's pen, and there is Emma's pencil. 10. George has a horse, and Robert has two dogs. 11. Give the book to John (give John the book). 12. Elizabeth's bonnet (Hut) is old. 13. Anne's bonnet is new. 14. We have seen the son of Mr. Peel (Mr. Peel's son). 15. Here is the horse of (the) king William. 16. I know the daughters of (the) queen Victoria.

### Conversation.

| | |
|---|---|
| Wo ist Karls [Carls] Vater? | Er ist hier. |
| Wo ist Luisens [Louisens] Tante? | Sie ist in Paris. |
| Für wen (for whom) sind diese Handschuhe? | Sie sind für Fräulein Julie. |
| Haben Sie den Kaiser Wilhelm gesehen? | Ja, ich habe ihn (him) in Berlin gesehen. |

Wie heißt die Königin von England?

Sie heißt Viktoria [Victoria].

Wo sind Emiliens Federn?

Sie (sie) liegen auf dem Tisch.

Für wen sind diese Bücher?

Sie sind für Herrn Maier.

Für wen sind jene Bänder?

Sie sind für Madame Huet.

Haben Sie Miltons Gedichte
gelesen?

Ja, ich habe sie gelesen.

Kennen Sie den Bruder des
Herrn Thomas?

Ich kenne den Herrn Thomas,
aber nicht seinen Bruder.

# LESSON XIII.

## Proper Names of Countries, Places etc.

1) Names of countries, towns and islands have in
German, as in English, no article:

England  England.      London  London.
Deutschland  Germany.   Berlin  Berlin.

*Except:* All *feminine* names, like **die** Schweiz Switzerland, and **die** Türkei' Turkey, which are used as common
names:

*Gen.* and *Dat.* **der** Schweiz; *Acc.* **die** Schweiz.

2) They form their genitive by the addition of **s**:

Die Flüsse Deutschlands  the rivers of Germany.

Die Straßen Berlins, Londons 2c.
The streets of Berlin, of London etc.

3) But when they end in **s, z** or **x**, no termination
can be added, and the genitive is expressed by the preposition **von**, as:

Die Straßen **von** Paris  the streets of Paris.

4) The use of the preposition **von** is also allowed with all other names of countries and towns; but the genitive is better.  Thus we may say:

Die Küsten **von** England  the coasts of England.
Die Straßen **von** London  the streets of London.

5) *To* before names of countries and towns must be translated **nach**, *at* or *in* **in**, *from* **von** or **aus**, as:

Ich gehe **nach** Amerika  I go *to* America.

My brother is in America, — at Rome, — in Paris.
Mein Bruder ist **in** Amerika, — **in** Rom, — **in** Paris.

I come from Paris, — from Lyons, — from America.
Ich komme **von** Paris, — **von** Lyon, — **aus** Amerika.

6) Names of the principal countries:

Europa  Europe.
Asien  Asia.
Afrika  Africa.
Amerika  America.
England  England.
Frankreich  France.
Deutschland  Germany.
Österreich [Oesterreich]  Austria.
Indien  India.
Spanien  Spain.
Italien  Italy.
Griechenland  Greece.
Preußen  Prussia.
Rußland  Russia.
China  China.
Belgien  Belgium.
die Schweiz  Switzerland.
die Türkei  Turkey.

7) Most of the (national) appellations, formed from these names of countries, end in **er**, as:

der Europä'er  the European.
der Amerika'ner  the American.
der Engländer  the Englishman.
der Holländer  the Dutchman.
der Spa'nier  the Spaniard.
der Italie'ner  the Italian.
der Schweizer  the Swiss.
der Römer  the Roman.

*Gen.* des Europäers, des Engländers, des Amerikaners.
*Plur.* die Spanier, *Gen.* der Spanier, *D.* den Spaniern 2c.

8) The feminine is formed by adding **in**.  Ex.:

bie Engländer**in**, bie Italiener**in**,
bie Französ**in**, bie Spanier**in**.

9) The following national appellations and some
others end in **e**, and follow the second declension:

| | | | |
|---|---|---|---|
| ber Deutſche | the German. | ber Schwebe | the Swede. |
| ber Franzoſe | the Frenchman. | ber Ruſſe | the Russian. |
| ·ber Preuße | the Prussian. | ber Türfe | the Turk. |

*Gen.* beß Deutſchen ; *Plur.* bie Deutſchen, bie Franzoſen 2c.

## Words.

| | |
|---|---|
| baß Produkt [Product] the product. | wir leben or wohnen we live. |
| Wien Vienna. | ich gehe I go ; geht goes. |
| baß Gebirge the mountain. | hübſch pretty. |
| baß Land the country. | ſo so ... alß as. |
| bie Hauptſtabt the capital. | angefommen arrived (*past part.*). |
| ich fomme I come. | falt cold. |
| ber Teil [Theil] (*plur.* -e) the part. | warm warm. |
| | fruchtbar fertile ; fruitful. |
| | hoch high. |
| | lang long. |

## Exercise 25.

1. Aſien iſt ſehr groß.  2. Die Flüſſe Rußlandß ſind groß.
3. Welcheß (what) ſind bie Produkte [Producte] Englandß?
4. Die Straßen Berlinß (or von Berlin) ſind ſchön.  5.
Napoleon war ber Kaiſer ber Franzoſen.  6. Ich war (was)
in Öſterreich [Deſterreich] und in Preußen.  7. Waß für ein
Land iſt dieß?  8. Dieß iſt Griechenland.  9. Kennen Sie
Philadelphia?  10. Ja, eß iſt eine Stadt in Amerifa.  11. Iſt
dieſer Mann ein Franzoſe?  12. Nein, er iſt ein Italiener;

er geht nach Amerika.   13. Mein Sohn geht nach Paris.
14. Paris ist die Hauptstadt Frankreichs (or von Frank=
reich).

### Exercise 26.

1. Europe is large, but America is much larger (viel
größer).   2. The mountains of Spain are high.   3. We
live in Germany.   4. Paris is the capital of France, and
London the capital of England.   5. India and China
are parts of Asia.   6. Prussia is not so large as Russia.
7. The products of England.   8. Switzerland is very
small.   9. William the First (der Erste) is king of (von)
Prussia and emperor of Germany.   10. I have seen
two Prussians and four Turks.   11. Has (is) the
Englishman arrived from Spain?   12. No, Sir, but the
Frenchman has arrived from Russia.   13. I have an
uncle in America and an aunt in Belgium.   14. I go
to Vienna.

### Conversation.

| | |
|---|---|
| Wo ist dein Bruder? | Er ist in Frankfurt. |
| Welches ist die Hauptstadt von Spanien? | Madrid ist die Hauptstadt von Spanien. |
| Kennen Sie die Schweiz? | Ja, ich kenne die Schweiz. |
| Wie heißt dieses Land? | Dieses Land ist Italien. |
| Sind diese Herren Franzosen? | Nein, mein Herr, sie sind Spanier. |
| Wohin gehen Sie? | Ich gehe nach Rußland. |
| Gehen Sie auch nach Paris? | Ja, nach Paris und nach London. |
| Wie sind die Straßen Berlins? | Sie sind lang und schön. |

# LESSON XIV.

## Demonstrative and Interrogative Adjectives.

### I. The Demonstrative Adjectives are:

| | Singular. | | Plural |
|---|---|---|---|
| Masc. | Fem. | Neuter. | for all genders. |
| biefer | biefe | biefes this, that. | biefe these. |
| jener | jene | jenes that. | jene those. |
| folcher | folche | folches such. | folche such. |

ber felbe bie felbe bas felbe [baffelbe] the same.  biefelben.
ber, bie, bas nämliche  the same.  die nämlichen.
ber, bie, bas anbre  the other.  die anbern.

(The Declension of **biefer** etc. see page 18.)

### Examples.

Diefes Buch ift gut  This book is good.
Diefe Bäume finb hoch  These trees are high.
Geben Sie mir biefen Bleiftift  Give me this pencil.
Kennen Sie jene Damen?  Do you know those ladies?

### *Declension with a Noun.*

| Singular. | Plural. |
|---|---|
| N. biefer Hut  this hat (bonnet) | biefe Hüte  these hats |
| G. biefes Hutes  of this hat | biefer Hüte  of these hats |
| D. biefem Hut(e)  to this hat | biefen Hüten  to these hats |
| A. biefen Hut  this hat. | biefe Hüte  these hats. |

*Note.* Derfelbe, ber nämliche and ber anbre are declined like adjectives: *N.* berfelbe, *G.* besfelben [beffelben], *D.* bem= felben, *A.* benfelben; *Plur.* biefelben ꝛc.

Die nämlichen Wörter  the same words.
Ich habe einen anbern Stock  I have another stick.

## II.  The **Interrogative Adjectives.**

1) welcher? welche? welches? *which? what?*

### Declension.

|  | *Singular.* | | | *Plural* |
|---|---|---|---|---|
|  | *Masc.* | *Fem.* | *Neuter.* | *for all genders.* |
| N. | welcher | welche | welches  which? | welche  which? |
| G. | welches | welcher | welches  of which? | welcher  of which? |
| D. | welchem | welcher | welchem  to which? | welchen  to which? |
| A. | welchen | welche | welches  which? | welche  which? |

### Examples.

Welchen Brief haben Sie?  Which letter have you?
Welche Federn haben Sie gekauft?
What pens have you bought?

2) was für ein? was für eine? was für ein?
what (sort of)? *plur.* was für?

Here the article only is declined, and agrees with
the following noun:

Was für eine Stadt ist dies?  what (sort of a) town is that?
Was für einen Hut haben Sie?  what (sort of a) hat have you?
Mit was für einer Feder?  with what (sort of a) pen?

a) In the plural, there is no article: was für?
Ex.:

Was für Bücher brauchen Sie?  what books *do you* need?
Was für Bäume sind dies?  what kind of trees are these?

b) The same form, was für? without the article, is
employed before names of materials:

Was für Fleisch kaufen Sie?  what sort of meat *do you* buy?
Was für Wein trinken Sie?  what kind of wine *do you* drink?

## Words.

das Tuch  the cloth.

der Apfelbaum  the apple-tree.

das Kalbfleisch  the veal.

das Rindfleisch  the beef.

die Eltern  the parents.

die Farbe  the color.

schwarz  black.

tot [todt]  dead.

der Ring  the ring.

der Fehler  the mistake.

das Wort ( *plur.* Wörter)  the word.

der Lehrer  the teacher.

gelernt  learned.

schlecht  bad.

dies, das  this *or* that (see page 135).

### Exercise 27.

1. Dieser König ist reich.  2. Diese Dame ist schön. 3. Dieses Tuch ist schwarz.  4. Jener Ring ist von Gold. 5. Jene Feder ist sehr schlecht.  6. Jenes Papier ist sehr gut. 7. Derselbe Mann.  8. Dieselbe Stadt.  9. Jene Bäume sind sehr hoch.  10. Welche Wörter haben Sie gelernt?  11. Ich habe die nämlichen Wörter gelernt.  12. Welchen Wein haben Sie gekauft?  13. Ich habe diesen Wein gekauft.  14. Was für ein Baum ist dies?  15. Dies ist ein Apfelbaum. 16. Was für Fleisch ist dies?  17. Dies ist Kalbfleisch. 18. Was für einen Lehrer haben Sie?  19. Mein Lehrer ist ein Deutscher.

### Exercise 28.

1. This book is good.  2. That ink is not good. 3. I have bought this paper and these pencils.  4. The color of this flower is beautiful.  5. Which house have you bought?  6. I have bought that house.  7. These pupils are very young.  8. I know the father of those children  9. The cap of this boy is new.  10. Give this bread to that woman.  11. This pen is not good, the other pen is better.  12. What (2) tree is this?  13. What (was für) beautiful (schöne) flowers!  14. What (welches)

is the name of these flowers?   15. These flowers are roses.   16. What *sort of* a hat have you?   17. I have no hat, I have a cap.

### Conversation.

| | |
|---|---|
| Ift biefer Herr reich? | Ja, er ift fehr reich. |
| Wie find die Früchte jener Bäume? | Sie find fehr füß (sweet). |
| Was für ein Bogel ift dies? | Es ift ein Adler (eagle). |
| Was für eine Blume haben Sie da? | Es ift ein Beilchen (violet). |
| Was für Pferde haben Sie ge= fauft? | Ich habe zwei junge Pferde gefauft. |
| Hat Heinrich den nämlichen Stock? | Nein, er hat einen andern. |
| Was für Wein haben Sie ge= trunfen (drunk)? | Unfer Wein war rot [roth]. |
| Welches Buch haben Sie ge= lefen? | Ich habe Eduards Buch ge= lefen. |
| Was für Fleifch ift das? | Das ift Rindfleifch. |

## LESSON XV.

### III. The Possessive Adjectives are:

| | Singular. | | Plural for all genders. |
|---|---|---|---|
| Masc. | Fem. | Neuter. | |
| mein | meine | mein my. | meine my. |
| dein | deine | dein thy. | deine thy. |
| fein | feine | fein his (its). | feine his (its). |
| ihr | ihre | ihr her (its). | ihre her (its). |
| unfer | unfre | unfer our. | unfre our. |
| euer | euere | euer ⎱ your. | euere, eure ⎱ your. |
| Ihr | Ihre | Ihr ⎰ | Ihre ⎰ |
| ihr | ihre | ihr their. | ihre their. |

## *Declension with Nouns.*

(See also page 19.3.)

### *Singular.*

|  | *Masc.* | *Fem.* | *Neuter.* |
|---|---|---|---|
| N. | unſer Vater | unſre Mutter | unſer Kind |
| G. | unſres Vaters | unſrer Mutter | unſres Kindes |
| D. | unſerm Vater | unſrer Mutter | unſerm Kind |
| A. | unſern Vater. | unſre Mutter. | unſer Kind. |

### *Plural.*

|  | | | |
|---|---|---|---|
| N. | unſre Väter | — Mütter | — Kinder |
| G. | unſrer Väter | — Mütter | — Kinder |
| D. | unſern Vätern | — Müttern | — Kindern |
| A. | unſre Väter. | — Mütter. | — Kinder. |

### *Singular.*

|  | | | |
|---|---|---|---|
| N. | ihr Bruder | ihre Schweſter | ihr Buch |
| G. | ihres Bruders | ihrer Schweſter | ihres Buches |
| D. | ihrem Bruder | ihrer Schweſter | ihrem Buch(e) |
| A. | ihren Bruder. | ihre Schweſter. | ihr Buch. |

### *Plural.*

|  | | | |
|---|---|---|---|
| N. | ihre Brüder | — Schweſtern | — Bücher |
| G. | ihrer Brüder | — Schweſtern | — Bücher |
| D. | ihren Brüdern | — Schweſtern | — Büchern |
| A. | ihre Brüder. | — Schweſtern. | — Bücher. |

## IV. The **Indefinite Numeral Adjectives** are:

| *Masc.* | *Fem.* | *Neuter.* | *Plural.* |
|---|---|---|---|
| jeder every, each | jede | jedes. | *(wanting).* |
| aller (all) all | alle | alles (all). | alle all. |
| kein no | keine | kein. | keine no. |
| viel much | viel(e) | viel. | viele many. |
| wenig little | wenig(e) | wenig. | wenige few. |
| wieviel? how much? | wie viel(e)? | wieviel? | wie viele? how many? |

beide, *plur.* both.      einige, *plur.* some, any, a few.

mehrere, *plur.* several.      die meiſten, *plur.* most.

### Declension.

#### Singular.

| Masc. | Fem. | Neuter. |
|---|---|---|
| N. aller (all) | alle | alles (all) all. |
| G. alles | aller | alles of all. |
| D. allem | aller | allem to all. |
| A. allen | alle | alles (all) all. |

#### Plural.

| N. alle Briefe | alle meine Briefe | einige Freunde |
|---|---|---|
| all the letters | all my letters | some friends |
| G. aller Briefe | aller meiner Briefe | einiger Freunde |
| D. allen Briefen | allen meinen Briefen | einigen Freunden |
| A. alle Briefe. | alle meine Briefe. | einige Freunde. |

### REMARK.

When in English the definite article follows the numeral adjective *all*, it must not be translated, as:

All the money    alles Gelb.

All the boys    alle Knaben (not alle bie Knaben).

### Words.

der Wagen  the carriage.

bie Überſetzung [Ueberſetzung] the translation.

bie Seite  the page, the side.

das Heft ( *plur.* -e) the copy-book.

koſtbar  precious.

liebt  loves.

glücklich  happy.

das Gelb  the money.

bie Minute  the minute.

nur  only.

verloren  lost.

gegeſſen  eaten.

bie Stunde  the hour.

hatte, hatten  had.

### Exercise 29.

1. Mein Vater iſt alt.  2. Deine Schweſter iſt jung.  3. Friedrich hat ſeinen Hut verloren.  4. Emilie hat ihre Hand= ſchuhe verloren.  5. Wo ſind unſre Hefte?  6. Ihre Hefte

find hier. 7. Die Eltern lieben ihre Kinder. 8. Unser Oheim ist nicht reich. 9. Die Eltern dieser Kinder sind tot [todt]. 10. Ich habe die Pferde ihres Oheims und den Wagen unsres Nachbars gekauft. 11. Jeder Vater liebt seine Söhne. 12. Jede Stunde ist kostbar. 13. Sie haben keinen Fehler in Ihrer Übersetzung [Uebersetzung]. 14. Meine beiden Brüder sind krank. 15. Alle Häuser dieser Stadt sind groß. 16. Alle meine Federn sind schlecht. 17. Wir haben einige Vögel. 18. Ich habe mehrere Seiten gelesen (read).

### Exercise 30.

1. My brother is ill. 2. Her mother is very good. 3. His horse is bad. 4. Where is your aunt? 5. She is in Paris. 6. Our friends have (are) arrived. 7. Are these your copy-books? 8. I go with my cousin to Italy. 9. All your books are new. 10. Every day, every minute is precious. 11. All the wine. 12. All the flowers are fresh (frisch). ✓ 13. I have no friend. 14. Charles has no mistakes in his exercise. 15. Many men are not happy. 16. Every child has his book. 17. I have bought several sticks. 18. Had you many mistakes in your translation? 19. I had only three or four. 20. All the papers are lost. 21. All my friends are in Berlin. 22. Our neighbor has lost all the money. 23. Most roses are red.

### Conversation.

| | |
|---|---|
| Wer hat mein Geld gefunden? | Dein Bruder hat dein Geld gefunden. |
| Wie viele Fehler habe ich in meiner Übersetzung [Ueber=setzung]? | Sie haben mehrere Fehler, vier oder fünf. |
| Wer ist jener junge Mann? | Es ist der Neffe unsres Nachbars. |
| Hast du einige gute Federn? | Nein, alle meine Federn sind schlecht. |

| | |
|---|---|
| Haben Sie viele Bücher? | Ich habe wenige Bücher. |
| Mit wem (with whom) sind Sie angekommen? | Ich bin mit einigen Freunden gekommen. |
| Haben Sie einen Brief von Berlin erhalten (received)? | Nein, ich habe keinen Brief erhalten. |
| Haben Sie alle Äpfel [Aepfel] gegessen? | Nein, ich habe nur einige ge= gessen. |

---

# LESSON XVI.

## Auxiliary Verb haben to have.

*Present Tense.*

ich **habe** I have
du hast thou hast
er hat he has
sie hat she has
es hat it has

wir haben we have
ihr habt or ⎫
Sie haben*) ⎬ you have
⎭
sie haben they have.

*Imperfect.*

ich **hatte** I had
du hattest thou hadst
er hatte he had
sie hatte she had
es hatte it had

wir hatten we had
ihr hattet ⎫
Sie hatten ⎬ you had
⎭
sie hatten they had.

*Future.*

ich werde .. †) haben I shall have
du wirst haben thou wilt have
er wird haben he will have

*Conditional.*

ich würde .. haben I should have
du würdest haben thou wouldst have
er würde haben he would have

---

*) *General observation.* It may be stated, once for all, that the 2d person plural of all verbs has two forms: ihr and Sie. The latter written with a capital S, to distinguish it from the 3d person, is the only one to be used by *foreigners* in conversation. On the other hand the 2d pers. sing. and its plur. ihr are much used in familiar conversation.

†) These two points indicate the place of the object. Ex.:

Ich werde **das Brot [Brod]** haben, — wenn ich **das Brot** hätte.

*Future.*

wir werden haben  we shall have

ihr werdet haben  ⎫
Sie werden haben  ⎬ you will have

sie werden haben  they will have.

*Conditional.*

wir würden haben  we should have

ihr würdet haben  ⎫
Sie würden haben  ⎬ you would have

sie würden haben  they would have.

*Imperative.*

habe have (thou)!
habet have (ye)!
haben Sie have!

*Infinitive.*

haben ⎫
zu haben ⎬ to have.

*Part. Past.* **gehabt** had.

## Subjunctive Mood.

### Present Tense.

ich habe  I (may) have
du habeſt  thou have
er (ſie, eś) habe  he (she, it) have

wir haben  we have
ihr habet ⎫
Sie haben ⎬ you have
sie haben  they have.

### Imperfect (Preterite).

wenn ich .. †) **hätte**  if I had
wenn du .. hätteſt  if thou hadst
wenn er .. hätte  if he had

wenn wir .. hätten  if we had
wenn ihr .. hättet  if you had
wenn Sie .. hätten  if you had
wenn ſie .. hätten  if they had.

### Words.

das Vergnügen  the pleasure.
die Klaſſe [Claſſe]  the class.
die Schülerin  the school-girl.

ein Strohhut  a straw-hat.
die Uhr  the watch; jetzt now.
Ferien  vacation, holidays.

### Exercise 31.

1. Ich habe ein Pferd.  2. Mein Bruder hat auch ein Pferd.  3. Du haſt einen Hund.  4. Wir haben viele Freunde in England.  5. Die Kinder haben viel Vergnügen.  6. Ich

†) See the footnote page 66.

hatte keinen Fehler in meiner Aufgabe. 7. Du hatteſt zwei
oder drei Fehler. 8. Der Lehrer hatte viele Schüler in ſeiner
Klaſſe [Claſſe]. 9. Wir hatten zuviel [zu viel] Brot [Brod].
10. Ihr hattet zuviel Butter. 11. Sie werden einen Strohhut
haben. 12. Du wirſt eine Kappe haben. 13. Heinrich wird
einen Rock haben. 14. Wir werden Ferien haben. 15. Die
Schüler und Schülerinnen würden viel Vergnügen haben. 16.
Wenn ich ein Pferd hätte. 17. Wenn wir unſre Bücher hätten.

### Exercise 32.

1. I have a book. 2. Thou hast a pencil. 3. He
has a copy-book. 4. She has a pen. 5. We have friends.
6. You have two horses. 7. They have no money. 8.
You had a brother. 9. I had three brothers; now 'I
'have only two. 10. The children had many apples;
they will also 'have 'pears.—11. I shall have a straw-
hat. 12. Robert will have a cap. 13. Have patience
(Geduld)! 14. I should 'have 'a 'carriage. 15. The
pupils had no paper. 16. I have not your cap. 17. Has
your brother a friend? 18. No, Sir, he has no friend.
19. Charles has no penknife. 20. I shall have a book.
21. Thou wilt have a copy-book. 22. My mother will
have three pounds of coffee and four pounds of sugar.

# LESSON XVII.

## Interrogative and Negative Form of haben.

### 1. Interrogative Form.

#### Present Tense.

| *Sing.* | | *Plur.* | |
|---|---|---|---|
| habe ich? | have I? | haben wir? | have we? |
| haſt du? | hast thou? | habt ihr? | have you? |
| hat er? | has he? | haben Sie? | |
| hat ſie? | has she? | haben ſie? | have they? |
| hat es? | has it? | | |

*Imperfect.*

| *Singular.* | | *Plural.* | |
|---|---|---|---|
| hatte ich? | had I? | hatten wir? | had we? |
| hatteft bu? | hadst thou? | hattet ihr? | } had you? |
| hatte er? | had he? | hatten Sie? | |
| | | hatten fie? | had they? |

*Future.*

| werbe ich .. haben? | shall I have? |
|---|---|
| wirft bu haben? | wilt thou have? |
| wirb er haben? | will he have? |
| werben wir haben? | shall we have? |
| werbet ihr haben? | } will you have? |
| werben Sie haben? | |
| werben fie haben? | will they have? |

*First Conditional.*

| w ü r b e  ich .. haben? | should I have? |
|---|---|
| würbeft bu haben? | wouldst thou have? |
| würbe er haben? | would he have? |
| würben wir haben? | should we have? |
| etc. | etc. |

## 2.  Negative Form.

*Present Tense.*

| *Singular.* | | *Plural.* | |
|---|---|---|---|
| ich habe nicht | I have not | wir haben nicht | we have not |
| bu haft nicht | thou hast not | ihr habt nicht | } you have |
| er hat nicht | he has not | Sie haben nicht | not |
| | | fie haben nicht | they have not. |

*Imperfect.*

| ich hatte nicht | I had not | wir hatten nicht | we had not |
|---|---|---|---|
| bu hatteft nicht | etc. | ihr hattet nicht | etc. |
| er hatte nicht | | Sie hatten nicht | |
| | | fie hatten nicht. | |

*Future.*

ich werde nicht haben   I shall not have
du wirst nicht haben ꝛc.

*Conditional.*

ich w ü r b e nicht haben   I should *or* would not have
du würdest nicht haben ꝛc.

**Words.**

die Tinte [Dinte] the ink.

das Tintenfaß [Dintenfaß] the inkstand.

das Schreibheft the copy-book.

das Wetter the weather.

Geduld haben to have patience.

brauchen to want, need.

genug enough.

das Hemb (*plur.* –en) the shirt.

die Zeit the time.

recht [Recht] haben to be right.

unrecht [Unrecht] haben to be wrong.

morgen to-morrow.

**Exercise 88.**

1. Haben Sie ein Pferd?   2. Ja, ich habe ein Pferd. 3. Hast du mein Buch?   4. Nein, ich habe dein Buch nicht. 5. Hat Wilhelm auch ein Schreibheft?   6. Haben Sie Tinte [Dinte]?   7. Ja, wir haben Tinte in dem Tintenfaß [Dintenfaß].   8. Hatte der König ein Schloß?   9. Wird Ihr Freund einen Strohhut haben?   10. Hat der Lehrer nicht viele Schüler? 11. Wo ist Ihr Buch?   12. Haben Sie es verloren?   13. Hat der Schüler sein Buch?   14. Der Schüler hat sein Buch nicht.   15. Hatte das Kind sein Brot [Brob]?   16. Nein, das Kind hatte sein Brot nicht.   17. Werden Sie Ihr Schreibheft haben?   18. Würden Sie morgen Geld haben?   19. Wenn die Königin die Rose in dem Garten gesehen hätte.   20. Was haben Sie da?   21. Ich habe ein Glas Bier.   22. Wollen Sie auch Bier haben?   23. Ja, geben Sie mir auch ein Glas Bier, wenn es Ihnen beliebt (if you please).   24. Werden wir ein Tintenfaß haben?   25. Hier sind zwei Tintenfässer

[Dintenfäffer]. 26. Habe ich recht [Recht]? 27. Nein, Sie haben unrecht [Unrecht].

### Exercise 84.

1. Have I enough? 2. Yes, you have enough. 3. Have you a pencil? 4. I have two pencils. 5. Has Henry [any] ink? 6. He has an inkstand with ink. 7. Had you much pleasure? 8. We had not much pleasure. 9. Have you not money enough? 10. No, Sir, we have not enough. 11. Will Charles 'have 'a 'horse? *) 12. He will not have a horse, but he will have a dog. ⟨ 13. Have you no ink? 14. No, I want [some] ink. 15. I shall have two dozen shirts. 16. How many shirts has that boy? 17. He has not many, he has only four. 18. Would you have patience? 19. I should not have patience enough. 20. We had not seen our friends. 21. Have you not bought many gloves? 22. I have bought two dozen gloves, and my aunt has bought five pounds of coffee. 23. Will your niece have a bonnet? 24. She will have a straw-hat.

### Conversation.

| | |
|---|---|
| Haben Sie einen Bruder? | Ja, ich habe zwei Brüder. |
| Haft du Brot [Brod] genug? | Nein, ich habe nicht genug. |
| Hatten Sie genug Butter und Käse? | Wir hatten Käse genug; aber nicht Butter genug. |
| Hatten Sie viel Vergnügen auf dem Lande (in the country)? | Ja, wir hatten sehr viel Vergnügen. |
| Werden wir schönes Wetter haben? | Ich glaube nicht (I think not). |
| Werden Sie Zeit haben, dieses Buch zu lesen (read)? | Wir werden heute keine Zeit haben; aber morgen. |
| Haben Sie meine Stahlfeder? | Nein, ich habe sie (it) nicht. |

---

*) See the footnote page 26.

# LESSON XVIII.

## Compound Tenses of the Auxiliary Verb haben.

| *Perfect Tense.* | *Pluperfect.* |
|---|---|
| ich habe .. **gehabt** *) I have had | ich hatte .. gehabt I had had |
| du haft gehabt thou hast had | du hatteft gehabt thou hadst had |
| er hat gehabt he has had | er hatte gehabt he had had |
| wir haben gehabt we have had | wir hatten gehabt we had had |
| ihr habt gehabt } you have | ihr hattet gehabt } you had |
| Sie haben gehabt } had | Sie hatten gehabt } had |
| fie haben gehabt they have had. | fie hatten gehabt they had had. |

| *Second Future.* | *Second Conditional.* |
|---|---|
| ich werde .. gehabt haben I shall have had | ich würde .. gehabt haben I should have had |
| du wirft gehabt haben | du würdeft gehabt haben |
| er wird gehabt haben | er würde gehabt haben |
| wir werden gehabt haben | wir würden gehabt haben |
| ihr werdet gehabt haben | ihr würdet gehabt haben |
| Sie werden gehabt haben | Sie würden gehabt haben |
| fie werden gehabt haben. | fie würden gehabt haben. |

## Interrogative Form.

| | | |
|---|---|---|
| *Perfect.* | habe ich .. gehabt? | have I had? |
| *Pluperf.* | hatte ich .. gehabt? | had I had? |
| *2d Fut.* | werde ich .. gehabt haben? | shall I have had? |
| *2d Cond.* | würde ich .. gehabt haben? | should I have had? |

---

*) See footnote †) page 66. The *past part.* stands *last.*

## Negative Form.

*Perfect.*    i𝔠𝔥 𝔥𝔞𝔟𝔢 𝔫i𝔠𝔥𝔱 𝔤𝔢𝔥𝔞𝔟𝔱   I have not had.
*Pluperf.*   i𝔠𝔥 𝔥𝔞𝔱𝔱𝔢 𝔫i𝔠𝔥𝔱 𝔤𝔢𝔥𝔞𝔟𝔱   I had not had.
         𝔦𝔠.              etc.

## Negative-interrogative Form.

*Perfect.*    𝔥𝔞𝔟𝔢 i𝔠𝔥 𝔫i𝔠𝔥𝔱 𝔤𝔢𝔥𝔞𝔟𝔱?   have I not had?
*Pluperf.*   𝔥𝔞𝔱𝔱𝔢 i𝔠𝔥 𝔫i𝔠𝔥𝔱 𝔤𝔢𝔥𝔞𝔟𝔱?   had I not had?
         𝔦𝔠.             etc.

## Subjunctive Mood.

𝔴𝔢𝔫𝔫 i𝔠𝔥 . . 𝔤𝔢𝔥𝔞𝔟𝔱 **𝔥ä𝔱𝔱𝔢**   if I had had
𝔴𝔢𝔫𝔫 𝔡𝔲 . . 𝔤𝔢𝔥𝔞𝔟𝔱 𝔥ä𝔱𝔱𝔢𝔰𝔱   if thou hadst had
𝔴𝔢𝔫𝔫 𝔢𝔯 . . 𝔤𝔢𝔥𝔞𝔟𝔱 𝔥ä𝔱𝔱𝔢   if he had had etc.

## Negative.

𝔴𝔢𝔫𝔫 i𝔠𝔥 𝔫i𝔠𝔥𝔱 𝔤𝔢𝔥𝔞𝔟𝔱 𝔥ä𝔱𝔱𝔢   if I had not had.

### REMARKS ON GERMAN CONSTRUCTION.

1) In principal clauses with *compound tenses* the German past participle is placed *at the end.* The *subject* comes then first, secondly the auxiliary, thirdly the personal pronoun, next the adverb of time, in the fifth place the object (*acc.* or *dat.*), then the other adjuncts, and finally the past participle or the infinitive Ex.:

ℑ𝔠𝔥 𝔥 𝔞 𝔟 𝔢 ein 𝔅𝔲𝔠𝔥 𝔤 𝔢 𝔥 𝔞 𝔟 𝔱   I have had a book.

𝔇𝔢𝔯 𝔎𝔫𝔞𝔟𝔢 𝔥 𝔞 𝔱 ein 𝔅𝔲𝔠𝔥 i𝔫 𝔡𝔢𝔯 𝔖𝔱𝔯𝔞ß𝔢 𝔤 𝔢 𝔣 𝔲 𝔫 𝔡 𝔢 𝔫.
The boy has found a book in the street.

𝔇i𝔢 𝔐𝔲𝔱𝔱𝔢𝔯 𝔴 i 𝔯 𝔡 einen 𝔅𝔯i𝔢𝔣 𝔳𝔬𝔫 i𝔥𝔯𝔢𝔯 𝔗𝔬𝔠𝔥𝔱𝔢𝔯 𝔥 𝔞 𝔟 𝔢 𝔫.
The mother will have a letter from the daughter.

2) Adverbs of time generally precede the object:

Der Knabe hat **gestern** ein Buch gefunden.
The boy found a book yesterday.

3) When any adverbial expression begins the sentence, then the auxiliary precedes the subject, as:

Gestern **habe ich** ein Buch gefunden.
Yesterday I found a book.

4) When the verb is in a simple tense, it takes the place of the auxiliary, as:

Ich gehe in den Hof  I go into the yard.

5) The negation „**nicht**" stands before the word it modifies, as:

Ich habe das Buch **nicht** gelesen.
I have not read the book.

*Lit.:* I have the book not read.

### Words.

| | |
|---|---|
| der Sonnenschirm  the parasol. | die Milch  the milk. |
| der Regenschirm  the umbrella. | ein Feiertag  a holiday. |
| der Mut [Muth]  the courage. | auf dem Land  in the country. |
| der Thee  the tea. | mehr  more. |

### Exercise 85.

1. Ich habe Geld gehabt.  2. Du hast Wein gehabt.  3. Wilhelm hat einen Apfel gehabt.  4. Wir haben Kirschen gehabt.  5. Habt ihr auch Kirschen gehabt or haben Sie auch Kirschen gehabt?  6. Die Kinder haben kein Vergnügen gehabt. 7. Haben Sie nicht einen Hund gehabt?  8. Hat Ihr Vater nicht ein Pferd gehabt?  9. Hat Ihre Mutter nicht einen Sonnenschirm gehabt?  10. Wird Karl [Carl] Geld genug

gehabt haben? 11. Werden die Schüler Zeit genug gehabt haben? 12. Sie werden nicht Zeit genug gehabt haben. 13. Wenn ich einen Fehler gehabt hätte. 14. Wenn du Geld gehabt hätteſt. 15. Wenn mein Vater ſeinen Regenſchirm nicht verloren hätte.

### Exercise 36.

1. I have had a house. 2. My friend has had a horse. 3. Has Emily not had [any] bread and butter? 4. She has had bread, but no butter. 5. Had I had [any] sugar in my tea? 6. Yes, you had had two pieces (Stück) of sugar. — 7. The children will have had [some] milk, but no coffee. 8. I should have had much pleasure in the country. 9. Henry has had two mistakes in the exercise. 10. Have I also had [any] mistakes? 11. No, you have had no mistakes. 12. We should have had more pleasure. 13. Will the boys not have a holiday? 14. Yes, they will have two holidays.

### Conversation.

| | |
|---|---|
| Haben Sie Wein gehabt? | Nein, wir haben Bier gehabt. |
| Wieviel Bier haben Sie gehabt? | Wir haben eine Flaſche Bier gehabt. |
| Hat Ihr Bruder Geld genug gehabt? | Nein, er hat nicht genug gehabt. |
| Hatte der Schüler ſein Buch gehabt? | Ja, er hatte es (it) gehabt. |
| Wer hat mein Federmeſſer gehabt? | Ich habe es nicht gehabt. |
| Haben Sie nicht viel Vergnügen auf dem Lande gehabt? | Nein, das Wetter war (was) ſehr ſchlecht. |
| Haben die Kinder nicht genug Brot [Brod] gehabt? | Doch (Oh! yes); ſie haben genug gehabt. |
| Wann (when) werden die Knaben einen Feiertag haben? | Sie werden morgen einen Feiertag haben. |

# LESSON XIX.

## Auxiliary Verb ſein to be.

*Present Tense.*

ich **bin** I am
du biſt  thou art
er (ſie, es) iſt  he (she, it) is

wir ſind  we are
ihr ſeid  }
Sie ſind  } you are
ſie ſind  they are.

*Imperfect.*

ich **war** I was
du warſt  thou wast
er (ſie, es) war  he (she, it) was

wir waren  we were
ihr waret  }
Sie waren  } you were
ſie waren  they were.

*Future.*

ich werde ſein  I shall be
du wirſt ſein  thou wilt be

er (ſie, es) wird ſein  he will be

wir werden ſein  we shall be
ihr werdet ſein  } you will
Sie werden ſein  }   be
ſie werden ſein  they will be.

*Conditional.*

ich würde ſein  I should be
du würdeſt ſein thou wouldst be

er (ſie, es) würde ſein  he would be

wir würden ſein  we should be
ihr würdet ſein  } you
Sie würden ſein  } would be
ſie würden ſein  they would be.

*Note.* The Conditional appears also in the following form :

*Singular.*

ich **wäre** I should be
du wäreſt  thou wouldst be
er (ſie, es) wäre  he would be.

*Plural.*

wir wären  we should be
ihr wäret  }
Sie wären  } you would be
ſie wären  they would be.

## Subjunctive Mood.

### Present Tense.

(daß) ich ſei  I [may] be

du ſeieſt  thou be

er (ſie, es) ſei  he (she, it) be

wir ſeien  we be

ihr ſeiet ⎱
Sie ſeien ⎰ you be

ſie ſeien  they be.

### Imperfect (Preterite).

(daß) ich wäre  (that) I were

du wäreſt  thou were

er (ſie, es) wäre  he (she, it) were

wir wären  we were

ihr wäret ⎱
Sie wären ⎰ you were

ſie wären  they were.

## Imperative.

| *Singular.* | *Plural.* |
|---|---|
| ſei be! | ſeib, ſeien Sie  be! |
| ſeien Sie  be! | ſeien wir, laßt uns ſein  let us be! |

## Infinitive Mood.

ſein, zu ſein  to be.

## Participle Past.

geweſen  been.

## Conditional Form with *if.*

| | |
|---|---|
| wenn ich wäre  if I were | wenn wir wären  if we were |
| wenn du wäreſt      etc. | wenn ihr wäret      etc. |
| wenn er (ſie, es) wäre | wenn Sie wären |
| | wenn ſie wären. |

## Words.

| | |
|---|---|
| die Kirche the church. | zufrieden contented. |
| glücklich happy. | unzufrieden discontented. |
| unglücklich unhappy. | müde tired; leicht easy. |
| der Kuchen the cake. | das Mädchen the girl. |
| artig good; zu too. | die Übersetzung [Uebersetzung] |
| fleißig diligent. | the translation. |
| das Theater the theatre. | ruhig quiet. |
| arm poor. | gestern yesterday. |
| ich wünsche I wish. | heute to-day. |

### Exercise 37.

1. Ich bin jung.  2. Du bist glücklich.  3. Ich bin un= glücklich.  4. Sie ist schön und reich.  5. Wir sind arm und krank.  6. Ihre Kinder sind sehr artig.  7. Ich war glücklich. 8. Du warst fleißig.  9. Dieser Mann war gut.  10. Ihr waret (or Sie waren) gestern in der Kirche.  11. Wir waren zu Hause; unsre Mutter war krank.  12. Die Schüler waren sehr fleißig.  13. Ich werde ruhig sein.  14. Julius wird morgen in Paris sein.  15. Die Mädchen werden in der Schule sein.  16. Ich würde unglücklich sein.  17. Du würdest zu= frieden sein.  18. Mein Nachbar würde unzufrieden sein. 19. Sei zufrieden!  20. Seien Sie ruhig!  21. Karl [Carl] würde sehr glücklich sein, wenn er viel Bücher hätte.

### Exercise 38.

1. I am poor.  2. Thou art rich.  3. He is old, she is young.  4. We are in the country.  5. Charles is tired; I am also very tired.  6. Robert's translation was very bad.  7. My uncle was poor, but now ²he ¹is rich. 8. I was in London.  9. You were in Berlin.  10. Henry was in Paris.  11. My son will be here to-morrow. 12. I should be here also.  13. Henry and William were ²very ³diligent ⁴to-day.  14. Their teacher will be con-

tented with them (ihnen). 15. Be quiet! 16. Let us be diligent! 17. I wish 'to 'be 'happy. 18. You would be contented, if you were in London. 19. It would be very easy.

# LESSON XX.

## Interrogative and Negative Form of ſein.

### 1. Interrogative Form.

*Present Tense.*

| *Singular.* | *Plural.* |
|---|---|
| bin ich? am I? | ſind wir? are we? |
| biſt du? art thou? | ſeid ihr? } are you? |
| iſt er? is he? | ſind Sie? } |
| iſt ſie? is she? iſt es? is it? | ſind ſie? are they? |

*Imperfect.*

| *Singular.* | *Plural.* |
|---|---|
| war ich? was I? | waren wir? were we? |
| warſt du? wast thou? | waret ihr? } were you? |
| war er? was he? | waren Sie? } |
| war ſie? was she? | waren ſie? were they? |
| war es? was it? | |

| *Future.* | *Conditional.* |
|---|---|
| werde ich ſein? shall I be? | würde ich ſein? should I be? |
| wirſt du ſein? wilt thou be? | würdeſt du ſein? wouldst thou be? |
| wird er (ſie, es) ſein? will he be? | würde er (ſie, es) ſein? would he be? |
| etc. | etc. |

## 2.　Negative Form.

| *Present Tense.* | *Imperfect.* |
|---|---|
| ich bin nicht  I am not | ich war nicht  I was not |
| du bift nicht  thou art not | du warft nicht  thou wast not |
| er ift nicht  he is not | er war nicht  he was not |
| fie ift nicht  she is not | fie war nicht  she was not |
| es ift nicht  it is not | es war nicht  it was not |

| | | |
|---|---|---|
| wir find nicht  we are not | wir waren nicht  we were not |

ihr feid nicht  } you are not
Sie find nicht  }

fie find nicht  they are not.

ihr waret nicht  } you  were
Sie waren nicht  }      not

fie waren nicht  they were not.

### *Future.*

ich werde nicht fein  I shall not be
du wirft nicht fein  thou wilt not be
er (fie, es) wird nicht fein  he will not be
wir werden nicht fein  we shall not be etc.

### *Conditional.*

ich würde nicht fein  I should not be
du würdeft nicht fein  thou wouldst not be etc.

## Imperative.

fei nicht!  be (thou) not, do not be!
feid nicht!  be (ye) not, do not be!
feien Sie nicht!  be not, do not be!

## Conditional Form with *if.*

wenn ich nicht **wäre**  if I were not
wenn du nicht wäreft  if thou were not
wenn er (fie, es) nicht wäre  if he were not
wenn wir nicht wären  if we were not etc.

## Words.

die Eltern  the parents.

die Freundin the *(fem.)* friend.

zu Hauſe  at home.

gewiß  certainly.

unwohl  unwell.

in d e r Schule  at school.

träge  idle ; wo ?  where ?

immer  always.

ſtark  strong.

ruhig  quiet.

die Küche  the kitchen.

Kopfweh  a headache.

wann ?  when ?

hier  here ; da  there.

## Exercise 39.

1. Wo bin ich ?  2. Biſt du krank ?  3. Iſt er in der Schule ?  4. Iſt Heinrich auch in der Schule ?  5. Sind wir glücklich ?  6. Wir ſind nicht glücklich.  7. Wo ſind Sie (or wo ſeid ihr) ?  8. Biſt du nicht in der Kirche ?  9. Sind Sie nicht in der Kirche ?  10. Sind die Schüler fleißig ?  11. Sind die Schüler nicht träge ?  12. Wo war Ihr Vater ?  13. Er war in Paris.  14. War Ihre Mutter auch in Paris ?  15. Nein, ſie war nicht in Paris; ſie war in Lyon.  16. Waren Sie geſtern in der Schule ?  17. Nein, wir waren zu Hauſe, unſre Mutter war krank.  18. Wirſt du ruhig ſein ?  19. Ja, ich werde ruhig ſein.  20. Werden Ihre Freundinnen morgen hier ſein ?  21. Nein, ſie werden nicht hier ſein.  22. Würdeſt du glücklich ſein ?  23. Ja gewiß, ich würde ſehr glücklich ſein, wenn ich nicht unwohl wäre.  24. Meine Eltern würden glücklich ſein, wenn ſie hier wären.  25. Der Schüler würde nicht zufrieden ſein, wenn er nicht viele Bücher hätte.

## Exercise 40.

1. Where are you?  2. I am here.  3. Is he contented?  4. No, he is discontented.  5. Was Charles 'at 'school 'yesterday?  6. Yes, he was at school, but his brother Richard was not there.  7. Were you in the kitchen?  8. No, I was not there.  9. She would be

happy, if she were not unwell.   10. Was Henry not
diligent?   11. Yes, he was diligent, but he could (konnte)
not work (arbeiten); he had [a] headache.   12. Were
you not in the garden, Margaret?   13. No, mamma, I
was in my room.   14. Was your pupil good?   15. Yes,
he is always good.   16. When will you be at home?
17. I shall not be at home to-day, but to-morrow.
18. My exercise was not easy to-day.

### Conversation.

| | |
|---|---|
| Sind Sie glücklich? | O ja, ich bin sehr glücklich. |
| Wo waren Sie gestern abend [Abend]? | Ich war im Theater. |
| Und wo war Ihr Freund? | Er war zu Hause. |
| War der Wein gut? | Nein, er war nicht sehr gut. |
| Waren Sie in Stuttgart? | Nein, ich war nicht da. |
| Warum (why) war der Lehrer unzufrieden? | Die Schüler waren nicht artig. |
| Ist Karl [Carl] oft (often) krank? | Ja, er ist immer krank. |
| Würden Sie zufrieden sein, wenn Sie reich wären? | Ich würde sehr zufrieden sein, wenn ich reich wäre. |
| Seid ihr fertig (ready)? | Wir werden gleich (directly) fertig sein. |
| Werden Sie glücklich sein, wenn (when) Ihr Vater kommt? | Gewiß, ich werde sehr glücklich sein. |

### READING-LESSON.

#### Die Frau und die Henne.
The Woman and the Hen.

Eine Frau hatte eine Henne.   Diese Henne legte
                                                    laid
jeden Tag ein Ei.   Aber die Frau war nicht damit
                                                    with it
zufrieden; sie wollte jeden Tag zwei Eier haben; denn
                wanted                                        for

bie Eier waren ſehr teuer [theuer]. Sie mäſtete baher bie
<small>dear</small> <small>fattened therefore</small>
Henne, in ber Hoffnung mehr Eier zu bekommen. Aber
<small>hope more</small> <small>to get</small>
bie Henne wurbe zu fett unb legte keine Eier mehr.
<small>became too fat</small>

# LESSON XXI.

## Compound Tenses of fein.

These tenses are formed with the past participle
**geweſen** and the auxiliary verb to be **fein,** not with
haben.

*Perfect.*

ich **bin geweſen** I *have* been
bu **biſt** geweſen thou hast been
er **iſt** geweſen he has been

wir **ſinb** geweſen we have been
ihr **ſeib** geweſen } you have been
Sie **ſinb** geweſen }
ſie **ſinb** geweſen they have been.

*Pluperfect.*

ich **war** geweſen I had been
bu warſt geweſen thou hadst been
er war geweſen he had been

wir waren geweſen we had been
ihr waret geweſen } you had been
Sie waren geweſen }
ſie waren geweſen they had been.

| *Second Future.* | *Second Conditional.* |
|---|---|
| ich werde **gewesen sein** I shall have been | ich würde **gewesen sein** \*) I should have been |
| du wirst gewesen sein etc. | du würdest gewesen sein etc. |
| er wird gewesen sein | er würde gewesen sein |
| wir werden gewesen sein | wir würden gewesen sein |
| ihr werdet gewesen sein | ihr würdet gewesen sein |
| Sie werden gewesen sein | Sie würden gewesen sein |
| sie werden gewesen sein. | sie würden gewesen sein. |

## Conditional Form with *if*.

wenn ich gewesen **wäre**   if I had been
wenn du gewesen **wärest**   if thou hadst been
wenn er gewesen **wäre**   if he had been
wenn wir gewesen **wären**   if we had been etc.

## Interrogative Form.

*Perfect.*    **bin** ich gewesen?   have I been?
         **bist** du gewesen?   hast thou been?
         **ist** er gewesen?   has he been? etc.
*Pluperf.*   **war** ich gewesen?   had I been? etc.
*2d Fut.*   werde ich gewesen **sein?**   shall I have been? etc.
*2d Cond.* würde ich gewesen **sein?**   should I have been? etc.

## Negative Form.

ich **bin** nicht gewesen   I have not been etc.

## Negative-interrogative Form.

**bin** ich nicht . . gewesen?   have I not been? etc.

## Negative-conditional Form.

wenn ich nicht gewesen **wäre**   if I had not been
wenn du nicht gewesen wärest   if thou hadst not been
wenn er nicht gewesen wäre   if he had not been
wenn wir nicht gewesen wären   if we had not been etc.

---

\*) Or ich **wäre** gewesen, du **wärest** gewesen, er **wäre** gewesen.

## Words.

der Großvater the grand-  
  father.  
die Großmutter ✦the grand-  
  mother.  
die Klaſſe [Claſſe] the class.  
gerecht just; der erſte the first.

Wien Vienna.  
beſſer better.  
ſchwer difficult, hard.  
treu faithful.  
oft often.  
nie or niemals never.

## Exercise 41.

1. Ich bin krank geweſen. 2. Du biſt auch krank geweſen. 3. Wilhelm iſt ſehr fleißig geweſen. 4. Luiſe [Louiſe] iſt nicht fleißig geweſen. 5. Unſer Nachbar war in Paris geweſen. 6. Iſt Ihre Tante in der Kirche geweſen? 7. Nein, ſie iſt zu Hauſe geweſen. 8. Du wirſt in der Schule geweſen ſein. 9. Alfred wird nicht in der Schule geweſen ſein. 10. Der Lehrer war nicht zufrieden; die Aufgaben werden ſchlecht geweſen ſein. 11. Die Mädchen würden unglücklich geweſen ſein, wenn ſie nicht im Theater geweſen wären.

## Exercise 42.

1. Where have you been? 2. I have been in Vienna. 3. Has your grandmother been ill? 4. Yes, she was very ill. 5. I have never been ill. 6. Henry has often been the first in his class. 7. My pen has been better than (als) Charles' pen. 8. Had I not been there? 9. Has my brother not been there also? 10. No, he has not been there; I have not seen him (ihn). 11. Mr. Bell had always been my friend. 12. Your translation has been very easy. 13. I should have been rich, if I had been in America. 14 'To 'be 'contented is often better than to be rich. 15. Would Emily not have been contented? 16. No, she would not have been contented. 17. Who was (has been) in my room? 18. It was your

grandmother. 19. She (has) brought (gebracht) a letter for you. 20. Has the tailor not been here? 21. I have not seen him; he has not been here.

---

# LESSON XXII.

### Third Auxiliary.

**Werden** to become, to get, to grow.

| *Present Tense.* | *Imperfect.* |
|---|---|
| ich **werde** I become, I get | ich **wurde** (ich ward) I became |
| du **wirſt** thou becomest | du wurdeſt (wardſt) thou becamest |
| er **wird** he becomes | er wurde (ward) he became |
| ſie wird she becomes | ſie wurde she became |
| es wird it becomes | es wurde it became |
| wir werden we become | wir wurden we became |
| ihr werdet ⎫ you become | ihr wurdet ⎫ you became |
| Sie werden ⎭ | Sie wurden ⎭ |
| ſie werden they become. | ſie wurden they became. |

*Perfect.*

ich **bin geworden** (or worden) I have become (*or* been)
du **biſt** geworden thou hast become
er **iſt** geworden *) he has become·

wir **ſind** geworden we have become
ihr ſeid geworden ⎫ you have become
Sie ſind geworden ⎭
ſie ſind geworden they have become.

---

*) *What has become of . . . ?* is translated: **was iſt aus . . . geworden?**

*Pluperfect.*

ich **war** geworden (or worden)  I had become (*or* been)
du warſt geworden (or worden)              etc.
er (ſie, es) war geworden.

*Future.*

ich werde werden  I shall become *or* get
du wirſt ⎫
er wird ⎪
          ⎬ werden        etc.
wir werden ⎪
ihr werdet ⎪
Sie werden ⎪
ſie werden ⎭

*Conditional.*

ich würde werden  I should become *or* get
du würdeſt ⎫
er würde ⎪
          ⎬ werden        etc.
wir würden ⎪
ihr würdet ⎪
Sie würden ⎪
ſie würden ⎭

## Infinitive.

werden or zu werden  to become.

### Words.

| | |
|---|---|
| müde tired. | groß tall. |
| naß wet. | grün green. |
| nie or niemals never. | die Nacht the night. |
| träge idle. | jetzt now. |
| ſpät late. | der Regenſchirm  the umbrella. |
| ſchmutzig dirty. | |
| dunkel dark. | verloren lost. |
| ſchläfrig sleepy. | die Leute people. |

### Exercise 43.

1. Ich werde müde. 2. Sie wird alt. 3. Sie werden niemals träge werden. 4. Zwei Kinder wurden krank. 5. Es wird spät. 6. Ich wurde gestern naß. 7. Ich bin jung; aber ich werde alt werden. 8. Es regnet (it rains); Sie werden naß werden. 9. Dieses Papier ist schmutzig geworden. 10. Es wird Nacht; es wird dunkel. 11. Diese Knaben sind krank geworden, sie essen zuviel [zu viel]. 12. Das Mädchen wurde schläfrig. 13. Unser Nachbar ist reich geworden. 14. Was ist aus dem Sohn des Herrn Müller geworden? 15. Er ist Soldat geworden.

### Exercise 44.

1. She becomes rich. 2. I shall also become rich. 3. He became my friend. 4. The child became ill. 5. The boys got tired and sleepy. 6. The trees become green in spring (im Frühling). 7. I am now rich, but I may (kann) ²become ¹poor. 8. We shall become contented. 9. Your children have grown very tall. 10. It had grown dark. 11. I was once (einst) young; but now ¹I ²have grown old. 12. It rains (es regnet), our friends will get wet; they have no umbrella. 13. This man has become [a] soldier. 14. What has become of your book? 15. It is lost.

### Conversation.

| | |
|---|---|
| Warum sind Sie nicht ge= kommen (come)? | Ich wurde unwohl. |
| Gehen Sie nach Hause? | Ja, es wird spät. |
| Wann werden die Bäume grün? | Im Frühling. |
| Sind Sie Soldat geworden? | Nein, ich bin Offizier [Officier] geworden. |
| Sind Sie reich geworden? | Nein, noch nicht (not yet). |

Sind Sie naß geworden?

Was ist aus (of) Ihrem Bruder geworden?

Wer wurde träge?

Was ist aus meinem Buch geworden?

Ich bin nicht naß geworden; ich hatte einen Regenschirm.

Er ist gestorben (has died).

Der Schüler wurde träge.

Ich habe es nicht gesehen.  •

---

# LESSON XXIII.

## Auxiliary Verbs of Mood.

### 1. Können (konnte, gekonnt) to be able.

*Present Tense.*

ich **kann**  I can *or* I may
du **kannst**  thou canst
er (sie, es) **kann**  he (she, it) can

wir **können**  we can, we may
ihr könnt or könnet ⎱
Sie können          ⎰ you can
sie können  they can, they may.

*Imperfect.*

ich **konnte**  I could
du konntest  thou couldst
er (sie, es) konnte  he (she, it) could

wir konnten  we could
ihr konntet ⎱
Sie konnten ⎰ you could
sie konnten  they could.

*Future.*

ich werde können  I shall be able
du wirst können  thou wilt be able
er wird können  he will be able etc.

*Perfect.*

ich habe gekonnt or ⎱
ich habe .. können ⎰ I have been able etc.

## 2. Wollen (wollte, gewollt) to be willing.

*Present.*

ich will　I will, I wish
du willſt　thou wilt *or* wishest
er will　he will *or* wishes
ſie will　she will *or* wishes

es will　it will *or* wishes

wir wollen　we will *or* wish

ihr wollt ⎱ you will *or*
Sie wollen ⎰　wish
ſie wollen　they will *or* wish.

*Imperfect.*

ich wollte　I wished *or* would
du wollteſt　thou wouldst
er wollte　he wished *or* would
ſie wollte　she wished *or* would

es wollte　it wished *or* would

wir wollten　we wished *or* would

ihr wolltet ⎱ you wished *or*
Sie wollten ⎰　would
ſie wollten　they wished *or* would.

*Future.*

ich werde . . wollen　I shall wish.

*Perfect.*

ich habe gewollt or ⎱ I have wished *or*
ich habe . . wollen ⎰ I have been willing.

### Words.

auf die Poſt　to the post-office.
kommen　to come.
bleiben　to remain, to stay.
tragen　to carry, to take.
kaufen　to buy.
gehen　to go.
machen ⎱ to make,
thun　⎰ to do.
ſchreiben　to write.

helfen　to help.
lieber　rather.
brauchen　to want.
ſpielen　to play.
abreiſen　to set out.
bezahlen　to pay.
eſſen　to eat.
zu klein　too small.
trinken　to drink.
leſen　to read.

### Exercise 45.

1. Kannſt du kommen? 2. Ja, ich kann kommen. 3. Können Sie 'Ihre 'Überſetzung [Ueberſetzung] machen? 4. Nein, ich kann nicht. 5. Sie können bleiben. 6. Ich konnte nicht bleiben. 7. Wollen Sie 'mich (me) 'bezahlen oder nicht? 8. Ja, ich will Sie bezahlen, wenn ich kann. 9. Warum können Sie nicht abreiſen? 10. Ich habe kein Geld. 11. Wir konnten den Wein nicht trinken. 12. Kann Ihr Diener den Brief auf die Poſt tragen? 13. Nein, er kann nicht. 14. Wollen Sie kommen? 15. Nein, ich will nicht kommen. 16. Ich wollte heute abreiſen, aber ich konnte nicht.

### Exercise 46.

1. I can write. 2. Charles cannot write. 3. Can you come? 4. No, I can 'not 'come*) 'now; I will come to-morrow. 5. Can we do it? 6. Yes, you can do it. 7. Will you 'help 'me (mir)? 8. Yes, I will. 9. Will you have some water? 10. No, I do not want [any] water (transl.: I will no water). 11. Could you go to (in die) school? 12. I could not go. 13. I could not write my exercise. 14. The children could not play in the room; it was too small. 15. Will you drink a glass of beer? 16. No, [Sir]; I will rather have a glass of wine. 17. How much money do you want (transl.: want you)? 18. I want six marks (Mark). 19. What will you buy? 20. I will buy two pounds of butter. 21. Will you pay the money? 22. I will pay it. 23. How much is it? 24. It is three marks.

---

*) Put the infinitive mood last.

# LESSON XXIV.

## Auxiliary Verbs.

### 3. Sollen (sollte, gesollt) shall.

| *Present Tense.* | *Imperfect.* |
|---|---|
| ich soll  I am to . . . | ich sollte  I was to, I ought to |
| du sollst  thou art to (shalt) | du solltest  thou wast to, shouldst |
| er soll  he is to (shall) | er sollte  he was to, should |
| wir sollen  we are to | wir sollten  we were to, we ought to |
| ihr sollt  } ye *or* you are to | ihr solltet  } you were to *or* |
| Sie sollen  }    (shall) | Sie sollten  }    you should |
| sie sollen  they are to (shall). | sie sollten  they should, ought to. |

### 4. Müssen (mußte, gemußt) to be obliged to.

| *Present Tense.* | *Imperfect.* |
|---|---|
| ich muß  I must | ich mußte  I was obliged to |
| du mußt  thou must | du mußtest  thou wast obliged |
| er muß  he must | er mußte  he was obliged |
| wir müssen  we must | wir mußten  we were obliged |
| ihr müßt  } ye *or* you must | ihr mußtet  } ye *or* you were |
| Sie müssen  } | Sie mußten  }    obliged |
| sie müssen  they must. | sie mußten  they were obliged. |

### *Future.*

ich werde . . müssen  I shall be obliged.

## 5. Mögen (mochte, gemocht) may.

### Present Tense.

| Singular. | Plural. |
|---|---|
| ich **mag** I may | wir **mögen** we may |
| du **magst** thou mayst | ihr **möget** } you may |
| er **mag** he may | Sie **mögen** } you may |
| | sie **mögen** they may. |

### Imperfect.

ich **mochte** I might, liked.

### Subjunctive.

ich **möchte** I should like, might.

NB. *May I?* means **darf** ich? *May we?* **dürfen** wir?

## 6. Dürfen (durfte, gedurft) may (to have the permission).

| Present Tense. | Imperfect. |
|---|---|
| ich **darf** I may (see 5) | ich **durfte** I was allowed |
| du **darfst** etc. | du durftest etc. |
| er **darf** | er durfte |
| wir dürfen we may *or* are permitted | wir durften we were permitted |
| ihr dürft } you may | ihr durftet } you were permitted |
| Sie dürfen } you may | Sie durften } you were permitted |
| sie dürfen they may. • | sie durften they were permitted. |

### Words.

| | |
|---|---|
| lernen to learn. | der Baron' the baron. |
| die Lektion [Lection] the lesson. | wahr true. |
| sagen to say. | tadeln to blame. |
| ausgehen to go out. | glauben to believe. |
| der Hof the yard. | behalten to keep. |
| loben to praise. | arbeiten to work. |
| | sehen to see. |

### Exercise 47.

1. Ich soll artig sein. 2. Du sollst fleißig sein. 3. Er soll bleiben, wo er ist. 4. Wir sollen lernen. 5. Ich soll nicht träge sein. 6. Mein Nachbar sollte heute abreisen. 7. Ich muß ihn (him) sehen. 8. Wir müssen abreisen. 9. Der Knabe soll jetzt nicht spielen. 10. Müssen Sie aus= gehen? 11. Nein, ich muß nicht ausgehen. 12. Karl [Carl] mußte heute in der Schule bleiben. 13. Wilhelm mußte zu Hause bleiben. 14. Ich möchte einen Brief schreiben. 15. Die Kinder dürfen spielen. 16. Ich darf heute nicht aus= gehen. 17. Was mußten Sie gestern lernen? 18. Ich mußte meine Lektion [Lection] lernen.

### Exercise 48.

1. I *am* to stay. 2. You *are to* 'write (you shall 'write) 'a 'letter. 3. We must go out. 4. *Am I to* (shall I) learn my lesson? 5. Yes, you must learn your lesson. 6. You may stay where you are. 7. I must write a letter. 8. We must learn our lesson. 9. The children must not play in the garden; they may play in the yard. 10. You may believe it; it is true. 11. I might write, if I had time. 12. You may see the church. 13. The professor shall blame the lazy (trägen) boys. 14. May I see what you write? 15. Yes, you may; it is a letter to (an) my uncle. 16. May we go into your garden? 17. Oh! yes, you may. 18. I ought to be at home at seven o'clock. 19. The baron ought [*to*] keep his servant. 20. Your cousins ought [to] stay here; they ought not to go to Paris.

### Conversation.

| | |
|---|---|
| Wollen Sie Wein trinken? | Nein, ich will keinen Wein trinken. |
| Wann müssen Sie ausgehen? | Ich muß um sechs Uhr aus= gehen. |

Können Sie nicht hier bleiben?　　Nein, ich muß abreisen.

Kannst du schreiben?　　Ich kann lesen, aber nicht schreiben.

Wollen Sie Butter und Käse?　　Nein, ich will Fleisch haben.

Wer will spielen?　　Friedrich will spielen.

Können Sie nicht kommen?　　Nein, ich habe keine Zeit,

Warum (why) will dieser Mann den Brief nicht lesen?　　Er kann nicht lesen.

Muß Wilhelm abreisen?　　Nein, er kann [darf] hier bleiben.

---

# LESSON XXV.

## Adjectives.

1) The adjective, in German, is used **predicatively**, accompanying a verb to state *how* a thing or a person is. In this case, it is placed after the verb, and undergoes no alteration at all; it remains the same for the three genders and for both numbers, as in English. Ex.:

*Sing.* Der Garten ist **groß** the garden is large.
Dieses Haus ist **klein** this house is small.

*Plur.* Die Gärten sind **groß** the gardens are large.
Diese Häuser sind **klein** these houses are small.

2) Or it is used **attributively**, to qualify a noun. Then it *precedes* the noun which it qualifies, and is declined according to the gender, number or case of the noun, with which it must agree in all these particulars, as:

*Sing.* der runde Tisch, *Plur.* die runden Tische.
ein großes Haus. rotes [rothes] Papier.

3) The declension of the adjective in its *attributive* use varies according to its being preceded:

    I. by the *definite* article (*or* a substitute of it);
    II. by the *indefinite* article (*or* a substitute of it);
    III. by neither of them.

### First Form.

The terminations of adjectives, when preceded by the *definite* article, are:

*Singular.*

N. –e  ⎫
G. –en  ⎬ for all genders.
D. –en  ⎭
A. –en, m., –e fem. & neut.

*Plural.*

N. –en  ⎫
G. –en  ⎬ for all genders.
D. –en  ⎭
A. –en

### Declension.

#### Masculine.

| *Singular.* | | *Plural.* |
|---|---|---|
| N. ber **gute** Freunb | the good friend | bie **guten** Freunbe |
| G. beß **guten** Freunbeß | of the good friend | ber **guten** Freunbe |
| D. bem **guten** Freunb(e) | to the good friend | ben **guten** Freunben |
| A. ben **guten** Freunb | the good friend | bie **guten** Freunbe. |

#### Feminine.

| | | |
|---|---|---|
| N. bie **gute** Mutter | the good mother | bie **guten** Mütter |
| G. ber **guten** Mutter | of the good mother | ber **guten** Mütter |
| D. ber **guten** Mutter | to the good mother | ben **guten** Müttern |
| A. bie **gute** Mutter | the good mother. | bie **guten** Mütter. |

#### Neuter.

| | | |
|---|---|---|
| N. baß **gute** Kinb | the good child | bie **guten** Kinber |
| G. beß **guten** Kinbeß | of the good child | ber **guten** Kinber |
| D. bem **guten** Kinb(e) | to the good child | ben **guten** Kinbern |
| A. baß **gute** Kinb | the good child. | bie **guten** Kinber. |

This form is also employed after the following words:

| | | | |
|---|---|---|---|
| **biefer,** e, e8 | this | **jener,** e, e8 | that; |
| **welcher,** e, e8 | which? | **jeber,** e, e8 | every. Ex.: |

*Singular.*      *Plural.*

biefer gute Bater  this good father.    biefe guten Bäter.
biefe8 neue Hau8  this new house.    biefe neuen Häufer.
welche gute Feber  which good pen?    welche guten Febern?

## Words.

| | |
|---|---|
| bie Erbe  the earth. | bie Farbe  the color. |
| runb  round. | ba8 Blatt (*plur.* –er) the leaf. |
| lieb  dear. | |
| ber Sommer  the summer. | hart  hard. |
| breit  broad, wide. | loben  to praise. |
| prächtig  beautiful, fine, splendid. | ber Name(n)  the name. |
| | groß  large. |
| lang  long. | grün  green. |
| furz  short. | ba8 Kleib  the dress. |
| englifch  English. | artig  good. |
| franzöfifch  French. | unreif  unripe. |

## Exercise 49.

1) 1. Der Garten ift klein.  2. Da8 Hau8 ift groß. 3. Die Erbe ift runb.  4. Diefe Häufer finb nicht groß. 5. Der große Tifch.  6. Die runde Erbe.  7. Die kleine Straße.  8. Da8 liebe Kind.  9. Diefe8 liebe Kind.  10. Diefe lieben Kinder finb fehr artig.  11. Der alte Mann ift fehr krank.  12. Der Sohn de8 alten Manne8 ift auch krank. 13. Wo ift ba8 neue Zimmer der guten Mutter?  14. Geben Sie ba8 Brot [Brob] dem armen Kinde.  15. Ich liebe die fchönen Blumen.  16. Diefe fleißigen Knaben gehen (go) in

bie Schule. 17. Geben Sie diese neuen Bücher den fleißigen Schülern! 18. Ich habe den schönen Garten des Prinzen ge=sehen.

2) 19. Wir lieben die breiten Straßen. 20. Haben Sie die prächtigen Diamanten der Königin gesehen? 21. Hat der Knabe die langen Briefe seines Vetters gelesen? 22. Die langen Tage des Sommers sind besser als die kurzen Tage des Winters. 23. Wir loben die artigen Schülerinnen. 24. Wo haben Sie die französischen Bücher gekauft? 25. Luise [Louise] hat ihre grünen Bänder verloren.

### Exercise 50.

1) 1. The father is good. 2. The garden is large. 3. The little table. 4. These flowers are beautiful. 5. The beautiful flowers. 6. The little children. 7. I like the good children. 8. The green leaf. 9. The green leaves. 10. The red color. 11. The red cherries. 12. I love the good aunt. 13. Where are the good sisters? 14. Do you like the red dresses of the little girls? 15. Yes, I like them (sie). 16. I have seen the large river. 17. Who is this old man? 18. He is the good grandfather of Robert.

2) 1. Give these new books to your brother. 2. The teacher praises (lobt) the diligent boys. 3. These little books are very good. 4. Where have you bought these beautiful ribbons? 5. Give [to] these poor children [some] bread and butter! 6. I like (the) hard pens. 7. Do you know the names of these little boys? 8. Yes, Sir, they are called (sie heißen) Henry and Lewis.

# LESSON XXVI.

## Declension of Adjectives continued.

### SECOND FORM.'

1) With the *indefinite* article ein, eine, ein the declension is nearly the same as with the definite article; it differs only in the *nominative* case, *masculine* and *neuter*, and in the *accusative neuter*, because in these cases the article e i n has no particular termination to indicate the gender. In these cases, the *adjective* must take the termination of the respective gender, viz.:

*Singular.*

| Masc. | Fem. | Neuter. |
|---|---|---|
| *Nom.* –er, | *Nom. & Acc.* –e, | *Nom. & Acc.* –es, |

all other cases –en.

### Declension.

*Masculine.*

*N.* e i n guter Bater  a good father
*G.* eines guten Baters  of a good father
*D.* einem guten Bater  to a good father
*A.* ein e n guten Bater  a good father.

*Neuter.*

*N.* ein armes Kind  a poor child
*G.* eines armen Kindes  of a poor child
*D.* einem armen Kinde  to a poor child
*A.* ein armes Kind  a poor child.

2) This mode of inflexion is also used after all the possessive adjectives (their terminations being similar to the indefinite article), viz.: mein, dein, fein, unser, euer, Ihr, ihr and fein. Its plural is the same as that of the first form, viz.: en in all cases.

### Examples with Possessive Adjectives.

*Singular.*

mein kleiner Hund  my little dog.
ihre liebe Tochter  your dear daughter.
unser neues Haus  our new house.

*Plural.*

meine kleinen Hunde  my little dogs.
ihre lieben Töchter  your dear daughters.
unsre neuen Häuser  our new houses.

### Declension with a Possessive Adjective.

*Singular.*

N. mein guter Freund  my good friend
G. meines guten Freundes  of my good friend
D. meinem guten Freund  to my good friend
A. meinen guten Freund  my good friend.

*Plural.*

N. meine guten Freunde  my good friends
G. meiner guten Freunde  of my good friends
D. meinen guten Freunden  to my good friends
A. meine guten Freunde  my good friends.

3) If more than one adjective precede a substantive, each adjective must be declined in this manner, as:

N. ein armer, alter Mann  a poor old man
G. eines armen, alten Mannes  of a poor old man
D. einem armen, alten Mann  to a poor old man
A. einen armen, alten, kranken Mann  a poor old sick man.

### Words.

deutsch  German.
der Kaiser  the emperor.
der Ring  the ring.
kostbar  precious.
das Metall  the metal.
treu faithful.

die Trauben *plur.* the grapes.
schwarz  black; grau  gray.
süß  sweet.
das Silber  the silver.
die Handschuhe *plur.* the gloves.

**Exercise 51.**

1. Ein artiger Knabe. 2. Eine fleißige Schülerin. 3. Ich habe einen runden Tisch. 4. Kennen Sie den deutschen Kaiser? 5. Ich habe ein deutsches Blatt gelesen. 6. Wo ist mein kleiner Bruder? 7. Ihr kleiner Bruder ist in dem Garten. 8. Ein runder Tisch. 9. Ein fleißiges Kind. 10. Die Bücher des fleißigen Knaben. 11. Unsre neuen Häuser sind schön. 12. Mein alter Vater und meine alte Mutter. 13. Ich habe meine kostbaren Ringe verloren. 14. Die Blätter einer roten [rothen] Rose. 15. Mein guter Freund hat seinen treuen Hund verloren. 16. Haben Sie Ihren alten Freund gefunden? 17. Ja, er wohnt (lives) in einem schönen, neuen Hause. 18. Die reifen Trauben sind gut.

**Exercise 52.**

1. A good brother. 2. My good brother. 3. A dear sister. 4. My dear sister. 5. A beautiful town. 6. A diligent boy. 7. A large house. 8. Your large house. 9. Have you seen our little cousin? 10. I have seen your little cousin and your little girl (*neuter*). 11. I like (the) ripe grapes. 12. The green leaves of a large tree. 13. Our friend lives in a fine house. 14. Has Henry a black hat or a gray hat? 15. He has a gray hat. 16. (The) ripe cherries are sweet. 17. Mr. Bell is a rich man. 18. (The) rich people (Leute) are not always happy. 19. Here is a letter from (von) your dear mother. 20. My little girl has lost her new gloves. 21. Silver is a precious metal.

---

# LESSON XXVII.

## THIRD FORM.

*Adjectives not preceded by any Article.*

1) The third form is made use of, when the adjective precedes the substantives *without* any article or substi-

tute.  The gender not being indicated by an article, it
must be expressed by the ending of the adjective itself,
which borrows its terminations from the definite article.
We give here only the *nom.*, *dat.* and *accus.*, as being
most used.

### Table of Endings.

|  | Singular. |  |  |  | Plural. |  |
|---|---|---|---|---|---|---|
|  | *Masc.* | *Fem.* | *Neuter.* |  |  |  |
| N. | –er | –e | –es | N. & A. | –e | |
| D. | –em *) | –er | –em | G. | –er | for all genders. |
| A. | –en | –e | –es. | D. | –en | |

### Examples.

#### Singular.

| *Masc.* | *Fem.* | *Neuter.* |
|---|---|---|
| N. guter Wein | süße Milch | frisches Waſſer |
| good wine | sweet milk | fresh water |
| D. gutem Wein | süßer Milch | friſchem Waſſer |
| A. guten Wein. | süße Milch. | friſches Waſſer. |

#### Plural.

| | | |
|---|---|---|
| N. & A. gute Weine | schöne Blumen | neue Bücher |
| good wines. | pretty flowers. | new books. |

2) When two or more adjectives are placed before
the same substantive without an article, they are declined in the same way, as:

N. guter, alter, roter [rother] Wein    (some) good old
red wine

A. guten, alten, roten Wein  good old red wine.

#### Plural.

gute, alte, rote Weine  good old red wines.

---

*) The genitive sing. of this third form is seldom used; it has –en
in the masculine and neuter, and –er in the feminine.

3) This third form is also used for the *vocative* case:

Armer Mann! poor man!     Armes Mädchen! poor girl!
Liebes Kind! dear child!     Liebe Kinder! dear children!

4) After cardinal and indefinite numerals in the plural:

> zwei schöne Pferde two fine horses.
> einige deutsche Wörter some German words.

#### ADJECTIVES USED SUBSTANTIVELY.

Adjectives may be converted into substantives. In this case they take the article, and must begin with a capital letter, but retain their inflexion as adjectives, for instance from the adj. gelehrt:

> *Sing.* der Gelehrte the learned man;
> *Plur.* die Gelehrten. — Ein Gelehrter.

Such are:

| | |
|---|---|
| der Reisende the traveller | ein Reisender a traveller |
| der Bediente the (man-)servant | ein Bedienter a(man-)servant |
| der Deutsche the German | ein Deutsch e r a German |
| der Fremde the stranger. | ein Fremb e r a foreigner *or* stranger. |

### Declension.

| First Form<br>with the definite article. | Second Form<br>with the indefinite article. |
|---|---|
| *N.* der Fremde the stranger | ein Fremder a stranger |
| *G.* des Fremden of the stranger | eines Fremden of a stranger |
| *D.* dem Fremden to the stranger | einem Fremden to a stranger |
| *A.* den Fremden the stranger. | einen Fremden a stranger. |

#### *Plural.*

| First and Second Form. | Third Form. |
|---|---|
| *N. &A.* die Fremden the strangers | Fremde strangers |
| *G.* der Fremden of the strangers | Fremder of strangers |
| *D.* den Fremden to the strangers. | Fremden to strangers. |

**Words.**

| | |
|---|---|
| der Thee tea; ſtark strong. | die Suppe the soup. |
| das Bier the beer. | der Schinken the ham. |
| der Bäcker the baker. | gegeſſen eaten. |
| die Taſſe the cup. | vortrefflich excellent. |
| weiß white. | zwanzig twenty. |
| ein Stück a piece. | morgen to-morrow. |

**Exercise 53.**

1. Hier iſt guter Thee und warme Milch.   2. Wir haben ſtarken Wein getrunken (drunk).   3. Wollen Sie friſches Waſſer?   4. Nein, geben Sie mir friſches Bier!   5. Hat der Bäcker gutes Brot [Brod]?   6. Ja, er hat immer gutes Brot.   7. Er hat auch friſche Butter.   8. Hier ſind ſchöne Blumen und reife Früchte.   9. Ich habe viele franzöſiſche Soldaten geſehen.   10. Mein Bruder hat zwei deutſche Bücher geleſen.   11. Ihre Tante hat zwei Taſſen Kaffee [Caffee] getrunken.   12. Haben Sie weißen Zucker?   13. Hier iſt weißer Zucker.   14. Gute, alte Weine ſind teuer [theuer] (expensive). 15. Ich habe ſchönes, rotes [rothes] Papier gekauft.   16. Dieſe Frau verkauft (sells) gute, friſche, ſüße Milch.   17. Geben Sie mir ein Glas ſüße Milch und ein Stück gutes, weißes Brot!   18. Neue Freunde ſind nicht immer gute Freunde.

**Exercise 54.**

1. Here is good red wine.   2. Here is also fresh water.   3. Do you like warm soup?   4. Yes, bring me [some] warm soup.   5. I want also some good ham, white bread and fresh butter.   6. What (was für) paper have you bought?   7. I have bought white and red paper.   8. We have large rooms.   9. Three small houses.   10. We have eaten excellent fruit at (bei) my aunt's.   11. The gardener has drunk very strong beer.   12. My father drinks only good old white wine. 13. New wine is not so good as old wine.   14. Do you

want green tea or black tea? 15. I want neither green nor black tea, I want good coffee and sweet milk. 16. You must learn twenty German words for to-morrow.

### Conversation.

| | |
|---|---|
| Ist Karl [Carl] fleißig? | Ja, er ist ein fleißiger Knabe. |
| Wer hat dieses schöne Bild gemalt? | Ein deutscher Maler. |
| Haben Sie einen großen Garten? | Nein, er ist nicht sehr groß. |
| Lieben Sie den roten [rothen] Wein? | Ich liebe den roten und den weißen. |
| Was verkauft diese Frau? | Sie verkauft süße Milch und frische Butter. |
| Ist Herr Lafitte ein reicher Mann? | Ja, er ist ein sehr reicher Mann; er hat viele schöne Häuser. |
| Wer hat diesen goldenen Ring verloren? | Meine kleine Schwester hat ihn verloren. |
| Hat der Bäcker gutes Brot [Brod]? | Er verkauft immer gutes Brot. |
| Haben Sie einen neuen Hut? | Nein, ich habe einen alten. |

### READING LESSON

### Ariosto.

Der italienische Dichter Ariosto baute sich ein
<br>poet     built himself
kleines Haus. Ein Freund fragte ihn: „Wie können
<br>asked    how
Sie sich mit einem so kleinen Haus begnügen, nachdem
<br>yourself      content     after
Sie in Ihrem „Orlando" so schöne Paläste beschrieben
<br>described
haben?" Der philosophische Sänger erwiderte [erwiederte]:
<br>bard    replied
„Worte sind billiger als Steine."
<br>cheaper than   stones.

# LESSON XXVIII.

## Degrees of Comparison.

1) The comparison, in German as in English, is effected by two degrees, the *comparative* and *superlative*. The comparative degree is formed by the addition of **er**, or when the adjective ends in **e**, only **r**. Further the vowels **a, o, u** are changed, in most monosyllables, into **ä, ö, ü** in both degrees. Ex.:

| | | | |
|---|---|---|---|
| klein small, little | *Comparative* | kleiner | smaller. |
| schön handsome, fine | " | schöner | handsomer. |
| reich rich | " | reicher | richer. |
| alt old | | älter | older. |
| stark strong | | stärker | stronger. |
| jung young | | jünger | younger. |
| groß large, great | | größer | larger, greater. |
| lang long | | länger | longer. |

2) To form the *superlative*, **st** or **est** is added and the vowel softened.

These superlatives are declined like adjectives in the first form (see page 96). Ex.:

*N.* der kleinste Knabe    die schönste Blume    das längste Kleid
*G.* des kleinsten Knaben    der schönsten Blume    des längsten Kleides
*D.* dem kleinsten Knaben    der schönsten Blume    dem längsten Kleide
*A.* den kleinsten Knaben.    die schönste Blume.    das längste Kleid.

> *Plur.* die kleinsten Knaben, rc.    die schönsten Blumen, rc.
> die längsten Kleider, rc.

3) There is another form for the superlative, viz.: the latter takes the ending **en**, and is preceded by **am**, as: **am schönsten.**

reich — *Comp.* reicher; *Superl.* am reichsten the richest.

This form is invariable, and only used when the superlative is used as predicate without any noun or as adverb.

### Examples.

Dieſer Wein iſt **am** ſtärkſten  this wine is (the) strongest.
Dieſe Roſe iſt **am** ſchönſten  this rose is the most beautiful.

4) In the superlative of adjectives ending in a hissing sound (3, ß, ß, ſch), an **e** is inserted before **ſt** for euphony (**eſte**), as:

| Comp. | Superl. |
|---|---|
| kurz short | kürzer, der kürz(e)ſte or am kürz(e)ſten. |
| ſüß sweet | ſüßer, = ſüßeſte = am ſüßeſten. |

*Note.* Adjectives ending in **b, t, th** with another consonant and accented vowel before them likewise insert usually a euphonical **e** in the superlative; those ending in a diphthong or **h** preceded by a vowel sometimes have the same form, as:

ſchlecht,  *Sup.*  der ſchlechteſte;
alt,  = älteſte;
rauh rough,  = rauheſte.

5) Some adjectives are irregular in the degrees of comparison, viz.:

| | Comp. | | Superl. |
|---|---|---|---|
| hoch high | **höher** higher | der höchſte or am höchſten. | |
| nahe near | näher nearer | der **nächſte, am nächſten.** | |
| groß great, large | größer greater | der **größte, am größten.***) | |
| gut good | beſſer better | der beſte, am beſten the best. | |

6) In clauses containing a simple comparison, *as* — *as* is translated **ebenſo . . . . , als** or **wie,** whereas *not so* is simply **nicht ſo.** Ex.:

Ich bin **ebenſo** groß **wie** Sie  I am *as* tall *as* you.
Karl [Carl] war **nicht ſo** glücklich, wie ſein Freund Wilhelm.
Charles was not so happy as his friend William.

---

*) Instead of: der größeſte.

### Words.

| | |
|---|---|
| tief  deep. | die Klaſſe [Claſſe]  the class. |
| der See  the lake. | ſchwach  feeble, weak. |
| der Adler  the eagle. | weiſe  wise. |
| der Flügel  the wing. | das Veilchen  the violet. |
| der Frühling  the spring. | das Metall  (*plur.* –e),  the |
| das Eiſen  (the) iron. |    metal. |
| das Kupfer  (the) copper. | naß  wet. |
| b i e Sonne  the sun. | höflich  polite. |
| b e r Mond  the moon. | nützlich  useful. |
| der Muſiklehrer  the music- | ſchwer  difficult. |
|    master. | |

### Exercise 55.

1. Der Eſel iſt kleiner als das Pferd. 2. Der Fluß iſt tief; der See iſt tiefer als der Fluß. 3. Karl [Carl] iſt ſtärker als Wilhelm. 4. Er iſt der ſtärkſte Knabe. 5. Marie iſt fleißiger als Emilie. 6. Mein Kleid iſt ſchöner als dein Kleid. 7. Das Kleid meiner Schweſter iſt a m ſchönſten. 8. Der Adler iſt der ſtärkſte Vogel. 9. Er hat die längſten Flügel. 10. Im Frühling ſind die Tage kürzer als im Sommer; aber im Winter ſind die Tage am kürzeſten. 11. Das Silber iſt koſtbarer als das Kupfer. 12. Das Gold iſt das koſtbarſte Metall. 13. Der Wein iſt beſſer als das Bier. 14. Unſer Oheim iſt ebenſo reich als unſer Vetter. 15. Der beſte Kaffee [Caffee] kommt (comes) aus Arabien.

### Exercise 56.

1. My garden is larger than the garden of my neighbor. 2. The earth is smaller than the sun, and the moon is smaller than the earth. 3. This man is wiser than his brother; he is the wisest man in the town. 4. Is William younger than Thomas? 5. No, Thomas is younger, he is the youngest of Mr. Peter's

sons. 6. My music-master is the politest man.
7. This girl is smaller than Louisa, but she is the
handsomest girl in her class. 8. I am wetter than you,
and Charles is the wettest. 9. This tree is much
higher than the other. 10. We are happier here than
many other people.

### Exercise 57.

1. I am young, but my brother is younger than I.
2. You are strong, but your cousin is stronger than
you. 3. (The) iron is more useful than (the) silver.
4. This pupil is *as* diligent *as* Charles. 5. The cat is
smaller than the dog. 6. A woman is feebler than a
man, but a woman is stronger than a girl. 7. Is your
exercise difficult? 8. Yes, it is very difficult, it is more
difficult than that (die) of Henry. 9. This mountain is
much higher than that (jener). 10. Is this pen good?
11. Yes, it is very good, it is much better than yours
(Ihre).

### Conversation.

| | |
|---|---|
| Wer ift ftärfer, Friedrich oder Karl [Carl]? | Ich glaube (think), Karl ift ftärfer. |
| Ift das Veilchen schöner als die Rose? | Nein, die Rose ift schöner als das Veilchen. |
| Welches ift das foftbarfte Metall? | Das Gold ift das foftbarfte. |
| Welches Metall ift am nütz= lichften? | Das Eifen ift am nützlichften. |
| Woher' (whence) fommt der befte Kaffee [Caffee]? | Der befte Kaffee fommt aus Arabien. |
| Welches ift die schönfte Blume? | Die Rose ift die schönfte Blume. |
| Welches ift das ftärffte Tier [Thier]? | Der Elefant [Elephant] ift das ftärffte Tier. |

# LESSON XXIX.

## Numerals.

The numerals are of two kinds, namely: *cardinal* and *ordinal numerals*.

### I. Cardinal Numerals. Grundzahlen.

ein, eine, ein or c i n § one.
zwei two.
brei three.
vier four.
fünf five.
sechs six.
sieben seven.
acht eight.
neun nine.
zehn ten.
elf eleven.
zwölf twelve.
breizehn thirteen.
vierzehn fourteen.
fünfzehn fifteen.
sechzehn sixteen.
siebzehn seventeen.
achtzehn eighteen.
neunzehn nineteen.
zwanzig twenty.
einunbzwanzig [ein unb zwan= zig] twenty-one.
zweiunbzwanzig [zwei unb zwanzig, 2c.] twenty-two.

breiunbzwanzig twenty-three.
vierunbzwanzig twenty-four.
fünfunbzwanzig twenty-five.
sechsunbzwanzig twenty-six.
siebenunbzwanzig twenty-seven.
achtunbzwanzig twenty-eight.
neununbzwanzig twenty-nine.
breißig thirty.
einunbbreißig thirty-one etc.
vierzig forty.
fünfzig fifty.
sechzig sixty.
siebzig seventy.
achtzig eighty.
neunzig ninety.
hunbert a hundred.
hunbert unb cins a hundred and one.
zweihunbert [zwei hunbert, 2c.] two hundred.
breihunbert three hundred.
vierhunbert four hundred.
fünfhunbert five hundred etc.
taufenb a thousand.

*Note* 1. *A* hundred and *a* thousand are in German simply h u n b e r t and t a u f e n b (not einhunbert, 2c.); but the English *one* hundred, *one* thousand is rendered by e i n ḧ u n b e r t [ein ḧunbert] and e i n t a u ſ e n b [ein tauſenb], as:

1800 = eintauſenb acht̡hunbert or achtzeḧnḧunbert.

*Note* 2. *In* before a year must be translated i m J a ḧ r. Ex.:

In 1876 = im Jaḧr eintauſenb achtḧunbcrt ſechSunbſiebzig
 or achtzeḧnḧunbert ſechSunbſiebzig.

### Remarks.

1) The *hours* of the day or night are expressed as follows:

What o'clock is it? **Wiebiel [Wie biel] Uḧr iſt eŝ?**
Two o'clock **zwei Uḧr.**

A quarter *past* two { ein Biertel **nach** zwei or ein Biertel
 **auf** b r e i *(towards three).*

Half past two **ḧalb brei.**

A quarter *to* three { brei Biertel **auf** b r e i or ein
 Biertel **bor** brei.

*At* three o'clock **um brei Uḧr.**

*Note.* With minutes we reckon as in English. Ex.:
Ten minutes *to* five zeḧn Minuten **bor** (or biŝ) 5 Uḧr.
Five minutes *past* two fünf Minuten **nach** zwei.

2) A person's age is expressed as in English. Ex.:
How old are you? Wie alt ſinb Sie?
I am twenty years old ich bin zwanzig Jaḧre alt.

3) The numeral adverbs are:

einmal [ein mal] once; zweimal [zwei mal] twice;
 breimal [brei mal] three times etc.

## Words.

die Kuh (*plur.* Kühe) the cow.

das Schaf (*plur.* Schafe) the sheep.

das Wort the word.

die Woche the week.

der Monat the month.

der Januar January.

machen to make.

gelernt learned.

der Schäfer the shepherd.

mal times.

wie viele how many.

ist geboren was born.

### Exercise 58.

1. Ein Pferd.  2. Eine Stunde.  3. Ich habe einen Bruder und zwei Schwestern.  4. Mein Oheim hat sechs Kinder gehabt; er hat drei Söhne und zwei Töchter verloren. 5. Unser Nachbar hat sieben Pferde, acht Kühe und zwanzig Schafe.  6. Zweimal [zwei mal] drei ist sechs.  7. Fünfmal neun ist fünfundvierzig [fünf und vierzig].  8. Wie alt sind Sie?  9. Ich bin achtzehn Jahre alt.  10. Wie alt ist Ihre Schwester?  11. Sie ist sechzehn Jahre alt.  12. Wie viele Wörter haben Sie gelernt?  13. Wir haben dreißig Wörter gelernt.  14. Der Januar hat einunddreißig Tage.  15. Ein Jahr hat 52 Wochen oder 365 Tage.  16. Wieviel [Wie viel] Geld haben Sie?  17. Ich habe dreiundzwanzig Mark (marks).  18. 21 und 84 ist 105.  19. Der Schäfer des Grafen hat 36 Schafe verkauft.  20. Wieviel Uhr ist es? 21. Es ist vier Uhr oder halb fünf.  22. Es ist halb sechs.

### Exercise 59.

1. I have two dogs.  2. My aunt has three cats. 3. My uncle has four horses.  4. How many children has Mr. Jones?  5. He has seven children: four daughters and three sons.  6. How old is his eldest son? 7. He is eighteen years old, and his eldest daughter is fourteen years old.  8. A year has twelve months or fifty-two weeks.  9. A week has seven days.  10. How

old are you, Frederick? 11. I am fifteen years old. 12. And your sister Mary, how old is she? 13. She is thirteen years old. 14. How much are twenty and fifty? 15. Twenty and fifty make seventy. 16. Twice four make eight. 17. Seven times nine make sixty-three. 18. In three months. 19. My brother was born in (the year) one thousand eight hundred and sixty-one. 20. Is it ten o'clock? 21. No, it is a quarter *to* eleven or ten minutes *to* eleven.

---

# LESSON XXX.

### Ordinal Numerals.

These are formed by adding the syllable te to the cardinal numerals up to 19. Beginning with 20 the syllable fte is added; except: der erfte the first, and der dritte the third.

der **erfte** the first.
der zweite the second.
der **dritte** the third.
der vierte the fourth.
der fünfte the fifth.
der sechste the sixth.
der siebente the seventh.
der achte the eighth.
der neunte the ninth.
der zehnte the tenth.
der elfte the eleventh.
der zwölfte the twelfth.
der dreizehnte the thirteenth.
der vierzehnte the fourteenth.
der fünfzehnte the fifteenth.
der sechzehnte the sixteenth.
der siebzehnte the seventeenth.

der achtzehnte the eighteenth.
der neunzehnte the nineteenth.
der zwanzigfte the twentieth.
der einundzwanzigfte the twenty-first.
der zweiundzwanzigfte the twenty-second etc.
der dreißigfte the thirtieth.
der vierzigfte the fortieth.
der fünfzigfte the fiftieth.
der sechzigfte the sixtieth.
der siebzigfte the seventieth.
der achtzigfte the eightieth.
der neunzigfte the ninetieth.
der hundertfte the hundredth.
der tausendfte the thousandth.
der, die, das letzte the last.

## Names of the days of the week.

ber Sonntag  Sunday.      ber Donnerstag  Thursday.
ber Montag  Monday.      ber Freitag  Friday.
ber Dienstag  Tuesday.      ber Samstag }
ber Mittwoch  Wednesday.      ber Sonnabend } Saturday.

## Names of the months.

ber Januar  January.      ber August  August.
ber Februar  February.      ber September  September.
ber März  March.      ber Oktober [October]  Oc-
ber April  April.      tober.
ber Mai  May.      ber November  November.
ber Juni  June.      ber Dezember [December]  De-
ber Juli  July.      cember.

### Examples.

ber erste März  the first *of* March.
am zweiten April  on the second *of* April.
ber sechsundzwanzigste September  the 26th *of* September.

**The ordinal numerals are declined like the adjectives:**

bas erste Mal  the first time.
ber zweite Band  the 2d volume; *G.* bes zweiten Bandes.
     *D.* bem zweiten Band ; *A.* ben zweiten Band.
mein drittes Glas  my third glass.

### Words.

ber Band  the volume.      bie Flasche  the bottle.
bie Klasse [Classe]  the class.      ber Teil [Theil]  the part.
ber Platz  the place.      Schweden  Sweden.
ber Fehler  the mistake.      ber Stock  the story, floor.

### Exercise 60.

1. Der erste Band.  2. Haben Sie ben zweiten Band?  3. Nein, ich habe ben dritten Band.  4. Dies ist mein erstes Glas. 5. Emilie ist in der vierten Klasse [Classe], und ihre Schwester Anna ist in der fünften Klasse.  6. Der Montag ist der zweite

Tag der Woche, der Freitag ist der sechste. 7. Der November ist der elfte Monat des Jahres. 8. Mein Vetter Ludwig ist der siebente in seiner Klasse und Heinrich der letzte. 9. Der erste Platz ist immer der beste Platz. 10. Napoleon der Dritte war Kaiser der Franzosen. 11. Sein Onkel war Napoleon der Erste. 12. Ein Monat ist der zwölfte Teil [Theil] des Jahres.

### Exercise 61.

1. The first day. 2. The second week of January. 3. March is the third month of the year. 4. I am the fourth, Robert is the seventh, and Arthur the last in our class. 5. A month is the twelfth part of the year. 6. The fifth window of the third story. 7. July is the seventh, and December the last month of the year. 8. This is our second bottle. 9. Sunday is the first day of the week. 10. Come on (am) Tuesday or Friday. 11. To-day is the twenty-first of May. 12. Have you the sixth volume? 13. No, Sir, I have the eighth. 14. What o'clock is it? 15. It is five o'clock or a quarter past five. 16. You are wrong (Sie haben unrecht [Unrecht]), Sir, it is half past five. 17. I will go at a quarter past seven, and you must go at half past seven. 18. My sister *was* (ist) born on the (am) second [of] April 1863.

### Conversation.

| | |
|---|---|
| Wie viele Fehler hat Georg? | Er hat 6 oder 7 Fehler. |
| Wie alt ist Karoline [Caroline]? | Sie ist 18 Jahre alt. |
| Wieviel [Wie viel] ist 20 und 40? | 20 und 40 ist sechzig. |
| Wieviel ist 4mal 12? | 4mal 12 ist 48. |
| Welchen Platz hat Karl [Carl] in der Schule? | Er ist sehr fleißig, er hat immer den ersten Platz. |
| Wann starb (died) Ihr Onkel? | Im Jahr 1871. |
| Wie alt war er? | Er war 51 Jahre alt. |
| Wieviel Uhr ist es? | Es ist 11 Uhr oder halb zwölf. |
| Haben Sie den ersten Band? | Nein, ich habe den dritten Band. |

# LESSON XXXI.

## Regular Verb. Regelmäßiges Zeitwort.

### *Formation of the Tenses.*

1) The *Present tense* is formed by dropping the final **n** of the infinitive, as: Ich lobe I praise *or* I am praising (from loben to praise); ich suche (from suchen to seek).

2) In the *Imperfect* the syllable **te** (sometimes ete) is added to the radical, as: lob=te from loben; hör=te from hören; redete from red=en.

The terminations of the different *persons* of the Present and Imperfect tenses are the following:

| Present. | | Imperfect. | |
|---|---|---|---|
| *Singular.* | *Plural.* | *Singular.* | *Plural.* |
| 1. –e | –en | 1. –te or ete | –ten or eten |
| 2. –ft or eft | –t, et or en | 2. –teft or eteft | –tet or etet(n) |
| 3. –t or et | –en. | 3. –te or ete | –ten or eten. |

The *Past Participle* is formed by prefixing the syllable **ge**, and by the addition of t (sometimes e t) to the radical, as: ge=lob=t, ge=hör=t, ge=red=et. All simple and separable compound verbs (Lesson 49) take this **ge**.

The *first Future* is formed by combining the auxiliary **ich werde** with the *Infinitive:* ich werde loben, ich werde hören, ich werde reden.

The *Perfect* and *Pluperfect* are formed by combining the auxiliary ich habe, ich hatte, ꝛc. with the *Past Participal*, as:

*Perfect.* ich habe gelobt, ich habe gehört, ich habe geredet.
*Pluperf.* ich hatte gelobt, ich hatte gehört, ꝛc.

This is quite analogous to the conjugation of the English regular verbs.

The *Conditional* is the *Infinitive* preceded by ich würde. Ex.:

> ich würde loben  I should praise.

The *Imperative* in the form of politeness is the *Infinitive* followed by Sie. Ex.:

> geben Sie  give; suchen Sie  seek, look for.

### Conjugation of a Regular Verb.

**lachen  (lach-te, ge-lacht)  to laugh.**

## Indicative.

#### Present Tense.

| | | | |
|---|---|---|---|
| ich lache | I laugh | wir lachen | we laugh |
| du lachst | thou laughest | ihr lacht (lachet) | } you laugh |
| er lacht | he laughs | Sie lachen | |
| sie lacht | she laughs | sie lachen | they laugh. |
| es lacht | it laughs. | | |

#### Imperfect.

| | | | |
|---|---|---|---|
| ich lachte | I laughed | wir lachten | we laughed |
| du lachtest | thou laughedst | ihr lachtet | } you laughed |
| er lachte | he laughed | Sie lachten | |
| sie lachte | she laughed | sie lachten | they laughed. |
| es lachte | it laughed. | | |

#### Future.

ich werde lachen  I shall laugh
du wirst lachen  thou wilt laugh
er wird lachen  he will laugh

wir werden lachen  we shall laugh
ihr werdet lachen } you will laugh
Sie werden lachen
sie werden lachen  they will laugh.

*Conditional.*

ich würde lachen   I should laugh
du würdest lachen      etc.
er würde lachen

wir würden lachen   we should laugh
ihr würdet lachen  }
Sie würden lachen  }    etc.
fie würden lachen.

## Imperative.

lache (du)! lachet (ihr)! } laugh.    lachen wir, laßt uns lachen!
lachen Sie!                        let us laugh.

## Infinitive.

lachen      } to laugh.
zu lachen }

## Participles.

*Pres.* lachend laughing.      *Past.* gelacht laughed.

### REMARK.

The English mode of conjugating the verb *to be* with the addition of a *pres. part.* cannot be rendered literally in German; the corresponding simple form of the verb is to be employed instead of them:

*Present.*
I am learning ich lerne; he is learning er lernt, ꝛc.

*Imperfect.*
I was learning ich lernte; he was learning er lernte.

*Perfect.*
I have been learning ich habe gelernt, ꝛc.

## Subjunctive.

### Present Tense.

*Singular.*           *Plural.*

ich lache  I (may) laugh     wir lachen  we laugh

du lacheſt  you laugh      ihr lachet $\big\}$ you laugh

er lache  he laughs        Sie lachen

                              fie lachen  they laugh.

### Imperfect.

ich lachte  I might laugh, I laughed etc.

(Quite like the Imperfect of the Indicative.)

## Interrogative Form.

### Present.

*Singular*           *Plural.*

lache ich?  do I laugh?      lachen wir?  do we laugh?

lachſt du?  dost thou laugh?   lacht ihr? $\big\}$ do you laugh?

lacht er?  does he laugh?     lachen Sie?

                             lachen fie?  do they laugh?

### Imperfect.

*Singular.*           *Plural.*

lachte ich?  did I laugh?     lachten wir?  did we laugh?

lachteſt du?     etc.        lachtet ihr?          etc.

lachte er?                lachten Sie?

                         lachten fie?

## Negative Form.

### Present.

*Sing.*  ich lache nicht  I do not laugh

       du lachſt nicht          etc.

       er lacht nicht

*Plur.*  wir lachen nicht  we do not laugh

       ihr lachet nicht                etc.

       Sie lachen nicht

       fie lachen nicht.

*Imperfect.*

ich lachte nicht   I did not laugh
du lachtest nicht     etc.

lachte ich nicht?   did I not laugh?
lachte er nicht?     etc.

The following verbs are conjugated in the same manner:

| | |
|---|---|
| machen to make, to do. | lernen to learn. |
| lieben to love, to like. | strafen to punish. |
| loben to praise. | bauen to build. |
| kaufen to buy. | wohnen to live, to reside. |
| hören to hear. | sagen to say, to tell. |
| suchen to look for, to seek. | fragen to ask. |
| holen to go for, to fetch. | weinen to cry, to weep. |
| zeigen to show. | wünschen to wish. |
| leben to live. | glauben to believe. |
| spielen to play. | schicken to send. |

### Words.

| | |
|---|---|
| die Lektion [Lection] the lesson. | Obst fruit. |
| die Musik the music. | immer always. |
| die Brieftasche the pocketbook. | morgen früh to-morrow morning. |
| die Schülerin the (*fem.*) pupil. | das Schloß the castle. |
| französisch French. | träge idle. |
| das Dutzend the dozen. | daß that. |
| früher formerly. | lang(e) long (time). |
| | jetzt now. |

### Exercise 62.

1. Ich lache. 2. Warum lachst du? 3. Was machst du? 4. Was machen Sie? 5. Ich mache meine Aufgabe. 6. Ich lobe den Knaben. 7. Du lobst deine Schwester. 8. Der

Lehrer lobt den Schüler. 9. Wir lieben die artigen Kinder. 10. Die Kinder lieben ihre Eltern. 11. Was suchen Sie? 12. Ich suche meine Brieftasche. 13. Mein Nachbar baute ein Haus. 14. Das Kind weinte. 15. Die Kinder weinten. 16. Die Schülerin lernte ihre Aufgabe. 17. Du lerntest deine Aufgabe nicht gut (well). 18. Wo wohnt Herr Morel? 19. Er wohnt in der Karlsstraße. 20. Hörten Sie die Musik? 21. Nein, ich hörte sie (it) nicht. 22. Zeige mir das Haus deines Vaters! 23. Ich werde meine Lektion [Lection] lernen. 24. Du würdest lachen. 25. Der Vater würde auch lachen, wenn er hier wäre. 26. Mein Freund wird einen Stock kaufen; er würde auch einen Regenschirm kaufen, wenn er genug Geld hätte. 27. Sagen Sie mir alles [Alles] (all)!

### Exercise 68.

1. I love my brother. 2. Thou praisest the servant. 3. Mary buys a book for her sister. 4. I learnt my lesson yesterday. 5. Robert learns French and English. 6. The teacher praises the industrious pupils. 7. He will not praise the lazy boys. 8. The children like apples and pears. 9. My uncle lived in Switzerland. 10. Ask the man. 11. Children, where do you play? 12. We play in the yard. 13. We played before (vorher) in the garden. 14. I should also play, if I had time. 15. I wish to learn music. 16. Will you ask me (mich)? 17. Yes, I shall ask you.

### Exercise 64.

1. I learn English. 2. Thou learnest German. 3. He learns his lesson. 4. We love our parents. 5. You live at (in) Frankfort. 6. They live in Paris. 7. Our friends live also in Paris. 8. What are you doing

(what do you make)?  9. I am learning my French lesson.  10. What is Charles doing (what makes Ch.)? 11. He is seeking his little dog; he has lost it (ihn). 12. What did you buy?  13. I bought a horse.  14. The teacher formerly praised his pupils; they formerly learnt their lesson.  15. What did the man fetch? 16. He fetched (or went for) [some] water.  17. Do you love your friend?  18. I loved him formerly; but now 'I 'love him no more (nicht mehr); he is no more my friend.

### READING LESSON.

### Die Römer.

**The Romans.**

Romulus baute die Stadt Rom.  Die Einwohner
      built                      inhabitants

wurden Römer genannt.  Sie waren ein sehr tapferes
         called.                          brave

Volk.  Sie liebten ihr Vaterland und kämpften, um es zu
people.                           fought          to

verteidigen [vertheidigen].  Sie wollten lieber sterben, als
  defend                        rather     die    than

ihre Freiheit verlieren.  Diese war ihnen teurer [theurer]
  liberty      lose.               to them  dearer

als das Leben.  Sie führten viele Kriege mit den
      life.           made        wars

Karthagern [Carthagern], mit wechselndem Erfolg.  Zuletzt
                    changing   success.   At last

besiegten sie (Nomin.) die Karthager (Acc.) und
conquered

zerstörten ihre Stadt.
destroyed

# LESSON XXXII.

## Regular Verbs continued.

### Compound Tenses.

*Perfect Tense.*

**ich habe gelacht** I have laughed *)
du haft gelacht  you have laughed
er hat gelacht  he has laughed
fie hat gelacht  she has laughed
es hat gelacht  it has laughed

wir haben gelacht  we have laughed
ihr habt gelacht          etc.
Sie haben gelacht
fie haben gelacht.

*Pluperfect.*

ich **hatte** gelacht  I had laughed
du hatteft gelacht  thou hadst laughed
er hatte gelacht  he had laughed
fie hatte gelacht  she had laughed
es hatte gelacht  it had laughed

wir hatten gelacht  we had laughed
ihr hattet gelacht          etc.
Sie hatten gelacht
fie hatten gelacht.

*Second Future.*

ich **werde** gelacht **haben**  I shall have laughed
du wirft gelacht haben  thou wilt have laughed
er wird gelacht haben  he will have laughed

wir werden gelacht haben  we shall have laughed
ihr werdet gelacht haben          etc.
Sie werden gelacht haben
fie werden gelacht haben.

*) Or also *I laughed.*

*Second Conditional.*

ich würde gelacht haben  I should have laughed
du würdest gelacht haben  thou wouldst have laughed
er würde gelacht haben  he would have laughed
wir würden gelacht haben        etc.

*NB.* Instead of ich würde gelacht haben one may also say: ich hätte gelacht etc.

## Negative Form.

ich habe nicht gelacht  I have not laughed *or* did not laugh
du hast nicht gelacht        etc.
er hat nicht gelacht.

## Interrogative Form.

habe ich gelacht?  have I laughed? *or* did I laugh?
haben Sie gelacht?  have you laughed? *or* did you laugh?

## Negative-interrogative Form.

habe ich nicht gelacht?  have I not laughed? *or* did I not laugh?
haben Sie nicht gelacht?  have you not laughed? *or* did you not laugh?

### Words.

die Zeit  the time.
der Lärm  the noise.
das Gemälde  the picture.
traurig  sad.
die Nadel (*plur.* -n) the needle.
der Uhrmacher  the watchmaker.

ich weiß nicht  I do not know.
verkauft (*part. past*) sold.
Strümpfe  stockings.
die Musik  the music.
jemand [Jemand]  anybody, somebody.
gefunden  found.

### Exercise 65.

1. Ich habe meine Aufgabe gestern gemacht; aber Karl [Carl] hat seine Aufgabe nicht gemacht. 2. Ludwig, warum hast du deine Lektion [Lection] nicht gelernt? 3. Ich habe

nicht Zeit gehabt. 4. Wer hat gelacht? 5. Emilie hat
gelacht. 6. Haben Sie die Musik gehört? 7. Ich habe die
Musik nicht gehört; aber ich habe einen Lärm gehört. · 8. Mein
Nachbar wird dieses Haus gekauft haben; er würde auch den
Garten gekauft haben, wenn er mehr Geld hätte. 9. Wer
hat in diesem Schloß gewohnt? 10. Der Lord A. hat
früher in diesem Schloß gewohnt; aber er wohnt jetzt nicht
mehr darin (in it); er wohnt jetzt in Paris. 11. Der
Lehrer würde die Schüler gelobt haben, wenn sie fleißiger
gewesen wären.

## Exercise 66.

1. Have you laughed? 2. Yes, I have laughed.
3. I have made a mistake. 4. Thou hast made three
mistakes in thy exercise. 5. Charles has not learnt
his lesson. 6. He must learn it again (wieder). 7. The
watchmaker has sold all (the) watches. 8. Louisa and
Mary are very sad; they have lost all their needles.
9. Has anybody found them (sie)? 10. I do not know.
11. The count has built a new house. 12. Formerly
'he 'had built a castle. 13. The teacher had praised
his pupils. 14. Which tailor has made this coat?
15. Who has bought this looking-glass? 16. I do not
know, I have not bought it (ihn). 17. My aunt has sent
to the mother of the poor children six pairs (Paar) of
stockings.

### Conversation.

| | |
|---|---|
| Was sagen Sie? | Ich sage nichts. |
| Wen lieben die Kinder? | Die Kinder lieben ihre Eltern. |
| Was sucht Karl [Carl]? | Er sucht sein Federmesser. |
| Hat er auf dem Tische ge= sucht? | Er hat überall (everywhere) gesucht. |
| Wer hat diese Aufgabe gemacht? | Ich habe sie gemacht. |

| | |
|---|---|
| Wo wohnt Ihr Oheim? | Er wohnt in der Friedrichs=straße. |
| Was kauften Sie auf dem Markte? | Wir kauften Butter und Eier. |
| Haben Sie auch Obst gekauft? | Ja, wir haben Birnen gekauft. |
| Was machen Sie da (there)? | Ich lerne meine Lektion [Lec=tion. |
| Warum lachen Sie, mein Herr? | Ich lache nicht über (at) Sie. |

## LESSON XXXIII.

### Remarks on the Regular Verbs.

1) In all verbs ending in **eln**, like h a n b e l n to act (instead of handelen), the first person singular of the Present, and the second of the Imperative drop the **e** before **l**.

#### Example.

*Present Tense.*

| *Singular.* | *Plural.* |
|---|---|
| ich handle I act | wir handeln we act |
| du handelst etc. | ihr handelt ⎫ etc. |
| er handelt | Sie handeln ⎭ |
| sie handelt | sie handeln. |
| es handelt. | |

*Imperfect.*

ich handelte I acted; du handeltest, er handelte, ꝛc.

*Perfect.*

ich habe gehandelt I have acted; du hast gehandelt, ꝛc.

*Imperative.*

handle, handeln Sie act.

Such are:

| | |
|---|---|
| tadeln  to blame. | segeln  to sail. |
| lächeln  to smile. | schütteln  to shake. |

2) Regular verbs in **ben, ten, gnen,** and **chnen** preserve the **e** before the termination in all the persons of the Present and Imperf., and in the Participle past. Ex.:

### Warten to wait.

|  |  |
|---|---|
| *Present Tense.* | *Imperfect.* |
| ich warte  I wait | ich wartete  I waited |
| bu warteſt  etc. | bu warteteſt    etc. |
| er wartet | er wartete |
| wir warten  we wait | wir warteten  we waited |
| ihr wartet    etc. | ihr wartetet    etc. |
| Sie warten | Sie warteten |
| ſie warten. | ſie warteten. |
| *Part. past.* | *Perfect.* |
| gewartet  waited. | ich habe gewartet  I have waited. |

Such are:

| | |
|---|---|
| baben  to bathe. | töten [töbten]  to kill. |
| beten  to pray. | fürchten  to fear. |
| arbeiten  to work. | regnen  to rain. |
| antworten  to answer. | reben  to talk. |
| achten  to esteem. | begegnen  to meet. |

*Imperfect.*

ich babete, arbeitete, antwortete, fürchtete, ꝛc.

*Participle past.*

gebabet, gearbeitet, geantworte , gefürchtet, ꝛc.

3) Verbs of foreign origin ending in **i e r e n,** are regularly conjugated; only in the Participle past they do not admit of the prefix **ge**:

| | *Imperfect.* | *Perfect.* |
|---|---|---|
| ſtubieren [ſtubiren]  to study. | ich ſtubierte. | ich habe ſtubiert. |
| probieren [probiren]  to try. | ich probierte. | ich habe probiert. |
| regieren  to govern. | ich regierte. | ich habe regiert. |

4) Verbs having an *unaccented prefix* before them, do not take the syllable ge in their past participle. Such prefixes are: be, emp, ent, er, ver, zer, ge, miß, voll, wider and hinter. Ex.:

| | Imperfect. | Participle. |
|---|---|---|
| bewoh'nen  to inhabit. | ich bewohnte. | bewohnt. |
| verkaufen  to sell. | ich verkaufte. | verkauft. |
| zerstören  to destroy. | ich zerstörte. | zerstört. |
| vermieten [vermiethen]  to let. | ich vermietete. | vermietet. |

(Further particulars on such verbs are given in Lesson XLVIII.)

5) The following verbs and those derived from them, though quite regular in their terminations, change in the *Imperfect* and *Participle past* the root-vowel into a:

| Infinitive. | Present. | Imperfect. | Part. past. |
|---|---|---|---|
| brennen  to burn. | ich brenne | ich brannte | gebrannt. |
| kennen  to know. | ich kenne | ich kannte | gekannt. |
| nennen  to name, call. | ich nenne | ich nannte | genannt. |
| rennen  to run. | ich renne | ich rannte | gerannt. |

6) Further the three following, which are a little more irregular:

| Infinitive. | Present. | Imperfect. | Participle past. |
|---|---|---|---|
| denken  to think. | ich denke | ich dachte | gedacht  thought. |
| bringen  to bring. | ich bringe | ich brachte | gebracht  brought. |
| wissen  to know*). | ich weiß | ich wußte | gewußt  known. |

*Remark.* The present *singular* of the indicative of wissen is also a little irregular, viz.:

ich weiß I know, du weißt, er weiß; *plur.* wir wissen, ihr wißt, Sie wissen, sie wissen.

---

*) French *savoir*, je sais.

### Words.

recht rightly.

der Briefträger the postman.

der Regen the rain.

der Schuhmacher the shoe-
maker.

etwas something, anything.

die Sonne the sun.

nicht mehr no more, no
longer.

alle Tage every day.

### Exercise 67.

1. Ich warte in dem Garten. 2. Ich wartete eine Stunde.
3. Ich handle recht. 4. Der Knabe badete gestern in dem
Flusse; er badet alle Tage. 5. Was fürchtest du? 6. Ich
fürchte nichts. 7. Es regnet sehr stark (hard). 8. Ich achte
diesen Mann nicht; denn (for) er arbeitet nichts. 9. Die
armen Soldaten haben viel gelitten. 10. Ich habe vier
Stunden studiert [studirt]. 11. Man hat lange probiert
[probirt]. 12. Ich denke an Sie. 13. Ich dachte nicht an
Sie. 14. Der Briefträger hat meinem Vater einen Brief
gebracht. 15. Haben Sie Herrn Butler gekannt? 16. Ich
habe ihn früher gekannt; jetzt kenne ich ihn nicht mehr.
17. Wissen Sie, wo meine Schwester ist? 18. Nein, ich weiß
es nicht. 19. Ich wußte nicht, daß Sie hier waren.

### Exercise 68.

1. You act rightly. 2. Why do you smile? 3. I
sail for (nach) America. 4. For whom (Auf wen) do you
wait? 5. I wait for the shoemaker. 6. Did you fear
anything? 7. No, I feared nothing. 8. It has rained
all (die ganze) night. 9. I have sold my house.
10. What did you study in Germany? 11. I studied
German. 12. Do you know Mr. Butler? 13. I have
known him formerly. 14. Have you thought of (an)
me? 15. I ²always ¹think of you. 16. Who ·has
brought the letter? 17. The postman has brought it
(ihn). 18. He brought two letters. 19. Do you know

that (daß) my teacher ²is ¹ill? 20. Yes, I know (it). 21. I knew it yesterday. 22. This house is not inhabited. 23. These rooms are let.

## READING LESSON.

### Alexander und Parmenio.

Darius, der König von Persien, wollte (dem) Alexander

zehntausend [zehn tausend] Talente bezahlen, wenn er
ten thousand          pay.    if

Asien mit ihm teilen [theilen] wollte. Aber Alexander
     him    divide

antwortete: „Die Erde kann nicht zwei Sonnen tragen,
answered    The   earth        suns    bear,

noch Asien zwei Könige." Parmenio, ein Freund Alexan=
nor

ders, hatte das Anerbieten des Darius gehört. Er sagte
        offer         heard.

zu Alexander: „Wenn ich Alexander w ä r e , würde ich

es annehmen." Aber der König antwortete ihm: „Ich
accept.

würde es auch annehmen, wenn ich Parmenio w ä r e ."

---

# LESSON XXXIV.

## Pronouns.

The German pronouns are divided into six classes, viz.: 1) *personal*, 2) *interrogative*, 3) *demonstrative*, 4) *possessive*, 5) *relative* and *correlative*, 6) *indefinite pronouns*.

### PERSONAL PRONOUNS.

1) These are: ich I; du thou; er he; sie she; es it; *plur.:* wir we; ihr, Sie you; sie they.

They are declined as follows:

### First Person : idj I.

| *Singular.* | *Plural.* |
|---|---|
| *N.* id) I | wir we |
| *G.* meiner (mein) of me | unſrer (unſer) of us |
| *D.* mir to me, me | uns to us, us |
| *A.* mid) me. | uns us. |

### Second Person : bu thou.

| *Singular.* | *Plural.* |
|---|---|
| *N.* bu thou | ifjr (ye) or Sie you |
| *G.* beiner (bein) of thee | eurer (euer) or Jfjrer of you |
| *D.* bir to thee, thee | eud) or Jfjnen to you, you |
| *A.* bid) thee. | eud) or Sie you. |

### Third Person : er, ſie, es.

| *Masc.* | *Fem.* | *Neuter.* |
|---|---|---|
| *N.* er he | ſie she | es it |
| *G.* ſeiner (ſein) of him | ifjrer of her | ſeiner (ſein) of it |
| *D.* ifjm to him, him | ifjr to her, her | ifjm to it |
| *A.* ifjn him, it. | ſie her, it. | es it. |

*Plural for all three genders.*

| | |
|---|---|
| *N.* ſie they | |
| *G.* ifjrer of them | |
| *D.* ifjnen (ſid)) to them, them | |
| *A.* ſie them. | |

### 4) Reflexive Form : ſid).

*D.*} ſid) {(to) himself, herself, itself,  {*All genders,*
*A.*}       yourself, yourselves, themselves. {*sing.* and *pl.*

*NB.* Observe the following expressions :

It is I id) bin es (id) bins [bin's]).    it is we wir ſinb es.
it is he (she) er (ſie) iſt es.    it is you Sie ſinb es.
It was I id) war es.    it was you Sie waren es.

*Interrog.:* Is it you? Sinb Sie es?

2) In German, the names of inanimate beings and abstract ideas being either masculine, or feminine, or neuter, proper attention must be paid that the right personal pronoun of the *third* person in the singular (*nomin.* er, ſie, es; *dat.* ihm, ihr, ihm; *accus.* ihn, ſie, es) be used, whereas in English *it* serves for all inanimate beings. For example, when answering to the question: *Where is my hat?* *It is in your room, it* must be translated with er, because the noun it refers to, viz.: der Hut, is masculine.

1) *Nominative case* (subject): it = er, ſie, es.

| | |
|---|---|
| Where is my hat? | *It* is in your room. |
| Wo iſt mein Hut *(masc.)?* | Er iſt in Ihrem Zimmer. |
| Where is my pen? | *It* lies on the table. |
| Wo iſt meine Feder? | Sie liegt auf dem Tiſch. |
| Where is my book? | *It* is there. |
| Wo iſt mein Buch? | Es iſt da. |

2) *Accusative* (after the verb): it = ihn, ſie, es.

| | |
|---|---|
| Have you my hat? | Yes, I have it. |
| Haben Sie meinen Hut? | Ja, ich habe ihn (viz.: den Hut). |
| Do you see that flower? | I do not see *it.* |
| Sehen Cie dieſe Blume? | Ich ſehe ſie nicht. |
| Will you buy the house? | Yes, I will buy *it.* |
| Wollen Sie das Haus kaufen? | Ja, ich will es kaufen. |

In the plural there is no difference, since there is only one form for all three genders, viz.: *nom.* and *accus.* ſie; *dat.* ihnen:

I will see *them* ich will ſie ſehen.
I give *them* bread ich gebe ihnen Brot [Brod].

3) The pronoun *myself*, *yourself* etc., joined to a noun or another pronoun, is translated by ſelbſt. Ex.:

The king himself der König ſelbſt.

I will go myself ich will ſelbſt gehen.

## Words.

| | |
|---|---|
| reden to talk; leihen to lend. | erzählen to relate. |
| hören to hear; ehrlich honest. | ſchicken to send. |
| die Schachtel the box. | verzeihen *(dat.)* to pardon. |
| die Überſetzung [Ueberſetzung] the translation. | erwarten to expect. |
| | ſchon already. |
| achten to esteem. | rufen to call. |
| Brüſſel Brussels. | die Geſchichte the story. |
| ſtrafen to punish. | ſprechen to speak. |

### Exercise 69.

1. Ich rede. 2. Du lobſt mich. 3. Er ſtraft ihn. 4. Sie kennt uns. 5. Wir hören Sie. 6. Wir hören ſie. 7. Ich und mein Bruder. 8. Machſt du deine Überſetzung [Ueberſetzung]? 9. Ja, ich mache ſie. 10. Wo haſt du dein Buch? 11. Ich habe es verloren. 12. Haben Sie Ihre Aufgabe gelernt? 13. Ja, wir haben ſie gelernt. 14. Achten Sie dieſen Mann? 15. Nein, ich achte ihn nicht, er iſt nicht ehrlich. 16. Von wem ſprechen Sie? 17. Wir ſprechen von ihm — von ihr — von Ihnen — von ihnen. 18. Hat Ihr Vater es ſelbſt geſagt? 19. Er hat es nicht ſelbſt geſagt. 20. Mein Oheim hat es mir geſagt. 21. Kommen Sie!*) 22. Erzählen Sie*) ihm dieſe Geſchichte! 23. Ich habe ſie ihm ſchon erzählt. 24. Wer iſt da? 25. Ich bin es. 26. Er iſt es. 27. Sind Sie es, mein Herr? 28. Ja, ich bin es (ich bins [bin's]).

---

*) Sie in the imperative is not translated in English.

### Exercise 70.

1. My father and I.   2. She and her sister.   3. I speak of (von) him and of her.   4. Do you speak of me?   5. Yes, I speak of you.   6. Give the book [to] me and not to him.   7. Give her this flower. 8. Will you lend *me* your penknife?   9. I cannot lend it [to] you; I have lost it.   10. Have you done it?   11. No, Sir, not I.   12. The teacher praised him and me.   13. Where are your brothers?   14. Call them.   15. Who will go to Brussels?   16. I will go myself.   17. Who has seen it?   18. We have seen it ourselves.   19. Who is there?   20. It is he,—it is she, — it is we.   21. Is it you, dear Emily? 22. Yes, it is I.   23. Are these boots for you? 24. No, they are not for me; they are for Henry. 25. Have you seen my hat?   26. Yes, I have seen *it*.

### Conversation.

| | |
|---|---|
| Wo ift Ihr Pferd? | Ich habe es verkauft. |
| Wer hat es gekauft? | Ein Engländer hat es ge= kauft. |
| Wer hat Ihnen diefe Blume gegeben (given)? | Meine Schwefter hat fie mir gegeben. |
| Liebft du mich? | Ja, ich liebe dich. |
| Haben Sie meinen Brief er= halten? | Ja, ich habe i h n erhalten. |
| Haben Sie heute die Zeitung (newspaper) gelefen? | Ich habe f i e noch nicht ge= lefen. |
| Wie finden Sie diefe Kirfchen? | Ich finde fie fehr füß. |
| Wo ift Ihre Tante? | Ich weiß nicht; ich habe fie heute noch nicht gefehen. |
| Denken Sie oft an (of) mich? | Ich denke fehr oft an Sie. |

# LESSON XXXV.
## Demonstrative Pronouns.

1) The *demonstrative* pronouns are:

| *Singular.* | *Plural.* |
|---|---|

dies, das  this *or* that.

dieser, e, s  this one         diese these.
jener, e, s  that one         jene  those.

derjenige, diejenige, dasjenige ⎫ that (of), he, she, that (who,
der,       die,      das      ⎭     which).

*Plur.* diejenigen *or* die  those.

derselbe,      dieselbe,      dasselbe [daſſelbe] ⎫ the same.
der nämliche,  die nämliche,  das nämliche        ⎭

### Examples.

Dieser hat es gethan  this one has done it.
Dieser ist neu, jener ist alt  this one is new, that is old.
Mein Hut und derjenige (*or* der') meines Bruders.
My hat and that of my brother.
Das ist gut  that is good.

### OBSERVATIONS.

1) When the *demonstrative* pronoun *this* or *that*, is
used pronominally, or is not immediately followed by
its noun, but separated from it by the verb *to be*, as for
instance: "*this is my hat*," it takes in German the
*neuter* form of the singular, then spelled: dies or das,
without any regard to the gender or number of the
following noun.  Ex.:

### Examples.

This is my father  dies (*or* das) ist mein Vater.
These are my books  das (dies) sind meine Bücher.
Are these your gloves?  sind das Ihre Handschuhe?

2) Frequently a contraction takes place of **ba**, *there*, with prepositions; the contracted forms are usually translated into English by a pronoun and a preposition, as:

damit  with it *or* with them.
darin  in it *or* in them.
dadurch  through it, them.
davon  of *or* from it, them.
dafür  for it *or* for them.

daraus from *or* out of it, them.
dazu  to it *or* to them.
daran  at it *or* at them.
darüber about *or* over it, them.
darunter  among them.

### Examples.

Ich bin d a m i t zufrieden  I am contented *with it.*
Wie viele sind d a r i n?  how many are *in it* (therein)?
Wir werden d a r ü b e r sprechen  we will talk *about it.*

### Words.

schlecht  bad.
das Band  the ribbon.
der Apfelbaum  the apple-tree.
der Pflaumenbaum  the plum-tree.

die Violine  the violin.
der Schinken  the ham.
teuer [theuer]  dear.
richtig  correct.
gelesen  read; gerufen  called.

### Exercise 71.

1. D i e s e r hat es mir gesagt (told), nicht jener.  2. Ich habe j e n e gerufen, nicht d i e s e.  3. Wir sprechen von diesem und von jenem.  4. Das ist gut.  5. Ist d a s Ihr Pferd?  6. Ja, das ·ist mein Pferd.  7. Sind das Ihre Kinder?  8. Ja, das sind meine Kinder.  9. Hier ist mein Buch und dasjenige (or d a s) meines Bruders.  10. Ihre Handschuhe sind schöner als diejenigen (d i e) meiner Schwester.  11. Dieses Band ist teurer [theurer] als jenes.  12. Haben Sie noch von derselben Tinte [Dinte]?  13. Ja, ich habe noch d a v o n.  14. Ist der Knabe in dem Hofe?  15. Ja, er ist d a r i n.  16. Wir sprechen d a v o n.  17. Ich war d a m i t zufrieden.

### Exercise 72.

1. This ham is good, that is bad.   2. These are apple-trees, those are plum-trees.   3. This is not my hat, it is that of my brother.   4. These are not your pencils, they are those of Henry.   5. These pears are unripe, those are ripe.   6. I have not seen your garden, but that of Mr. Brown.   7. Here is my pen and that of Caroline.   8. Have you sold your [own] horses? 9. No, Sir, I have not sold my horses, but those of my father (*or* but my father's).   10. Are these your gloves? 11. Yes, these are my new gloves.   12. Are those your brother's children?   13. No, they are my cousin's children.   14. Are you contented with your violin? 15. Yes, Sir, I am contented *with it.*   16. Is your father in the garden?   17. Yes, he is *in it.*   18. Here is ham, will you have [some] *of it?*   19. Yes, give me [some] *of it.*

---

# LESSON XXXVI.

## Interrogative Pronouns.

These are: 1) **wer** who? **was** what?

#### Declension.

| | | | |
|---|---|---|---|
| *N.* | **wer** who? | **was** what? |
| *G.* | **weſſen** whose? | (weſſen) of what? |
| *D.* | **wem** to whom? | (was) to what? |
| *A.* | **wen** whom? | **was** what? |

**wer?** applies to persons, without distinction of sex; **was?** to inanimate beings. Ex.:

Wer iſt da? who is there?

Wer hat dies gethan? who has done this?

Weſſen Hut iſt das? whose hat is this?

Wem geben Sie diese Rose? to whom do you give this rose?
Von wem sprechen Sie? of whom do you speak?
Was wollen Sie? what do you want?

*Note.* The **wo?** where? is sometimes contracted with a preposition into one word, in the following manner:

wovon = von was? of what?   woran = an was? at *or* of
womit = mit was? with what?       what?
wofür = für was? for what?   woraus? from *or* out of
                          what?
wozu = zu was? to what?    worüber? about what? etc.

### Examples.

Wovon (or von was) sprechen Sie? Of what are you speaking?
Woran (or an was) denken Sie? Of what are you thinking?

2) **welcher? welche? welches?** *which (of)?* and was für einer, e, es? *what (sort of)?* used without a substantive joined to them in the same case, must agree in gender with the noun that is understood; (in the expression was für einer the last word only is declinable).

Welcher von Ihren Söhnen? which of your sons?

Welches von diesen Büchern haben Sie gelesen?
Which of these books have you read?

Hier sind zwei Federmesser; welches wollen Sie haben?
Here are two penknives; which will you have?

Sie haben ein Buch verloren? Was für eines?
You have lost a book? What (sort of a) book (was it)?

*NB.* *What* before a *noun* is not a pronoun, but an *interrogative* **adjective,** and already explained p. 60.

3) The rule given page 135, Observ. 1, is to be applied to the interrogative *which* or *what?* viz.: it is

**welches** before the verb ſein *to be*, both in singular and plural, as:

Which is your pen? welches iſt Ihre Feder?

Which are your pens? welches ſind Ihre Federn?

What is your name? welches iſt Ihr Name?

## Words.

| | |
|---|---|
| der Briefträger the postman. | abgereiſt departed. |
| der Spaziergang the walk. | ſchwarz black; ſchwer heavy. |
| nehmen to take. | Irland Ireland. |
| die Kouſine [Couſine] the cousin, *fem.* | die Sprache the language. |
| | leicht easy. |
| erhalten to receive, received. | der Weg the way. |
| brauchen to want. | die Poſt the post-office. |

### Exercise 73.

1. Wer kommt da? 2. Es iſt der Briefträger; er bringt einen Brief. 3. Von wem iſt der Brief? 4. Er iſt von Ihrem Vater. 5. Wem geben Sie dieſes Brot [Brod]? 6. Ich gebe es einem armen Kinde. 7. Wen lieben Sie? 8. Ich liebe meinen Vater und meine Mutter. 9. Von wem ſprechen Sie? 10. Ich ſpreche von unſerm Profeſſor. 11. Was machen Sie da? 12. Ich lerne meine Aufgabe. 13. An was denken Sie jetzt? 14. Ich denke an unſern Spaziergang. 15. Welche von dieſen Federn iſt die beſte? 16. Dieſe iſt am beſten. 17. Welches von dieſen Pferden iſt das jüngſte? 18. Das ſchwarze iſt das jüngſte. 19. Hier ſind zwei Grammatiken, welche wollen Sie nehmen? 20. Ich will die leichteſte nehmen.

### Exercise 74.

1. Who is there? 2. It is my brother. 3. Who is in your room? 4. It is one (einer) of my pupils. 5. Whose hat is this? 6. It is Robert's hat. 7. From whom have you received this letter? 8. It (er) is from my [female] cousin. 9. What do you want? 10. I

want a penknife. 11. Which of your sons is ill? 12. Charles is ill. 13. Which of these books is the best? 14. This is the best; the other is not so good. 15. Here are two knives, which will you take? 16. I will take the smallest. 17. Which of your [female] cousins has (is) departed? 18. My cousin Louisa has (is) departed. 19. Which of these flowers do you like best (am meiſten)? 20. I like the rose best.

### Exercise 75.

1. Which of these hats is the oldest? 2. The black [one]. 3. Which of the two countries is larger, England or Ireland? 4. Which is the finest country in Europe? 5. Which is the heaviest of all metals? 6. Which of your friends will go to America? 7. Which of the two languages is easier to learn, the German or the French? 8. Which of those gentlemen speak German? 9. Pray (bitte), which is the nearest (nächſte) way to (zu) the post-office? 10. Which of those needles are the best? 11. The dearest are also the best.

# LESSON XXXVII.

## Possessive Pronouns.

1) These are formed from the *possessive adjectives,* mein, dein, ſein, unſer, euer, Ihr, ihr, by adding the termination –ige or simply –e. This form is always preceded by the definite article. They are:

| Masc. | Fem. | Neuter. |
|---|---|---|
| der mein(ig)e | die mein(ig)e | das mein(ig)e mine. |
| der dein(ig)e | die dein(ig)e | das dein(ig)e thine. |
| der ſein(ig)e | die ſein(ig)e | das ſein(ig)e his. |
| der ihr(ig)e | die ihr(ig)e | das ihr(ige) hers. |

*Plur.* die meinigen, die deinigen, ꝛc.

der, die, das unfr(ig)e ; *plur.* die unfr(ig) e n ours.
der, die, das eur(ig)e or Ih r (i g) e , *plur.* die eur(ig)en or die
  Ih r (ig) e n yours.
der, die, das ihr(ig)e; *plur.* die ihr(ig)en theirs.

2) There is also another form, which is oftener used
in conversation, but without article; it is declined like
diefer, diefe, diefes, viz.:

| | | |
|---|---|---|
| meiner | meine | meines mine. |
| deiner | deine | deines thine. |
| feiner | feine | feines his. |
| ihrer | ihre | ihres hers. |
| unfrer | unfre | unfres ours. |
| eurer | eure | eures ⎫ yours. |
| Ihrer | Ihre | Ihres ⎬ |
| ihrer | ihre | ihres theirs. |

### Declension.

| | Masc. | Singular.<br>Fem. | Neuter. | Plural<br>for all genders. |
|---|---|---|---|---|
| N. | meiner | meine | meines mine | meine |
| G. | meines | meiner | meines of mine | meiner |
| D. | meinem | meiner | meinem to mine | meinen |
| A. | meinen | meine | meines mine | meine. |

### Examples.

Ift das Ihr Heft?      Ja, es ift das meinige or meines.
Is this your copy-book?    Yes, it is mine.

Ift das mein Platz?      Ja, es ift der Ihrige or Ihrer.
Is that my place (*or* seat)?   Yes, it is yours.

Sind das Ihre Stiefel?    Nein, das find nicht meine.
Are these your boots?     No, these are not mine.

### Words.

| | |
|---|---|
| die Stahlfeder  the steel-pen. | finden  to find. |
| gehören  to belong. | hübsch  pretty. |
| blau  blue. | die Gräfin  the countess. |
| er schreibt  he writes. | das Klavier [Clavier] the piano. |
| der Mantel  the cloak. | gebrochen  broken. |

### Exercise 76.

1. Ist das Ihr Zimmer? 2. Nein, dies ist nicht das meinige (or meines); das nächste (next) ist meines. 3. Sind das Ihre Handschuhe? 4. Ja, das sind meine; ich hatte sie verloren. 5. Die Pferde des Herrn Braun sind besser als die unsrigen. 6. Wem gehören jene Federn? 7. Welche? 8. Jene Stahlfedern. 9. Ich glaube, es sind die meinigen (or meine). 10. Welches von diesen Messern wollen Sie? 11. Geben Sie mir Ihres! 12. Mein Haus ist neu, das Ihrige (or Ihres) ist alt. 13. Sein Mantel ist blau, Ihrer (der Ihrige) ist schwarz. 14. Ich schreibe an meinen Vater, du schreibst an deinen (den deinigen), Albert schreibt an seinen. 15. Wie finden Sie meinen Garten? 16. Ich finde ihn größer als den meinigen.

### Exercise 77.

1. Is that (das) your garden? 2. Yes, it is mine. 3. It is very large; it is larger than yours. 4. My father is older than thine, but my mother is younger than thine. 5. My sister is not so diligent as yours. 6. Your house is prettier than mine. 7. His horse is younger than ours. 8. Who has lost a pencil? 9. Charles has lost his pencil and mine. 10. My uncle has lost his watch and mine. 11. Have you read his letter? 12. Yes, Sir, I have read his letter and hers. 13. Why has Henry bought a stick? 14. He has lost his. 15. Has the countess received my letter? 16. She has received a letter, but not yours. 17. This cloak is not so pretty

as yours. 18. My sister has lost her penknife; my brother has broken his; he is very discontented. 19. Do you find my piano better than yours? 20. Yes, I find it much better.

---

## LESSON XXXVIII.

### Relative Pronouns.

These are:

> der, die, das
> welcher, welche, welches } who, which, that.

They are employed indifferently.

### Declension of welcher, welche, welch=s.

| | Singular. | | | Plural |
|---|---|---|---|---|
| Masc. | Fem. | | Neuter. | for all genders. |
| N. welcher | welche | welches | who, which | welche |
| G. dessen | deren | dessen | whose, of which | deren |
| D. welchem | welcher | welchem | to whom, to which | welchen |
| A. welchen | welche | welches | whom, which | welche. |

### Declension of the relative pronoun der, die, das.

| | Singular. | | | Plural |
|---|---|---|---|---|
| Masc. | Fem. | | Neuter. | for all genders. |
| N. der | die | das | which, that, who | die |
| G. dessen | deren | dessen | of which, whose | deren |
| D. dem | der | dem | to which, to whom | denen |
| A. den | die | das | whom, that, which | die. |

#### OBSERVATIONS.

1) These pronouns must agree in gender and number with the noun they refer to, and have a comma before them. Ex.:

| Singular. | Plural. |
|---|---|
| der Mann, welcher or der .., | die Frau, welche or die .., |
| das Buch, welches or das .., | die Bücher, welche or die ... |

2) It is peculiar to them, that *the verb is placed at the end of the clause* which they introduce, the *auxiliary*, if there is any, being the *last*.   Ex.:

Das Geld, welches ich in der Straße gefunden **habe**.

3). In English the relative pronouns *whom, which, that*, are sometimes left out and understood after the nouns; in German they must always be expressed, as:

The boy I saw with you yesterday (instead of *whom* I saw).
Der Knabe, **den** (or w e l ch e n) ich gestern bei Ihnen sah.
Here are the books you have ordered.
Hier sind die Bücher, d i e (or w e l ch e) Sie bestellt haben.

### Examples.

Wo ist der Mann, welcher (or der) den Brief gebracht hat?
Where is the man who has brought the letter?
Hier ist der Thee, den (or welchen) Sie verlangt haben.
Here is the tea (which) you have asked for.
Da sind die Taschentücher, welche (or die) Sie gekauft haben.
There are the pocket-handkerchiefs you have bought.

4) When the relative pronouns referring to things are preceded by prepositions, they are often joined with the latter, so that the pronoun assumes the form of **wo•** or **wor•** (before a vowel), and the preposition follows it, answering to the English *whereof, whereby, wherefore* etc.   In this case the verb is likewise at the end of the clause.   Such are:

| | |
|---|---|
| wozu  to which *or* to what. | woraus  from which *or* what. |
| wodurch  by which *or* what. | worin  in which *or* what. |
| womit  with which *or* what. | worüber  at (over) which *or* what. |
| wobei  at which *or* what. | |
| wofür  for which *or* what. | worauf  upon which *or* what. |
| wovon  of which *or* what. | woran  at which *or* what. |
| | worunter  among which. |

## Examples.

Ift das der Schlüffel, w o m i t Sie die Thüre geöffnet haben?
Is that the key with which you have opened the door?

Das Zimmer, w o r i n ich schlafe, ift fehr kalt.
The room, in which I sleep, is very cold.

Das Glas, w o r a u s ich getrunken habe, ift zerbrochen.
The glass out of which I drank, is broken.

## Words.

| | |
|---|---|
| der Schneider the tailor. | der Reifende the traveller. |
| dort ift, dort find there is, there are. | unterhaltend amusing. |
| | ich schlafe I sleep. |
| erhalten to receive, received. | geschrieben written. |
| bekannt known; geliehen lent. | feucht damp. |
| ankommen to arrive. | geftorben dead. |
| geöffnet opened. | letztes Jahr last year. |
| der Dieb the thief. | die Pflanze the plant. |
| weinen to cry, to weep. | verbeffert corrected. |

## Exercise 78.

1. Hier find die Handschuhe, welche (or die) Sie gekauft haben. 2. Hier ift ein Mann, welcher einen Brief bringt. 3. Dort ift eine Frau, welche weint. 4. Der Hut, welchen (or den) Sie für Ihren Sohn gekauft haben, ift fehr teuer [theuer]. 5. Ich kenne die Frau nicht, von welcher Sie einen Brief erhalten haben. 6. Kennen Sie den Schneider, von welchem wir sprechen? 7. Hier ift der Knabe, dem ich mein Buch geliehen habe. 8. Der Engländer, deffen Sohn Sie kennen, ift geftorben. 9. Die Dame, deren Tochter Ihre Schülerin ift, wird morgen ankommen. 10. Das Haus, worin ich wohne, ift fehr groß. 11. Die Bücher, wovon Sie sprechen, find fehr teuer.

### Exercise 79.

1. Here is the man who *brought* 'the 'letter.
2. Where is the woman who sells cherries? 3. I bring
you the ribbons which Miss Mary has bought. 4. Where
is the letter . . you have received from your aunt?
5. Here 'it 'is, you may read it. 6. The room in which
I sleep, is very damp; I must have another room.
7. The plants, I have seen in your garden, are beautiful. 8. Is this the exercise which your teacher has
corrected? 9. Yes, it is. 10. Here is the pen *with
which* I have written my English letter. 11. My neighbor, whose horse you *bought* 'last 'year, is now in
America. 12. The town *of which* I speak, lies (liegt) in
Spain; it is not well-known. 13. I have found the key
*with which* the thief has opened the room.

### READING LESSON.

#### Die wilde Taube und die Biene.

#### (The wild Pigeon and the Bee.)

Eine wilde Taube, welche auf einer Erle am Bache
                                         alder           brook
saß, erblickte eine Biene, die in das Wasser gefallen war,
sat,   saw                                     fallen
und die mit den Wellen des Baches kämpfte, welche
                waves                  struggled
drohten, sie fortzureißen. „Warte, armes Vög(e)lein!"
threatened    to carry it away.      Wait,
rief die Taube, „ich will dir ein Schiffchen schicken, auf
cried                            a little boat     send,
welchem du dich retten kannst." Sie pickte ein
                save                     picked   a
Baumblatt ab und warf es ihr hinunter. Die Biene
leaf      off      threw        down.
rettete sich und dankte ihrer Wohlthäterin.
saved        thanked   her     benefactress.

# LESSON XXXIX.

## Indefinite Pronouns.

1) They are:

man  one (French *on*), they, people.
einander  each other, one another.
jedermann [Jedermann]  everybody, every one.
jemand [Jemänd]  somebody, some one, anybody.
niemand [Niemand]  nobody (not — anybody).
selbst (selber), . . . self (myself, etc.).
etwas  something, anything.

2) The *indefinite numeral adjectives* are also used as indefinite *pronouns*, when the substantives are dropped. We repeat them here:

jeder, e, es or ein jeder  each, every one.
einer, eine, eines  one, some one.
der and(e)re, die and(e)re, das and(e)re  the other.
der eine —, der and(e)re  the one —, the other.
  *plur.* die einen —, die andern  some —, the others.
einige  some *or* a few.
einige —, andre  some —, others.
mancher  many a man; *plur.* manche (many).
beide  both; both of them.
viel  much; *plur.* viele  many.
mehrere several; — mehr  more (is indeclinable).
die meisten  most (of them).
wenig  little; *plur.* wenige  few.
alles  everything; *plur.* alle  all.
der nämliche (*neut.* das nämliche)  the same.
keiner, keine, keines  none, no one.

## Words.

| | |
|---|---|
| die Stimme the voice. | stellen to put; spielen to play. |
| der Fehler the fault. | der Preis the prize. |
| das Gewissen the conscience. | höflich polite. |
| die Erfahrung the experience. | klopfen to knock. |
| gewonnen won. | bereit ready. |
| gelehrt learned. | der Platz the place. |

### Exercise 80.

1. Man ist glücklich, wenn man jung ist. 2. Diese zwei Mädchen lieben einander. 3. Ich kenne niemand [Niemand] in dieser Stadt. 4. Klopft jemand [Jemand]? 5. Ich höre jemandes Stimme. 6. Thun Sie nie (never do) etwas gegen Ihr Gewissen! 7. Keiner ist ohne Fehler. 8. Keiner von uns hat den ersten Preis gewonnen. 9. Jedermann wünscht reich zu sein. 10. Der eine [Eine] ist ein Franzose, der andre [Andre] ein Amerikaner. 11. Einige sind fleißig, andre sind träge. 12. Jeder (or ein jeder) hat seine Fehler. 13. Viele haben die nämliche Erfahrung gemacht. 14. Mehrere haben das nämliche [Nämliche] gesehen. 15. Die meisten von meinen Freunden sind gestorben (dead). 16. Nur einer ist noch am Leben (alive).

### Exercise 81.

1. One is happy, when one is contented. 2. Do not wish 'to 'please 'every one. 3. I know somebody who is more learned than you. 4. Do you know any one in this town? 5. No, Sir, I know nobody. 6. Of these pupils each has won a prize. 7. Some are too old, some are too young. 8. Everybody was ready. 9. Be polite to everybody. 10. Animals eat (fressen) one another. 11. My sister and I love one another. 12. Of whom have you spoken? 13. I have spoken of nobody.

14. I see nothing. 15. Put these books each in its (feinen) place. 16. Do not speak evil (Böfes) of (von) others. 17. Give me something better (Befferes)! 18. Where are your two nephews, Edward and John? 19. They are both in America. 20. Most of the apples were ripe. 21. Give me some soup, but very little.

### Conversation.

| | |
|---|---|
| Klopft jemand [Jemand] an die Thüre? | Nein, niemand [Niemand] ist da. |
| Was sagte Jhr Freund? | Er sagte nichts. |
| Wie viele Schüler haben Sie? | Jch habe mehrere. |
| Was machen diese Leute? | Die einen lefen, die andern schreiben. |
| Gegen wen soll man höflich sein? | Gegen jedermann [Jeder=mann]. |
| Lieben die Mädchen einander? | Ja, sie lieben einander. |
| Wer wünscht glücklich zu sein? | Jedermann wünscht es zu sein. |
| Wer ist angekommen? | Einige von unfern Freunden. |
| Was haben Sie gehört? | Jch habe alles [Alles] gehört. |

# LESSON XL.

## Passive Voice.

The Passive Voice, both for the regular and irregular active verbs, is formed by means of the third auxiliary **werden** with the past participle of a *transitive verb:*

geliebt werden to be loved.
getadelt werden to be blamed.
geschickt werden to be sent.

## Conjugation of a Passive Verb.

**gelobt werden** to be praised.

### *Present Tense.*

ich **werde** gelobt  I am praised
du **wirst** gelobt  thou art praised
er, sie, es **wird** gelobt  he, she, it is praised

wir **werden** gelobt  we are praised
ihr werdet gelobt ⎫
Sie werden gelobt ⎬ you are praised
fie werden gelobt  they are praised.

### *Imperfect.*

ich **wurde** gelobt  I was praised
du **wurdest** gelobt  thou wast praised
er **wurde** gelobt  he was praised

wir wurden gelobt  we were praised
ihr wurdet gelobt ⎫
Sie wurden gelobt ⎬ you were praised
fie wurden gelobt  they were praised.

### *Future.*

ich **werde** gelobt **werden**  I shall be praised
du wirst gelobt werden  thou wilt be praised
er wird gelobt werden  he will be praised, etc.

### *Conditional.*

ich **würde** gelobt **werden**  I should be praised
du würdest gelobt werden  thou wouldst be praised
er würde gelobt werden  he would be praised, etc.

*Perfect.*

ich **bin** gelobt **worden**  I have been praised
du **bift** gelobt **worden**  thou hast been praised
er **ift** gelobt **worden**  he has been praised

wir find gelobt worden  we have been praised
ihr feid gelobt worden } you have been praised
Sie find gelobt worden }
fie find gelobt worden  they have been praised.

## Infinitive.

*Present:* gelobt **werden** or gelobt zu werden  to be praised.

**Such are:**

geliebt werden  to be loved.

getadelt werden  to be blamed.

geftraft werden  to be punished.

geachtet werden  to be respected.

verbeffert werden  to be corrected.

zerftört werden  to be destroyed.

*Remark* 1. The preposition *by* joined to a verb in the passive voice is translated **von.** Ex.:

Diefes Haus wurde v o n meinem Nachbar gebaut.
This house was built *by* my neighbor.

*Remark* 2. When a past participle belongs to an intransitive verb denoting motion or transition from one state to the other, or when it has the meaning of an adjective, *to have* and *to be* are rendered by f e i n. Ex.:

My friend has arrived  mein Freund **ift** angekommen.
I am disposed  ich **bin** geneigt.
The castle is destroyed  das Schloß **ift** zerftört.
The glasses are broken  die Gläfer **find** zerbrochen.

### Words.

| | |
|---|---|
| der Muſiklehrer the music-master. | der Ring the ring. |
| artig good, well-mannered. | ehrlich honest. |
| unartig naughty. | zerſtört (*past part.*) destroyed. |
| der Feind the enemy. | geſchickt (*past part.*) sent. |
| nachläſſig negligent, care-less. | der Arbeiter the workman. |
| | geſtohlen stolen. |
| | beſiegt conquered. |

### Exercise 82.

1. Ich w e r d e v o n meiner Mutter geliebt. 2. Du w i r ſt von deinem Lehrer gelobt. 3. Die artigen Knaben w e r b e n gelobt, aber die unartigen Knaben w e r d e n ge= ſtraft. 4. Marie w u r d e von ihrem Muſiklehrer getadelt; ſie iſt ſehr nachläſſig. 5. Die Stadt w u r d e von den Feinden zerſtört. 6. Karl [Carl] iſt beſtraft w o r d e n. 7. Die Aufgaben ſ i n d von dem Lehrer verbeſſert w o r d e n. 8. Die Arbeiter ſ i n d gut bezahlt w o r d e n, denn (for) ſie haben viel gearbeitet. 9. Iſt dieſe Aufgabe verbeſſert worden? 10. Nein, ſie iſt noch nicht verbeſſert (worden). 11. Von wem wurde dieſer Brief geſchrieben? 12. Er iſt von einem jungen Mädchen geſchrieben worden.

### Exercise 83.

1. I *am* loved by my father. 2. Thou *art* loved by thy mother. 3. This professor *is* loved by his pupils. 4. Lewis *is* always praised by his master, for (denn) he is very diligent. 5. The naughty pupils *were* punished. 6. My exercise *has been* corrected by my teacher. 7. This ring *was* given me by my grandmother. 8. This letter must *be* sent to the post-office (auf die Poſt). 9. My watch *has been* stolen. 10. Your exer-cise will *be* corrected to-morrow. 11. The village *was* entirely (ganz) destroyed.

**Conversation.**

| | |
|---|---|
| Von wem wird Ihr Sohn gelobt? | Er wird von seinen Lehrern gelobt. |
| Wann wurde die Schlacht bei Sedan geliefert (fought)? | Am 2. September 1870. |
| Wer ist besiegt worden? | Die Franzosen sind besiegt worden. |
| Wann (when) wurde dieser Brief gebracht? | Er wurde gestern abend [Abend] gebracht. |
| Von wem ist Karthago [Carthago] zerstört worden? | Von den Römern. |
| Warum ist dieser Mann gestraft worden? | Er hat eine goldene Uhr gestohlen (stolen). |
| Von wem ist Cäsar ermordet (slain) worden? | Von Brutus und Cassius, und einigen andern [Andern]. |
| Wann ist dieses Haus gebaut (was . . built) worden? | Es ist im Jahre 1851 gebaut worden. |

# LESSON · XLI.

## Irregular Verbs.

Those verbs are commonly called *irregular* (unregelmäßig) which deviate from the formation and conjugation of the modern or r,gular verbs, though they are indeed sufficiently regular after their own fashion of conjugation. The deviation from the regular form takes place only in the *imperfect* and the *past participle;* all the other tenses are formed regularly.

1) The peculiar character of the *imperfect indicative* of the irregular verbs consists in their *adding no termination at all* to the stem in the 1st and 3d persons singular, *but in changing its radical vowel*, as from geben:

*imp.* idj ga6. The difference of the changed vowel causes these verbs to be divided into four conjugations, according to the prevailing four vowels **a, i, o** and **u**.

    a) The ancient verbs which take the vowel **a** in the imperfect, compose the *first* conjugation. Ex.:

        geben — idj g a b ;

    b) those with **i** or **ie,** the *second.* Ex.:

        ſdjreiben — idj ſdj r i e b ;

    c) those which take **o,** the *third.* Ex.:

        ſdjießen — idj ſ dj o ß, and

    d) those which take **u,** the *fourth.* Ex.:

        ſdjlagen — idj ſ dj l u g.

The 3d person singular of the imperfect is always like the first, as in English.

    2) The *imperfect* of the *subjunctive* mood is formed by adding **e** to the imperfect indicative, and modifying the vowel, when it is **a, o** or **u,** as :

    idj gäbe, bu g ä b e ſt, er g ä b e, ꝛc. (wenn idj g ä b e).

    3) The ***past participle*** of all verbs of the ancient form ends in **en** instead of **t,** as: **gegeben** given; **geſdjrie=ben** written, etc.; but, as the vowel does not always remain the same in the past participle, the first two conjugations have three subdivisions or classes, according to the prevailing vowel of the past participle.

    4) Concerning the terminations of the *present tense,* the irregular verbs are the same as the regular verbs, but several of the former change besides, in the second

and third persons singular, and in the second person singular of the imperative mood, their radical vowel **a** into **ä**, and **e** into **i** or **ie**, as:

ich schlage, du **schlägst**; ich gebe, er **giebt** [gibt]; **gieb** [gib].

## Conjugation of an Irregular Verb.

### geben to give.

<table>
<tr><td>Present Tense.</td><td>Imperfect.</td></tr>
<tr><td>ich gebe I give</td><td>ich gab I gave</td></tr>
<tr><td>du giebst [gibst] thou givest</td><td>du gabst thou gavest</td></tr>
<tr><td>er giebt [gibt] he gives</td><td>er gab he gave</td></tr>
<tr><td>wir geben we give</td><td>wir gaben we gave</td></tr>
<tr><td>ihr gebt ⎱ you give<br>Sie geben ⎰</td><td>ihr gabt ⎱ you gave<br>Sie gaben ⎰</td></tr>
<tr><td>sie geben they give.</td><td>sie gaben they gave.</td></tr>
</table>

*Imperfect Subjunctive* ich **gäbe.**

### Imperative.

**geben Sie** (or gieb [gib], gebet) give!

### Perfect.

ich habe **gegeben** I have given.

### First Future.

ich werde geben I shall give.

### Second Future.

ich werde gegeben haben I shall have given.

### First Conditional.

ich würde geben I should give.

### Second Conditional.

ich würde gegeben haben I should have given.

We subjoin here a list of the most used German irregular verbs.

## First Conjugation.   (A-Conjugation.)

### First Class.

*Imperfect* in **a**.   *Past participle* in **e**.

| INFINITIVE. | PRESENT INDICATIVE. | IMPERFECT. a | PAST PART. e |
|---|---|---|---|
| geben  to give. | ich gebe, du giebſt [gibſt], er giebt [gibt], wir geben, ihr gebet, Sie geben, ſie geben. | ich gab, du gabſt, er gab, wir gaben, ꝛc. | gegeben given. |
| eſſen  to eat. | ich eſſe, du iſſeſt, er iſſt, wir eſſen, ihr eſſet, ꝛc. | ich a ß. *pl.* wir aßen. | gegeſſen eaten. |
| freſſen to eat, devour. | (das Tier | Thier]) fri ß t, (die Tiere) freſſen. | fra ß. | gefreſſen devoured. |
| leſen  to read. | ich leſe, du lieſeſt, er lieſt, wir leſen, ihr leſet, ꝛc. | ich la s. *pl.* wir laſen. | geleſen read. |
| ſehen  to see. | ich ſehe, du ſiehſt, er ſieht, wir ſehen, ihr ſehet, ꝛc. | ich ſa h. | geſehen seen. |
| †geſchehen*) to happen. | 3d pers. es geſchieht. (impers. verb). | es ge ſ ch a h. | geſchehen happened. |
| vergeſſen to forget. | ich vergeſſe, du vergiſſeſt, er vergißt, wir vergeſſen, ꝛc. | ich v e r g a ß. | vergeſſen forgotten. |
| bitten  to beg, ask. | ich bitte, du bitteſt, er bittet, wir bitten, ꝛc. | ich ba t. | gebeten asked. |
| †ſitzen*) to sit. | ich ſitze, du ſitzeſt, er ſitzt, wir ſitzen, ihr ſitzet, ꝛc. | ich ſa ß. | geſeſſen seated. |
| †liegen*) to lie. | ich liege, du liegſt, er liegt, wir liegen, ꝛc. | ich la g. | gelegen lain. |
| †ſtehen*) to stand. | ich ſtehe, du ſteheſt or ſtehſt, er ſteht, wir ſtehen, ꝛc. | ich ſtand. | geſtanden stood. |

Thus: verſtehen to understand. *Past participle* verſtanden understood.

*) Verbs marked with † are neuter, and generally form their compound tenses with the auxiliary ſein (to be), as: es iſt geſchehen it *has*

## First Conjugation.—Continued.

| INFINITIVE. | PRESENT INDICATIVE. | IMPERFECT. a | PAST PART. |
|---|---|---|---|
| thun to do, to make. | ich thue, du thuſt, er thut, wir thun, ihr thut, ſie thun. | ich that, du thatſt, ꝛc. | gethan done. |

### Words.

der Blinde  the blind man.

das Heu  the hay.

der Hafer  the oats.

das Gras  the grass.

unterhaltend  amusing.

der Teller  the plate.

der Kuchen  the cake.

leiſe  low.

zu  too.

der Turm [Thurm]  the tower.

### Exercise 84.

1. Ich gebe Ihnen eine Mark. 2. Du giebſt [gibſt] mir zwei Franken. 3. Der Briefträger gab mir einen Brief. 4. Was ißt dieſes Mädchen da? 5. Sie ißt Kirſchen. 6. Ich habe kein Fleiſch gegeſſen. 7. Der Ochſe frißt Heu. 8. Die Pferde freſſen Hafer. 9. Was lieſt der Schüler? 10. Er lieſt ein deutſches Buch. 11. Ich habe es auch ge= leſen. 12. Der Blinde ſieht nichts. 13. Sehen Sie den Vogel dort? 14. Wir ſahen ein Schiff. 15. Ich habe nie einen Elefanten [Elephanten] geſehen. 16. Ich vergaß, Sie zu fragen, wo Ihr Freund wohnt. 17. Der Schüler hat das Wort vergeſſen. 18. Zwei Männer ſtanden an der Thüre. 19. Der Rabe ſaß auf einem hohen Baume. 20. Wo lag der Hund? 21. Er hatte unter dem Tiſch ge= legen, aber jetzt liegt er nicht mehr da. 22. Wer hat das gethan? 23. Heinrich that es. 24. Thun Sie es nicht mehr!

happened; ich bin gegangen I *have* gone; ich bin gekommen I *have* come etc.; yet some are construed with haben, thus even ſitzen, liegen, ſtehen, which three, however, in the south of Germany, are mostly employed with ſein.

### Exercise 85.

1. I give you (*dat.*) the permission.  2. My father gives me a watch; my mother gave me a ring.  3. Give me that plate, please (gefälligſt)!  4. I eat [some] bread; thou eatest [some] cherries, Robert eats a cake.  5. We ate pears.  6. The cows eat (devour) hay and grass.  7. Thou readest too low, my son. 8. Read louder (lauter), children.  9. I have read an amusing book.  10. Do not forget ²to ³do ¹it. 11. What dost thou see?  12. Do you not see that tower on the mountain?  13. Yes, I see *it*.  14. I forgot ²to ³eat ¹my ²bread.*)  15. Who will do this?  16. I have already (ſchon) done it.  17. Will you stand? 18. No, I will sit.  19. You sit too high.  20. What must I do?  21. What have I done?  22. I shall do it no more (nicht mehr).

### Conversation.

| | |
|---|---|
| Wem geben Sie dieſe Blumen? | Ich gebe ſie meiner Tante. |
| Was eſſen Sie da? | Ich eſſe Brot [Brod] und Käſe. |
| Wer hat es Ihnen gegeben? | Meine Mutter gab es mir. |
| Haben Sie die Zeitung (the newspaper) geleſen? | Ich habe ſie geleſen; aber ich habe nichts Neues darin ge= ſehen. |
| Haben Sie vergeſſen, die Wörter zu lernen? | Nein, ich habe es nicht ver= geſſen; ich habe ſie gelernt. |
| Wo ſaß die Dame? | Sie ſaß auf dem Sofa [Sopha]. |
| Wo lag der Hund? | Er lag unter dem Tiſch. |
| Warum ſtehen Sie? | Ich habe keinen Stuhl (chair). |
| Was hat der Knabe gethan? | Er hat ein Glas zerbrochen. |

---

*) The object always precedes the Infinitive mood, which generally stands *last*.

# LESSON XLII.

## First Conjugation.—Continued.

### Second Class.

*Imperfect* in **a**.   *Past participle* in **o**.

| Infinitive. | Present Indicative. | Imperfect. a | Past Part. o |
|---|---|---|---|
| **befehlen** to order. | ich befehle, du **befiehlst**, er **befiehlt**, wir befehlen, ꝛc. | ich **befahl** I ordered. | **befohlen** ordered. |
| **brechen** to break. | ich breche, du brichst, er bricht, wir brechen, ꝛc. | ich **brach** I broke. | **gebrochen** broken. |

Thus: **zerbrechen** to break. *Imperfect* **zerbrach**.
*Past part.* **zerbrochen**.

| | | | |
|---|---|---|---|
| **helfen** (*dat.*) to help. | ich helfe, du hilfst, er hilft, wir helfen, ꝛc. | ich half. | geholfen helped. |
| **nehmen** to take. | ich nehme, du n i m m ſt, er n i m m t, wir neh= men, ꝛc. | ich nahm. | **genommen** taken. |
| **sprechen** to speak. | ich spreche, du sprichst, er spricht, wir sprechen, ꝛc. | ich sprach. | gesprochen spoken. |

Thus: **versprechen** to promise. *Past part.* **versprochen**.

| | | | |
|---|---|---|---|
| **stehlen** to steal. | ich stehle, du stiehlst, er stiehlt, wir stehlen, ꝛc. | ich stahl. | gestohlen stolen. |
| † **sterben** to die. | ich sterbe, du stirbst, er stirbt, wir sterben, ꝛc. | ich starb. | gestorben died. |
| **verderben** to spoil. | ich verderbe, du verdirbst, er verdirbt, wir ver= derben, ꝛc. | ich verdarb. | verdorben spoiled. |
| **verbergen** to hide. | ich verberge, du ver b i r g ſt, er verbirgt, wir ver= bergen, ꝛc. | ich verbarg. | verborgen hidden. |
| **werfen** to throw. | ich werfe, du wirfſt, er wirft, wir werfen, ꝛc. | ich warf. | geworfen thrown. |

## First Conjugation.—Continued.

| INFINITIVE. | PRESENT INDICATIVE. | IMPERFECT. a | PAST PART. o |
|---|---|---|---|
| **beginnen** to begin. | ich beginne, du beginnst, er beginnt, wir beginnen, 2c. | ich begann. | begonnen begun. |
| **gewinnen** to gain, win. | ich gewinne, du gewinnst, er gewinnt, wir ge= winnen, 2c. | ich gewann. | gewonnen gained. |
| †**schwimmen***) to swim. | ich schwimme, du schwimmst, er schwimmt, wir schwim= men, 2c. | ich schwamm. | geschwom= men swum. |
| †**kommen** to come. | ich komme, du kommst, er kommt, wir kommen, 2c. | ich kam. | gekommen come. |

Thus: †an'kommen to arrive; bekommen to get. *Past part.* the same.

### Words.

der Spiegel  the looking-glass.
die Tasse  the cup.
der Gefangene  the prisoner.
die Eisenbahn  the railroad.
die Mauer  the wall.
die Arznei  the medicine.
der Matrose  the sailor.
der Dieb  the thief.
der Stein  the stone.

die Mark  the mark.
der Fremde  the stranger.
das Geld  the money.
das Ziel  the aim.
der Arzt  the physician.
das große Los [Loos]  the first prize.
noch  still.
noch nicht  not yet.

### Exercise 86.

1. Du zerbrichst den Stock. 2. Der Knabe zer= bricht das Glas. 3. Der Diener zerbrach den Spiegel, er hat auch die Tasse zerbrochen. 4. Ich befehle Ihnen, hier zu bleiben. 5. Der General befiehlt den Soldaten. 6. Der König hat befohlen, eine Eisenbahn zu bauen. 7. Der Gefangene war hinter einer Mauer ver= borgen. 8. Helfen Sie mir? 9. Ich half meinem Bruder. 10. Warum nimmt die Frau Arznei? 11. Sie

---

*) This verb is also construed with haben.

ift kranf. 12. Ein Dieb hat mein Geld geftohlen. 13. Der alte Mann ift geftorben. 14. Wer hat den Stein geworfen? 15. Der unartige Sohn des Nachbars warf ihn in unfern Garten. 16. Hat der Fremde Französisch oder Deutsch gesprochen? 17. Er sprach Deutsch. 18. Das Kind hat das Messer genommen. 19. Was gewannen Sie in der Lotterie? 20. Ich habe hundert Mark gewonnen. 21. Warum kamst du nicht? 22. Die Matrosen schwammen über den Fluß. 23. Unser Vetter ift nicht gekommen.

### Exercise 87.

1. Who has broken the glass? 2. John has broken it; he breaks everything. 3. Order him (*dat.*) to come. 4. Who will help me (*dat.*)? 5. I will help you. 6. I have also helped your brother. 7. Take this pen; it is better than the other. 8. Little Louisa took all [the] cherries; she has taken also my bread. 9. Does your brother speak French? 10. He speaks French and German. 11. The thieves have stolen our money. 12. We have spoken of (von) you. 13. Who has thrown the stone against the window? 14. I have seen nobody. 15. Do not throw stones! 16. Mr. Blair died yesterday. 17. My neighbor has won the first prize (great lot). 18. I swam across (over) the river. 19. He came to (zu) me. 20. Our cousin *has* not yet come. 21. The meat was spoiled; we could not eat it.

### Conversation.

| | |
|---|---|
| Wer hat meinen Stock zerbrochen? | Ich habe ihn nicht zerbrochen. |
| Wer hat Ihnen befohlen, auszugehen (to go out)? | Der Arzt hat es mir befohlen. |
| Hat Ihnen jemand [Jemand] geholfen? | Niemand hat mir geholfen. |
| Wovon haben Sie gesprochen? | Wir haben von unsrer deutschen Aufgabe gesprochen. |

| | |
|---|---|
| Ist die Feder noch gut? | Nein, sie ist verdorben. |
| Hat Karl [Carl] diesen Stein geworfen? | Nein, Heinrich hat ihn geworfen. |
| Hat ihr Nachbar etwas gewonnen? | Ja, er hat das große Los [Loos] gewonnen. |
| Haben Sie Ihre Uhr nicht mehr? | Nein, man hat sie mir gestohlen. |
| Sind Sie gestern gekommen? | Nein, ich kam diesen Morgen. |

---

# LESSON XLIII.

## First Conjugation.—Continued.

### THIRD CLASS.

*Imperfect* in **a**.    *Past Participle* in **u**.

All the verbs belonging to this class have either **ind** or **ing** or **inl** in their radical syllable.

| INFINITIVE. | PRESENT INDICATIVE. | IMPERFECT. a | PAST PART. u |
|---|---|---|---|
| **binden** to bind, tie. | ich binde, du bindest, er bindet, wir binden, ꝛc. | ich **band.** | **gebunden** tied, bound. |
| **finden** to find. | ich finde, du findest, er findet, wir finden, ꝛc. | ich **fand.** | gefunden found. |
| Thus : **erfinden** to invent. *Imperfect* **erfand.** *Past Participle* **erfunden.** | | | |
| †**verschwinden** to disappear. | ich verschwinde, du verschwindest, er verschwindet, wir verschwinden, ꝛc. | ich **verschwand.** | verschwunden disappeared. |
| **singen** to sing. | ich singe, du singst, er singt, wir singen, ꝛc. | ich **sang.** | gesungen sung. |
| †**springen** to spring. | ich springe, du springst, er springt, wir springen, ꝛc. | ich **sprang.** | gesprungen jumped. |
| †**sinken** to sink. | ich sinke, du sinkst, er sinkt, wir sinken, ꝛc. | ich **sank.** | gesunken sunk. |
| **trinken** to drink. | ich trinke, du trinkst, er trinkt, wir trinken, ꝛc. | ich **trank.** | getrunken drunk. |
| **zwingen** to force. | ich zwinge, du zwingst, er zwingt, wir zwingen, ꝛc. | ich **zwang.** | gezwungen forced. |

## Words.

das Veilchen  the violet.
der Gärtner  the gardener.
der Pfahl  the stake, post.
der Nebel  the mist, fog.
das Konzert [Concert]  the concert.
der Graben  the ditch.
das Schiff  the ship, boat.

Fräulein  Miss.
der Gefangene  the prisoner.
die Stecknadel  the pin.
das Lied  the song.
die Tasche  the pocket.
ich danke Ihnen  I thank you.
das Pulver  the gunpowder.

### Exercise 88.

1. Ich f i n d e meinen Stock nicht, und Karl [Carl] f i n d e t seinen Hut nicht. 2. Wo haben Sie dieses Veilchen g e = f u n d e n? 3. Ich f a n d es in meinem Garten. 4. Der Gärtner hat das Bäumchen an einen Pfahl g e b u n d e n. 5. Der Nebel ist v e r s c h w u n d e n. 6. Fräulein Karoline [Caroline] f i n g t sehr schön; sie f a n g gestern in einem Konzert [Concert] einige hübsche Lieder. 7. Das Pferd f p r a n g über einen breiten Graben. 8. Das Schiff ist g e f u n k e n. 9. Wie haben Sie sich gestern abend [Abend] unterhalten (amused)? 10. Wir haben g e f u n g e n und gespielt. 11. Haben Sie Wasser g e t r u n k e n? 12. Nein, ich habe Bier g e t r u n k e n. 13. Wollen Sie auch t r i n k e n? 14. Ja, geben Sie mir ein Glas.

### Exercise 89.

1. I do not find my copy-book; have you not seen it? 2. No, Miss, I have not seen it. 3. I found these violets in your garden. 4. The maid-servant has found a pin. 5. They (man) found a letter in the pocket of the prisoner. 6. What do you drink there? 7. I drink wine, but my sister takes (trinkt) coffee. 8. What have you drunk? 9. Nothing; they gave me nothing to drink. 10. Emily sang formerly pretty songs; but now 'she 'sings no more. 11. She has sung too much. 12.

Will you take a cup of tea?   13. No, thank you, I have
already taken two.   14. The dog sprang upon the wall.
15. Who invented gunpowder?   16. A German named
(Namens) Schwarz.

## READING LESSON.
### Der hungrige Araber.
#### The hungry Arab.

Ein Araber hatte sich in der Wüste (desert) verirrt[1])
und seit mehreren Tagen nichts g e g e s s e n.   Er fürchtete
vor Hunger zu s t e r b e n.   Endlich[2]) kam er an einen jener
Brunnen[3]), wo die Karawanen [Karavanen] ihre Kamele
[Kameele] tränken[4]) und s a h einen ledernen[5]) Sack[6]) auf
dem Sande l i e g e n.   Er n a h m[7]) ihn a u f[7]) und
befühlte[8]) ihn.

„Gott sei Dank!" r i e f[9]) er a u s, „das sind gewiß[10])
Datteln oder Haselnüsse"[11]).   Er öffnete schnell den Sack;
aber er fand sich in seiner Hoffnung (hope) getäuscht[12]).
Der Sack war mit Perlen gefüllt.

Da wurde er traurig[13]) und s a n k (fell) auf seine
Knie[14]) und b a t Gott, daß er ihn von seiner Not [Noth][15])
erretten[16]) und ihm Hülfe schicken möchte.   Sein Gebet[17])
wurde erhört; bald k a m der Mann, der den Sack v e r =
l o r e n hatte, auf einem Kamel reitend z u r ü c k, um ihn zu
suchen.   Er war sehr glücklich, ihn w i e d e r zu f i n d e n,
hatte Mitleid[18]) mit dem armen Araber, erquickte[19])ihn mit

1) lost his way.   2) at length.   3) wells, fountains.
4) water.   5) leathern.   6) sack, bag.   7) took it up.
8) felt.   9) exclaimed.   10) certainly.   11) hazel-nuts.
12) deceived.   13) sad.   14) knees.   15) misery, trouble.
16) to save.   17) prayer.   18) compassion.   19) to refresh.

Speise²⁰) und Trank, nahm ihn zu sich auf sein Kamel und brachte ihn zu der Karawane.

20) food.

---

# LESSON XLIV.

## Second Conjugation. (I-Conjugation.)

The second Conjugation has in the *imperfect* the letter **i**, which is either a short **i**, or a long **i** spelled **ie**. The *past participle* takes the same vowel **i** or **ie** as the *imperfect;* but the 3d class retains the vowel of the *infinitive*. Most verbs of this Conjugation are recognizable by the radical diphthong **ei**.

### FIRST CLASS.

*Imperfect* and *Past Participle* with **i**.

| INFINITIVE. | PRESENT INDICATIVE. | IMPERFECT. i | PAST PART. i |
|---|---|---|---|
| **beißen** to bite. | ich beiße, du **beißest**, er **beißt**, wir beißen, 2c. | ich **biß**, du **bissest**, er **biß**. | **gebissen** bitten. |
| **greifen** to grasp. | ich greife, du greifst, er greift, wir greifen, 2c. | ich griff. | gegriffen grasped. |

Thus: **begreifen** to conceive; **aufgreifen** to attack.

| | | | |
|---|---|---|---|
| **gleichen** to resemble. | ich gleiche, du gleichst, er gleicht, wir gleichen, 2c. | ich glich. | geglichen resembled. |
| **leiden** to suffer. | ich leide, du leidest, er leidet, wir leiden, 2c. | ich litt. | gelitten suffered. |
| **pfeifen** to whistle. | ich pfeife, du pfeifst, er pfeift, wir pfeifen, 2c. | ich pfiff. | gepfiffen whistled. |
| **zerreißen** to tear. | ich zerreiße, du zerreißest, er zerreißt, wir zerreißen, 2c. | ich zerriß. | zerrissen torn. |
| **†reiten** to ride. | ich reite, du reitest, er reitet, wir reiten, 2c. | ich ritt. | geritten ridden. |
| **schneiden** to cut. | ich schneide, du schneidest, er schneidet, wir schneiden, 2c. | ich schnitt. | geschnitten cut. |

## SECOND CLASS.

*Imperfect* and *Past Participle* in **ie.**

|  | *Imperfect.* | *Past Participle.* |
|---|---|---|
| †bleiben to stay. | ich blieb. | geblieben. |
| schreiben to write. | ich schrieb. | geschrieben. |
| reiben to rub. | ich rieb. | gerieben. |
| leihen to lend. | ich lieh. | geliehen. |
| schreien to cry. | ich schrie. | geschrieen. |
| verzei'hen to pardon. | ich verzieh. | verziehen. |
| †steigen to mount. | ich stieg. | gestiegen. |
| scheinen to seem, to shine. | ich schien. | geschiener |

### Words.

der Finger the finger.
der Fremde the stranger.
die Pfeife the whistle.
der Schmerz the pain.
das Musikheft the music-book.

der Feind the enemy.
das Vergnügen the pleasure.
der Thron the throne.
das Wörterbuch the dictionary.

### Exercise 90.

1) 1. Die Hunde beißen. 2. Ein Hund hat mich ge=
bissen. 3. Die Tochter gleicht ihrer Mutter. 4. Der
Kranke leidet viele Schmerzen. 5. Die armen Gefangenen
haben viel gelitten. 6. Wer pfeift? 7. Ich pfiff
mit einer Pfeife. 8. Zerreißen Sie Ihre Hefte nicht!
9. Meine Schuhe sind zerrissen. 10. Dieser Soldat
reitet zu schnell. 11. Ich bitte Sie, mir ein Stückchen Brot
[Brod] zu schneiden. 12. Das Kind hat sich in den
Finger geschnitten. 13. Wer gab ihm ein Messer?
14. Es hat es selbst genommen. 15. Ich begreife das
nicht.

2) 16. Bleiben Sie hier? 17. Die Knaben sind heute
vier Stunden in der Schule geblieben. 18. Ich schreibe viele
Briefe. 19. Haben Sie diese Aufgabe geschrieben? 20. Ja,

ich habe sie geschrieben. 21. Leihen Sie mir eine Mark! 22. Ich habe mein Pferd Ihrem Nachbar geliehen. 23. Reiben Sie Ihre Hände! 24. Ich habe sie schon gerieben. 25. Schreien Sie nicht so laut! 26. Ich habe meinem Feinde verziehen. 27. Die Sonne schien sehr warm. 28. Der Fremde ist auf den Berg gestiegen.

### Exercise 91.

1) 1. The dog has bitten me.  2. Has it also bitten you?  3. No, it (he) has not bitten me.  4. It does not bite (the) children.  5. Henry resembles his father (*dat.*).  6. My brother had not so much to suffer as I. 7. I have suffered much.  8. Who has lent my pen? 9. Your brother has lent it.  10. Cut me a piece of bread, please (bitte).  11. Why have you whistled? 12. I have tried my whistle.  13. I went on horseback (I rode) yesterday.

2) 14. You (have) stayed too long in the garden. 15. To whom (an wen) do you write?  16. I am writing (I write) to my friend Henry.  17. He has also written to me.  18. The sun shines.  19. Who cried so loud (laut)?  20. I think it was Frederick who cried so loud. 21. I lent my music-book [to] Louisa.  22. Will you lend me two francs.  23. I will do so (it) with pleasure. 24. The son of the king *has* ascended (mounted on) the throne.  25. Does the sun shine?  26. It (sie) shone an hour ago (vor . .), and I think it will soon shine again. 27. Pardon me (*dat.*) my faults.

### Conversation.

| | |
|---|---|
| Was thun die Hunde? | Sie beißen. |
| Hat der Hund Sie gebissen? | Nein, er hat mich nicht gebissen. |
| Wem gleicht dieses Mädchen? | Es gleicht seiner Mutter. |
| Können Sie reiten? | Ja, ich reite jeden Tag. |

Wie lange find Sie in Paris geblieben?

Ich bin sechs Monate dort (there) geblieben.

War Ihr Onkel sehr krank?

Ja, er hat viele Schmerzen (pain) gelitten.

Wer hat diesen Brief geschrieben?

Karoline [Caroline] hat ihn geschrieben.

Wollen Sie mir Ihr Wörterbuch ein wenig leihen?

Ich werde es Ihnen mit Vergnügen leihen.

Wollen Sie mir verzeihen?

Ich habe Ihnen schon verziehen.

Warum hat der Knabe so laut geschrieen?

Ein Hund hat ihn in die Hand gebissen.

---

# LESSON XLV.

## Third Class of the Second Conjugation.

The *Imperfect* is in **ie,** the *Past Participle* retains the vowel of the Infinitive mood.

| INFINITIVE. | PRESENT INDICATIVE. | IMPERFECT. ie | PAST PART. a |
|---|---|---|---|
| **blasen** to blow. | ich blase, du **bläsest,** er **bläst,** wir blasen, 2c. | ich **blies.** | **geblasen** blown. |
| **braten** to roast. | ich brate, du brätst, er brät, wir braten, 2c. | ich briet. | gebraten roasted. |
| †**fallen** to fall. | ich falle, du fällst, er fällt, wir fallen, 2c. | ich fiel. | gefallen fallen. |

Thus: **gefallen** to please. *Imperfect* gefiel. *Past part.* gefallen.

| **fangen** to catch. | ich fange, du fängst, er fängt, wir fangen, 2c. | ich fing. | gefangen caught. |
|---|---|---|---|

Thus: **an'fangen** to commence. *Past part.* **angefangen.**

| **halten** to hold, take. | ich halte, du hältst, er hält, wir halten, 2c. | ich hielt. | gehalten held. |
|---|---|---|---|

Thus: **behalten** to keep; **erhalten** to receive. *Past part.* **erhalten** received.

# Third Class of the Second Conjugation.—Cont'd.

| INFINITIVE. | PRESENT INDICATIVE. | IMPERFECT. ie | PAST PART. a |
|---|---|---|---|
| laffen to leave. | ich laffe, du läffeft, er läßt, wir laffen, ꝛc. | ich ließ. | gelaffen left. |

Thus : **verlaffen** to leave (a place). *Past part.* **verlaffen** left.

| | | | |
|---|---|---|---|
| fchlafen to sleep. | ich fchlafe, du fchläfft, er fchläft, wir fchlafen, ꝛc. | ich fchlief. | gefchlafen slept. |

Thus : **ein'fchlafen** to fall asleep. *Past part.* **eingefchlafen.**

| | | | |
|---|---|---|---|
| †laufen to run. | ich laufe, du läufft, er läuft, wie laufen, ꝛc. | ich lief. | gelaufen run. |
| †gehen to go. | ich gehe, du gehft, er geht, wir gehen, ꝛc. | ich ging. | gegangen gone. |

Thus : †**aus'gehen** to go out. *Past part.* **ausgegangen.**

| | | | |
|---|---|---|---|
| rufen to call. | ich rufe, du rufft, er ruft, wir rufen, ꝛc. | ich rief. | gerufen called. |

## Words.

der Wind  the wind.
der Reifende  the traveller.
gleich  directly.
kochen (*reg. v.*) to boil.
die Leiter  the ladder.
allein  alone.

raten [rathen]  (*irr. v.*) to advise.
das Netz  the net.
die Angel  the fishing-hook.
Kopfweh  a headache.
das Bettchen  the little bed.

## Exercise 92.

1) 1. Der Wind bläft ftark; geftern blies er nicht fo ftark. 2. Das Fleifch ift nicht gut gebraten. 3. Der Vogel fiel tot [todt] vom Baume. 4. Warum weint das Kind? 5. Es ift gefallen. 6. Wollen Sie Vögel fangen? 7. Ja, ich habe fchon drei gefangen. 8. Wollen Sie das Buch behalten? 9. Ja, ich behalte es. 10. Der Gärtner hat einen Brief von feinem älteften Sohn aus Amerika erhalten.

2) 11. Was r a t e n [rathen] Sie mir; soll ich bleiben oder gehen? 12. Ich rate [rathe] Ihnen zu bleiben. 13. Wo ist das kleine Kind? 14. Es s ch l ä f t. 15. Der Reisende s ch l i e f unter einem Baum. 16. Wie haben Sie die vorige (last) Nacht g e s ch l a f e n? 17. Ich habe sehr gut ge= schlafen. 18. Wohin g e h e n Sie? 19. Ich g e h e in die Schule; ich g i n g gestern auch in die Schule. 20. Wer r u f t mich? 21. Ihr Vater ruft Sie, gehen Sie gleich zu ihm!

### Exercise 98.

1) 1. The wind blows very hard (ſtarf). 2. Is the meat roasted? 3. No, it is boiled. 4. *Has* little Charles fallen? 5. Yes, he has fallen from the ladder. 6. (The) cats catch mice. 7. The concert began at seven o'clock. 8. I have begun to learn German. 9. My hat *has* fallen into the water. 10. (The) fish(es) are caught in nets and with hooks.

2) 11. Let me alone (in Ruhe). 12. The mother left the young lady alone at home. 13. Why did you not sleep well last night? 14. I had a headache. 15. The child slept in his little bed (*dimin.*). 16. Where (wohin') do you run? 17. I run to my professor's; I am late. 18. Do you not go to the (ins [in's]) theatre this evening? 19. No, Sir, I am going into the garden with my aunt. 20. Henry *has* gone out.

### READING LESSON.

#### Ein teurer [theurer] Kopf und ein wohlfeiler.

A dear Head and a cheap one.

Als der letzte König von Polen noch regierte[1]), b r a ch[2]) eine Empörung[3]) gegen ihn a u s. Einer von den Em=

1) was reigning.  2) broke out.  3) an insurrection, revolt.

pörern⁴), ein polnischer Fürst, setzte einen Preis⁵) von 20,000 Gulden auf den Kopf des Königs und hatte sogar⁶) die Freiheit⁷), es dem König selbst zu schreiben, um⁸) ihn zu erschrecken⁸).

Aber der König schrieb ihm ganz kaltblütig⁹) folgende¹⁰) kurze Antwort: „Ihren Brief habe ich erhalten und gelesen. Es hat mir einiges Vergnügen gemacht¹¹), daß mein Kopf Ihnen noch so viel wert [werth]¹²) ist; ich kann Sie versichern¹³), für den Ihrigen gebe ich nicht einen Pfennig"¹⁴).

4) rebels. 5) a prize. 6) even. 7) insolence. 8) in order to frighten him. 9) quite cooly. 10) the following. 11) given. 12) worth. 13) assure. 14) a farthing.

---

# LESSON XLVI.

### Third Conjugation. (O-Conjugation.)

The third conjugation has both in the *Imperfect* and *Past Participle* o as characterizing vowel.

| INFINITIVE. | PRESENT INDICATIVE. | IMPERFECT. o | PAST PART. o |
|---|---|---|---|
| **bieten** to offer. | ich biete, du bietest, er bietet, wir bieten, ꝛc. | ich **bot**. | **geboten** offered. |
| Thus : **verbieten** to forbid. *Past part.* **verboten** forbidden. | | | |
| †**fliegen** to fly. | ich fliege, du fliegst, er fliegt, wir fliegen, ꝛc. | ich flog. | geflogen flown. |
| †**fließen** to flow. | ich fließe, du fließest, er fließt, wir fließen, ꝛc. | ich floß. | geflossen flowed. |
| **frieren** to freeze, to be cold. | ich friere, du frierst, er friert, wir frieren, ꝛc. | ich fror. | gefroren frozen. |

## Third Conjugation.—Continued.

| INFINITIVE. | PRESENT INDICATIVE. | IMPERFECT. | PAST PART. |
|---|---|---|---|
| schießen to shoot, kill. | ich schieße, du schießest, er schießt, wir schießen, ꝛc. | ich schoß. | geschossen shot. |
| schließen lock, shut. | ich schließe, du schließest, er schließt, wir schließen, ꝛc. | ich schloß. | geschlossen locked. |
| verlieren to lose. | ich verliere, du verlierst, er verliert, wir verlieren, ꝛc. | ich verlor. | verloren lost. |
| betrügen to cheat. | ich betrüge, du betrügst, er betrügt, wir betrügen, ꝛc. | ich betrog. | betrogen cheated. |
| wiegen to weigh. | ich wiege, du wiegst, er wiegt, wir wiegen, ꝛc. | ich wog. | gewogen weighed |
| lügen to tell a lie. | ich lüge, du lügst, er lügt, wir lügen, ꝛc. | ich log. | gelogen lied. |
| schmelzen to melt. | ich schmelze, du schmilzest, er schmilzt, wir schmelzen, ꝛc. | ich schmolz. | geschmolzen melted. |

### Words.

der Kanarienvogel [Canarien=vogel] the canary-bird.
der Rhein the Rhine.
das Vaterland the native country.
der Keller the cellar.
das Gewehr the gun, rifle.
der Sperling the sparrow.
verlangen to ask (for).
seit since.
töten [tödten] to kill.

der Schnee the snow.
der Kaufmann the merchant.
der Hirsch the stag.
der Graf the count.
die Magd or das Dienstmädchen the (*fem.*) servant.
das Kilogramm the kilo-gram.
seit wann? since when? how long?
das Eis the ice.

### Exercise 94.

1) 1. Ich biete Ihnen zwanzig Mark für Ihren Stock; wollen Sie mir ihn geben? 2. Nein, ich gebe ihn nicht für dreißig. 3. Wieviel [Wie viel] bot man Ihnen für Ihr Pferd?

4. Man hat mir fünfhundert Mark geboten. 5. Der Vogel fliegt. 6. Die Vögel fliegen. 7. Der Kanarienvogel [Canarienvogel] ist über das Haus geflogen. 8. Letzten Winter war der Rhein gefroren. 9. Das Wasser floß in den Keller. 10. Was machen Sie mit diesem Gewehr? 11. Ich schieße Vögel. 12. Gestern habe ich sechs Sperlinge geschossen.

2) 13. Wollen Sie die Thüre schließen? 14. Sie ist schon geschlossen. 15. Wieviel [Wie viel] verlor Ihr Oheim im Spiel? 16. Er hat nur einige Mark verloren. 17. Wieviel wiegt dieser Koffer? 18. Er ist noch nicht gewogen worden; aber ich glaube nicht, daß er fünfundzwanzig Kilogramm wiegt. 19. Lügen Sie nicht? 20. Ich habe nicht gelogen. 21. Der Schnee ist geschmolzen.

### Exercise 95.

1) 1. The merchant asked eleven shillings (Mark). 2. I offered him ten. 3. The count has offered me 400 pounds for my two horses. 4. The bird flew through the open window into the room. 5. The river flows between two mountains. 6. I am cold. 7. Are you also cold? 8. The water is frozen. 9. I have shot at (auf) a stag, but I did not kill him. 10. Who has locked my door? 11. The servant has locked it. 12. Have you shut the window? 13. No, I have not shut it.

2) 14. Have You lost anything? 15. Yes, I have lost my gloves. 16. You lose everything. 17. The servant of my neighbor has *told a lie (lied)*. 18. Since when is the snow melted? 19. Since some days. 20. Who has cheated you? 21. A stranger, whom I do not know, has cheated me. 22. The children shall

(ſollen) not lie.    23. Have you weighed the meat? 24. Yes, it weighs two kilograms.    25. The ice is melted.

### Conversation.

| | |
|---|---|
| Wer kann fliegen? | Die Vögel können fliegen. |
| Wieviel [Wie viel] hat der Offi= zier [Officier] Ihnen für ihr Pferd geboten? | Er hat mir 150 Pfund Sterling geboten. |
| Darf man hier rauchen (smoke)? | Nein, es iſt verboten. |
| Wo haben Sie Ihren Vogel? | Er iſt durch das Zimmer ge= flogen. |
| Iſt es heute kalt? | Ja, das Waſſer iſt ge= froren. |
| Waren Sie auf der Jagd (a hunting)? Haben Sie etwas geſchoſſen? | Ja, ich habe zwei Haſen (hares) geſchoſſen. |
| Warum haben Sie Ihre Fenſter geſchloſſen? | Es iſt zu kalt; ich friere; ich habe Feuer in dem Ofen (stove). |
| Hat der kleine Knabe kein Taſchentuch (pocket-hand- kerchief)? | Nein, er hat es verloren. |
| Warum gehen Sie nicht in Ihr Zimmer? | Ich kann nicht; die Thüre iſt geſchloſſen. |

---

# LESSON XLVII.

## Fourth Conjugation.    (U-Conjugation.)

This conjugation consists only of nine verbs having a for their radical vowel. Here the distinguishing vowel in the *Imperfect* is u: the *Past Participle* retains the radical vowel a of the infinitive. In the second and third person singular of the indicative present seven of them change their a into ä.

| INFINITIVE. | PRESENT INDICATIVE. | IMPERFECT. u | PAST PART. a |
|---|---|---|---|
| **baden** to bake. | ich bade, bu bädſt, er bädt, wir baden, ꝛc. | ich buk or *reg.* ich badte. | **gebaden** baked. |
| **†fahren** to drive, to ride in a vehicle, *etc.* | ich fahre, bu fährſt, er fährt, wir fahren, ꝛc. | ich fuhr. | **gefahren** gone in a carriage. |

Thus : **††ſpazieren fahren** to take a drive.

| | | | |
|---|---|---|---|
| **laden** to load. | ich lade, bu läbſt, er läbt, wir laben, ꝛc. | ich lub. | gelaben laden & loaded. |

Thus : **ein'laben** to invite. *Past Participle* **eingelaben.**

| | | | |
|---|---|---|---|
| **ſchaffen** to create, make. | ich ſchaffe, bu ſchaffſt, er ſchafft, wir ſchaffen, ꝛc. | ich ſchuf. | geſchaffen created. |
| **ſchlagen** to strike, beat. | ich ſchlage, bu ſchlägſt, er ſchlägt, wir ſchla= gen, ꝛc. | ich ſchlug. | geſchlagen struck. |
| **tragen** to carry, wear. | ich trage, bu trägſt, er trägt, wir tragen, ꝛc. | ich trug. | getragen carried. |
| **waſchen** to wash. | ich waſche, bu wäſcheſt, er wäſcht, wir waſchen, ꝛc. | ich wuſch. | gewaſchen washed. |
| **†wachſen** to grow. | ich wachſe, bu wächſt, er wächſt, wir wachſen, ꝛc. | ich wuchs. | gewachſen grown. |

## Words.

der Kuchen  the cake.
bas Mehl  the flour.
weich  soft.
der Kutſcher  the coachman.
der Wagen  the carriage.
bie Jagb  chase, hunting.
bie Eiſenbahn  the railroad.

der Ball  the ball.
der Bauer  the peasant.
der Bäcker  the baker.
prächtig  magnificent, stately.
bie Piſtole  the pistol.
bas Taſchentuch  the pocket-handkerchief.

das Holz  the wood.     der Karren  the cart.
der Sack  the sack, bag.     das Feld  the field.
der Rücken  the back.     schmutzig  dirty.
das Heu  the hay.     schnell  quick.

### Exercise 96.

1) 1. Bäckt Ihre Mutter heute Kuchen? 2. Nein, sie hat kein Mehl; sie wird morgen backen. 3. Dieses Brot [Brod] ist nicht gut gebacken; es ist zu weich. 4. Der König fährt mit sechs Pferden. 5. Wohin fahren Sie? 6. Ich fahre spazieren. 7. Gestern fuhren wir nach Versailles. 8. Sind Sie in einem Wagen gefahren? 9. Nein, wir fuhren mit der Eisenbahn. 10. Warum laden Sie das Gewehr? 11. Ich will auf die Jagd gehen.

2) 11. Der Mann lud den Sack auf den Rücken des Esels. 12. Das Holz wurde auf einen Wagen geladen. 13. Der Knabe schlägt den Hund. 14. Die Bauern schlagen oft die Pferde. 15. Haben Sie Ihr Pferd auch geschlagen? 16. Nein, ich habe meinen Esel geschlagen. 17. Wohin' haben Sie den Brief getragen? 18. Ich habe ihn auf die Post getragen. 19. Der Gärtner wusch seine Hände. 20. Diese Rosen sind in meinem Garten gewachsen.

### Exercise 97.

1) 1. What does the baker bake? 2. He bakes bread; yesterday he also baked cakes. 3. The coachman drives too quickly. 4. We have (sind) *taken a drive*. 5. The prince drove in a stately carriage and four (vierspännig). 6. The cart was laden with hay. 7. Is your pistol loaded? 8. No, it is not loaded. 9. Are you invited to (zu) the ball? 10. No, 'not 'I, but my sisters are invited.

2) 11. Do not beat this dog; it will bite you. 12. Who will take (carry) my letter to the post-office?

13. The man-servant may (can) take it; he has nothing to do now. 14. Wash your hands, they are dirty. 15. Are my pocket-handkerchiefs washed? 16. The girl is washing them just now (eben jetzt). 17. The best coffee grows in Arabia (Arabien). 18. Where did you find these violets? 19. They *have* grown in the field behind our garden (*dat.*).

---

# LESSON XLVIII.

## Inseparable Verbs.

Most German verbs may have certain syllables or prepositions, as prefixes, before them. Unaccented particles or prefixes assimilate themselves with the simple verb so as to form one inseparable combination, such as:

bezahlen to pay; ich **bezahle** I pay; ich **bezahlte** I paid.

Verbs of this kind are called *inseparable verbs*. The following particulars are to be observed concerning them:

1) The prefixes remain attached to the verb through the whole conjugation.

2) The prefixes are always unaccented.

3) These verbs do not admit of the syllable **ge** in the past participle, as: **bezahlt'** (not gebezahlt).

4) They are conjugated conformably to their root-verb being regular or irregular. The following eleven prefixes are inseparable:

> **be, emp, er, ent, ver, zer ;**
> **ge, miß, voll, wider** and **hinter.**

## CONJUGATION OF INSEPARABLE VERBS.

### bewohnen  to inhabit.

#### Present Tense.

ich bewohne  I inhabit          wir bewohnen  we inhabit
du bewohnst  thou inhabitest    ihr bewohnt  } you inhabit
er bewohnt  he inhabits         Sie bewohnen }
                                sie bewohnen  they inhabit.

#### Imperfect.

ich bewohnte  I inhabited; du bewohntest, er bewohnte, ꝛc.

#### Future.

ich werde bewohnen  I shall inhabit; du wirst bewohnen, ꝛc.

#### Perfect.

ich habe bewohnt  I have inhabited; du hast bewohnt, ꝛc. ꝛc.

### Thus are conjugated:

| INFINITIVE. | PRESENT. | IMPERFECT. | PAST PARTICIPLE. |
| --- | --- | --- | --- |
| be: behalten, irr. v. to keep | ich behalte | ich behielt | behalten kept. |
| emp: empfangen, irr. v. to receive | ich empfange | ich empfing | empfangen received. |
| er: erhalten, irr. v. to receive | ich erhalte | ich erhielt | erhalten received. |
| ent: †entgehen, irr. v. to escape | ich entgehe | ich entging | entgangen escaped |
| ver: verlieren, irr. v. to lose | ich verliere | ich verlor | verloren lost. |
| zer: zerstören  to destroy | ich zerstöre | ich zerstörte | zerstört destroyed. |

Conjugation of Inseparable Verbs.—*Continued.*

| Infinitive. | Present. | Imperfect. | Past Participle. |
|---|---|---|---|
| **ge**: gefallen, *irr. v.* to please | ich gefalle | ich gefiel | gefallen pleased. |
| **miß**: mißfallen, *irr. v.* to displease | ich mißfalle | ich mißfiel | mißfallen displeased. |
| **voll**: vollbringen, *irr. v.* to accomplish | ich vollbringe | ich vollbrachte | vollbracht accomplished. |
| **wider**: widerstehen, *irr. v.* to resist | ich widerstehe | ich widerstand | widerstanden resisted. |
| **hinter**: hinterlassen, *irr. v.* to leave behind | ich hinterlasse | ich hinterließ | hinterlassen left behind. |

*Remark.* A few other verbs, though compounded with inseparable particles, take in the *past participle* the prefix **ge,** because their first component is accented. Such are:

**frühstücken** to breakfast ich frühstücke ich frühstückte gefrühstückt.

**antworten** to answer ich antworte ich antwortete geantwortet.

**urteilen** [urtheilen] to judge. ich urteile ich urteilte geurteilt.

### Words.

die Gefahr the danger.
der Sonnenschirm the parasol.
das Schauspiel the play.
die Frage the question.
verstehen (*irr. v.*) to understand.
bedecken (*reg. v.*) to cover.

das Land the land.
gehorchen to obey.
bewundern to admire.
das Gemälde the picture.
gewöhnlich common(ly), usual(ly).

### Exercise 98.

1. Ich bewohne ein kleines Haus; mein Vater bewohnt ein großes Haus. 2. Der Schüler hat das Buch behalten. 3. Wir empfangen oft Briefe von unsern Eltern; aber heute haben wir keine erhalten. 4. Die

Soldaten ſind der Gefahr entgangen. 5. Fräulein Luiſe [Louiſe] hat ihren Sonnenſchirm verloren; ſie verliert oft etwas. 6. Die Feinde zerſtörten die Stadt. 7. Wie hat Ihnen das Schauſpiel gefallen? 8. Es hat mir ſehr gut gefallen. 9. Wann frühſtücken Sie? 10. Ich frühſtücke um 8 Uhr. 11. Haben Sie mir geantwortet? Nein. 12. Warum antworten Sie mir nicht? 13. Ich habe Ihre Frage nicht verſtanden.

### Exercise 99.

1. Snow covers the mountains in (im) winter. 2. Water covered the land. 3. We inhabit a large house. 4. I have not received your letter. 5. You will lose your money. 6. Good children obey their parents (*dat.*). 7. Don't you admire this beautiful picture? 8. We have already (ſchon) admired it, and we admire it still (noch). 9. What have you lost? 10. I have lost my pencil. 11. This picture pleases me much (ſehr). 12. The castle of the count was destroyed by the enemy. 13. The poor man *has* died and has left five children (behind). 14. They (man) have sold his little house. 15. At what o'clock do you breakfast? 16. We breakfast commonly at nine o'clock, but to-day we have breakfasted at eight. 17. Answer me (*dat.*), if you please (gefälligſt or wenn es Ihnen beliebt).

### Conversation.

| | |
|---|---|
| Wer bewohnt jenes Schloß? | Der Graf Douglas. |
| Wird er es behalten? | Nein, er will es verkaufen. |
| Haben Sie einen Brief von Ihrem Freunde erhalten? | Ich erhalte oft Briefe von ihm. |
| Haben Sie Ihren Vater verloren? | Ich habe meinen Vater und meine Mutter verloren. |
| Haben Sie meine Frage verſtanden? | Ja, ich habe ſie verſtanden. |

Hat Fräulein Luise [Louise] etwas verloren?

Ja, sie hat ihren Sonnenschirm verloren.

Haben Sie auf den Brief Ihres Freundes geantwortet?

Ich werde ihm in einigen Tagen antworten.

Wer hat dieses Glas zerbrochen?

Ich weiß es nicht; ich habe es nicht zerbrochen.

Um wieviel [wie viel] Uhr frühstücken Sie gewöhnlich?

Ich frühstücke gewöhnlich um halb acht Uhr.

---

# LESSON XLIX.

## Separable Verbs.

*Separable verbs* are such as consist of a verb and of a prefix which may be detached from it, as: **aus-gehen** to go out; **weg-gehen** to go away; **an-fangen** to begin.

When conjugated in the *Present* and *Imperfect* of the indicative, and in the *Imperative*, these prefixes are detached from the verb, and placed at the end of the principal clause; in dependent clauses they join, however, the verb, which must be at the end after relative pronouns and subordinating conjunctions.

| *Present.* | *Imperfect.* |
|---|---|
| ich **gehe** diesen Abend **aus**. | ich **ging** gestern nicht **aus**. |

*Imperative.*

**Gehen** Sie mit mir **aus**! — **Fangen** Sie jetzt **an**!

*Dependent Construction.*

Der Knabe, welcher diesen Abend **ausgeht**, ist kein guter Knabe.

The prefix remains with the verb in the *Infinitive*, in those tenses formed with the Infinitive (*First Future* and *First Conditional*), and in both *Participles*. Ex.: **anfangen** to begin; *Future* ich werde anfangen; *Present Participle* anfangend.

In the *Past Participle* the syllable ge is placed between the particle and the verb, as: an=ge=fangen, aus= gegangen. The same rule is applied to the word „zu", when this is required in the Infinitive, as: an=zu=fangen, auszugehen, ꝛc. All the *separable* verbs have a double accent, one on the separable particle, the other on the verb, as: an'fang'en, aus'geh'en, an'gefang'en.

### Conjugation of the Separable Verb: anfangen.

#### Present Indicative.

| Singular. | Plural. |
|---|---|
| ich fange — an I begin *or* commence | wir fangen — an we begin |
| du fängst — an | ihr fangt — an |
| er fängt — an | Sie fangen — an |
| | sie fangen an. |

#### Imperfect.

| Singular. | Plural. |
|---|---|
| ich fing — an I began *or* commenced | wir fingen — an we begun |
| du fingst — an. | ihr fingt — an |
| er fing — an. | Sie fingen — an |
| | sie fingen — an. |

#### Future.
ich werde anfangen I shall begin *or* commence.

#### Perfect.
ich habe angefangen I have begun *or* commenced.

#### Pluperfect.
ich hatte angefangen I had begun, etc.

#### First Conditional.
ich würde anfangen I should begin.

### Imperative.

fange — an, fanget an } begin *or* commence!
fangen Sie an
fangen wir — an let us begin *or* commence.

## Infinitive.

anfangen and anzufangen to begin, to commence.

## Participles.

*Present.*
anfangenb beginning.

*Past.*
angefangen begun, commenced.

# A List of the most used Separable Particles.

## 1. Simple separable Particles.

| INFINITIVE. | PRESENT. | PAST PARTICIPLE. |
|---|---|---|
| **ab** : †abreifen, *irr. v.* to depart. | ich reife — ab | abgereif. |
| **an** : †an'kommen, *irr. v.* to arrive. | ich komme — an | angekommen. |
| **auf** : †auf'ftehen, *irr. v.* to get up. | ich ftehe — auf | aufgeftanden. |
| **aus** : †aus'gehen, *irr. v.* to go out. | ich gehe — aus | ausgegangen. |
| **bei** : †bei'ftehen, *irr. v.* to assist. | ich ftehe — bei | beigeftanden. |
| **ein** : ein'laden, *irr. v.* to invite. | ich lade — ein | eingeladen. |
| **fort** : †fort'gehen, *irr. v.* to go away. | ich gehe — fort | fortgegangen. |
| **mit** : mit'teilen [mittheilen], *reg. v.* to communicate. | ich teile — mit | mitgeteilt. |
| **nach** : †nach'laufen, *irr. v.* to run after. | ich laufe — nach | nachgelaufen. |
| **vor** : vor'ftellen, *reg. v.* to introduce. | ich ftelle — vor | vorgeftellt. |
| **weg** : weg'nehmen, *irr. v.* to take away. | ich nehme — weg | weggenommen. |
| **zu** : zu'machen, *reg. v.* to shut. | ich mache — zu | zugemacht. |
| zu'bringen, to spend. | ich bringe — zu | zugebracht. |

*Note.* Verbs compounded with **durch, um, unter** and **über** are partly separable and partly inseparable, according to their signification. Ex.:

ich ſetze über I cross, — ich überſetze I translate.

2. There are also compound separable particles added to verbs, such as: hinauf, herauf, herab, herein, hinein, heraus, vorbei, zurück zuſammen. Ex.:

hinaufgehen to go up.
hereinkommen to come in.
vorherſagen to foretell.
hineingehen to go in.
vorbeifahren to drive by.
zurückkommen to come back, etc.

These are conjugated in the same way.

ich gehe hinauf; er kam herein — herauf — heraus.
ich komme morgen zurück; ich bin zurückgekommen, ꝛc.
ich ſage vorher; — ich habe vorhergeſagt.

### Words.

| | |
|---|---|
| das Schauſpiel the play. | das Mittageſſen the dinner. |
| ab'ſchreiben to copy. | die Arbeit the work. |
| die Stunde the lesson. | der Wind the wind. |
| der Geſandte the ambassador. | der Abend the evening. |
| das Konzert [Concert] the concert. | ſpät late. |
| | jeden Tag every day. |
| die Nachricht the news. | vor'leſen to read (aloud). |
| das Gedicht the poem. | auf'hören to cease, stop. |
| an'ziehen to put on. | aus'geben to spend. |

### Exercise 100.

1) 1. Ich fange meine Aufgabe an. 2. Das Schauſpiel fängt um ſechs Uhr an. 3. Haben Sie Ihren Brief

abgeſchrieben? 4. Nein, ich habe ihn angefangen.
5. Morgen werden meine deutſchen Stunden anfangen.
6. Meine Tante reiſt morgen früh ab. 7. Der engliſche
Geſandte iſt geſtern abgereiſt (left). 8. Ich ſchreibe
dieſe Aufgabe ab. 9. Wer ſchrieb dieſen Brief ab? 10.
Karl [Carl] hat ihn abgeſchrieben. 11. Der Kaiſer iſt
um ſechs Uhr angekommen. 12. Die Kaiſerin wird
morgen ankommen.

2) 13. Ich ziehe mein neues Kleid an. 14. Stehen
Sie auf! 15. Es iſt Zeit, aufzuſtehen. 16. Gehen
Sie aus? 17. Ja, ich gehe aus; ich ging geſtern nicht
aus, da ich krank war. 18. Man hat mir dieſe Nachricht
mitgeteilt [mitgetheilt]. 19. Ich lade Sie zum Mittag=
eſſen ein; ich habe auch Ihren Bruder eingeladen.
20. Leſen Sie mir dieſes Gedicht vor! 21. Der Regen
hat aufgehört. 22. Machen Sie das Fenſter zu!
23. Ich bringe meine Abende bei meinen Eltern zu.

### Exercise 101.

1) 1. Charles, begin! 2. I began to copy (abzu=
ſchreiben) my exercise. 3. The concert begins at seven
o'clock. 4. You have not yet commenced your work.
5. When do you go out? 6. I go out every day at
eight o'clock. 7. I also went out yesterday. 8. My
brother *has left* (departed) for (nach) London. 9. Our
uncle leaves (departed) this evening; and my brother
*has* left this morning. 10. Put on your shoes. 11.
The rain has ceased, but the wind does not cease.
12. I must go out at four o'clock.

2) 13. *Has* Charles gone out? 14. No, Sir, he *has*
not yet gone out. 15. Have you spent much money?
16. No, not much, I spent two or three marks. 17. He

who*) 'gets up (aufſteht†) 'late, loses much time.
18. Take away these papers!  19. I shall introduce
you [to] the count *(dat.);* he will invite you to
the ball (zum Ball).  20. Introduce me to your
friend.  21. Shut the door.  22. It is already shut.
23. My sister spends her evenings at (bei) her aunt's.
24. Come in (herein), Sir!

### Conversation.

| | |
|---|---|
| Wann fängt das Konzert [Con= cert an? | Es fängt um 7 Uhr an. |
| Hat Emilie ihre deutſchen Stunden (lessons) ange= fangen? | Sie hat ſie vorgeſtern ange= fangen. |
| Wann reiſt Ihre Tante ab? | Sie reiſt dieſen Abend ab. |
| Haben Sie Ihre Überſetzung [Ueberſetzung] ſchon abge= ſchrieben? | Noch nicht; aber ich ſchreibe ſie jetzt ab. |
| Um wieviel [wie viel] Uhr gehen Sie dieſen Abend aus? | Heute gehe ich nicht aus; ich werde morgen ausgehen. |
| Sind Sie geſtern auch nicht aus= gegangen? | Nein, ich hatte keine Zeit, aus= zugehen. |
| Iſt das Kind angekleidet? | Ja, die Mutter hat es ange= kleidet. |
| Wann geht (rise) die Sonne auf? | Im Sommer geht ſie um 3 Uhr (des) Morgens auf. |
| Sind Sie zu dem Ball einge= laden? | Nein, ich bin nicht eingeladen. |
| Warum machen Sie das Fenſter zu? | Der Wind iſt zu kalt. |
| Wie bringen Sie Ihre Abende zu? | Ich leſe deutſche Bücher. |

*) Derjenige welcher.

†) After a relative pronoun there is no separation.

# LESSON L.

## Neuter and Intransitive Verbs.

*Neuter verbs* are those which ascribe to the subject a *state* or *condition;* they often, too, as *intransitive verbs,* express an *action,* but this does not pass over to an object in the accusative case. Ex.:

ich ſtehe I stand, ich ſitze I sit, ich gehe I walk, ich komme I come, ich folge bir (*dat.*) I follow you.

Their conjugation does not differ from that of the active verb, except in the *compound tenses* where *most\*)* of them are conjugated with the auxiliary ſein (to be).

We subjoin here an example of a regular and an irregular neuter or intransitive verb.

### 1. reiſen to travel.

*Present.*

ich reiſe I travel
bu reiſeſt thou travellest ‒
er reiſt he travels.

*Imperfect.*

ich reiſte I travelled.

*Future.*

ich werde reiſen I shall travel.

*Conditional.*

ich würde reiſen I should travel.

---

\*) Yet a certain number are construed with haben. Such are: ſchlafen to sleep, lachen to laugh, leben to live, weinen to cry, wohnen to live, etc. Perfect: ich habe geſchlafen, habe gelacht, gewohnt, ꝛc. See footnote page 156.

*Perfect.*

ich **bin** gereist  I *have* travelled
du **bift** gereist  thou hast travelled
er **ift** gereist  he has travelled

wir **find** gereist  we have travelled
ihr **feib** gereist  } you have travelled
Sie **find** gereist  }
fie **find** gereist  they have travelled.

*Pluperfect.*

ich war gereist  I *had* travelled
du warft gereist          etc.
er war gereist.

*Second Future.*

ich werde gereist fein  I shall *have* travelled.

*Second Conditional.*

ich würde gereist fein  I should *have* travelled.

## 2.  gehen to go.

*Present*

ich gehe  I go
du gehft  thou goest
er geht  he goes, etc.

*Imperfect.*

ich ging  I went.

*Future.*

ich werde gehen  I shall go.

*Conditional.*

ich würde gehen  I should go.

*Perfect Tense.*

| *Singular.* | *Plural.* |
|---|---|
| ich **bin** gegangen I *have* gone | wir **ſind** gegangen we *have* gone |
| du **biſt** gegangen thou *hast* gone | ihr **ſeid** gegangen etc. |
| er **iſt** gegangen he *has* gone | Sie **ſind** gegangen |
| | ſie **ſind** gegangen. |

## Such are:

abreiſen to set out; ich **bin** ab=
  gereiſt.
ankommen (*irr.*) to arrive.
aufſtehen (*irr.*) to get up.
bleiben (*irr.*) to remain, stay.
einſchlafen (*irr.*) to fall asleep.
entgehen (*irr.*) to escape.
fahren (*irr.*) to drive.
fallen (*irr.*) to fall.
fliegen (*irr.*) to fly.
fliehen (*irr.*) to flee, run
  away.
geſchehen (*irr.*) to happen.
klettern (*reg.*) to climb.
kommen (*irr.*) to come.

laufen (*irr.*) to run.
marſchieren [marſchiren] (*reg.*)
  to march.
reiten (*irr.*) to go on horse-
  back.
ſcheitern (*reg.*) to run a-
  ground, to be wrecked.
ſchwimmen (*irr.*) to swim.
ſpazieren gehen (*irr.*) to walk.
ſteigen (*irr.*) to mount.
ſterben (*irr.*) to die.
um'kommen (*irr.*) to perish.
werden (*irr.*) to become.
zurückkommen (*irr.*) to come
  back.

## Words.

das Land the country.
außer Atem [Athem] out of
  breath.
der Schuhmacher the shoe-
  maker.
die Wunde the wound.
die Mannſchaft the crew.

das Schiff the ship, boat.
die Küſte the coast.
der Matroſe the sailor.
der Gärtner the gardener.
der Tod the death.
holländiſch Dutch.
das Frühſtück the breakfast.

## Exercise 102.

1) 1. Ich reiſe viel (a great deal); ich bin letztes Jahr
in Spanien gereiſt; mein Bruder reiſte in Italien.  2. Wohin

gehen Sie? 3. Ich gehe ins [in's] Theater. 4. Meine Schwester ist vor einer halben Stunde ins Konzert [Concert] gegangen. 5. Wird Heinrich nach Paris gehen? 6. Nein, er wird nach London gehen. 7. Wann sind Sie aufge= standen? 8. Ich bin um sieben Uhr aufgestanden. 9. Das Kind ist gefallen. 10. Der Knabe ist zu schnell gelaufen; er ist außer Atem [Athem]. 11. Mein Nachbar, der Schuh= macher, starb diesen Morgen.

2) 12. Der Soldat ist an seinen Wunden gestorben. 13. Das Kind hat sehr gut geschlafen. 14. Das Buch liegt auf dem Tische. 15. Ich sitze unter einem Baume. 16. Der Soldat stand am Thore. 17. Die Mädchen sind in den Garten gegangen. 18. Meine Mutter ist gestern vom Lande zurückgekommen, sie war drei Wochen da geblieben. 19. Was ist dem Kinde geschehen? 20. Es ist gefallen. 21. Ein holländisches Schiff ist an der Küste Afrikas gescheitert. 22. Der größte Teil [Theil] (part) der Mannschaft ist um= gekommen; nur einige Matrosen sind dem Tode entgangen.

### Exercise 108.

1. Lewis travels a great deal. 2. Last year he travelled in Italy. 3. *Has* your cousin also travelled a great deal? 4. No, Sir, he *has* never travelled. 5. He would perhaps travel also, if he were rich. 6. Who goes into the garden? 7. It is the gardener. 8. The professor *has* gone to Paris. 9. Where is your brother? 10. He is gone out. 11. I *have* swum in the river. 12. We have marched all (die ganze) night; we wished to arrive before eight o'clock. 13. I stayed two years in Lyons; now I live in Geneva (Genf). 14. The boy *(has)* climbed on a tree *(acc.)*. 15. When did you fall asleep? 16. I fell asleep at ten o'clock. 17. Why have you not come to (zum) breakfast? 18. I was not yet up (auf).

## Conversation.

| | |
|---|---|
| Sind Sie in Frankreich gereist? | Ich bin zwei Jahre dort gereist. |
| Wann sind Sie abgereist? | Ich bin um halb sechs abgereist. |
| Wann sind Sie hier ange= kommen? | Gegen sechs Uhr abends [Abends]. |
| Wann stehen Sie des Morgens auf? | Gewöhnlich um 6 Uhr; aber heute bin ich um 7 Uhr auf= gestanden. |
| Mit wem sind Sie nach Berlin gegangen? | Ich bin mit meinem Bruder gegangen. |
| Wollen Sie ein wenig mit uns spazieren gehen? | Ich werde mit Vergnügen mit Ihnen gehen. |
| Haben Sie gut geschlafen? | O ja, ziemlich (pretty) wohl. |

## READING LESSON.

### Eine lächerlich gemachte Lüge (Lie).

Ein Reisender erzählte eines Abends ganz ernsthaft[1]) in einer Gesellschaft[2]), daß er viel gereist sei und daß er unter andern Seltenheiten[3]) eine angetroffen[4]) habe, deren[5]) noch kein Schriftsteller[6]) Erwähnung[7]) gethan habe. Dieses Wunder war, wie er sagte, ein so großer und dicker Kraut= kopf[8]), daß fünfzig wohlbewaffnete Reiter[9]) unter einem seiner Blätter sich hätten in Schlachtordnung[10]) stellen und manövrieren [manövriren] können.

Einer der Anwesenden[11]) hielt diese Übertreibung [Uebertreibung][12]) keiner Antwort wert [werth]; aber er sagte ihm mit der größten Ruhe[13]), daß er auch gereist sei,

1) earnestly. 2) party. 3) curiosity. 4) met. 5) which. 6) author. 7) mention. 8) cabbage. 9) well armed horsemen. 10) in battle-array. 11) present. 12) exaggeration. 13) calmness.

und daß er, in Japan angekommen, zu seinem größten
Erstaunen[14]) gesehen hätte, wie mehr als dreihundert
Kesselschmiede[15]) an einem ungeheuern[16]) Kessel arbeiteten,
in welchem sich mehr als hundert Leute (or Personen)
befanden, die damit beschäftigt[17]) waren, ihn zu polieren
[poliren][18]).

„Was wollte man denn mit diesem ungeheuern Kessel
machen?" fragte der Reisende.

„Man wollte den Krautkopf darin kochen, wovon (or
von dem) Sie eben gesprochen haben."

14) astonishment.   15) kettle-maker, copper-smith.
16) immense.   17) occupied.   18) to polish.

---

# LESSON LI.

### Impersonal Verbs.

Impersonal verbs have, as in English, besides the
*Infinitive* and the *Past Participle* only the third person
*singular* throughout. Most of them are of the same
kind in both languages, as:

| *Infinitive.* | *Present.* |
|---|---|
| regnen  to rain. | es regnet  it rains. |
| schneien  to snow. | es schneit  it snows. |
| donnern  to thunder. | es donnert  it thunders. |
| blitzen  to lighten. | es blitzt  it lightens. |
| hageln  to hail. | es hagelt  it hails. |
| frieren  to freeze. | es friert  it freezes. |
| geben  there to be. | es giebt [gibt]  **there is,**<br>**there are.** |

They are all regular verbs except two: es friert; (*Past participle* gefroren, see page 171), and es giebt [gibt] (*Past participle* gegeben).

All are conjugated with the auxiliary haben. Ex.:

es hat geschneit, es hat gedonnert, es hatte geblitzt, 2c.

### 1. regnen to rain.

| | | |
|---|---|---|
| *Present.* | es regnet | it rains. |
| *Imperfect.* | es regnete | it rained. |
| *Future.* | es wird regnen | it will rain. |
| *Condit.* | es würde regnen | it would rain. |
| *Perfect.* | es hat geregnet | it has rained. |
| *Pluperfect.* | es hatte geregnet | it had rained, etc. |

### 2. es giebt [gibt] there is, there are.

| | | |
|---|---|---|
| *Present.* | es giebt | there is, there are. |
| *Imperfect.* | es gab | there was, there were. |
| *Perfect.* | es hat gegeben | there has (have) been. |
| *Pluperfect.* | es hatte gegeben | there had been. |
| *First Fut.* | es wird geben | there will be. |
| *First Cond.* | es würde geben (es gäbe) | there would be. |

### REMARKS.

1) es giebt [gibt] indicates a general existence. Ex.:

Es giebt Leute, welche sehr reich sind.
There are people who are very rich.

Was giebt es Neues?
What is the news?

2) *There is* may also be translated by es ist, *there are* es sind; *there was* es war, plur. *there were* es waren. This is always the case, when a *definite existence* is

expressed, *i. e.* when a *distinct small place* or *space* is added.  Ex.:

**Es ist** eine Katze i n b e m Zimmer.
There is a cat in the room.

**Es ist** kein Wasser i n b e r Flasche.
*There is* no water in the bottle.

### REFLEXIVE IMPERSONALS.

Some verbs occur impersonally with a personal pronoun in the objective case:

*es freut **mich***) I am glad.    es thut **mir** leid ⎱
*es wundert **mich***) I wonder.   es ist **mir** leid  ⎰ I am sorry.
es ist **mir** warm  I am warm.   es scheint mir  it seems to me.

### Words.

| | |
|---|---|
| die Kälte  the cold. | nennen  to call. |
| Leute  people; daß  that. | die Nuß  the nut. |
| stumm  dumb. | früh  early. |
| benn  for. | früher  earlier. |

### Exercise 104.

1) 1. Regnet es?  2. Nein, es regnet nicht, es schneit.  3. Gestern schneite es auch.  4. Es wird bald hageln.  5. Es wäre gut, wenn es regnete.  6. Es würde schneien, wenn es nicht zu kalt wäre.  7. Es donnert, hören Sie es?  8. Es wird noch mehr donnern.  9. Hat es auch geblitzt?  10. Ja, es hat zweimal [zwei mal] geblitzt.  11. Ich gehe nicht aus, wenn es regnet; denn ich habe meinen Regenschirm verloren.  12. Wie ist das Wetter heute?  13. Es ist nicht kalt; es ist ein wenig warm.

2) 14. Es ist sehr schönes Wetter.  15. Wenn es morgen schön ist, werde ich auf das Land gehen.  17. Es giebt [gibt] Leute, welche nicht sprechen können; man nennt sie stumm.  17. Was ist in diesem Glas?  18. Es ist Wasser darin.

---

*) We may also say: **ich** freue mich, **ich** wundre mich.

19. Giebt es Kirschen dieses Jahr? 20. Ja, es giebt viele Kirschen. 21. Es wundert mich, daß Sie so spät aufstehen; Sie müssen früher aufstehen. 22. Die Kälte ist noch nicht vorbei (past), es friert noch. 23. Ich glaube, daß es morgen auch frieren wird.

### Exercise 105.

1) 1. It rains. 2. It rained. 3. I think it will not rain to-morrow. 4. It lightens; do you see it? 5. Do you hear thunder? 6. Yes, it thunders; it has thundered. 7. Does it snow? 8. No, it does not snow now, but it has snowed all night. 9. How is the weather? 10. It is cold; it has frozen. 11. Is there [any] beer in that bottle? 12. No, there is wine in it (darin). 13. There are people who are always discontented. 14. Is it warm? 15. Yes, it is warm in this room. 16. Were there many people in the theatre? 17. Yes, there were many in it (darin). 18. There will be many nuts this year. 19. What is the news? 20. I know nothing. 21. I am glad to see you here. 22. I am sorry that you are ill.

### Conversation.

| | |
|---|---|
| Schneit es? | Nein, es schneit nicht. |
| Hat es gedonnert? | Ich glaube, daß es gedonnert hat. |
| Hat es geblitzt? | Ja, es hat sehr stark geblitzt. |
| Wird es bald frieren? | Ich glaube nicht, daß es bald frieren wird; es wird schneien. |
| Hat es letzte Nacht geregnet? | Ja, es hat ein wenig geregnet. |
| Was für Wetter ist es? | Es ist schlechtes Wetter, es regnet. |
| Giebt [Gibt] es etwas Neues? | Ich weiß (I know of) nichts. |

# LESSON LII.

## Reflexive Verbs.

The verb of a sentence is reflexive, when it returns the action upon the agent, viz., when there is a pronoun in an oblique case, generally in the accusative, representing the same being as the subject, which happens much oftener in German than in English. Ex.:

**Ich** ſetze **mich** I sit down (I place *myself*).

All such verbs are conjugated with the auxiliary h a b e n.

### EXAMPLE OF CONJUGATION.

**ſich irren** to be mistaken.

### Indicative.

*Present.*

**ich** irre **mich**\*) I am mistaken
**du** irrſt **dich** thou art mistaken
**er** irrt **ſich** he is mistaken
**ſie** irrt **ſich** she is mistaken
**es** irrt **ſich** it is mistaken

**wir** irren **uns** we are mistaken
**ihr** irrt **euch** }
**Sie** irren **ſich** } you are mistaken
**ſie** irren **ſich** they are mistaken.

*Imperfect.*

ich irrte mich I was mistaken
du irrteſt dich thou wast mistaken
er irrte ſich he was mistaken
ſie irrte ſich she was mistaken
es irrte ſich it was mistaken

---

\*) Lit.: I mistake myself.

wir irrten uns  we were mistaken
ihr irrtet euch ⎱
Sie irrten sich ⎰ you were mistaken
sie irrten sich  they were mistaken.

### Perfect.

ich habe mich ge=irrt*) I have been mistaken
du haft dich geirrt            etc.
er hat sich geirrt.

### Pluperfect.

ich hatte mich geirrt  I had been mistaken
du hatteft dich geirrt           etc.
er hatte sich geirrt.

## Imperative.

(Of the Verb: **sich gewöhnen** to accustom one's self.)

gewöhne **dich** accustom thyself!
gewöhnet **Euch** accustom yourselves!
gewöhnen wir **uns** let us accustom ourselves!
gewöhnen Sie **sich** accustom yourself (-selves)!

**Such are:**

sich befinden (*irr. v.*) to be in
  health, to *do*.
sich freuen  to rejoice.
sich erkälten  to catch cold.
sich beklagen  to complain.
sich beschäftigen  to occupy,
  busy one's self.
sich bemühen  to endeavor.
sich waschen (*irr. v.*)  to wash
  one's self.

sich erinnern  to remember.
sich betragen (*irr. v.*) to behave.
sich entschließen (*irr. v.*) to resolve.
sich schämen  to be ashamed.
sich setzen  to sit down.
sich unterhalten (*irr. v.*) to
  amuse one's self.
sich verirren  to stray.

---

*) I have mistaken myself.

## Words.

| | |
|---|---|
| die Hitze the heat. | möglich possible. |
| vorbei past; so thus, so. | der Christ the Christian. |
| die Ordnung the order. | der Handel commerce, trade |
| der Gebrauch the use. | sich bereichern to enrich one's |
| aufstehen to get up. | self. |
| sich rühmen to boast. | Dinge things. |
| der Wald the forest. | sich rächen (an) to avenge |
| das Gesicht the face. | one's self on. |
| gelehrt learned. | verwunden to wound. |

Wie befinden Sie sich? how do you do?

## Exercise 106.

1) 1. Sie glauben, daß (that) ich Ihr Freund bin? 2. Sie irren sich, mein Herr, ich bin es nicht. 3. Ich sehe, daß ich mich geirrt habe. 4. Karl [Carl] irrt sich, wenn er glaubt, daß die Hitze vorbei ist. 5. Die jungen Leute irren sich oft. 6. Als (when) wir jung waren, haben wir uns auch oft geirrt. 7. Befinden Sie sich wohl? 8. Nein, ich befinde mich nicht wohl. 9. Wie befindet sich Ihre Mutter? 10. Ich danke Ihnen, sie befindet sich wohl.

2) 11. Haben Sie sich erkältet? 12. Ja, ich habe mich ein wenig erkältet. 13. Hier ist frisches Wasser, waschen Sie sich! 14. Wir haben uns schon gewaschen. 15. Gewöhne dich, Ordnung in allen Dingen zu haben! 16. Gewöhnen Sie sich früh aufzustehen! 17. Ich habe mich gestern im Walde verirrt. 18. Ich würde mich schämen, so träge zu sein. 19. Schämen Sie sich, sich so zu betragen! 20. Ich werde mich bemühen, meine Aufgaben so gut als möglich zu machen.

## Exercise 107.

1) 1. I *am* often *mistaken*. 2. Thou *art* never mistaken. 3. John was mistaken yesterday. 4. He boasts to be learned. 5. We rejoice at it. 6. At (über) what

do you rejoice? 7. Of (über) what do you complain? 8. I complain of the heat. 9. With what do you occupy (*or* busy) yourself? 10. I occupy myself with the German language. 11. Is your professor still (noch) ill? 12. No, Sir, he is no longer (more) ill, he *is* now *in good health* (he finds himself well). 13. What ailed him (had he)? 14. He had caught cold. 15. Why will you avenge yourself? 16. A good Christian shall not avenge himself on his enemy.

2) 17. The English have enriched themselves by (the) trade. 18. Demosthenes has killed himself. 19. Accustom yourselves to make a good use of your time! 20. I rejoice to see my mother. 21. You are mistaken, if you think that (daß) I 'am 'ill; on the contrary (im Gegenteil [Gegentheil]) I am quite well. 22. And how do you do? 23. I thank you (*dat.*), I am not well; I have caught cold. 24. Has Charles washed his (himself the) face? 25. No, he has washed his hands (transl. himself the hands). 26. Lewis has wounded himself with his knife.

## Conversation.

| | |
|---|---|
| Wie befinden Sie sich, mein Herr? | Ich danke Ihnen, ich befinde mich recht wohl. |
| Wie befindet sich Ihre Tante? | Sie befindet sich nicht wohl. |
| Was fehlt ihr (what ails her)? | Sie hat sich ein wenig erkältet. |
| Haben Sie Ihr Haus verkauft? | Sie irren sich, ich werde es nicht verkaufen. |
| Womit beschäftigen Sie sich? | Ich lese deutsche Bücher. |
| Wie haben sich die Knaben betragen? | Sie haben sich sehr gut betragen. |
| Worüber beklagen Sie sich? | Wir beklagen uns über das schlechte Wetter. |

## READING LESSON.

### Die Erfindung des Glases.

Discovery of Glass.

Einst (one day) landeten die Phönizier [Phöni=
cier] (Phenicians) an der Nordküste[1]) Afrikas, wo
der Fluß Belus sich in das Meer ergießt[2]). Eine
weite Sandfläche[3]) lag vor ihren Augen. Sie suchten
Steine, um ihre Kessel und Pfannen[4]) über denselben
aufzustellen[5]); aber da fanden sie keine. Dann holten[6])
sie aus ihren Schiffen Salpetersteine[7]), die sie als
Ladung (load) mit sich führten, machten ein Feuer
an, kochten ihre Lebensmittel[8]), und aßen ihr einfaches[9])
Mahl[10]).

Als sie die Salpetersteine zurücktragen wollten, waren
sie von der Gewalt[11]) des Feuers geschmolzen und
hatten sich mit der Asche und dem glühenden[12]) Sande ver=
mischt[13]), und als die flüssige (liquid) Masse kalt geworden
war, lag eine helle, durchsichtige[14]) Masse auf der Erde —
das war Glas. — So wurden die Phönizier die Erfinder
des Glases.

1) northern coast. 2) empties itself. 3) a vast plain
of sand. 4) kettles and pans. 5) to put. 6) fetched.
7) saltpeter-stones. 8) provisions. 9) plain. 10) meal.
11) power, heat. 12) glowing. 13) mixed. 14) trans-
parent.

# LESSON LIII.

## Adverbs.

1) Adverbs are words used to modify verbs, adjectives or other adverbs. They are not variable, except that those of manner, quality and time, are partly subject to degrees of comparison.

2) Most *adjectives* are also used as *qualifying adverbs* without changing their form; not only in the positive but also in the comparative and superlative degrees. Ex.:

Dieſer Brief iſt ſ ch l e ch t geſchrieben.
This letter is *badly* written.

Der Diener wurde r e i ch belohnt.
The servant was *richly* awarded.

Ich lerne l e i ch t e r Deutſch als Franzöſiſch.
I learn German *more easily* than French.

### 1. Adverbs of Place.

wo?   ⎫
†wohin? *) ⎬ where?
†woher'? whence?
hier here.
†hierher here, hither.
da, dort there.
†dahin, †dorthin thither.
darin therein.
außen (draußen) ⎫ outside,
auswendig   ⎬ without.
innen (drinnen) ⎫ within, in-
inwendig   ⎬ side.
oben, droben above, upstairs.

hinten, dahinten behind.
unten, drunten below, down-
  stairs.
‡rechts *) to the right.
‡links to the left.
irgendwo somewhere.
anderswo elsewhere.
nirgends (— wo) nowhere.
überall everywhere.
weit far.
‡beiſammen together.
†nach Hauſe home.
zu Hauſe at home.

---

*) Adverbs under 1. marked with † are used with verbs of *motion;* those with ‡ both for *rest* and *motion;* the others not marked are generally used with verbs denoting *rest.*

## 2. Adverbs of Time.

wann? when?

jetzt, nun now.

jemals or je ever.

niemals or nie never.

meistens mostly.

sonst, ehemals formerly.

früher, eher sooner.

nach'her afterwards.

spät late; später later.

einst, einmal once, one day.

neulich the other day.

manchmal ⎰
zuweilen ⎱ sometimes.

oft, oftmals often.

bald soon.

gleich directly.

früh early; früher earlier.

das erste Mal the first time.

zuerst at first.

zuletzt at last.

endlich at length.

dann, damals then.

immer always.

schon, bereits already.

noch still, yet.

noch nicht not yet.

heute to-day.

gestern yesterday.

vorgestern the day before yesterday.

morgen to-morrow.

morgen früh to-morrow morning.

übermorgen the day after to-morrow.

lange, lange Zeit long.

jährlich yearly.

monatlich monthly.

täglich daily.

### Words.

langsam slowly.

schnell quick.

die Küche the kitchen.

der Speicher the garret.

der Kutscher the coachman.

(aus)zanken to scold.

spazieren gehen to take a walk.

die Regel the rule.

hübsch pretty.

die Arznei the medicine.

das Beispiel (*plur.* -e) the example.

lehren to teach, instruct.

kurz short.

besser better.

der Weg the road.

### Exercise 108.

1) 1. Sie gehen zu langsam; gehen Sie schneller! 2. Das Mädchen schreibt nicht schön; der Knabe schreibt besser. 3. Woher kommen Sie? 4. Ich komme von Baden. 5. Der

Herr, welchen Sie suchen, wohnt nicht hier, er wohnt weit von hier. 6. Gehen Sie nicht dahin (or dorthin); kommen Sie hierher! 7. Die Küche ist unten; der Speicher ist oben. 8. Ich saß draußen bei dem Kutscher; die Damen saßen drinnen im Omnibus. 9. Ich habe Sie überall gesucht.

2) 10. Man sieht diese Mädchen immer beisammen. 11. Mein Platz ist rechts, der Ihrige links. 12. Der Herr Professor ist nicht zu Hause, suchen Sie ihn anderswo! 13. Ist Ihr Bruder unten (drunten)? 14. Nein, er ist oben. 15. Ich finde meinen Stock nirgends; ich habe überall gesucht. 16. Gehen Sie jetzt nach Hause; es ist schon spät; Ihr Vater wird Sie auszanken. 17. Ich war neulich mit einigen Freunden im Theater. 18. Der Kranke muß täglich drei Löffelvoll [Löffel voll] (full) Arznei nehmen.

## Exercise 109.

1) 1. The ass goes slowly. 2. (The) time passes away (verfließt) quickly. 3. My sons learn 'German 'easily. 4. Your letter is very badly written. 5. (The) examples teach more easily than (the) rules. 6. Where is my stick? 7. There 'it 'is. 8. Did you seek it? 9. Yes, I have sought it everywhere. 10. Where do you live now? 11. I live here. 12. This house is very pretty outside, but inside 'it 'is not so pretty. 13. Is your father upstairs? 14. No, Sir, he is downstairs.

2) 15. The ox goes more slowly than the horse. 16. Do you go into the garden (acc.)? 17. No, I stay here. 18. Must I go to the right or to the left? 19. Go to the right; that road is shorter. 20. The traveller *has* arrived very late. 21. We 'often 'take a walk. 22. Come directly! 23. My friend Frederick wrote me *the other day* a long letter. 24. My cousin has (is) at length

departed. 25. Formerly my neighbor was rich, now
'he 'is poor. 26. This is the first time that I am in
Paris.

---

# LESSON LIV.

### 3. Adverbs of Quantity and Comparison.

wie? how?

wieviel [wie viel]? wie ſehr?
  how much?

viel much.

mehr more.

ſehr, recht very.

zu ſehr, zu viel too much.

nichts nothing.

etwas something, anything.

wenig little; ein wenig a little.

zu wenig too little.

genug enough.

kaum scarcely.

ungefähr about.

beinahe, faſt nearly, almost.

nur, allein only.

höchſtens at the highest.

wenigſtens at least.

ſo, ebenſo so, as.

ganz quite.

beſonders especially.

einmal once.

zweimal twice.

dreimal three times.

### 4. Adverbs of Affirmation, Doubt and Negation.

ja, ja doch, doch! yes, oh yes!

jawohl oh! yes.

gewiß to be sure.

wirklich really.

wahrſcheinlich       } prob-
vermutlich [vermuthlich] } ably.

vielleicht perhaps.

ohne Zweifel no doubt.

umſonſt, vergeblich in vain.

gern(e) willingly.

nein no.

nicht not.

gar nicht not at all.

nicht einmal not even.

niemals never.

nicht mehr no more.

### 5. Adverbs of Interrogation.

wann (wenn)? when?

warum? why?

weswegen? wherefore?

wie? how?

wieviel [wie viel]? how much?

wie viele? how many?

wie weit? how far?

wie lange? how long?

*Irregular Comparison.*

The following adverbs are irregular in the degrees of comparison:

viel much    mehr more    am meiſten (der meiſte) most.
gut, wohl well    beſſer better    am beſten best.
gern willingly    lieber (rather)    am liebſten (I like) best.
bald soon    eher, früher sooner    am eheſten (the) soonest.

## Words.

koſten to cost; davon of it.
der Frank the franc.
der Meter the metre.
begegnen to meet.
die Zeitung the newspaper.
im Gegenteil [Gegentheil] on
   the contrary.

geſchlafen slept.
danken to thank.
die Seite the page.
ausgeben to spend.
die Wegſtunde one hour's
   walk.
der Bahnhof the station.

## Exercise 110.

1. Wie haben Sie geſchlafen? 2. Ich habe ſehr wohl ge-
ſchlafen, ich danke Ihnen. 3. Wieviel [Wie viel] Geld haben
Sie? 4. Ich habe nicht viel; ich habe nur wenig.
5. Ich will keine Butter; ich will Käſe. 6. Haben Sie
Geld in Ihrem Beutel? 7. Nein, ich habe kein Geld in
meinem Beutel; ich habe alles ausgegeben. 8. Wie viele
Brüder haben Sie? 9. Ich habe nur zwei Brüder, aber vier
Schweſtern. 10. Iſt es weit von hier nach Frankfurt? 11.
Es iſt ungefähr ſechzig Kilometer. 12. Wieviel bezahlen Sie
jährlich für Ihr Zimmer? 13. Ich bezahle monatlich vierzig
Mark. 14. Gehen Sie rechts oder links? 15. Ich gehe rechts.
16. Ich war dieſen Morgen auf dem Bahnhof. 17. Mein Hut
iſt ganz neu. 18. Mein Freund hat mir nicht einmal geantwortet; er iſt warſcheinlich nicht mehr in Frankfurt.

## Exercise 111.

1. How do you like (find) this wine? 2. I find it
very good. 3. How much does it cost? 4. One franc
a (the) bottle. 5. This is not too much. 6. The child
was nearly dead. 7. You eat too little. 8. I have eaten
enough. 9. Will you have more of it (baoon)? 10. No,
thank you, I have enough. 11. I want about twenty
metres. 12. Have you eaten all? 13. On the contrary,
I have eaten nothing. 14. Where is Charles? 15. He
is perhaps in the garden. 16. He was there also this
morning. 17. I have sought [for] him in vain; I could
not find him. 18. You do not get up early. 19. Get up
earlier. 20. I (have) met him at least three times.
21. Go directly to your aunt'[s] and bring her the newspaper. 22. I have never seen that (this) man. 23. He
is probably a stranger.

### Conversation.

| | |
|---|---|
| Wie ſchreibt Wilhelm? | Er ſchreibt ſehr ſchön. |
| Wer geht langſam (slowly)? | Der Eſel geht langſam. |
| Wann kommen Sie zurück? | Ich werde bald zurückkommen. |
| Iſt Ihre Schweſter zu Hauſe? | Nein, ſie iſt ausgegangen. |
| Woher kommen Sie? | Ich komme aus dem Konzert [Concert]. |
| Wollen Sie auf mich warten? | Ein wenig, aber nicht lange. |
| Wie gefällt Ihnen das Haus des Herrn Buſch? | Es iſt inwendig ſehr ſchön, aber auswendig iſt es häßlich (ugly). |
| Wie viele Wörter ſoll ich lernen? | Lerne wenigſtens eine halbe Seite! |
| Wohnen Sie noch in Ihrem eigenen (own) Haus? | Nein, ich habe es vor ungefähr vier Monaten verkauft? |
| Eſſen Sie gern (do you like) Kirſchen? | Ja, ich eſſe ſie ſehr gern (I like them very much). |

# LESSON LV.

## Prepositions.

Prepositions are particles which serve to show the relation which exists between two words in a clause. This relation being of different kinds, the prepositions destined to indicate it, govern different cases; namely the *accusative, dative* or *genitive* case.

### 1. Prepositions with the Accusative Case.

| | |
|---|---|
| burch through, by. | ohne without, but for. |
| für for. | um about, round, at. |
| gegen towards, against, to. | wider against. |

#### Examples.

burch den Garten through the garden.
für Ihre Schwester for your sister.
gegen die Thüre against the door.
gegen den Fluß towards the river.
ohne einen Freund without a friend.
um die Stadt herum round about the town.
um den Tisch round the table.

### 2. Prepositions with the Dative Case.

| | |
|---|---|
| aus out of, from. | seit since, for. |
| außer except, besides. | von from, of, by. |
| bei near, with, by, at. | zu to, at. |
| mit with. | bis zu as far as, up to. |
| nach after, to, according to. | von — an from, since. |
| gegenüber opposite. | |

### Examples.

aus dem Garten  from the garden.
bei meinem Onkel  at my uncle's.
bei unsrer Ankunft  on our arrival.
nach dem Regen  after the rain.
seit jenem Tag  since that day.
ich gehe zu meinem Lehrer  I go to my teacher's.
der Kirche gegenüber  opposite the church.

### Words.

der Apotheker  the apothecary.
die Kindheit  the childhood.
der Wald  the forest.
die Sonne  the sun.
der Mond  the moon.
stoßen  to thrust, push.

die Erlaubnis [Erlaubniß]  permission.
die Eisenbahn  the railroad.
der Spiegel  the looking-glass.
der Spaziergang  the walk.
die Studien  the studies.
endigen  to finish.

### Exercise 112.

1) 1. Ich ging durch den Hof.  2. Wer hat einen Stein durch das Fenster geworfen?  3. Ich wollte ihn in den Garten werfen.  4. Seien Sie höflich gegen jedermann [Jedermann]!  5. Wir gingen um die Stadt (herum).  6. Ohne Freund ist man nicht glücklich.  7. Ludwig ist wider (or gegen) den Willen seines Vaters nach Berlin gegangen. 8. Wir wollen der Eisenbahn entlang (along) spazieren gehen.

2) 9. Woher kommen Sie?  10. Ich komme aus der Kirche.  11. Wohin gehen Sie jetzt?  12. Ich gehe nach Hause.  13. Bei wem wohnt Ihr Lehrer?  14. Er wohnt bei dem Apotheker, der Post gegenüber.  15. Seit wann sind Sie hier?  16. Ich bin seit drei Tagen hier.  17. Nach dem Regen scheint (shines) die Sonne.  18. Wir werden nach dem Mittagessen spielen.  19. Nach dem Abend kommt der Morgen. 20. Dieser arme Knabe ist von seiner Kindheit an blind.

1) 1. We went through the forest. 2. For whom are these books? 3. They are for my father. 4. Who has pushed against the door? 5. I do not know. 6. One cannot travel without money. 7. The earth turns (breht fid)) round the sun, and the moon turns round the earth. 8. Caroline has (is) gone out without my permission. 9. The young ladies (girls) have taken a walk along (entlang) the railroad. 10. Some one has thrown a stone through the window against the looking-glass.

2) 11. Do you come from the garden? 12. No, we come from a walk. 13. Go out of the room. 14. I have seen nobody besides your brother. 15. Mrs. Richard dined (fpeifte) yesterday at our house (bei uns). 16. When will you have finished your studies? 17. I shall have finished them in a year. 18. The post-office is opposite the station. 19. Shall we play after (the) breakfast? 20. No, we shall play after the lesson. 21. Mr. Bush has known me for a long time (knows me since long).

### 3. Prepositions with the Genitive Case.

anftatt or ftatt  instead of.
außerhalb  without, outside.
innerhalb  within *(place)*.
oberhalb  above *(higher up)*.
unterhalb  below  *(lower down)*.
dießfeits  on this side of.
jenfeits  on the other side of.
längs  along.
trotz *)  in spite of.
vermittelft (mittelft)  by means of.
während *)  during.
wegen  on account of.

---

*) Trotz and während are sometimes used with the dative case, as: während dem Regen for während des Regens.

### Examples.

anſtatt eines Briefes  instead of a letter.

außerhalb des Landes  without (out of) the country.

diesſeits des Fluſſes  on this side of the river.

jenſeits des Meeres  beyond the sea.

innerhalb der Stadt  within the town.

oberhalb des Dorfes  above the village.

unterhalb der Brücke  below the bridge, etc.


## 4.   Prepositions with both the Dative and the Accusative Cases.

| | | |
|---|---|---|
| an at, on. | in in, at, into. | über over. |
| auf on, upon. | neben near. | unter under, among. |
| hinter behind. | zwiſchen between. | vor before, ago. |

These nine prepositions govern sometimes the *dative*, sometimes the *accusative*. The *dative* is required, when the ruling verb signifies a *state of repose*, or sometimes an action within a place — the *accusative*, when it denotes a *motion from one place to another* or *direction towards a place*. This distinction may be rendered more evident by applying either the questions *at, in what place?* or *whither, to, into what place?* (See page 48, 4).   Ex.:

Das Buch liegt (lies) auf dem Tiſch *(dat.)*.

Die Kinder ſpielen im Garten.

But: Put the book upon the table! is translated:

Legen Sie das Buch auf den Tiſch *(acc.)!*

The question is here: *whereto, whither* or *to what place?*

## Examples.

Ich gehe in den Garten  I go into the garden.

Ich stehe an dem Fenster *(dat.)*.
I am standing at the window.

Der Hund liegt auf dem Boden (lies on the floor).

Die Fische leben in dem (im) Wasser.
(The) fish live *in* the water.

Mein Hut ist in das (ins [in's]) Wasser gefallen.
My hat fell *into* the water.

Der Hund liegt (or spielt) unter dem Tisch.
The dog lies (*or* plays) under the table.

Werfen Sie das Papier unter den Tisch!
Throw the paper under the table!

## Words.

der Zugvogel  the bird of passage.

der Pfau  the peacock.

die Köchin  the *(fem.)* cook.

die Kartoffeln  the potatoes.

die Kälte  the cold.

verlassen  to leave.

die Krankheit  the illness.

die Brücke  the bridge.

verbergen  to hide.

die Kapelle [Capelle]  the chapel.

die Kanone  the cannon, gun.

der Nachschlüssel  the master-key.

öffnen.  to open.

der Frühling  the spring.

die Schublade  the drawer.

die Mauer  the wall.

## Exercise 114.

1) 1. Die Mädchen sind diesseits des Flusses spazieren gegangen; sie sind nicht vor sechs Uhr nach Hause gekommen. 2. Wegen der großen Kälte konnte ich das Zimmer nicht verlassen. 3. Amerika liegt jenseits des atlantischen Meeres. 4. Die Post ist trotz des tiefen Schnees rechtzeitig (in time) angekommen. 5. Wir wohnen oberhalb der Brücke. 6. Der Garten liegt außerhalb des Dorfes.

2) 7. Der Vogel sitzt auf dem Baume.　8. Der Diener stand an der Thüre.　9. Im Winter ist es kalt.　10. Die Zugvögel verlassen uns im Herbst (autumn) und kehren im Frühling zu uns zurück.　11. Meine Eltern wohnen auf dem Lande.　12. Der Pfau ist der schönste unter den Vögeln. 13. Der Dieb lief in das Haus und suchte sich zu verbergen. 14. Die Köchin hat Kartoffeln gekocht anstatt gelber Rüben (carrots).　15. Während der Krankheit der Mutter konnte die Tochter nicht in die Schule gehen.

### Exercise 115.

1. Give me a pen instead of this pencil!　2. Eliza has taken an umbrella instead of a parasol.　3. The chapel stands (is) outside the town.　4. The guns were inside the walls.　5. The boat is below the bridge.　6. During (the) winter it is cold.　7. I do not go out during the rain.　8. My mother did not go out on account of the cold.　9. The thief opened the door by means of a false key.　10. Mr. Barry lives on the other side of the river.　11. Where is Henry?　12. He is at (in) (the) school.　13. I do not go to (in die) school to-day.　14. Put the inkstand upon the table and the pencils into the drawer.

### *Recapitulation.*

#### Words.

der Stock, das Stockwerk  the story.

stellen  to put, place.

der Keller  the cellar.

zeichnen  to draw.

das Muster  the pattern, model.

der Schrank  the press, wardrobe.

begleiten  to accompany.

die Alpen  the Alps.

gelegen  situated.

liegen  to lie.

klopfen  to knock.

der Bäcker  the baker.

die Kindheit  the childhood.

springen  to jump.

die Seide  the silk.

die Baumwolle  the cotton.

## Exercise 116.

1. An der Hand. 2. Im zweiten Stock. 3. Nach dem Frühstück. 4. Ich war im Garten während des Regens. 5. Stoßen Sie nicht gegen den Tisch! 6. Stellen Sie sich hinter die Thüre. 7. Man kann nicht reisen ohne Geld. 8. Unter dem Hause befindet sich der Keller. 9. Zeichnen Sie dies nach dem Muster? 10. Wir wohnen bei einem Bäcker. 11. Ich habe meinen Freund Alfred seit drei Jahren nicht gesehen. 12. Man hat mich bis an das Thor (die Thüre) begleitet. 13. Die Schüler sind mit ihrem Professor längs des Flusses spazieren gegangen. 14. Ich bleibe zu Hause wegen des Regens. 15. Die Kapelle [Capelle] liegt (ist gelegen) ober= halb des Schlosses. 16. Die Katze sprang über den Tisch.

## Exercise 117.

1. I live outside the town. 2. Instead of a good horse. 3. On the other side of the Alps. 4. At the window. 5. On the first floor. 6. After the lesson. 7. The children played after (the) breakfast. 8. The man knocked at the window. 9. My aunt lives at (bei) a baker's. 10. The little girl is blind since her child-hood. 11. Put yourself behind the press. 12. The dog jumped over the bed. 13. I have accompanied my cousin as far as (bis an, *acc.*) the station. 14. My sister has bought silk instead of cotton. 15. We have walked along the railroad. 16. The castle is situated (liegt) above the town. 17. Here is a wall round the garden. 18. I have remained in (the) bed on account of the bad weather. 19. The dog will jump over the wall.

### Conversation.

Wo liegt (ist) mein Buch?  Es liegt auf Ihrem Tisch.
Wo saß der Vogel?  Er saß auf dem Baum.
Wann gehen Sie nach London?  In einigen Tagen.

| | |
|---|---|
| Wer steht an dem Fenster? | Es ist ein junges Mädchen. |
| Was hat die Köchin gekocht? | Gelbe Rüben statt Kartoffeln. |
| Wohin geht die Köchin? | Sie geht in den Garten. |
| Wo lebt Ihre Tante? | Sie lebt im Sommer auf (in) dem Lande, im Winter in der Stadt. |
| Wohin geht die Gräfin? | Sie geht in die Kirche. |

# LESSON LVI.

## Conjunctions.

Conjunctions are particles, which serve to connect words with words, sentences with sentences, and clauses with clauses, in order to bring them into a certain relation with one another. This relation can be very different; it may express either a mere connection, or an opposition, a condition, comparison, cause, relation of time, just as in English.

They have a great influence upon the *position of the verb;* we therefore divide them into three classes.

### FIRST CLASS.

### Co-ordinating Conjunctions.

With these the place of the verb is not changed:

| | | | |
|---|---|---|---|
| und | and. | aber or allein | but. |
| oder | or. | sondern | but (after the negation not). |
| denn | for. | | |

### Examples.

Ich werde nicht ausgehen; denn ich bin krank.
I shall not go out. for I am ill.

Er wollte arbeiten; aber (or allein) er konnte nicht.
He wished to work, but he could not.

Ich habe einen Schlüssel, aber er öffnet die Thüre nicht.
I have a key, but it does not open the door.

Ich war nicht in London, sondern in Paris.
I was not in London, but in Paris.

### SECOND CLASS.

## Adverbial Conjunctions.

| | |
|---|---|
| also therefore. | indessen meanwhile. |
| auch also. | kaum scarcely. |
| außerdem besides. | folglich consequently. |
| bald — bald now — now or then. | nicht nur } sondern { not only, nicht allein } auch { but also. |
| da, dann then. | nichtsdestoweniger nevertheless. |
| daher, deswegen there-fore. | nun, jetzt now. |
| dennoch still, yet. | so thus, so. |
| entweder — (oder) either — (or). | sonst otherwise or else. |
| | weder — noch neither — nor. |
| | zwar indeed. |

Like all other *adverbial expressions*, the *adverbial* **Conjunctions** require the inversion, viz., the *subject* is placed after the *verb*, when these conjunctions begin the sentence or clause.

Mein Vetter ist krank, also (or deswegen, daher, folglich) kann er nicht kommen.
My cousin is ill, therefore he cannot come.

Kaum hatte der Lehrer dies gesehen . . .
Scarcely had the teacher seen this . . .

Nehmen Sie einen Regenschirm, sonst werden Sie naß werden.
Take an umbrella, else you will become wet.

Gehen Sie nach Hause, sonst werden Sie gezankt werden.
Go home, else you will be scolded.

**Words.**

abſchreiben  to copy.
der Beſuch  the visit.
deutlich  distinctly.
die Stimme  the voice.
die Arbeit  the work.
der Räuber  the robber.
verbinden  to bind up.
ſchwach feeble; reinlich clean.

der Schreiner  the joiner.
die Rechnung  the account, bill.
leidend  suffering, poorly.
die Pflanze  the plant.
übergeben  to hand (over).
dunkel  dark.
dann then; naß wet.

**Exercise 118.**

1) 1. Der Vater ſchreibt die Briefe, und der Sohn ſchreibt ſie ab.  2. Kommen Sie um vier Uhr oder um fünf Uhr?  3. Ich kann nicht mit Ihnen gehen; denn ich erwarte einen Beſuch.  4. Die Knaben haben die Lektion [Lection] gelernt; aber ſie haben die Aufgabe nicht geſchrieben.  5. Wir konnten den Mann ſehen; aber wir hörten ſeine Stimme nicht deutlich.  6. Die Mutter hat dich nicht gerufen, ſondern deine Schweſter.

2) 7. Das Pferd iſt zu ſchwach für dieſe Arbeit; außer= dem iſt es einäugig (one-eyed).  8. Bald lieſt er ein engliſches Buch, bald ein franzöſiſches.  9. Der Räuber verband mir zuerſt die Augen; dann führte er mich in den Wald.  10. Sie ſind nicht reinlich gekleidet; deswegen können Sie nicht mit uns gehen.  11. Die Arbeit des Schreiners war ſehr ſchlecht; dennoch bezahlte ich ihm ſeine Rechnung.  12. Mein Nachbar iſt zwar leidend; deſſenungeachtet (or nichtsdeſtoweniger) muß er den ganzen Tag arbeiten.  13. Ich habe weder Ihre Feder, noch Ihren Bleiſtift genommen.

**Exercise 119.**

1) 1. You and I.  2. The brother or the sister.  3. You must take a parasol or rather (lieber) an um- brella.  4. I cannot tell you the name of this plant;

for I do not know it. 5. They (one) could not hand (deliver) you the letter; for you were not at home. 6. Miss Emily, have you learnt your lesson? 7. Yes, Sir, I have learnt it, but I have not written the exercise. 8. My uncle was not in Berlin, but (fonbern) in Vienna.

2) 9. This room is not large enough for me; besides it is too dark. 10. The count is sometimes in Paris, sometimes in Rome. 11. Study German, then you can go to Germany. 12. I have not received my money; therefore I cannot pay my bills. 13. Our professor is somewhat (a little) unwell; nevertheless he gives four lessons every day. 14. Take an umbrella, else you will be wet. 15. He has deserved nothing; still I will give him the money.

### READING LESSON.

#### Der Pflaumenbaum.

##### The Plum-tree.

Der kleine Julius betrachtete[1]) mit gierigem[2]) Auge einen Pflaumenbaum, welcher mit reifen Früchten behangen war. Er hatte Lust[3]), einige davon zu pflücken[4]); aber sein Vater hatte es ihm verboten[5]). Er sagte zu sich: „Niemand ist hier, der mich sehen könnte; weder mein Vater, noch der Gärtner ist da, und ich könnte wohl einige von diesen Pflaumen pflücken, ohne daß man es bemerkte; aber ich will gehorsam sein; ich will meine Naschhaftigkeit[6]) nicht befriedigen[7]), sonst würde ich das Verbot übertreten[8]), das man mir gegeben hat." Und Julius wollte[9]) fortgehen.

1) to look at. 2) greedy. 3) a mind. 4) to pluck. 5) forbidden. 6) greediness. 7) to satisfy. 8) to infringe upon the prohibition. 9) was about to.

Sein Vater, der ihm hinter einem Baume zugehört hatte, lief ihm entgegen[10]) und sagte zu ihm: „Komm, mein lieber Julius, komm, mein Kind, jetzt wollen wir Pflaumen pflücken!" Der Vater schüttelte[11]) den Baum, und Julius durfte die Pflaumen auflesen[12]) und essen.

10) to meet him.  11) to shake.  12) pick up.

---

# LESSON LVII.

### THIRD CLASS.

## Subordinating Conjunctions.

1) All *subordinating* conjunctions, simple as well as compound, cause the verb to be put to the end of the clause (with a comma, semicolon or full stop after it); if the verb is in a compound tense, the auxiliary stands last.

a) *Simple Subordinating Conjunctions.*

als  when, as.
bevor, ehe  before.
bis  till, until.
da  as, since.
daß  that.
damit'  in order that.
falls (im Fall)  in case.
indem'  as.
nachdem'  after.
ob  if, whether.

obgleich' }
obschon' }  though, although.
seit or seitdem  since.
sobald (als)  as soon as.
so oft (als)  as often as.
so lange (als)  as long as.
während  while, whilst.
wann  when.
wenn  if, when.
weil  because.

### Examples.

Es war gerade zwei Uhr, **als** ich den Brief **erhielt.**
It was just two o'clock, when I received the letter.

Warten Sie, **bis** ich meine Aufgabe geschrieben **habe!**
Wait till I have written my exercise!

**Obgleich** ich diese Dame nicht **kenne.**
Though I do not know this lady.

Ich gehe nicht aus, **weil** ich krank **bin.**
I do not go out, because I am ill.

Es regnete oft, **während** ich in Deutschland **war.**
It often rained, while I was in Germany.

Wissen Sie, **ob** *) Herr Müller angekommen **ist?**
Do you know *if* Mr. Miller has arrived?

Ich weiß nicht, **ob** *) er ihm geantwortet **hat.**
I do not know if he has answered him.

### *Important Rules.*

1) If the verb thus placed at the end of the subordinate clause, is a *separable* one, the *separation* does not take place.   (See Lesson XLIX.)

### Examples.

Es war vier Uhr, **als** die Sonne **aufging.**
It was four o'clock, when the sun rose.

Ich war krank, **als** ich in Berlin **ankam.**
I was sick when I arrived at (in) Berlin.

2) When the subordinate or dependent clause or clauses of the sentence lead with one of the afore-named subordinating conjunctions, then the principal clause **begins with the verb**, and the subject follows it.

---

*) *If* is translated **ob,** when it means **whether.**

### Examples.

Als ich nach Hause kam, **fand ich** Ihren Brief.
When I came home, I found your letter.

Indem sie in das Zimmer eintrat, **weinte sie** (not sie weinte).
On entering the room she cried.

Nachdem wir gefrühstückt hatten, **gingen wir** (not wir gingen)
    in die Schule.
After having breakfasted, we went to school.

Wenn es regnet, **geht man** nicht spazieren.
When it rains, people do not take a walk.

Wenn ich heute einen Brief erhalte, **reise ich** morgen ab.
If I receive a letter to-day, I shall set out to-morrow.

### Words.

| | |
|---|---|
| laut aloud. | der Gefangene the prisoner. |
| verstehen to understand. | endigen to finish, to end. |
| belagern to besiege. | aufhören to cease, stop. |
| mildthätig charitable. | nehmen to take. |
| begegnen to meet. | das Examen the examination. |
| fast almost. | die Stelle the place. |
| speisen to dine. | verfehlen to miss. |
| der Krieg the war. | der Zug the train. |
| hoffen to hope. | öffnen to open. |
| wecken to wake. | borgen to borrow. |

### Exercise 120.

1) 1. Ich schlief noch, als mein Bedienter ins [in's]
Zimmer trat. 2. Machen Sie Ihre Aufgabe, ehe (or
bevor) Sie ausgehen! 3. Da der Schüler sehr fleißig war,
[so] wurde er gelobt. 4. Glauben Sie, daß der Lehrer
kommen wird? 5. Es scheint, daß er nicht kommen

wird. 6. Sprechen Sie lauter, damit man Sie beffer verstehe. 7. Nachdem ich mein Geld erhalten hatte, bezahlte ich meine Rechnungen. 8. Ich weiß nicht, ob diejes Haus bewohnt ist oder nicht. 9. Die Soldaten belagerten die Stadt, bis sie sich ergab (surrendered).

2) 10. Sobald (als) ich den Brief empfangen hatte, reiste ich ab. 11. Obgleich er nicht reich ist, ist er doch sehr mildthätig. 12. Luise [Louise] kann nicht ausgehen, weil sie krank ist. 13. Wenn Sie morgen ins [in's] Theater gehen, werde ich mit Ihnen gehen. 14. So oft ich ausgehe, begegne ich diesem Menschen. 15. Wenn ich mehr Geld hätte, würde ich ein Pferd kaufen. 16. Während ich auf dem Lande war, regnete es fast jeden Tag. 17. Da das Pferd zu alt ist, werde ich es nicht kaufen.

### Exercise 121.

1) 1. I had not yet breakfasted, when (als) your friend came (kam) in my room. 2. I take a walk before I dine. 3. Speak lower (leiser), *in order that* you do not wake the child. 4. Wait till I have finished my letter; then I will go with you. 5. Ask him if he will sell his horse. 6. I am very well, since I am in (auf) the country. 7. I hope that the war will soon be ended.

2) 8. Since (as) you do not work, I shall give you nothing. 9. After the door was opened, the prisoners came out (kamen . . heraus). 10. Though it is not cold, I shall take my cloak. 11. As soon as I had passed (gemacht) my examination, I got (received) a good place. 12. If you do not leave (go) directly, you will miss the train. 13. When the rain has stopped, I shall go out. 14. Although he does not know me, he wishes to borrow money of me.

*Recapitulation.*

**Words.**

| | |
|---|---|
| zeichnen to draw. | reinlich clean(ly). |
| stricken to knit. | helfen to help. |
| artig good; gelehrt learned. | das Herz the heart. |
| anfangen to commence, begin. | studieren [studiren] to study. |
| der Honig the honey. | abwesend absent. |
| Luſt haben to have a mind. | ſtehlen to steal; allein alone. |
| verheiratet [verheirathet] married. | umſonſt in vain. |
| eine Muſikſtunde a music- | verdienen to earn. |
| lesson. | irgendwo somewhere. |

**Exercise 122.**

1) 1. Die Knaben zeichnen, und die Mädchen ſtricken. 2. Die Kinder müſſen artig ſein, ſonſt werden ſie geſtraft werden. 3. Ich habe den Mann geſehen, aber ich kenne ihn nicht. 4. Der arme Mann hat Hunger, und doch will er nichts eſſen. 5. Da es heute regnet, werde ich zu Hauſe bleiben. 6. Als ich in Paris ankam, war es ſchönes Wetter; aber bald fing es an zu ſchneien. 7. Da Sie krank ſind, können Sie nicht arbeiten. 8. Ich glaube, daß Sie den Thee nicht lieben, ſonſt würden Sie gewiß eine Taſſe davon trinken; denn er iſt ſehr gut. 9. Ich habe Luſt zu ſpielen, aber ich habe nicht (die) Zeit dazu; denn meine Aufgaben ſind noch nicht fertig. 10. Wenn man viel ſtudiert [ſtudirt], wird man ein gelehrter Mann werden.

2) 11. Nicht nur ſeine Mutter, ſondern auch ſeine Großmutter war hier. 12. Sobald als ich meine Aufgabe beendigt haben werde, werde ich mit euch ſpielen. 13. Seit= dem meine Brüder verheiratet [verheirathet] ſind, bin ich ganz allein. 14. Selbſt (even) wenn es ſchneien würde, würde ich ausgehen. 15. Ludwig kann ſeine Aufgabe nicht machen, ſolange [ſo lange] als Sie ihm nicht helfen. 16. Ich habe die Kirſchen weggenommen, ſonſt würden die Kinder

fie alle gegeſſen haben.　17. Ich glaube, daß ich dieſen Herrn irgendwo geſehen habe.　18. Falls (im Fall), daß Ihr Freund morgen hier ankommt, geben Sie ihm dieſen Brief!

### Exercise 123.

1. The mother writes the letters, and the daughter copies them. 2. Work, then play! 3. I think it will be fine to-morrow. 4. We expected him, but in vain. 5. The professor is contented with his pupils, when · they are diligent; but when they are idle, he is not contented with them. 6. Since you are here, I will give you a music-lesson. 7. This little boy would be very happy, if he had some good books. 8. Ask him if (ob) he has money enough. 9. Every body loves him, because he has a good heart. 10. A thief has stolen my watch, while I was absent. 11. As long as you are (will be) here, you will live with (bei) me. 12. I shall show you the letter, as soon as I have read it. 13. When one works, one earns money.

# LESSON LVIII.

## b) *Compound Subordinating Conjunctions.*

Compound conjunctions are those consisting of two separate words. These, too, cause the verb to be placed at the end of the clause.

als ob' ⎫
als wenn ⎬ as if (with the *Impf. Subj.*).
wie wenn ⎭
bis daß until.
im Fall daß in case that.
damit .. nicht lest.
je — deſto the — the.
ſo or wie .. auch however.

ohne daß without.
ſo daß so that.
wenn .. nicht unless.
ſelbſt wenn even if.
wenn .. gleich ⎫ although.
wenn .. auch ⎭
wenn .. nur provided.
um .. zu (with the *Inf.*) in order to.

### Examples.

Das Kind sieht aus, **als ob** or **als wenn** es krank wäre.
The child looks as if it were ill.

**Wenn** er **auch** alt ist though he is (*or* be) old.

**Wenn** er mich **nicht** bezahlt unless he pay me.

**Wenn** er **nur** die Erlaubnis [Erlaubniß] erhält.
Provided he obtains the permission.

**Wie** gelehrt **auch** dieser Professor sein mag.
However learned this professor may be.

Gehen Sie schnell, **damit** Sie **nicht** überrascht werden.
Go quick, lest you be surprised.

#### FOURTH CLASS.

## Relative Conjunctions.

All adverbs of interrogation have in *indirect interrogations* the value of *relative conjunctions;* therefore they require the verb at the end of the clause, and if the verb is in a compound tense, the auxiliary stands last.

Such are:

| | | |
|---|---|---|
| wann  when. | wie lange how long. | worin |
| warum  why. | wo  where. | wherein. |
| weswegen [weß=]  where- | woher  whence. | woran ꝛc. |
| weshalb [weß=]  fore. | wohin  whereto. | wobei. |
| wie  how. | wodurch  whereby. | wovon. |
| wieviel [wie viel] how much. | womit  with which. | worauf. |
| | | worunter. |

#### Examples.

Ich weiß, w a r u m er gestern nicht gekommen ist *).
Sagen Sie mir, w i e lange Sie in der Schule geblieben s i n d!
Ist dies das Buch, w o v o n Sie gestern gesprochen h a b e n?
Ich fragte ihn, w a n n ich ihn zu Hause finden w ü r d e.

---

*) The *direct* interrogation is: warum ist er gestern nicht gekommen?

## Words.

ausſehen  to look.
die Ferien  the vacation, holidays.
bemerken  to perceive.
ungeſchickt  awkward.
der Beiſtand  the assistance.
die Luft  the air.

leicht  light.
überſetzen  to translate.
der Satz  the sentence, clause.
die Schulden  the debts.
die Wahrheit  the truth.
übergeben  to deliver.

### Exercise 124.

1. Das Kleid ſieht aus, als wenn es nicht neu wäre. 2. Der Schüler wird nicht in die Ferien gehen, bis daß er ſein Examen gemacht hat. 3. Ich ging aus dem Zimmer, ohne daß er es bemerkte. 4. Dieſes junge Mädchen iſt ſehr ungeſchickt; es nimmt nie etwas in die Hand, ohne es zu zer= brechen. 5. Die Schüler können dieſe Aufgabe nicht machen, wenn Sie ihnen nicht helfen. 6. Je fleißiger die Knaben ſind, deſto mehr werden ſie lernen. 7. Es donnerte und blitzte, ſo daß ich nicht ausgehen konnte. 8. Sie können die Arbeit leicht beendigen, wenn Sie nur nicht ſpäter als um ein Uhr beginnen. 9. Ich gehe nach Deutſchland, um Deutſch ſprechen zu lernen. ' 10. Je wärmer die Luft iſt, deſto leichter iſt ſie.

### Exercise 125.

1. Charles looks as if he were suffering. 2. The dead child lay on his bed as if it slept. 3. In case (that) you want my assistance, call me! 4. However learned you are, you cannot translate this sentence. 5. However rich your uncle may be, he has no mind (keine Luft) to pay your debts. 6. It was night, so that I could see nothing. 7. Even if you should speak the truth, I would not believe you (Ihnen). 8. I travel to see the world. 9. I have called you in order to deliver you (Ihnen) this money.

### Conversation.

| | |
|---|---|
| Sind Sie gestern spazieren gegargen? | Ja, ich ging spazieren, obschon es geregnet hat. |
| Warum soll ich diese Aufgabe noch einmal schreiben? | Damit du sie besser lernest. |
| Wird der Fürst hier bleiben? | Ich zweifle, ob er hier bleibt. |
| Werden die Arbeiter (workmen) belohnt werden? | Ja, wenn sie fleißig sind. |
| Können die Schüler diese Arbeit machen? | Nicht ohne daß Sie ihnen helfen. |
| Ist es gesund (healthy), sehr lange zu schlafen? | Nein, je länger man schläft, desto träger wird man. |
| Kennen Sie diesen Mann? | Nein, aber es scheint mir, als ob ich ihn schon gesehen hätte. |
| Wissen Sie, warum Robert nicht gekommen ist? | Nein, ich weiß es nicht, er hat es mir nicht gesagt. |
| Warum sprechen Sie so leise (low voice)? | Damit das schlafende Kind nicht geweckt werde. |

### READING LESSON.

### Außergewöhnliche Stärke.

#### Extraordinary Strength.

Als der Marschall, Prinz von Sachsen, eines Tages einen Beweis[1]) seiner Stärke[2]) geben wollte, trat[3]) er bei einem Hufschmied[4]) ein, unter dem Vorwand[5]), sein Pferd beschlagen[6]) zu lassen. Er untersuchte[7]) die Hufeisen[8]), die man ihm zeigte, und zerbrach sechs davon nacheinander

1) a proof. 2) strength. 3) eintreten to enter. 4) farrier. 5) pretence. 6) to have his horse shod. 7) to examine. 8) horse-shoe.

(or eins nach dem andern), indem er sagte, daß sie nichts taugten[9]), und daß man ihm beffere geben follte.

Endlich ftellte er fich[10]), als ob er paffende[11]) fände, und als das Pferd beschlagen war, gab er dem Schmied[4]) zwei Sechslivrethaler[12]). Diefer, indem er fich feiner= feits[13]) ftellte, als wenn er die Thaler fchlecht fände, zerbrach fie vor den Augen des Prinzen, der ihm dann einen Louisdor gab und geftand[14]), daß er feinen Meifter gefunden habe.

9) were good for nothing.   10) he pretended   11) fit ones.   12) pieces of six francs.   13) on his part.   14) ge= ftehen  to confess. ‑

# 1.

1. Die Flüsse Rußlands sind groß.   2. Die Thäler¹) der Schweiz sind schön.   3. Welches sind die Produkte [Producte] Englands?   4. Die Straßen Berlins (or von Berlin) sind schön.   5. Napoleon war in Ägypten [Aegypten].   6. Er starb²) auf der Insel Sankt [Sanct] Helena.   7. Ich war nicht in Österreich [Oesterreich]; aber ich war in Preußen. 8. Was ist das für ein Land?   9. Dies ist Griechenland. 10. Kennen Sie Philadelphia?   11. Nein, ich kenne es nicht, ich war nicht in Amerika.   12. Ist dieser Mann ein Holländer?   13. Nein, er ist ein Irländer; er geht nach Amerika. 14. Ich schicke meinen Sohn nach Paris.   15. Gustav Adolf [Adolph] war König von Schweden.   16. Kennen Sie die Stadt Frankfurt?   17. Nein, aber ich kenne die Stadt Köln [Cöln]³).   18. Der Monat Mai ist der schönste in Deutschland.   19. Der Rhein ist ein großer Fluß.   20. Mein Freund ist im Juni angekommen.

1) valleys.   2) died.   3) Cologne.

# 2.

1. I have seen a man and (a) woman.   2. Who is the emperor of Germany?   3. William II., king of (von) Prussia.   4. Henry's father and mother have arrived. 5. Victoria is the name of the Queen of England.

*) These "Exercises" may be now and then inserted, as soon as the pupils have passed Lesson 20 or 25.

6. Here are Mr. Bell's son and daughter. 7. My aunt is ill, but my uncle is not ill; he is very well. 8. The duchess¹) has no (feine) daughters, but two sons. 9. Do you know this gentleman? 10. Yes, Sir, it is Mr. Jones; he is Mr. Brown's brother-in-law and lives (lebt) in Germany. 11. The husband²) has lost his wife³); he is a widower⁴). 12. Have you seen my nephew? 13. I have not seen your nephew, but your niece. 14. This woman is a Jewess⁵). 15. The prince is the bene-factor⁶) of this country. 16. Charles is an industrious boy; he is my friend. 17. We have a very good servant.

1) Herzogin. 2) der Gatte, der Mann. 3) Frau, Gattin. 4) Witwer [Wittwer] (*masc.*). 5) Jüdin. 6) Wohlthäter (*masc.*).

### 3.

1. Ich habe zwanzig Schüler. 2. Herr Lang hat acht Kinder, drei Töchter und fünf Söhne. 3. Der König hat zehn Schlösser. 4. Meine Schwester hat vierundzwanzig Äpfel [Aepfel] gekauft. 5. Der Gärtner hat neun Vögel gefangen¹). 6. Wie alt sind Sie? 7. Ich bin zweiundzwanzig Jahre alt. 8. Wie alt ist Ihre Schwester? 9. Sie ist siebzehn Jahre alt. 10. Das Jahr hat zwölf Monate. 11. Der Monat März hat einunddreißig Tage. 12. In dieser Stadt sind viertausend Häuser. 13. Wieviel [Wie viel] Uhr ist es? 14. Es ist drei Uhr oder halb vier. 15. Der König hat viele Pferde; er hat mehr als²) hundert. 16. Wie viele Aufgaben hat der Schüler bis jetzt gemacht? 17. Er hat siebenund-neunzig gemacht. 18. Der Reisende³) hat zweiunddreißig Städte und sechsundneunzig Dörfer gesehen.

1) caught. 2) more than. 3) the traveller.

### 4.

1. I love my friend. 2. The brother loves his sister. 3. I see the dog. 4. I see also the horse. 5. I have

seen the hat.    6. Which (*acc.*) hat?    7. I have seen
your hat.    8. Which friend is good?    9. Which dress
is new?    10. *Do* you know my teacher?    11. I *do* not
know your teacher.    12. Has your cousin bought the
garden?    13. No, he has not bought the garden, but he
has bought the house.    14. My pocket-book[1]) is old; but
yours is new.    15. We love our father and our mother.
16. *Do* you know my friend?    17. I do not know your
friend, but I know your cousin.    18. Which garden has
your grand-father bought?    19. He has bought Mrs.
Brown's garden.    20. Has your sister [any] flowers?
21. Yes, she has two roses.

1) Taſchenbuch (*neut.*).

## 5.

1. Der erſte Tag.    2. Die dritte Woche des zweiten
Monats.    3. Die letzten[1]) Wochen des vorigen[1]) Jahres.    4.
Dieſer Knabe iſt ſehr fleißig; er iſt immer der zweite [Zweite]
oder dritte [Dritte] in ſeiner Klaſſe [Claſſe].    5. Ludwig iſt
der vierte [Vierte].    6. Der kleine Heinrich iſt der drei=
zehnte [Dreizehnte].    7. Guſtav war der letzte [Letzte].    8. Der
Januar iſt der erſte Monat des Jahres; der März iſt der
dritte, der April iſt der vierte, der Juni iſt der ſechſte.    9. Zwei
iſt der fünfte Teil [Theil] von zehn.    10. Zehn iſt der dritte
Teil von dreißig.    11. Den wievielten[2]) des Monats haben
wir heute?    12. Wir haben heute den zwanzigſten oder ein=
undzwanzigſten.    13. War geſtern nicht der achtzehnte?    14.
Nein, geſtern war der neunzehnte oder vielleicht der zwanzigſte.
15. Ludwig der Vierzehnte war König von Frankreich.    16.
Wilhelm der Erſte, König von Preußen, war ſeit 1871 auch
Kaiſer von Deutſchland.    17. Adam und Eva waren die erſten
Menſchen.

1) last.    2) what day of the month.

## 6.

1. This man is a peasant.   2. Those men are peasants.
3. They are very rich; they have fields and forests[1]).
4. (The) monkeys[2]) are in the forests.   5. The trees of
those forests are beautiful.   6. My cousin is ill.   7. My
cousins are ill.   8. This house belongs[3]) to my neighbor.
9. Those fields belong to our neighbors.   10. Are your
neighbors your friends?   11. Yes, they are my best
friends.   12. Here is the shoemaker.   13. What does
he bring?   14. He brings your shoes (Schuhe) and
(your) slippers[4]).   15. The rich count has many
houses, gardens, fields and forests.   16. (The) fish(es)
like (the) worms[5]).   17. Who are these men?
18. They are Frenchmen; they have bought my
horses, (my) oxen, (my) cows and calves.   19. Do you
want your slippers?   20. Yes, please (bitte), give them
to me!

1) ber Walb, (*plur.*) Wälber.  2) ber Affe.  3) gehört.  4) Pantoffeln.
5) ber Wurm, (*plur.*) see page 43.2.

## 7.

1. Der Fluß ift tief; ber See[1]) ift tiefer alß ber Fluß; baß
Meer ift a m tieffften.   2. Karl [Carl] ift ftärfer alß Wil=
helm; er ift ber ftärffte Knabe.   3. Der Abler[2]) ift ber ftärffte
Vogel.   4. Er hat bie längften Flügel unb bie fchärffften
Krallen[3]).   5. Im Frühling[4]) finb bie Tage fürzer alß im
Sommer; aber im Winter finb fie am fürzeften.   6. Daß
Silber ift foftbarer alß baß Kupfer.   7. Daß Golb ift baß
foftbarfte Metall.   8. Wein ift beffer alß Bier.   9. Die
fpanifchen Weine finb bie beften (Weine).   10. Diefer Maler
ift nicht fo berühmt[5]) alß fein Vater; aber feine Bilber[6]) finb

1) lake.  2) eagle.  3) sharpest claws.  4) spring.  5) renowned.
6) pictures.

ebenſo ſchön. 11. Unſer Onkel (Oheim) iſt ebenſo reich als unſer Vetter; aber er iſt nicht ſo glücklich. 12. Der beſte Kaffee [Caffee] kommt aus Arabien.

### 8.

1. The wings[1]) of the birds. 2. The coats of the tailor are new. 3. The fathers are wiser than the sons. 4. The love of the fathers is great. 5. Where is Charles? 6. He has (is) gone out with his brothers. 7. How many brothers has he? 8. He has two brothers. 9. Has he [any] sisters? 10. He has only[2]) one. 11. The gardens of the countess are beautiful, but the gardens of the queen are still (noch) more beautiful. 12. Many bakers are rich. 13. The birds have wings. 14. (The) tailors make (machen) coats; (the) shoemakers make boots and shoes; (the) watchmakers[3]) make watches. 15. The servant has lost four silver[4]) spoons and three silver knives. 16. These knives are not sharp[5]). 17. Is your penknife sharp? 18. Yes, it is very sharp. 19. These boots are too (zu) large. 20. Yours are too small. 21. (The) asses are the laziest animals; but they are very useful. 22. Where are the gardeners? 23. They are in the gardens.

1) Flügel (*masc.*). 2) nur. 3) Uhrmacher (*masc.*). 4) ſilberne. 5) ſcharf.

### 9.

1. Ich liebe meinen Bruder. 2. Du liebſt deine Schweſter. 3. Die Fiſche leben im Waſſer. 4. Was kaufen Sie? 5. Der König hat ein Schloß gebaut. 6. Der Knabe lernt. 7. Der Lehrer hat dieſen Schüler gelobt, weil er ſehr fleißig iſt. 8. Der Knabe hat ſeine Aufgabe nicht gelernt. 9. Der Vater ſtraft[1]) den trägen Knaben. 10. Die Mutter ſpielte mit

1) to punish.

dem Kind.   11. Die tapfern²) Soldaten werden die Stadt ver=
teidigen [vertheidigen]³).   12. Ich sehe das spielende Kind.
13. Die Mutter würde weinen⁴) wenn das Kind krank wäre.
14. Wir loben den fleißigen Schüler.   15. Niemand wird die
trägen Schüler loben.   16. Gestern ²hörte ¹ich schöne Musik.
17. Haben die Kinder gestern gespielt?   18. Ja, sie haben
gespielt, und sie werden auch morgen spielen.

2) brave.  3) to defend.  4) to cry.

## 10.

1. This boy is thankful¹); his brother is more thankful, but his sister is the most thankful.   2. Gold is useful; copper²) is more useful, but iron is the most useful
metal.   3. That word is more used³) than the other.
4. Henry is the handsomest young man.   5. The rose
is the most beautiful flower.   6. Who is more amiable⁴)
than your daughter?   7. We had a very pleasant⁵) walk⁶)
to-day; but our yesterday's walk was much more
pleasant.   8. This wine is good, the other is better; but
the wine in that bottle is the best.   9. My paper is bad;
but your paper is worse.   10. Is that the nearest⁷) way?
11. No, Sir, that is the farthest⁸).   12. A ring of (von)
gold is more precious than a ring of silver.

1) dankbar.  2) das Kupfer.  3) gebräuchlich.  4) liebenswürdig.  5)
angenehm.  6) Spaziergang (masc.).  7) nächste.  8) weiteste.

## 11.

1. Ich würde froh¹) sein, wenn mein Vater hier wäre.   2.
Du würdest mehr Freunde haben, wenn du gerechter²) wärest.
3. Er würde ein Pferd kaufen, wenn er Geld genug hätte.   4.
Meine Nichte würde ausgehen, wenn sie nicht unwohl wäre.

1) glad.  2) just.

5. Unfer Schneider²) würde nicht so arm sein, wenn er fleißiger wäre.   6. Die Kinder würden nicht so hungrig sein, wenn sie etwas gegessen hätten.   7. Würden Sie auf das Land gehen, wenn das Wetter nicht so schlecht wäre?   8. Wir würden Shakespeares „Macbeth" gesehen haben, wenn wir gestern im Theater gewesen wären.   9. Der Vater würde nicht so strenge⁴) sein, wenn der Sohn nicht so nachlässig⁵) wäre.   10. Wir würden diesen Hund nicht so gern⁶) haben, wenn er nicht so treu wäre.   11. Die Reisenden würden nicht so durstig⁷) sein, wenn sie Bier, Wein oder Wasser getrunken hätten.

3) tailor.  4) strict, severe.  5) careless.  6) gern haben = to like.
7) thirsty.

## 12.

1. Who is there?  2. It is a stranger¹); it is a traveller. 3. Do you know him?  4. I have never (nie) seen him. 5. He comes from (kommt aus) America.  6. What does he bring?  7. He brings a letter.  8. From whom?  9. From your cousin Richard.  10. At whose house²) does the young traveller live?  11. He lives at³) the book-seller's⁴). . 12. From whom have you received these apples?  13. From Louisa.  14. Who has made these tables and (these) chairs?  15. Our joiner⁵).  16. To whose house (to whom) do you go?  17. I go to my aunt's.  18. With whom do you go to your aunt's?  19. With my little sister Sarah. 20. Where is the prisoner⁶)? 21. He is in (the) prison⁷).  22. Who has seen the two travellers?  23. We have not seen the two travellers, but we have seen a foreigner at the merchant's.  24. [To] whom have you sent your money?  25. I have sent it to a bookseller in Munich⁸).

1) ein Fremder.  2) at whose house = bei wem?  3) bei.  4) der Buchhändler.  5) der Schreiner.  6) der Gefangene.  7) im Gefängnis [Gefängniß].  8) München.

## 13.

1. Ich komme aus dem Garten. 2. Diese Damen kommen aus dem Theater. 3. Das Haus steht bei dem Flusse. 4. Karl [Carl] wohnt bei seinem Oheim. 5. Herr Müller ist mit seinen Kindern ausgegangen. 6. Mit wem ist der Fremde angekommen? 7. Er ist mit zwei anderen Reisen= den aus Amerika angekommen. 8. Wohin gehen Sie? 9. Ich gehe zu meinem Lehrer. 10. Wo wohnt er? 11. Er wohnt bei der Kirche. 12. Wohin gehen Sie nach der Stunde¹)? 13. Nach meiner Stunde gehe ich nach Hause. 14. Der Schneider kann Ihren Rock nicht machen; er ist seit einigen Wochen krank. 15. Sind Sie mit Ihrem Diener zu= frieden? 16. Ja, ich bin mit ihm zufrieden. 17. Waren Sie gestern b e i Ihrer Tante? 18. Nein, ich hatte keine Zeit, dahin zu gehen. 19. Ich mußte bei meiner kleinen Schwester bleiben²). 20. Warum sehen³) Sie so bleich⁴) aus? 21. Ich bin nicht wohl.

1) lesson. 2) to remain. 3) to look. 4) pale.

## 14.

1. Do you expect¹) him? 2. Yes, he must bring me my new coat. 3. Have you ever²) been in Spain? 4. Yes, I was at (in) Madrid [for] two years. 5. I was (have been) formerly³) much happier than now. 6. How long were you in Paris? 7. I was (have been) there only three months. 8. Has the little boy been at his uncle's? 9. He has not yet been there, he will go this evening. 10. My son has never been more contented than to-day; he has received a reward⁴) from his teacher, who has praised him very [much]. 11. He had written his exercise without mistakes. 12. These gentlemen

1) erwarten. 2) je or schon. 3) früher. 4) eine Belohnung.

have never been at (in) my house; they have never
paid (made) me a visit⁵), and I have never spoken (ge=
ſprochen) to (mit) them.

5) Beſuch (*masc.*).

### 15.

1. Ich bin in meinem Garten geweſen.   2. Biſt du auf
dem Ball geweſen?   3. Karl [Carl] iſt geſtern nicht zu Hauſe
geweſen.   4. Wir ſind immer fleißig und aufmerkſam¹) ge=
weſen.   5. Ihr ſeid krank geweſen.   6. Sind Sie geſtern in
dem Konzert [Concert] geweſen?   7. Nein, mein Herr, ich bin
mit meiner älteſten Schweſter im Theater geweſen.   8. Wer
iſt hier geweſen?   9. Herr Bell iſt hier geweſen; er hat
dieſen Brief für Sie gebracht.   10. Iſt der Bediente bei dem
Schneider geweſen?   11. Ja, er iſt dort²) geweſen; aber Ihr
Rock war noch nicht fertig³).   12. Dieſer berühmte Reiſende
iſt lange in Amerika geweſen.   13. Wo ſind Ihre Söhne
dieſen Morgen geweſen?   14. Sie ſind in der Schule
geweſen.   15. Iſt Ihr Lehrer in England geweſen?   16. Ja,
er iſt zweimal dort geweſen; das erſte Mal vor⁴) fünf Jahren,
das letzte Mal vor zwei Jahren.

1) attentive.   2) there.   3) done.   4) ago.

### 16.

1. What do you fetch¹)?   I fetch [some] water.
2. The house is not sold.   3. We admire²) the beautiful
picture.   4. Louisa has not perceived³) the mistake.
5. Do not believe him (ihm).   6. What are you doing⁴)?
7. I am learning my lesson.   8. Charles is going to
church.   9. The servant was waiting⁵) for (auf) you.
10. We have been admiring your garden.   11. The
man *wishes*⁶) to clean⁷) the room.   12. This gentleman

1) holen.   2) bewundern.   3) bemerken (*reg. v.*).   4) to do = thun.
5) warten.   6) wünſchen.   7) zu reinigen.

dines⁶) here every day. 13. The mother loves her daughters. 14. Have you tried⁹) the wine? 15. No, but I shall try it to-morrow. 16. A poor man has found some money. 17. Our uncle *has* travelled a great deal (viel) in France. 18. When you go home, ²I ¹shall go with you. 19. Will the stranger remain¹⁰) here? 20. No, he would like¹¹) to remain here, but he must go to Berlin in a few days.

8) ſpeiſen. 9) probieren [probiren]. 10) bleiben. 11) möchte gern.

## 17.

1. Wer hat dieſe Schuhe gemacht? 2. Unſer Schuhmacher hat ſie gemacht. 3. Ich habe zwei Affen¹) geſehen. 4. Haſt du ſie auch geſehen? 5. Nein, ich habe ſie nicht geſehen. 6. Der Gärtner hat dieſe Blumen gebracht. 7. Für wen ſind ſie? 8. Sie ſind für meine Schweſter. 9. Wir haben viele Briefe geſchrieben. 10. Ihr habt viele Bücher geleſen. 11. Die Diener haben die Flaſchen nicht gefüllt²). 12. Ich habe eine goldene Uhr gekauft. 13. Haſt du den König nicht geſehen? 14. Hatte Emil nicht ſein Geld verloren? 15. Wir hatten früher³) viel Vergnügen gehabt. 16. Emilie hatte dieſe Geſchichte⁴) früher noch nicht geleſen. 17. Sie hatte das Buch nicht gehabt. 18. Hat der Schüler ſeine Aufgabe gemacht? 19. Ich weiß⁵) es nicht; ich habe ihn heute noch nicht geſehen. 20. Hat der Schneider den Rock des Herrn Baron gemacht? 21. Er hat ihn noch nicht gemacht; er wird ihn morgen machen.

1) monkey. 2) to fill. 3) formerly. 4) history. 5) I know.

## 18.

1. The butcher¹) who has bought these oxen, is very rich. 2. I have seen the man who has lost all his

1) der Metzger or Fleiſcher.

fortune³). 3. Where is the shoemaker who has made my shoes? 4. Show³) me the Jew⁴) whose brother has bought your horse! 5. Did you see the woman whose daughter has sold those cherries? 6. No, Sir, I have not seen her (fie). 7. Show me the pupil who has received a reward from his teacher! 8. The tailor to (ʒu) whom I have sent your coat, is here; he wants his money. 9. Is this the man whom I have seen at your house? 10. Is this the garden (which) you have sold? 11. Is this the house (that) you have hired⁵)? 12. This is the gardener's daughter whose exercise you have praised. 13. Is this the name of the merchant whom you met⁶) at Berlin last summer? 14. No, Sir, that is not his name; his name is Martin. 15. The pen which you have made⁷), is not good.

2) Vermögen (*neut.*). 3) zeigen. 4) der Jude. 5) gemietet [gemiethet].
6) begegnet. 7) geschnitten.

## 19.

1. Gustavus Adolphus, king of Sweden, was killed in the battle¹) of (bei) Lutzen. 2. Have the kindness to tell me what o'clock it is! 3. It is ten o'clock or half past ten. 4. At what o'clock do you breakfast? 5. I breakfast every day at eight o'clock. 6. Why have you not washed your hands? 7. I should have washed them, if I had had any water and soap²). 8. Where has the servant put³) my new gloves? 9. He has put them in the press. 10. I hope that your friend will obtain⁴) the situation⁵) (that) he wishes [for]. 11. What do I see! 12. You are still⁶) in bed! 13. Do you not

1) Schlacht (*fem.*). 2) Seife (*fem.*). 3) (hin)gelegt. 4) erlangen, erhalten. 5) die Stelle. 6) noch.

know what o'clock it is?    14. I suppose[7]), it is seven o'clock.    15. You are mistaken[8]); it is half past nine; you sleep too much.    16. The´ music-master said that he was (had been) at home yesterday; but his servant did not know it; he thought (glaubte) he had gone out. 17. I hope my teacher will be satisfied[9]) with my exercise, because I made very few mistakes in it (darin).

7) vermuten [vermuthen].    8) Sie irren sich.    9) befriedigt.

# Easy Conversations.

## 1.

| | |
|---|---|
| Was haben Sie da? | What have you there? |
| Ich habe mein Buch | I have my book. |
| Haben Sie Ihr Heft? | Have you (got) your copy-book? |
| Ja, mein Herr, ich habe es. | Yes, Sir, I have it. |
| Nein, ich habe es vergessen. | No, I have forgotten it. |
| Haben Sie etwas [Etwas, ge= kauft? | Have you bought anything? |
| Ja, ich habe etwas gekauft. | Yes, I have bought something. |
| Was haben Sie gekauft? | What have you bought? |
| Ich habe ein Paar Handschuhe gekauft. | I bought a pair *of* gloves. |
| Haben Sie Obst? | Have you any fruit? |
| Ja, ich habe (welches). | Yes, I have some. |
| Nein, ich habe keines. | No, I have none. |
| Haben Sie guten Wein? | Have you any good wine? |
| Ich habe immer guten Wein. | I always have good wine. |
| Haben Sie viele Freunde? | Have you many friends? |
| Ich habe wenige Freunde. | I have few friends. |
| Ist Ihr Freund hier ange= kommen? | Has your friend arrived here? |
| Er ist gestern angekommen. | He arrived yesterday. |

## 2.

| | |
|---|---|
| Haben Sie Geld genug? | Have you money enough? |
| Ich habe nicht genug. | I have not enough. |
| Was wollen Sie kaufen? | What do you want to buy? |

Ich will einen neuen Hut kaufen. — I will buy a new hat.

Haben Sie Thee gekauft? — Did you buy any tea?

Wieviel [Wie viel] (was) kostet das Kilogramm? — How much a kilogram?

Das Kilogramm kostet 8 Mark. — Eight marks a kilogram.

Ich finde das sehr teuer [theuer]. — I find that very dear.

Das ist sehr wohlfeil (billig). — That is very cheap.

Haben Sie Ihr Pferd verkauft? — Have you sold your horse?

Ich habe es noch nicht verkauft. — I have not yet sold it.

Werden Sie es verkaufen? — Will you sell it?

Nein, ich werde es nicht ver= kaufen. — No, I shall not sell it.

Bringen Sie mir Brot [Brob] und Butter! — Bring me some bread and butter!

Ich habe genug gegessen. — I have eaten enough.

Wollen Sie ein Glas Wein trinken? — Will you drink a glass *of* wine?

Hier ist auch frisches Wasser. — Here is also some fresh water.

### 3.

Kommen Sie herein! — Come in!

Machen Sie die Thüre zu! — Shut the door!

Machen Sie das Fenster auf! — Open the window!

Tragen Sie diesen Brief auf die Post! — Take this letter to the post-office!

Für wen ist er? — For whom is it?

Er ist für meine Tante. — It is for my aunt.

Haben Sie Lust, zu spielen? — Do you wish to play?

Ich habe jetzt keine Zeit. — I have no time now.

Hat der Schuhmacher gute Schuhe? — Has the shoemaker (any) good shoes?

Er macht immer gute Schuhe. — He always makes good shoes.

Was haben Sie zu thun? — What have you to do?

| | |
|---|---|
| Ich habe nichts [Nichts] zu thun. | I have nothing to do. |
| Ich bin fertig. | I have done. (I am ready.) |
| Karl [Carl] hat seine Aufgabe zu schreiben. | Charles has to write his exercise. |
| Was hat Ihr Bruder zu thun? | What has your brother to do? |
| Er hat einen Brief zu schreiben. | He has a letter to write. |

### 4.

| | |
|---|---|
| Haben Sie Ihren Ring gefunden? | Did you find your ring? |
| Ich habe ihn wieder gefunden. | I did. |
| Wo sind meine Stiefel? | Where are my boots? |
| Sie sind bei dem Schuhmacher. | They are at the shoe-maker's. |
| Was sagen Sie? | What do you say? |
| Ich sagte nichts. | I said nothing. |
| Mit wem sprechen Sie? | To whom do you speak? |
| Ich spreche mit dem Schneider. | I speak to the tailor. |
| Was wünschen Sie? | What do you want? |
| Ich bitte um ein Glas Wasser. | I ask for a glass of water. |
| Hier ist eines. | Here is one. |
| Sie sind sehr gütig. | You are very kind. |
| Was suchen Sie da? | What are you looking for? |
| Ich suche meine Uhr. | I am looking for my watch. |
| Was wollen Sie thun? | What are you about to do? |
| Ich will ausgehen. | I will go out. |
| Was machen (or thun) Sie da? | What are you doing there? |
| Ich lerne meine Aufgabe. | I am learning my lesson. |

### 5.

| | |
|---|---|
| Kennen Sie diesen Mann? | Do you know this man? |
| Ich kenne ihn sehr gut. | I know him very well. |
| Ich kenne ihn nicht. | I do not know him. |

Wie heißt er? — What is his name?

Er heißt Müller. — His name is Miller.

Wie schreibt man dieses Wort? — How do you spell this word?

Verstehen Sie mich? — Do you understand me?

Glauben Sie das? — Do you believe that?

Ich glaube es nicht. — I do not believe it.

Es ist wahr. — It is true.

Was ist zu thun? — What is to be done?

Sind Sie mit ihm zufrieden? — Are you contented with him?

Wir sind damit zufrieden. — We are contented (with it).

Das (es) freut mich sehr. — }

Ich bin sehr froh. — } I am very glad of it.

Das thut mir sehr, sehr leid. — I am very sorry.

## 6.

Guten Morgen, mein Herr. — Good morning, Sir.

Guten Abend, mein Fräulein. — Good evening, Miss A.

Nehmen Sie Platz! — Take a seat!

Setzen Sie sich! — Be seated (sit down)!

Wie befinden Sie sich? — How do you do?

Sehr gut, ich danke Ihnen. — Very well, I thank you.

Und Sie (selbst)? — And you (yourself)?

Wie geht es Ihnen? — How are you?

Nicht sehr gut. — Not very well.

Ziemlich gut. — Tolerably (pretty) well.

Ich bitte Sie, sagen Sie mir! — Please or pray tell me!

Geben Sie mir den Brief! — Give me the letter!

Ich bitte Sie darum. — I beg you.

Ich danke Ihnen. — I thank you.

Ist Herr N. zu Hause? — Is Mr. N. at home?

Ja, er ist zu Hause. — Yes, Sir, he is at home.

Nein, er ist ausgegangen. — No, Sir, he has gone out.

Es ist Zeit aufzustehen. — It is time to get up.

Stehen Sie auf! — Get up!

| | |
|---|---|
| Um wieviel [wie viel] Uhr stehen Sie auf? | At what o'clock do you get up? |
| Ich stehe um 8 Uhr auf. | I get up at eight o'clock. |

## 7.

| | |
|---|---|
| Wer ist es? | Who is it? |
| Wer ist da? | Who is there? |
| Ich bin es. | It is I. |
| Wir sind es. | It is we. |
| Wohin gehen Sie? | Where are you going? |
| Wir gehen in die Schule. | We are going to school. |
| Ich gehe nicht hin. | I do not go there. |
| Woher kommen Sie? | Where do you come from? |
| Ich komme von London. | I come from London. |
| Wir kommen aus dem Konzert [Concert]. | We come from the concert. |
| Fräulein Elise kommt vom Ball. | Miss Eliza comes from the ball. |
| Wann gehen Sie nach Hause? | When do you go home? |
| In einer Stunde. | In an hour. |
| Ist es Zeit zu gehen? | Is it time to go? |
| Es ist zehn Uhr. | It is ten o'clock. |
| Gehen Sie nicht so schnell! | Do not go so fast! |
| Wollen Sie mit mir kommen? | Will you come with me? |
| Wir wollen einen Spaziergang machen. | We will take a walk. |
| Wann kommen Sie wieder? | When do you come again? |
| Morgen abend [Abend]. | To-morrow evening. |

## 8.

| | |
|---|---|
| Heute. | To-day. |
| Morgen. | To-morrow. |
| Übermorgen [Uebermorgen]. | The day after to-morrow. |
| Gestern Morgen. | Yesterday morning. |
| Gestern Abend. | Yesterday evening. |

Vorgeſtern. | The day before yesterday.
Vor acht Tagen. | A week ago.
Vor vierzehn Tagen. | A fortnight ago.
In ſechs Wochen. | In six weeks.
Vor einigen Tagen. | Some days ago.
Nächſte Woche. | Next week.
Lézte Woche. | Last week.
Was für Wetter iſt heute | How is the weather to-day?
Es iſt ſchönes Wetter. | It is fine weather.
Es iſt ſchlechtes Wetter. | It is bad weather.
Was für herrliches Wetter! | What beautiful weather!
Es iſt ſehr warm (heiß). | It is very warm (hot).
Die Sonne ſcheint. | The sun shines.
Die Sonne geht unter. | The sun sets.
Es iſt dunkel (Nacht). | It is dark (night).
Die Sonne geht auf. | The sun rises.
Es regnet ein wenig. | It rains a little.
Es donnert. | It thunders.
Es blißt. | It lightens.
Iſt es Ihnen warm? | Do you feel warm?
Frieren Sie? | Are you cold?
Es ſchneit; es fällt Schnee. | It snows.

## 9.

Brauchen Sie etwas? | Do you want anything?
Ich brauche meine Pantoffeln. | I want my slippers.
Hier iſt alles [Alles] was Sie brauchen. | Here is all you want.

Sind Sie ſchläfrig? | Are you sleepy?
Ich bin ſehr ſchläfrig. | I am very sleepy.
Gehen Sie zu Bette! | Go to bed!
Kleiden Sie ſich aus! | Undress!
Ziehen Sie Ihre Schuhe aus! | Take off your shoes!
Ziehen Sie Ihren Schlafrock an! | Put on your dressing-gown!
Ich habe ſehr gut geſchlafen. | I slept very well.

Wieviel [Wie viel] Uhr ist es? What o'clock is it?

Es ist spät, es ist neun Uhr. It is late, it is nine o'clock.

Um wieviel Uhr gehen Sie aus? At what o'clock shall you go out?

Ich werde um 8 Uhr ausgehen. I shall go out at eight o'clock.

Sind Sie angekleidet? Are you dressed?

Ich kleide mich eben an. I am dressing.

Wann kommen Sie zurück? When will you be back?

Um halb 10 Uhr. At half past nine.

Um dreiviertel [drei Viertel] auf zehn. At a quarter to ten.

Um einviertel auf zwölf. At a quarter past eleven.

# Proverbs.

1. Aller Anfang ist schwer.

2. Gleich und Gleich gesellt sich gern.

3. Wer einmal lügt, dem glaubt man nicht,
   Und wenn er auch die Wahrheit spricht.

4. Unrecht Gut gedeiht nicht

5. Wie die Alten sungen*),
   So zwitschern die Jungen.

6. Wer zuletzt lacht,
   Lacht am besten.

7. „Morgen, morgen nur nicht heute",
   Sprechen alle faulen Leute.

8. Wie gewonnen,
   So zerronnen.

9. Rede wenig, aber wahr,
   Vieles Reden bringt Gefahr.

*) For sangen.

# Poetry.

1. Willst du immer weiter schweifen?
   Sieh das Gute liegt so nah.
   Lerne nur das Glück ergreifen,
   Denn das Glück ist immer da.

   Johann Wolfgang von Göthe (1749–1832).

## Wissenschaft.

2. Einem ist sie die hohe, die himmlische Göttin, dem Andern
   Eine tüchtige Kuh, die ihn mit Butter versorgt.

   Friedrich von Schiller (1759–1805).

3. Du schmähst mich hinterrücks? das soll mich wenig kränken.
   Du lobst mich ins [in's] Gesicht? das will ich dir gedenken!

   Gotthold Ephraim Lessing (1729–1781).

4. Möge jeder [Jeder] still beglückt,
   Seiner Freuden warten!
   Wenn die Rose selbst sich schmückt,
   Schmückt sie auch den Garten.

   Friedrich Rückert (1789–1866).

5. Anfangs wollt' ich fast verzagen,
   Und ich glaubt', ich trüg' es nie;
   Und ich hab' es doch getragen,
   Aber fragt mich nur nicht: wie?

   Heinrich Heine (1799–1856).

## Herbstgefühl.

6. Müder Glanz der Sonne!
Blasses Himmelsblau!
Von verklungner Wonne
Träumet still die Au.

An der letzten Rose
Löset lebenssatt,
Sich das letzte lose,
Bleiche Blumenblatt.

Goldenes Entfärben
Schleicht sich durch den Hain;
Auch Vergehn und Sterben
Deucht [Däucht] mir süß zu sein.

Karl Gerok (1815–1890).

# Alphabetical List of the Irregular Verbs.

| Infinitive. | Present, 2d and 3d Persons. | Imperfect, 1st Person. | Past Participle. |
|---|---|---|---|
| baden  to bake | bädſt, bädt | buk | gebaden |
| befehlen  to order | befiehlſt, befiehlt | befahl | befohlen |
| befleißen  to apply to, to study | | befliß | befliſſen |
| beginnen  to begin | | begann | begonnen |
| beißen  to bite | | biß | gebiſſen |
| bergen  to hide | birgſt, birgt | barg | geborgen |
| berſten  to burst | birſteſt, birſt | barſt | geborſten |
| beſinnen  to meditate | | beſann | beſonnen |
| beſiߟen  to possess | | beſaß | beſeſſen |
| betrügen  to cheat | | betrog | betrogen |
| bewegen *)  to induce | | bewog | bewogen |
| biegen  to bend | | bog | gebogen |
| bieten  to offer | | ' bot | geboten |
| binden  to bind, to tie | | band | gebunden |
| bitten  to ask, to request | | bat . | gebeten |
| blaſen  to blow | bläſeſt, bläſt | blies | geblaſen |
| bleiben  to remain | | blieb | geblieben |
| braten  to roast | brätſt, brät | briet | gebraten |
| brechen  to break | brichſt, bricht | brach | gebrochen |
| brennen  to burn | | brannte | gebrannt |
| bringen  to bring | | brachte | gebracht |
| denken  to think | | dachte | gedacht |
| dreſchen  to thrash | driſcheſt, driſcht | droſch | gedroſchen |
| bringen to  urge,  to penetrate | | brang | gebrungen |
| bürfen  to be allowed to, may, can | ich  barf,  bu barfſt, er barf | burfte | geburft |
| empfangen  to receive | empfängſt, em- pfängt | empfing | empfangen |
| empfehlen to  recom- mend | empfiehlſt, em- pfiehlt | empfahl | empfohlen |
| empfinden  to feel | | empfand | empfunden |

*) Bewegen is regular, when it means *to move* (*of bodily motion*).

| Infinitive. | Present, 2d and 3d Persons. | Imperfect, 1st Person. | Past Participle. |
|---|---|---|---|
| entrinnen to escape | | entrann | entronnen |
| erbleichen *) to turn pale | | erblich | erblichen |
| erküren to choose | | erkor | erkoren |
| erlöschen to become extinct | erlischeft, erlischt | erlosch | erloschen |
| erschallen to resound | | erscholl | erschollen |
| erschrecken to be frightened | erschrickst, erschrickt | erschrak | erschrocken |
| erwägen to consider | | erwog | erwogen |
| essen to eat | issest, ißt | aß | gegessen |
| fahren to drive | fähreft, fährt | fuhr | gefahren |
| fallen to fall | fällft, fällt | fiel | gefallen |
| fangen to catch | fängst, fängt | fing | gefangen |
| fechten to fight | fichtst, ficht | focht | gefochten |
| finden to find | | fand | gefunden |
| flechten to twist, to braid | flichtst, flicht | flocht | geflochten |
| fliegen to fly | | flog | geflogen |
| fliehen to flee | | floh | geflohen |
| fließen to flow | | floß | geflossen |
| fressen to eat (of animals) | frissest, frißt | fraß | gefressen |
| frieren to freeze | | fror | gefroren |
| gären [gähren] to ferment | | gor [gohr] | gegoren [gegohren] |
| gebären to bring forth | | gebar | geboren |
| geben to give | gi(e)bst, gi(e)bt | gab | gegeben |
| gebieten to command | | gebot | geboten |
| gedeihen to prosper | | gedieh | gediehen |
| gefallen to please | | gefiel | gefallen |
| gehen to go | | ging | gegangen |
| gelingen to succeed | | gelang | gelungen |
| gelten to be worth | giltst, gilt | galt | gegolten |
| genesen to recover | | genaß | genesen |
| genießen to enjoy | | genoß | genossen |
| geraten [gerathen] to fall into; to thrive | gerätst [geräthst], gerät [geräth] | geriet [gerieth] | geraten [gerathen] |
| geschehen to happen | geschieht (impers.) | geschah | geschehen |

*) The simple word bleichen is regular.

| Infinitive. | Present, 2d and 3d Persons. | Imperfect, 1st Person. | Past Participle. |
|---|---|---|---|
| gewinnen to gain | | gewann | gewonnen |
| gießen to pour | | goß | gegossen |
| gleichen to resemble | | glich | geglichen |
| gleiten to glide | | glitt | geglitten |
| glimmen to glow | | glomm | geglommen |
| graben to dig | gräbst, gräbt | grub | gegraben |
| greifen to seize | | griff | gegriffen |
| haben to have | | hatte | gehabt |
| halten to hold | hältst, hält | hielt | gehalten |
| hängen to hang | | hing | gehangen |
| hauen to hew | | hieb | gehauen |
| heben to lift | | hob | gehoben |
| heißen to be called | | hieß | geheißen |
| helfen to help | hilfst hilft | half | geholfen |
| kennen to know | | kannte | gekannt |
| klimmen to climb | | klomm | geklommen |
| klingen to sound | | klang | geklungen |
| kommen to come | | kam | gekommen |
| können to be able | ich kann, du kannst, er kann | konnte | gekonnt |
| kriechen to creep | | kroch | gekrochen |
| laden to load | | lud | geladen |
| lassen to let | lässest, läßt | ließ | gelassen |
| laufen to run | läufst, läuft | lief | gelaufen |
| leiden to suffer | | litt | gelitten |
| leihen to lend | | lieh | geliehen |
| lesen to read | liesest, liest | las | gelesen |
| liegen to lie | | lag | gelegen |
| löschen to extinguish | (lischest, lischt) | losch · | geloschen |
| lügen to lie, to utter a falsehood | | log | gelogen |
| meiden to avoid | | mied | gemieden |
| melken to milk | | molk | gemolken |
| messen to measure | missest, mißt | maß | gemessen |
| mißfallen to displease | mißfällst, fällt | mißfiel | mißfallen |
| mögen to like | ich mag (I may), du magst, er mag | mochte | gemocht |
| müssen to be obliged | ich muß, du mußt, er muß | mußte | gemußt |
| nehmen to take | nimmst, nimmt | nahm | genommen |

| Infinitive. | Present, 2d and 3d Persons. | Imperfect, 1st Person. | Past Participle. |
|---|---|---|---|
| nennen  to call |  | nannte | genannt |
| pfeifen  to whistle |  | pfiff | gepfiffen |
| pflegen  foster |  | pflog | gepflogen |
| preifen  to praise |  | pries | gepriesen |
| quellen  to spring forth | quillst, quillt | quoll | gequollen |
| raten [rathen]  to advise | rätest [räthest], rät [räth] | riet [rieth] | geraten [gerathen] |
| reiben  to rub |  | rieb | gerieben |
| reißen  to tear |  | riß | gerissen |
| reiten  to ride on horseback |  | ritt | geritten |
| rennen  to run |  | rannte | gerannt |
| riechen  to smell |  | roch | gerochen |
| ringen  to wrestle |  | rang | gerungen |
| rinnen  to flow |  | rann | geronnen |
| rufen  to call |  | rief | gerufen |
| salzen  to salt |  | salzte | gesalzen |
| saufen  to drink (of animals) | säufst, säuft | soff | gesoffen |
| saugen  to suck |  | sog | gesogen |
| schaffen  to create |  | schuf | geschaffen |
| schallen  to sound |  | scholl | geschallt |
| scheiden  to separate |  | schied | geschieden |
| scheinen  to seem |  | schien | geschienen |
| scheren · to shear | schierst, schiert | schor | geschoren |
| schelten  to scold | schiltst, schilt | schalt | gescholten |
| schieben  to shove |  | schob | geschoben |
| schießen  to shoot |  | schoß | geschossen |
| schinden  to flay |  | schund | geschunden |
| schlafen  to sleep | schläfst, schläft | schlief | geschlafen |
| schlagen  to beat | schlägst, schlägt | schlug | geschlagen |
| schleichen  to sneak |  | schlich | geschlichen |
| schleifen  to grind |  | schliff | geschliffen |
| schließen  to lock |  | schloß | geschlossen |
| schlingen  to wind; to devour |  | schlang | geschlungen |
| schmeißen  to throw |  | schmiß | geschmissen |
| schmelzen  to melt | schmilzst, schmilzt | schmolz | geschmolzen |
| schnauben  to snort |  | schnob | geschnoben |
| schneiden  to cut |  | schnitt | geschnitten |
| schreiben  to write |  | schrieb | geschrieben |

| Infinitive. | Present, 2d and 3d Persons. | Imperfect, 1st Person. | Past Participle. |
|---|---|---|---|
| ſchreien  to cry | | ſchrie | geſchrieen |
| ſchreiten  to stride | | ſchritt | geſchritten |
| ſchweigen  to be silent | | ſchwieg | geſchwiegen |
| ſchwellen to swell | ſchwillſt, ſchwillt | ſchwoll | geſchwollen |
| ſchwimmen to swim | | ſchwamm | geſchwommen |
| ſchwinden to vanish | | ſchwand | geſchwunden |
| ſchwingen  to swing | | ſchwang | geſchwungen |
| ſchwören  to swear | | ſchwor | geſchworen |
| ſehen  to see | ſieh(e)ſt, ſieht | ſah | geſehen |
| ſenden  to send | | ſandte | geſandt |
| ſieden  to boil | | ſott | geſotten |
| ſingen  to sing | | ſang | geſungen |
| ſinken  to sink | | ſank | geſunken |
| ſinnen  to meditate | | ſann | geſonnen |
| ſitzen  to sit | | ſaß | geſeſſen |
| ſollen  to should | Ich ſoll (I am to), du ſollſt, er ſoll | ſollte (I should) | geſollt |
| ſpeien  to spit | | ſpie | geſpieen |
| ſpinnen  to spin | | ſpann | geſponnen |
| ſprechen  to speak | ſprichſt, ſpricht | ſprach | geſprochen |
| ſprießen  to sprout | | ſproß | geſproſſen |
| ſpringen  to leap | | ſprang | geſprungen |
| ſtechen  to stitch | ſtichſt, ſticht | ſtach | geſtochen |
| ſtecken  to stick | . | ſtack | geſteckt |
| ſtehen  to stand | | ſtand | geſtanden |
| ſtehlen  to steal | ſtiehlſt, ſtiehlt | ſtahl | geſtohlen |
| ſteigen  to mount | | ſtieg | geſtiegen |
| ſterben  to die | ſtirbſt, ſtirbt | ſtarb | geſtorben |
| ſtieben  to fly off | | ſtob | geſtoben |
| ſtinken  to stink | | ſtank | geſtunken |
| ſtoßen  to push | ſtößeſt, ſtößt | ſtieß | geſtoßen |
| ſtreichen  to stroke ; to cancel | | ſtrich | geſtrichen |
| ſtreiten  to quarrel | | ſtritt | geſtritten |
| thun  to do | | that | gethan |
| tragen  to carry | trägſt, trägt | trug | getragen |
| treffen  to hit | triffſt, trifft | traf | getroffen |
| treiben  to drive | | trieb | getrieben |
| treten  to tread | trittſt, tritt | trat | getreten |
| trinken  to drink | | trank | getrunken |

| Infinitive. | Present, 2d and 3d Persons. | Imperfect, 1st Person. | Past Participle. |
|---|---|---|---|
| trügen  to deceive | | trog | getrogen |
| verbergen  to hide | verbirgst, birgt | verbarg | verborgen |
| verbieten  to forbid | | verbot | verboten |
| verbleichen  to discolor | | verblich | verblichen |
| verderben  to spoil | verdirbst, ver-birbt | verdarb | verdorben |
| verdrießen  to vex | . | verdroß | verdrossen |
| vergessen  to forget | vergissest, ver-gißt | vergaß | vergessen |
| verhehlen  to conceal | | verhehlte | verhohlen |
| verlieren  to lose | | verlor | verloren |
| verschwinden  to disappear | | verschwand | verschwunden |
| verwirren  to confuse | | verworr | verworren |
| verzeihen  to forgive | | verzieh | verziehen |
| wachsen  to grow | wächsest, wächst | wuchs | gewachsen |
| wägen  to weigh | | wog | gewogen |
| waschen  to wash | wäschest, wäscht | wusch | gewaschen |
| weben  to weave | | wob | gewoben |
| weichen  to yield | | wich | gewichen |
| weisen  to show | | wies | gewiesen |
| wenden  to turn | | wandte | gewandt |
| werben  to sue | wirbst, wirbt | warb | geworben |
| werfen  to throw | wirfst, wirft | warf | geworfen |
| wiegen  to weigh | | wog | gewogen |
| winden  to wind | | wand | gewunden |
| wissen  to know | ich weiß, du weißt, er weiß | wußte | gewußt |
| wollen  to be willing | ich will, du willst, er will | wollte | gewollt |
| zeihen  to accuse | | zieh | geziehen |
| ziehen  to draw | | zog | gezogen |
| zwingen  to force | | zwang | gezwungen. |

# ABBREVIATIONS.

*acc.* accusative.
*adj.* adjective.
*adv.* adverb.
*art.* article.
*comp.* comparative.
*conj.* conjunction.
*dat.* dative.
*def.* definite.
*dem.* demonstrative.
*fem.* feminine.
*fig.* figurative.
*gen.* genitive.
*imp.* imperfect.
*indef.* indefinite.
*interj.* interjection.
*interr.* interrogative.
*intrans.* intransitive.
*irr.* irregular.

*masc.* masculine.
*n.* noun.
*neut.* neuter.
*num.* numeral.
*part.* participle.
*pers.* personal.
*pl.* plural.
*poss.* possessive.
*pr. n.* proper noun.
*pron.* pronoun.
*refl.* reflexive.
*rel.* relative.
*sep.* separable.
*sing.* singular.
*superl.* superlative.
*trans.* transitive.
*v.* verb (regular verb in German).
( ) subject to omission.

# I. GERMAN-ENGLISH VOCABULARY.

Aal, ber, –(e)s. eel.
Aas, bas, –es. carrion.
ab, adv. off.
Abend, ber, –s. evening.
Abendbrot [Abendbrod], bas, –(e)s
or Abendessen, bas, –s. supper.
aber, conj. but.
Aberglaube(n), ber, –ns. superstition.
abschreiben, irr. v.; sep. to copy
(write off).
Abschrift, bie. copy.
abwesend, adj. absent.
acht, num. eight.
Acht, bie. heed, attention, care;
geben Sie acht [Acht], give heed,
pay attention; nehmen Sie sich
in acht, take care.
achten, v. to esteem, respect.
achtundzwanzig, num. twenty-
eight.
achtzehn, num. eighteen.
achtzig, num. eighty.
Achsel, bie. shoulder.
Acker, ber, –s. ploughed field.
Adam, ber, –s. Adam.
Adler, ber, –s. eagle.
Admiral, ber, –s. admiral.
Adolf or Adolph, ber, –s. Adolphus.
Advokat [Advocat], ber, –en.
lawyer.
Affe, ber, –n. ape, monkey.
Afrika, –s, pr. n. Africa.

Ägypten, –s, pr. n. Egypt.
Ägypter [Aegypter], ber, –s.
Egyptian.
Albert, ber, –s. Albert.
Alexander, ber, –s. Alexander.
Alfred, ber, –s. Alfred.
all (–er, –e, –es), adj. all, every;
Alles, everything.
allein, adj. alone; adv. only; conj.
but.
Allmacht, bie. omnipotence.
allmächtig, adj. almighty, omnip-
otent.
Alpen, bie, pl. Alps.
als, conj. as, than, when.
also, adv. so, thus, therefore.
alt, adj. old, of age.
am for an bem.
Amalia or Amalie, bie, –s or –ns.
Amelia.
Ameise, bie. ant.
Amerika, –s, pr. n. America.
Amerikaner, ber, –s. American
(man); Amerikanerin, bie. American (woman).
amerikanisch, adj. American.
Amsel, bie. black-bird.
Amt, bas, –(e)s. office.
an, prep. at, in, to.
ander, adj. other.
anderswo, adv. elsewhere.
Anerbieten, bas, –s. offer.
Anfang, ber, –(e)s. beginning;
Anfangs, at first.

anfangen, *irr. v.; sep.* to begin.

Angel, die. fishing-hook *and* rod.

angenehm, *adj.* agreeable, pleasant.

angreifen, *irr. v.; sep.* to touch; to attack.

anhalten, *irr. v.; sep.* to stop.

ankleiden, *v.; sep.* to dress.

ankommen, *irr. v.; sep.* to arrive.

Ankunft, die. arrival.

anmachen, *v.; sep.* to make up, kindle.

Anna, die, –s. Anna.

annehmen, *irr. v.; sep.* to accept.

ansehen, *irr. v.; sep.* to look at.

anstatt, *prep.* instead.

antreffen, *irr. v.; sep.* to meet, find (at a place).

Antwort, die. answer.

antworten, *v.* to answer.

anwesend, *adj.* present.

anziehen, *irr. v.; sep.* to pull on, put on; to attract.

anzünden, *v.; sep.* to kindle.

Apfel, der, –s. apple.

Apfelbaum, der, –s. apple-tree.

Apotheker, der, –s. apothecary, druggist.

April, der, –s. April.

Araber, der, –s. Arab.

Arabien, –s. Arabia.

Arbeit, die. work, labor.

arbeiten, *v.* to work, labor.

Arbeiter, der, –s. workman, laborer.

arm, *adj.* poor.

Arm, der, –(e)s. arm.

Armband, das, –(e)s. bracelet.

artig, *adj.* well-mannered, well-behaved, good.

Artikel, der, –s. article.

Arznei, die. medicine.

Arzt, der, –es. physician.

Asche, die, *sing.* ashes.

Asien, –s, *pr. n.* Asia.

Ast, der, –(e)s. branch.

Atem [Athem], der, –s. breath.

atlantisch, *adj.* Atlantic.

Aue, die. meadow.

auch, *adv.* also, too.

auf, *prep.* on, upon, at, to; *adv.* up.

Aufgabe, die. lesson, exercise, task.

aufgehen, *irr. v.; sep.* to rise (of sun, etc.).

aufhören, *v.; sep.* to leave off, cease.

auflesen, *irr. v.; sep.* to pick up.

aufmachen, *v.; sep.* to make open, open.

aufmerksam, *adj.* attentive.

aufnehmen, *irr. v.; sep.* to take (up); to receive.

aufstehen, *irr. v.; sep.* to stand up, get up, rise.

aufstellen, *v.; sep.* to set up.

Auftrag, der, –(e)s. order, commission.

Auge, das, –s; *pl.* –en. eye.

August, der, –s. August.

aus, *prep.* out of, from; *adv.* out.

ausbrechen, *irr. v.; sep.* to break out.

Ausfuhr, die. export.

ausführen, *v.; sep.* to carry out; to export.

ausgeben, *irr. v.; sep.* to spend, expend.

ausgehen, *irr. v.; sep.* to go out.

auskleiden, *v.; sep.* to undress.

ausrufen, *irr. v.; sep.* to call out, exclaim.

Ausrufungswort, das, –(e)s. interjection.

ausschicken, *v.; sep.* to send out.
außen, *adv.* on the outside.
außer, *prep.* outside of, without, beside.
außerdem, *adv.* besides.
außerhalb, *prep. and adv.* outside.
außerordentlich, *adj.* extraordinary.
auswendig, *adj.* external; *adv.* inside out; by heart; auswendig können, to know by heart.
auszanken, *v. sep.* to scold.
Axe, die. Axle.

Bach, der, –(e)s. brook; Bächlein, das, –s. brooklet.
backen, *irr. v.* to bake.
Bäcker, der, –s. baker.
Bad, das, –es. bath.
baden, *v.* to bathe.
Baden, –s, *pr. n.* Baden.
Bahnhof, der, –(e)s. railway-station.
bald, *adv.* soon; in Bälde, in a short time.
Balken, der, –s. beam (wooden).
Ball, der, –(e)s. ball.
Band, das, –(e)s; *pl.* –er. ribbon.
Band, der, –es; *pl.* –e. volume.
Bank, die. bench; bank.
Bär, der, –en. bear.
Baron, der, –(e)s. baron.
Bart, der, –(e)s. beard.
Bau, der, –(e)s. structure.
bauen, *v.* to build.
Bauer, der, –s *or* –n; *pl.* –n. farmer, peasant.
Bauerngut, das, –(e)s. farm.
baufällig, *adj.* out of repair (tumble-down).
Baum, der, –(e)s. tree.
Baumblatt, das, –es. leaf of a tree.
Baumwolle, die. cotton.

bedecken, *v.* to cover.
Bediente, der, –en; *participial adj. used as a noun.* man-servant.
Befehl, der, –(e)s. command, order.
befehlen, *irr. v.; sep.* to command.
befinden, *irr. v.; refl.* to find one's self, to be, to do; wie befinden Sie sich? how do you do?
befriedigen, *v.* to satisfy.
befühlen, *v.* to feel (by touch).
begegnen, *v.* to meet.
beginnen, *irr. v.* to begin.
begleiten, *v.* to accompany.
beglückt, *adj.* contented.
begnügen, *v.; refl.* to content one's self.
begreifen, *irr. v.* to conceive.
behalten, *irr. v.* to keep.
behängen, *v.* to hang (with).
bei, *prep.* by, near, at the house of, with.
beider, –e, –es, *adj.* both.
beim *for* bei dem.
Bein, das, –(e)s. leg.
beinahe, *adv.* nearly, almost.
beisammen, *adv.* together.
Beispiel, das, –(e)s. example.
Beistand, der, –(e)s. assistance.
beistehen, *irr. v.; sep.* to assist.
bejahrt, *adj.* aged.
bekannt, *adj.* known.
beklagen, *v.* to lament; *refl.* to complain.
bekommen, *irr. v.* to get, receive.
belagern, *v.* to besiege.
Belgien, –s, *pr. n.* Belgium.
belohnen, *v.* to reward.
Belohnung, die. reward.
Belus, der, *pr. n.* Belus.
bemerken, *v.* to notice, perceive.
bemitleiden, *v.* to pity.
bemühen, *v.* to trouble; *refl.* to endeavor.

bereichern, *v.* to enrich.

bereit, *adj.* ready.

Berg, der, –(e)s. mountain.

bergen, *irr. v.* to hide.

Berlin, –s, *pr. n.* Berlin.

Beruf, der, –(e)s. calling, profession.

berufen, *irr. v.* to call.

berühmt, *adj.* renowned, celebrated.

beschäftigen, *v.* to occupy; *refl.*
to busy one's self, be busy.

beschlagen, *irr. v.* to shoe.

beschreiben, *irr. v.* to describe.

besiegen, *v.* to conquer.

besser, *adj.; comp. of* gut. better.

best, *adj.; superl. of* gut. best.

Bestellung, die. order.

bestimmt, *adj.* definite.

Bestimmungswort, das, –(e)s.
article.

Besuch, der, –(e)s. visit.

besuchen, *v.* to visit.

Besuchszimmer, das –s. parlor.

beten, *v.* to pray.

betrachten, *v.* to look at.

betragen, *irr. v.* to amount; *refl.*
to behave.

betreffen, *irr. v.* to befall : to concern.

betrügen, *irr. v.* to cheat.

Bett, das, –(e)s; *pl.* –en. bed.

Betttuch, das, –(e)s. sheet.

Beutel, der, –s. purse.

bevor, *conj.* before.

Beweis, der, –es. proof.

bewohnen, *v.* to inhabit.

Bewohner, der, –s. inhabitant.

bewundern, *v.* to admire.

bezahlen, *v.* to pay.

biegen, *irr. v.* to bend.

Biene, die. bee.

Bier, das, –(e)s. beer.

bieten, *irr. v.* to offer.

Bild, das, –(e)s. image, likeness,
picture.

Billet, das, –(e)s. ticket.

billig, *adj.* fair, cheap.

binden, *irr. v.* to bind.

Bindewort, das, –(e)s. conjunction.

binnen, *prep.* within.

Birne, die. pear.

bis, *adv., prep. and conj.* as far
as ; up to, till ; until.

bitten, *irr. v.* to beg, ask, request ;
bitte, pray, please.

blasen, *irr. v.* to blow.

blaß, *adj.* pale.

Blatt, das, –es. leaf; journal.

blau, *adj.* blue.

Blei, das, –(e)s. lead.

bleiben, *irr. v.* to remain, stay.

bleich, *adj.* pale.

Bleistift, der, –(e)s. lead-pencil.

blind, *adj.* blind.

blitzen, *v.* lighten.

bloß, *adj.* bare ; *adv.* only.

Blume, die. flower , Blumenblatt,
das, –(e)s. leaf of a flower.

Blut, das, –(e)s. blood.

Boden, der, –s. ground, floor.

Bohne, die. bean.

Boot, das, –es. boat.

Börse, die. exchange.

böse, *adj.* bad ; angry ; Böses,
evil, wrong.

Bosheit, die. malice.

braten, *irr. v.* to roast.

Braten, der, –s. roast.

brauchen, *v.* to use; to want, need.

Braun, –s, *pr. n.* Brown.

brechen, *irr. v.* to break.

breit, *adj.* broad, wide.

brennen, *irr. v.* to burn.

Brief, der, –(e)s. letter.

Briefbote, der, -n. postman.

Brieftasche, die. portfolio, pocket-book.

Briefträger, der, -s. letter-carrier.

Brille, die, *sing.* pair of spectacles.

bringen, *irr. v.* to bring.

Brot [Brod], das, -(e)s. bread.

Brücke, die. bridge.

Bruder, der, -s. brother.

Brunnen, der, -s. well, fountain.

Brüssel, -s, *pr. n.* Brussels.

Brust, die. breast.

Brutus, der. Brutus.

Buch, das, -(e)s. book; *dim.* Büchlein, das, -s. little book.

Buchbinder, der, -s. bookbinder.

Buchhändler, der, -s. bookseller.

Bund, der, -(e)s. confederation.

Bund, das, -(e)s. bundle.

Bündel, das, -s. bundle.

Burg, die. castle.

Busch, der, -es. bush.

Butte, die. tub.

Butter, die. butter.

Cäsar, der, -s. Cæsar.

Cassius, der. Cassius.

Cato, der. -s. Cato.

Ceder, die. cedar.

Certifikat [Certificat], das, -(e)s. certificate.

Charakter, der, -s. character.

Chemie, die. chemistry.

Chili, -s, *pr. n.* Chili.

China, -s, *pr. n.* China.

Citat, das, -(e)s. quotation.

Citrone, die. lemon.

Claudius, der. Claudius.

Colonel, der, -s. colonel.

Cuba, -s, *pr. n.* Cuba.

Cypern, -s, *pr. n.* Cyprus.

Da, *adv. and conj.* there, here, then; as.

Dach, das, -(e)s. roof.

Dachstube, die. garret.

dadurch, *adv.* thereby, through it or them; through this or that, through these or those.

daher, *adv.* thence, therefore.

dahin, *adv.* thither, there.

dahinten, *adv.* behind.

damals, *adv.* at that time.

Dame, die. lady.

damit, *adv. and conj.* therewith, with it or them; in order that; damit nicht, lest.

Damm, der, -(e)s. dam.

Dank, der, -(e)s. thanks.

dankbar, *adj.* thankful.

danken, *v.* to thank.

dann, *adv.* then.

daran, *adv.* thereat, at it or them.

darauf, *adv.* thereon, thereupon, on or upon it, etc.

daraus, *adv.* thence, out of it, etc.

darin, *adv.* therein, in it, etc.

Darius, der. Darius.

darüber, *adv.* over it, etc.

darum, *adv.* therefore.

darunter, *adv.* under it, among it, etc.

das, *art. and pron.* the; this, that, it; which.

daß, *conj.* that.

Dattel, die. date (fruit).

Datum, der, -s; *pl.* -ta. date (day).

däucht, *old form* = deukt; mir däucht. methinks.

davon, *adv.* thereof, of it, etc.

dazu, *adv.* thereto, to it, etc.

dazwischen, *adv.* between it, etc.

dazwischenlegen, *v. sep.* to put between.

Decke, die. covering, blanket; ceiling.

dein, -e, deiu, poss. adj. thy, your.

deiner, gen. of pers. pron. du. of thee, of you, of thyself, of yourself.

deiner, -e, -es, poss. pron. thine, yours; der, die, das deine, thine, yours; der, die, das deinige, thine, yours.

denen, dat. pl. of dem. and rel. pron. to these, etc.

denken, irr. v. to think.

denn, conj. for.

dennoch, adv. still, yet.

der, die, das, art. and pron. the; he, she, it, this, that; who, which.

deren, gen. sing. fem. and gen. pl. of dem. and rel. pron.

derjenige, diejenige, dasjenige, pron. the one, he, she, that.

derselbe, dieselbe, dasselbe [daffel-be], pron. and adj. the same, he, she, it.

des for deffen.

deffen, gen. sing. masc. and neut. of dem. and rel. pron.

desto, adv. so much, the; je ... desto, the ... the.

deutlich, adj. distinct.

deutsch, adj. German; das Deutsch, -en, the German (language); der Deutsche, -en, the German (man); die Deutsche, -en, the German (woman); ein Deutscher, -en, a German (man); eine Deutsche, -en, a German (woman).

Deutschland, -s, pr. n. Germany.

Dezember [December], der, -s. December.

Diamant, der, -en. diamond.

dich, acc. of du. thee.

Dichter, der, -s. poet.

dick, adj. thick.

Dieb, der, -(e)s. thief.

Diener, der, -s. man-servant.

Dienstag, der, -(e)s. Tuesday.

dies for dieses.

dieser, diese, dieses, pron. this, this one.

diesseits, adv. and prep. on this side.

Ding, das, -(e)s. thing.

dir, dat. of du.

doch, adv. still, yet, however; oh yes; I hope.

Dom, der, -(e)s. cathedral.

Domkirche, die. cathedral.

donnern, v. to thunder.

Donnerstag, der, -s. Thursday.

Dorf, das, -(e)s. village.

dort, adv. there, yonder.

dorthin, adv. thither.

Dose, die. box.

Douglas, der. Douglas.

draußen, adv. outside, without.

drehen, v. to turn, twist.

drei, num. three.

dreihundert, num. three-hundred; der, die, das dreihundertste, the three-hundredth.

dreimal, adv. thrice, three-times.

dreißig, num. thirty; der, die, das dreißigste, the thirtieth.

dreiundzwanzig, num. twenty-three; der, die, das dreiundzwanzigste, the twenty-third.

dreizehn, num. thirteen; der, die, das dreizehnte, the thirteenth.

drinnen, adv. inside.

dritte, adj. third.

droben, adv. above.

drohen, v. to threaten.

drunten, adv. below.

du, pron. thou.

dumm, adj. stupid.

**dunkel,** *adj.* dark.

**durch,** *prep.* through, by.

**durchſehen,** *irr. v.; sep.* to look through, over.

**dürfen,** *irr. v.* to be allowed.

**durſtig,** *adj.* thirsty.

**Dutzend,** das, -(e)s. dozen.

**eben,** *adj. and adv.* even; just; **ebenſo,** just as, as, so.

**Eduard,** der, -s. Edward.

**ehe,** *conj.* ere, before; **eher,** *adv.* sooner.

**ehemals,** *adv.* formerly.

**Ehre,** die. honor.

**ehrlich,** *adj.* honest.

**Ei,** das, -(e)s. egg.

**Eigenſchaftswort,** das, -(e)s. adjective.

**ein, eine, ein,** *art. and num.* a, an; one; **einer, eine, ein(e)s,** (*without noun*) one, some one.

**einander,** *adv.* each other.

**einäugig,** *adj.* one-eyed.

**einfach,** *adj.* simple, plain.

**einführen,** *v.; sep.* to introduce.

**einig,** *adj. and adv.* united; in concord.

**einig,** *adj. and pron.* some, any, a few.

**einladen,** *irr. v.; sep.* to invite.

**einmal,** *adv.* once, even.

**einſchlafen,** *irr. v.; sep.* to fall asleep.

**einſt,** *adv.* once, one day, some day.

**eintreten,** *irr. v.; sep.* to enter.

**einunddreißig,** *num.* thirty-one; **der, die, das einunddreißigſte,** the thirty-first.

**einundzwanzig,** *num.* twenty-one; **der, die, das einundzwanzigſte,** the twenty-first.

**Einwohner,** der, -s. inhabitant.

**Einzahl,** die. singular.

**einzig,** *adj.* single, only, one.

**Eis,** das, -es. ice.

**Eiſen,** das, -s. iron.

**Eiſenbahn,** die. rail-road.

**eiſern,** *adj.* iron.

**eitel,** *adj.* vain.

**Elbe,** die. the river Elbe.

**Elend,** das, -(e)s. misery.

**Elefant** [**Elephant**], der, -en. elephant.

**elf,** *num.* eleven; **der, die, das elfte,** the eleventh.

**Eliſabeth,** die, -s. Elizabeth.

**Eliſe,** die, -ns. Eliza.

**Elle,** die. yard.

**Eltern,** die, *pl.* parents.

**Emilie,** die, -ns. Emily.

**Empfang,** der, -(e)s. reception.

**empfangen,** *irr. v.* to receive.

**Empfänger,** der, -s. receiver.

**Emma,** die, -s. Emma.

**Empörer,** der, -s. rebel.

**Empörung,** die. rebellion, revolt, insurrection.

**Ende,** das, -s; *pl.* -n. end.

**endigen,** *v.* to end, finish.

**endlich,** *adv.* at length.

**England,** -s, *pr. n.* England.

**Engländer,** der, -s. Englishman; **die Engländerin,** English-woman.

**engliſch,** *adj.* English; **das Engliſch,** -en, the English (language).

**Enkel,** der, -s. grandson; **Enkelin,** die. granddaughter.

**entdecken,** *v.* discover.

**Entfärben,** das, -s. discoloring.

**Ente,** die. duck.

**entfliehen,** *irr. v.* to escape.

**entgegen,** *adv. and prep.* to meet; towards; **entgegengehen,** *irr. v.; sep.* to go to meet.

entgehen, *irr. v.* to escape.

entlang, *adv. and prep.* along.

entschließen, *irr. v.; refl.* to resolve.

entsprechen, *irr. v.* to answer to (figuratively).

entweder, *conj.* either.

Ephen, der, –s. ivy.

er, *pron.* he, she, it.

erbauen, *v.* to build up; to edify.

erblicken, *v.* to espy, see.

Erbse, die. pea.

Erde, die. earth.

erfahren, *irr. v.* to experience; to learn.

Erfahrung, die. experience.

erfinden, *irr. v.* to invent, discover.

Erfindung, die. invention, discovery.

Erfolg, der, –(e)s. success.

ergeben, *irr. v.; refl.* to surrender.

ergießen, *irr. v.; refl.* to empty.

ergreifen, *irr. v.* to seize.

erhalten, *irr. v.* to receive.

erhören, *v.* to listen to.

erinnern, *v.* to remind; *refl.* to remember.

erkälten, *v.; refl.* to take cold.

erkennen, *irr. v.* to recognize.

erlangen, *v.* to obtain.

erlassen, *irr. v.* to release; to issue.

erlauben, *v.* to allow, permit.

Erlaubnis [Erlaubniß], die. permission.

ermorden, *v.* to slay, murder.

ernsthaft, *adj.* earnest.

Ernte, die. harvest.

erquicken, *v.* to refresh.

erretten, *v.* to save.

erschrecken, *v.* to frighten; *irr. v.* to be frightened.

erst, *adj. and adv.* first; at first, not till.

Erstaunen, das, –s. astonishment.

erstrecken, *v.; refl.* to extend.

ersuchen, *v.* to request, ask.

Erwähnung, die. mention.

erwarten, *v.* to expect.

erwidern [erwiedern], *v.* to reply.

erzählen, *v.* to relate, tell.

es, *pron.* he, she, it, they; there.

Esel, der, –s. ass.

essen, *irr. v.* to eat.

Essen, das, –s. meal, dinner.

Essig, der, –s. vinegar.

etwas, *pron. and adv.* something, anything, some; a little.

euch, *dat. and acc. of* ihr. to you; you.

euer, *gen. of* ihr. of you.

euer, eu(e)re, euer, *poss. adj.* your.

euer, eure, eures, *poss. pron.* yours; der, die, das eure, yours; der, die, das eurige, yours.

Eva, die, –s. Eva.

ewig, *adj.* eternal.

Examen, das, –s. examination.

Exempel, das, –s. example.

Fächer, der, –s. fan.

Fähigkeit, die. faculty.

fahren, *irr. v.* to drive, ride (in any vehicle).

Fall, der, –(e)s. fall; case; falls, *conj.* in case.

fallen, *irr. v.* to fall.

Familie, die. family.

fangen, *irr. v.* to catch, take, capture.

Fanny, die, –s. Fanny.

Farbe, die. color.

Faß, das, –es. cask, barrel.

fassen, v. to seize, grasp.

fast, adv. almost.

fasten, v. to fast.

faul, adj. lazy.

Februar, der, –s. February.

Feder, die. pen.

Federmesser, das, –s. pen-knife.

fehlen, v. to be missing; to err; was fehlt Ihnen? what ails you? what is the matter with you?

Fehler, der, –s. mistake, fault.

fehlschlagen, irr. v.; sep. to fail.

Feiertag, der, –(e)s. holiday.

fein, adj. fine.

Feind, der, –(e)s. enemy.

Feld, das, –(e)s. field.

Feldmesser, der, –s. surveyor.

Feldzeugmeister, der, –s. general-in-chief.

Feldzug, der, –(e)s. campaign.

Felsen, der, –s. rock.

Fenster, das, –s. window.

Ferien, die, pl. vacation.

fertig, adj. ready, done.

Festung, die. fortress.

fett, adj. fat.

feucht, adj. damp.

Feuer, das, –s. fire.

finden, irr. v. to find.

Finger, der, –s. finger.

Fingerhut, der, –(e)s. thimble.

finster, adj. dark.

Fisch, der, –es. fish.

Flasche, die. bottle.

Flecken, der, –s. spot; borough.

Fleisch, das, –es. flesh, meat.

fleißig, adj. diligent.

fliegen, irr. v. to fly.

fliehen, irr. v. to flee.

fließen, irr. v. to flow.

Flinte, die. gun, rifle.

Flügel, der, –s. wing.

Flur, die. field; floor.

Fluß, der, –es. river.

flüssig, adj. liquid.

Föhre, die. fir.

folgen, v. to follow.

folglich, adv. consequently.

fort, adv. off, away, on.

fortfahren, irr. v.; sep. to drive off; to continue (go on).

fortgehen, irr. v.; sep. to go away.

forttreiben, irr. v.; sep. to carry away.

Frage, die. question.

fragen, irr. v., sometimes used regularly. to ask.

Franc, der, –en. franc (French coin).

Frankfurt, –s, pr. n. Frankfort.

Frankreich, –s, pr. n. France.

Franzose, der, –n. Frenchman; die Französin, French woman.

französisch, adj. French; das Französisch, –en. the French (language).

Frau, die. woman; wife; Mrs.

Fräulein, das, –s. young lady; damsel; Miss.

frech, adj. insolent.

Frechheit, die. insolence.

frei, adj. free.

Freiheit, die. freedom, liberty.

freilich, adv. indeed, certainly, to be sure.

Freitag, der, –s. Friday.

fremd, adj. strange, foreign; der Fremde, –n, the stranger; ein Fremder, –en, a stranger; die Fremde, eine Fremde, strange woman or country.

fressen, irr. v. to eat (of animals), devour.

Freude, die. joy.

freuen, *v.* to make glad; es freut mich, it makes me glad, I am glad; *refl.* to rejoice, ich freue mich, I rejoice, am glad.

Freund, der, –(e)s. friend.

Freundin, die. friend *(fem.)*.

Freundschaft, die. friendship.

Frevel, der, –s. outrage.

Friedrich, der, –s. Frederick; Friedrichstraße, Frederick Street.

frieren, *irr. v.* to freeze; to be cold; es friert mich, I am cold.

frisch, *adj.* fresh.

froh, *adj.* glad.

Frucht, die. fruit.

fruchtbar, *adj.* fruitful, fertile.

früh, *adj. and adv.* early, soon; früher, earlier, sooner, former(ly).

Frühling, der, –(e)s. spring.

Frühstück, das, –(e)s. breakfast.

frühstücken, *v.* to breakfast.

Fuchs, der, –es. fox.

führen, *v.* to lead; Krieg führen, to wage war.

Führer, der, –s. leader, guide.

füllen, *v.* to fill.

fünf, *num.* five; der, die, das fünfte, the fifth.

fünfhundert, *num.* five-hundred; der, die, das fünfhundertste, the five-hundredth.

fünfmal, *adv.* five times.

fünfundvierzig, *num.* forty-five; der, die, das fünfundvierzigste, the forty-fifth.

fünfundzwanzig, *num.* twenty-five; der, die, das fünfundzwanzigste, the twenty-fifth.

fünfzehn, *num.* fifteen; der, die, das fünfzehnte, the fifteenth.

fünfzig, *num.* fifty; der, die, das fünfzigste, the fiftieth.

für, *prep.* for.

fürchten, *v.* to fear.

Fürst, der, –en. prince.

Fürwort, das, –(e)s. pronoun.

Fuß, der, –es. foot.

Fußboden, der, –s. ground, floor.

Fußteppich, der, –(e)s. carpet.

Gabel, die. fork.

Gans, die. goose.

ganz, *adj. and adv.* whole, entire, all; quite.

gar, *adj. and adv.* done; very, even; garnicht, not at all.

Garten, der, –s. garden.

Gärtner, der, –s. gardener; die Gärtnerin, gardener's wife.

Gasthof, der, –(e)s. tavern, inn.

Gatte, der, –n. husband.

Gattin, die. wife.

Gebäude, das, –s.· building.

geben, *irr. v.* to give; es gi(e)bt, there is, there are.

Gebet, das, –(e)s. prayer.

Gebirge, das, –s. mountain-range.

geboren, *past part. of* gebären. born.

Gebrauch, der, –(e)s. use, custom.

gebräuchlich, *adj.* usual, customary.

Geburtstag, der, –(e)s. birthday.

gedeihen, *irr. v.* to thrive.

gedenken, *irr. v.* to remember.

Gedicht, das, –(e)s. poem.

Geduld, die. patience.

Gefahr, die. danger.

gefallen, *irr. v.* to please.

gefälligst, *adv.* if you please, please.

gefangen, *adj.* captive; der Gefangene, –en, prisoner; ein Gefangener, –en, a prisoner (*participial adj. used as noun*).

Gefängnis [Gefängniß], das, -es. prison.

gegen, *prep.* towards, against, to, about.

Gegend, die. region.

Gegenteil [Gegentheil], das, -(e)s. contrary; im Gegenteil, on the contrary.

gegenüber, *adv. and prep.* opposite.

gehen, *irr. v.* to go, to walk; wie geht es Ihnen? how are you?

Gehirn, das, -(e)s. brain.

gehorchen, *v.* to obey.

gehören, *v.* to belong.

gehorsam, *adj.* obedient.

geistreich, *adj.* intelligent, witty.

gelb, *adj.* yellow.

Geld, das, -(e)s. money.

gelegen, *adj.* situate; convenient, opportune.

gelehrt, *adj.* learned.

gelingen, *irr. v.* to succeed; es gelingt mir, I succeed.

Gemahl, der, -(e)s. husband.

Gemahlin, die. wife.

Gemälde, das, -s. painting.

Gemse, die. chamois.

Gemüse, das, -s. vegetable.

General, der, -(e)s. general.

Genf, -s, *pr. n.* Geneva.

genug, *adv.* enough.

Geographie, die. geography.

Georg, der, -s. George.

gerade, *adj. and adv.* straight, direct; just.

gerecht, *adj.* just.

gern, *adv.* willingly; gern mögen, gern haben, *and* gern *with any verb, equivalent to the English,* to like; er singt gern, he likes to sing (*lit.* he sings willingly).

gesandt, *past. part.* sent; der Ge-

sandte, -en, ein Gesandter, -en, ambassador (*participial adj. used as noun*).

Gesang, der, -(e)s. singing, song.

Geschäft, das, -(e)s. business.

geschehen, *irr. v.* to happen.

Geschenk, das, -(e)s. present.

Geschichte, die. history, story.

Geschlechtswort, das, -(e)s. article.

gesellen, *v.; refl.* to associate.

Gesellschaft, die. society, company.

Gesetz, das, -es. law.

Gesicht, das, -(e)s. face.

Gespräch, das, -(e)s. conversation.

gestehen, *irr. v.* to confess.

gestern, *adv.* yesterday.

gesund, *adj.* healthy, wholesome.

Getreide, das, -s. grain.

Gevatter, der, -s. godfather.

Gewalt, die. force, power.

Gewehr, das, -(e)s. musket, gun, rifle.

gewinnen, *irr. v.* to win.

gewiß, *adj.* certain.

Gewissen, das, -s. conscience.

gewöhnen, *v.* to accustom.

gewöhnlich, *v.* usual, common.

gierig, *adj.* greedy.

Gierigkeit, die. greediness.

Glanz, der, -es. splendor.

Glas, das, -es. glass.

glauben, *v.* to believe, to think.

gleich, *adj. and adv.* like; directly, immediately.

gleichen, *irr. v.* to be like, resemble.

Gleichgültigkeit, die. indifference.

Glocke, die. bell.

glücklich, *adj.* happy, fortunate.

glühen, *v.* to glow.

Gnade, die. grace.

Gold, das, –(e)s. gold.

golden, adj. golden, gold, of gold.

Gott, der, –es. God.

Göttin, die. goddess.

Grab, das, –(e)s. grave.

graben, irr. v. to dig.

Graben, der, –s. ditch.

Graf, der, –en. count.

Gräfin, die. countess.

grämen, v. to grieve.

Grammatik, die. grammar.

Gras, das, –es. grass.

grau, adj. gray.

greifen, irr. v. to grasp, seize.

Griechenland, –s, pr. n. Greece.

groß, adj. great, big, tall, large.

Großmutter, die. grandmother.

Großvater, der, –s. grandfather.

grün, adj. green.

grüßen, v. to greet.

Gulden, der, –s. florin.

Gustav, der, –s. Gustavus.

gut, adj. and adv. good; well; Gut, das, –es. possession.

Güte, die. goodness, kindness.

gütig, adj. kind.


Haar, das, –(e)s. hair.

haben, irr. v. to have.

Hafen, der, –s. harbor.

Hafer, der, –s. oats.

hageln, v. to hail.

Hahn, der, –(e)s. cock.

Haide, die. heath.

Hain, der, –(e)s. grove.

halb, adj. half.

Hals, der, –es. neck.

Halsbinde, die. neck-tie, cravat.

Halstuch, das, –(e)s. kerchief.

halten, irr. v. to hold; für ... halten, to consider as.

Hammelfleisch, das, –(e)s. mutton.

Hammer, der, –s. hammer.

Hand, die. hand.

Handel, der, –s. commerce, trade.

handeln. to act; to deal.

bändigen, v. to hand.

Handschuh, der, –(e)s. glove.

Handtuch, das, –(e)s. towel.

Handwerk, das, –(e)s. handicraft, trade.

hangen, irr. v. to hang, to be suspended.

hängen, v. to hang.

Harmonie, die. harmony.

hart, adj. hard.

Hase, der, –n. hare.

Haselnuß, die. hazel-nut.

Haß, der, –es. hatred.

häßlich, adj. ugly.

Haube, die. cap.

Haupt, das, –(e)s. head.

Hauptstadt, die. capital (city).

Hauptstraße, die. main-street.

Hauptwort, das, –(e)s. noun.

Haus, das, –es. house; zu Hause, at home; nach Hause, home.

Hausthür, die. street-door.

heben, irr. v. to lift.

Heer, das, –(e)s. army.

Herde [Heerde], die. herd.

Heft, das, –(e)s. book (of sheets put together).

heilen, v. to heal, cure.

Heimat [Heimath], die. home.

Heinrich, der, –s. Henry.

heirathen [heirathen], v. to marry.

heiß, adj. hot.

heißen, irr. v. to bid; to be called, to mean; das heißt, that means, that is; wie heißen Sie? what is your name?

Held, der, –en. hero.

helfen, irr. v. to help.

hell, adj. bright.

Hemd, das, -(e)s; pl. -en. shirt, chemise

Henne, die. hen.

her, adv. hither.

herab, adv. down.

herauf, adv. up (toward the speaker).

heraus, adv. out (toward the speaker).

Herbst, der, -(e)s. autumn ; Herbst= gefühl, das, -(e)s. autumn-thoughts.

Herde [Heerde], die, herd.

herein, adv. in (towards the speaker); herein! come in !

hereinkommen, irr. v.; sep. to come in.

Herr, der, -n ; pl. -en. master; gentleman ; lord ; Mr.; mein Herr, Sir.

herrlich, adj. lordly ; glorious.

herum, adv. round.

herunter, adv. down (toward the speaker).

Herz, das, -ens; pl. -en. heart.

Herzogin, die. duchess.

Heu, das, -(e)s. hay.

heucheln, v. to feign, to be a hypocrite.

Heuchler, der, -s. hypocrite.

hier, adv. here.

hierher, adv. hither.

Himmel, der, -s. heaven, sky ; Himmelsblau, das, -s. blue sky.

hin, adv. away.

hinab, adv. down.

hinauf, adv. up.

hinauffahren, irr. v.; sep. to drive up.

hinaufgehen, irr. v.; sep. to go up.

hinaus, adv. out (away from the speaker).

hinein, adv. in (away from the speaker).

hineingehen, irr. v.; sep. to go in.

hinten, adv. behind.

hinter, prep. behind.

hinterlassen, irr. v. to leave.

hinterrücks, adv. behind the back.

hinunter, adv. down (away from the speaker).

hinunterwerfen, irr. v.; sep. to throw down.

Hirsch, der, -(e)s. stag.

Hirse, der, -s. millet.

Hirt(e), der, -en. shepherd.

Hitze, die. heat.

hoch, adv. high ; comp. höher, higher.

höchst, superl.; adj. and adv. highest ; extremely ; höchstens, at the utmost.

Hof, der, -(e)s. court, yard.

hoffen, v. to hope.

Hoffnung, die. hope.

höflich, adj. polite.

Höhe, die. height.

Höhle, die. cave.

holen, v. to fetch, to go for, to get.

Holländer, der, -s. Dutchman.

Hölle, die. hell.

Holz, das, -es. wood.

hölzern, adj. wooden, of wood.

holzicht or holzig, adj. ligneous.

Honig, der, -s. honey.

hören, v. to hear.

Hotel, das, -s. hotel.

Hose, die. trowsers.

hübsch, adj. pretty, nice.

Huf, der, -(e)s. hoof; Hufschmied, der, -(e)s. farrier.

Hügel, der, -s. hill.

Huhn, das, -(e)s. hen ; das Hühn= chen, -s. chicken.

Hund, der, –(e)s. dog.
hundert, num. hundred; der, die, das hundertste, hundredth.
hungrig, adj. hungry.
hüpfen, v. to leap.
Hut, der, –(e)s. hat, bonnet.
Hütte, die. hut, cottage.

ich, pron. I.
ihm, dat. of er, pron. (to) him, her, it.
ihn, acc. of er, pron. him, her, it.
ihnen, dat., pl. of er, fie, es. (to) them.
Ihnen, dat. of Sie. (to) you.
ihr, dat. of fie, pron. (to) him, her, it.
ihr, pron. ye, you.
ihr, ihre, ihr, poss. adj. his; her; its; their.
Ihr, Ihre, Ihr, poss. adj. your.
ihrer, gen. of fie. of her; of them; of herself, of themselves.
Ihrer, gen. of Sie. of you, of yourself, of yourselves.
ihrer, ihre, ihres, poss. pron. his, hers, its, theirs; der, die, das ihre, his, hers, its, theirs; der, die, das ihrige, his, hers, its, theirs.
Ihrer, Ihre, Ihres, poss. pron. yours; der, die, das Ihre, yours; der, die, das Ihrige, yours.
im for in dem.
immer, adv. always.
in, prep. in, at; into.
indem, conj. whilst, as.
indessen, adv. meanwhile; however.
innen, adv. inside.
innerhalb, adv. and prep. within.
ins [in's] for in das.

Insel, die. island.
inwendig, adj. and adv. inside.
irgendwo, adv. somewhere.
Irland, –s. pr. n. Ireland.
irren, v. to err; refl. sich irren, to be mistaken.
Italien, –s, pr. n. Italy.
Italiener, der, –s. Italian (man); die Italienerin, the Italian (woman).
italienisch, adj. Italian.

ja, adv. yes, yea; jawohl, yes, indeed.
Jacke, die. jacket.
Jagd, die. chase, hunting.
Jäger, der, –s. hunter.
Jahr, das, –(e)s. year.
jährlich, adj. yearly, annual.
Jacob [Jakob], der, –s. James.
Januar, der, –s. January.
Japan, –s, pr. n. Japan.
je, adv. ever; je ... desto, the ... the.
jeder, jede, jedes, pron. and adj. every, each.
jedermann [Jedermann], pron. everybody.
jedoch, conj. still, yet, however.
jemand [Jemand], pron. somebody, anybody.
jener, jene, jenes, pron. that (dem).
jenseits, prep. and adv. on that (the other) side.
jetzt, adv. now, at present.
Johann, der, –s. John.
Jude, der, –n. Jew; Jüdin, die. Jewess.
Jugend, die. youth.
Juli, der, –s. July.
Julie, die, –ns. Juliet.
Julius, der. Julius.

jung, *adj.* young.

Jüngling, der, –s. youth (young man).

Jünglingsalter, das, –s. youthful age.

Kaffee, der, –s. coffee.

Käfig, der, –(e)s. cage.

kahl, *adj.* bald.

Kaiser, der, –s. emperor.

Kaiserreich, das, –(e)s. empire.

Kalb, das, –(e)s. calf.

Kalbfleisch, das, –(e)s. veal.

kalt, *adj.* cold.

kaltblütig, *adj.* cold-blooded, cool.

Kälte, die. cold (weather); coldness.

Kamel [Kameel], das, –(e)s. camel.

Kamin, der, –(e)s. chimney.

kämmen, *v.* to comb.

kämpfen, *v.* to fight, struggle.

Kanone, die. cannon, gun.

Kapelle [Capelle], die. chapel.

Kappe, die. cap.

Karawane [Karavane], die. caravan.

Karl [Carl], der, –s. Charles.

Karlsstraße, die. Charles Street.

Karoline [Caroline], die, –ns. Caroline.

Karren, der, –s. cart.

Karte, die. card, ticket.

Karthager, der, –s. Carthaginian.

Karthago, –s, *pr. n.* Carthage.

Kartoffel, die. potato.

Kasino [Casino], das, –s. Casino.

Käse, der, –s; *pl.* Käse, die. cheese.

Katze, die. cat.

kaufen, *v.* to buy.

Kaufmann, der, –(e)s. merchant.

kaum, *adv.* scarcely.

kein, keine, kein, *adj.* no, not any.

keiner, keine, keines, *pron.* none, no one.

Keller, der, –s. cellar.

kennen, *irr. v.* to know, to be acquainted with.

Kerze, die. candle.

Kessel, der, –s. kettle.

Kesselschmied, der, –(e)s. coppersmith.

Kette, die. chain.

Kilogramm, das, –(e)s. kilogram.

Kind, das, –(e)s. child.

Kindheit, die. childhood.

kindisch, *adj.* childish.

Kinn, das, –(e)s. chin.

Kirche, die. church.

Kirsche, die. cherry.

Kissen, das, –s. pillow.

klar, *adj.* clear.

Klasse [Classe], die. class.

Klavier [Clavier], das, –(e)s. piano.

Klee, der, –s. clover.

Kleid, das, –(e)s. dress; *pl.* clothes.

Kleidung, die. clothing.

klein, *adj.* small, little.

klettern, *v.* to climb.

Klingel, die. bell.

klopfen, *v.* to knock.

Knabe, der, –n. boy.

Knie, das, –s. knee.

kochen, *v.* to cook, boil.

Koffer, der, –s. trunk.

Kohl, der, –s. cabbage; Blumenkohl, cauliflower.

Kohle, die. coal; Steinkohle, hard coal.

Köhler, der, –s. charcoal-burner.

Köln [Cöln], –s. *pr. n.* Cologne.

kommen, *irr. v.* to come.

Kommode [Commode], die. chest (of drawers).

Kompliment [Compliment], das, –(e)s. compliment.

König, der, –(e)s. king.
Königin, die. queen.
Königreich, das, –(e)s. kingdom.
können, irr. v. to be able, can, may.
Konzert [Concert], das, –(e)s. concert.
Kopf, der, –(e)s. head.
Kopfweh, das, –s. headache.
Korb, der, –(e)s. basket.
Korn, das, –(e)s. corn, rye.
Körper, der, –s. body.
kostbar, adj. costly, precious.
kosten, v. to cost.
Cousine [Cousine], die. cousin (fem.).
Kraft, die. n. power.
Kralle, die. claw.
krank, adj. ill, sick.
kränken, v. to hurt (of feelings).
Krankheit, die. illness, sickness.
Kraut, das, –(e)s. cabbage.
Krautkopf, der, –(e)s. cabbage-head.
Kreuz, das, –es. cross.
Krieg, der, –(e)s. war.
Kriegszahlamt, das, –(e)s. army pay-office.
Küche, die. kitchen.
Kuchen, der, –s. cake.
Kuh, die. cow.
kühl, adj. cool.
Kunst, die. art.
Kupfer, das, –s. copper; Kupferschmied, der, –(e)s. coppersmith.
kurz, adj. short.
Küste, die. coast.
Kutscher, der, –s. coachman.

laben, v. to refresh.
Labsal, das, –(e)s. refreshment.
lächeln, v. to smile.
lachen, v. to laugh.

lächerlich, adj. ridiculous.
Laden, der, –s. shutter; shop, store.
laden, irr. v. to load; to invite, summon.
Ladung, die. load, cargo; summon.
Lage, die. situation.
lahm, adj. lame.
Land, das, –(e)s. land, country.
landen, v. to land.
lang, adj. long; lang(e), adv. a long time, long; drei jahrelang [Jahre lang], for three years; eine zeitlang [Zeit lang], for a time.
Länge, die. length.
langsam, adj. slow.
Lärm, der, –(e)s. noise.
lassen, irr. v. to let; to leave.
lau, adj. tepid.
Laub, das, –(e)s. foliage.
Lauf, der, –(e)s. course.
Laura, die, –s. Laura.
lauschen, v. to listen.
Laut, der, –(e)s. sound.
laut, adj. and adv. loud; aloud.
leben, v. to live.
Leben, das, –s. life; am Leben, alive.
Lebensmittel, die. pl. provisions.
lebenssatt, adj. tired of life.
Leder, das, –s. leather.
ledern, adj. leathern, of leather.
leeren, v. to empty.
legen, v. to lay, put, place.
lehren, v. to learn.
Lehrer, der, –s. teacher, master.
leicht, adj. light, easy.
Leid, das, –(e)s; pl. –en. sorrow, grief; es ist or es thut mir leid, I am sorry.
leiden, irr. v. to suffer.

leihen, *irr. v.* to lend.
leife, *adj.* soft; low.
Leiter, die. ladder.
Lektion [Lection], die. lesson.
lernen, *v.* to learn.
lefen, *irr. v.* to read.
letzt, *adj.* last.
Leuchter, der, –8. candlestick.
Leute, die. *pl.* people.
Licht, das, –(e)8. light.
Lichtputze, die or Lichtschere [Licht= scheere], die. *sing.* snuffers.
Lichtstock, der, –(e)8. candlestick.
lieb, *adj.* dear.
Liebe, die. love.
lieben, *v.* to love, like.
liebenswürdig, *adj.* amiable.
Liebenswürdigkeit, die. amiability.
lieber, *adv.; comp.* rather; am liebsten, *adv.; superl.* most, best.
liebkofen, *v.* to caress.
Lied, das, –(e)8. song.
liefern, *v.* furnish; to give (battle).
liegen, *irr. v.* to lie.
Lilie, die. lily.
link, *adj.* left.
links, *adv.* to or on the left.
Linfe, die. lentil.
Lippe, die. lip.
loben, *v.* to praise.
Loch, das, –(e)8. hole.
Löffel, der, –8. spoon.
London, –8, *pr. n.* London.
Los [Loos], das, –e8. lot; große Los, das. first prize.
Lord, der, –8; *pl.* –8. Lord (title).
Lorelei, die, *pr. n.* Loreley.
los, *adj.* loose.
löfen, *v.* to loosen.
Lotterie, die. lottery.
Lotfe, der, –n. pilot.

Louisdor, der, –8; *pl.* –8. louisd'or (coin).
Löwe, der, –n. lion.
Löwin, die. lioness.
Ludwig, der, –8. Louis.
Luft, die. air.
Lüge, die. lie.
lügen, *irr. v.* to lie, tell a false-hood.
Luife [Louife], die, –n8. Louisa.
Lunge, die. lung.
Luft, die. desire, pleasure; Luft haben, to have a mind (to).
Lützen, –8, *pr. n.* Lutzen.
Lyon, –8, *pr. n.* Lyons.
Lyfias, der. Lysias.

machen, *v.* to make, to do; es macht mir Vergnügen, it gives me pleasure; ich mache einen Befuch, I pay a visit.
Macht, die. might, power.
Madam(e), die. madam; Mrs.
Mädchen, das, –8. girl; das Dienst= mädchen, maid-servant.
Magd, die. servant (*fem.*).
Magen, der, –8. stomach.
Mahl, das, –(e)8. meal.
Mai, der, –8. May.
Main, der, –8. Main (river).
Mal, das, –(e)8. time (*in multipli-cative sense*); einmal, once; vier= mal, four times.
malen, *v.* to paint.
Maler, der, –8. painter.
Mama [Mamma], die. mamma.
man, *indef. pron.* (French on). one, they, we, you, people.
mancher, manche, manches, *pron.* many a; many a one.
manchmal, *adv.* sometimes.
Mann, der, –(e)8. *pl.* –er. man; husband.

manöbrieren [manöbriren], v. to manoeuvre.

Mannſchaft, die. crew.

Mantel, der, –s. cloak.

Margarete [Margarethe], die, –ns. Margaret.

Marie, die, –ns. Mary.

Mark, die; pl. Mark. mark (coin = 25 cents).

Markt, der, –(e)s. market.

marſchieren [marſchiren], v. to march.

Marſchall, der, –s. marshal.

März, der, –es. March.

Maſſe, die. mass.

mäſten, v. to fatten.

Matraſe, die. mattress.

Matroſe, der, –n. sailor.

Mauer, die. wall.

Maulbeerbaum, der, –s. mulberry-tree.

Maurer, der, –s. mason.

Maus, die. mouse.

Meer, das, –(e)s. sea.

Mehl, das, –(e)s. flour.

mehr, adv. more.

mehrere, adj.; pl. several.

Mehrzahl, die. plural.

mein, meine, mein, poss. adj. my.

mein(er) gen. of ich. of me.

meiner, meine, mein(e)s, poss. pron. mine; der meine, die meine, das meine, mine; der meinige, die meinige, das meinige, mine.

meiſt, adj. most; adv. am meiſten, most, best.

meiſtens, adv. mostly.

Meiſter, der, –s. master.

Melodie, die. melody.

Menſch, der, –en. man (mankind).

Meſſer, das, –s. knife.

Metall, das, –(e)s. metal.

Meter, der, –s. metre.

Metzger, der, –s. butcher.

mich, acc. of ich, pron. me.

mieten [miethen], v. to hire.

Milch, die. milk.

mild, adj. mild.

mildthätig, adj. charitable.

mindeſt, adj. least; mindeſtens, adv. at least.

Minute, die. minute.

mir, dat. of ich, pron. (to) me.

mißfallen, irr. v. to displease.

mit, prep. with, together with, by.

Mitleid(en), das, –(en)s. compassion.

mitleidig, adj. compassionate.

Mittageſſen, das, –s. dinner.

Mittel, das, –s. means, remedy.

mittelſt, prep. by means.

mitteilen [mittheilen], v.; sep. to communicate.

Mittwoch, der, –s. Wednesday.

Möbel, die; pl. furniture.

möblieren [möbliren], v. to furnish.

mögen, irr. v. may, can; to like.

möglich, adj. possible.

Mohr, der, –en. moor; negro.

Möhre, die. carrot.

Monat, der, –(e)s. month.

monatlich, adj. monthly.

Mond, der, –(e)s. moon.

Montag, der, –(e)s. Monday.

Moor, das, –(e)s. moor, marsh.

Moos, das, –es. moss.

morgen, adv. to morrow; morgen früh, to-morrow morning.

Morgen, der, –s. morning.

Moritz, der, –ens. pr. n. Maurice.

müde, adj. tired, faint.

Mühe, die. trouble.

Mühle, die. mill.

Müller, der, -s. miller.
Mund, der, -(e)s. mouth.
Mundkoch, der, -(e)s. head-cook (at court).
murren, v. to murmur.
Musik, die. music.
Musikheft, das, -(e)s. music-book.
Musiklehrer, der, -s. music-teacher.
Musikstunde, die. music-lesson.
müssen, irr. v. must, to be obliged, to have to.
Muster, das, -s. pattern, model.
Mut [Muth], der, -(e)s. courage; mood.
Mutter, die. mother.
Mütze, die. cap.

nach, prep. after; to; according to.
Nachbar, der, -s or -n; pl. -n. neighbor.
Nachbarin, die. neighbor (fem.).
Nachbarschaft, die. neighborhood.
nachdem, adv. and conj. after.
nachher, adv. afterwards.
nachlässig, adj. negligent.
nachlaufen, irr. v.; sep. to run after.
Nachricht, die. news.
Nachschlüssel, der, -s. master-key.
nachsetzen, v.; sep. to put after.
nächst, adj. nearest, next.
nachsuchen, v.; sep. to search after.
Nacht, die. night.
Nacken, der, -s. neck.
Nadel, die. needle.
Nagel, der, -s. nail.
nah(e), adj. near.
Name(n), der, -ns. name; Namens, by name.
nämlich, adj. same; adv. namely.

Narcisse, die. narcissus.
Narr, der, -en. fool.
Nase, die. nose.
Naschhaftigkeit, die. greediness.
naß, adj. wet.
Nation, die. nation.
Nebel, der, -s. fog, mist.
neben, prep. at the side of, by.
Neffe, der, -n. nephew.
nehmen, irr. v. to take.
nein, adv. no.
nennen, irr. v. to name, call.
Nest, das, -(e)s. nest.
Netz, das, -es. net.
neu, adj. new.
Neugierde, die. curiosity.
neulich, adv. lately.
neun, num. nine; der, die, das neunte, the ninth.
neunundzwanzig, num. twenty-nine; der, die, das neunund-zwanzigste, the twenty-ninth.
neunzehn, num. nineteen; der, die, das neunzehnte, the nineteenth.
neunzig, num. ninety; der, die, das neunzigste, the ninetieth.
nicht, adv. not.
Nichte, die. niece.
nichts, pron. nothing.
nichtsdestoweniger, adv. nonetheless, nevertheless.
nie, adv. never.
niedrig, adj. low.
niemals, adv. never.
niemand [Niemand], pron. nobody, no one.
nirgends, adv. nowhere.
noch, adv. and conj. yet, still; nor; noch ein etc., another; noch einmal, once more; weder ... noch, neither ... nor.
Nord(en), der, -ens. north.

Nordküſte, die. north-shore.
Not [Roth], die. need, distress, misery, trouble.
Notdurft [Nothdurft], die. necessity.
Null, die. zero.
nun, adv. now.
nur, adv. only.
Nuß, die. nut.
Nußbaum, der, -(e)s. nut-tree.
nützlich, adj. useful.

ob, conj. whether.
oben, adv. above, up stairs.
oberhalb, adv. above.
Oberſt, der, -en. colonel.
obgleich or obſchon, conj. though, although.
Obſt, das, -(e)s. fruit (collective).
Ochs or Ochſe, der, -en. ox.
öde, adj. desolate.
oder, conj. or.
Ofen, der, -s. stove.
offen, adj. open.
Offizier [Officier], der, -s. officer.
öffnen, v. to open.
oft, adv. often; öfter, oftener.
oftmals, adv. oftentimes.
Oheim, der, -s. uncle.
ohne, prep. without, but for.
Ohr, das, -(e)s; pl. -en. ear.
Oktober [October], der, -s. October.
Öl [Oel], das, -(e)s. oil.
Omnibus, der, -ſſes. omnibus.
Onkel, der, -s. uncle.
Ordnung, die. order.
Öſterreich or Öſtreich [Oeſterreich], -s, pr. n. Austria.
Oſtwind, der, -(e)s. east-wind.

Paar, das, -(e)s. pair.
Pack, das, -(e)s. pack.

packen, v. to pack; to seize.
Palaſt, der, -(e)s. palace.
Pantoffel, der, -s. slipper.
Papier, das, -(e)s. paper.
Paris, pr. n. Paris.
Park, der, -(e)s. park.
Parmenio, der, -s. Parmenio.
paſſen, v. to fit; to suit.
paſſend, adj. convenient; fit.
Pate [Pathe], der, -n. godfather.
Perle, die. pearl.
Perſien, -s, pr. n. Persia.
Perſon, die. person.
Pfad, der, -(e)s. path.
Pfahl, der, -(e)s. stake, post, pole.
Pfanne, die. pan.
Pfau, der, -(e)s. peacock.
Pfeffer, der, -s. pepper.
Pfeife, die. whistle; pipe.
pfeifen, v. to whistle.
Pfeil, der, -(e)s. arrow.
Pfennig, der, -s. penny, farthing.
Pferd, das, -(e)s. horse.
Pflanze, die. plant.
Pflaſter, das, -s. plaster; pavement.
Pflaume, die. plum.
Pflaumenbaum, der, -s. plum-tree.
Pflicht, die. duty.
pflücken, v. to pick; to pluck.
Pflug, der, -(e)s. plough.
Pfund, das, -(e)s. pound.
Philoſoph, der, -en. philosopher.
Philoſophie, die. philosophy.
philoſophiſch, adj. philosophical.
Phönizier [Phönicier], der, -s. Phoenician (man).
Photograph, der, -en. photographer.
Piano(forte), das, -s. piano (-forte).
picken, v. to pick, to peck.

Pistole, die. pistol.

Platz, der, -es. place; seat; square.

Polen, -s, pr. n. Poland.

polieren [poliren], v. to polish.

polnisch, adj. Polish.

Portion, die. portion.

Post, die. post, mail.

prächtig, adj. splendid, magnificent.

Präsident, der, -en. president.

Preis, der, -es. price; prize.

Preuße, der, -n. Prussian (man).

Preußen, -s, pr. n. Prussia.

Prinz, der, -en. prince (of the royal blood).

Prinzessin, die. princess.

probieren [probiren], v. to try, to test.

Produkt [Product], das, -(e)s. product.

Professor, der, -s; pl. -en. professor.

Pulver, das, -s. powder.

Punkt, der, -(e)s. dot, point.

Qual, die. torment.

Quarz, das, -es. quartz.

Quelle, die. fountain, source, spring.

quer, adv. and adj. across; cross.

Quirl, der, -s. twirling-stick.

Rabe, der, -n. raven.

Rahm, der, -s. cream.

raten [rathen], irr. v. to guess; to advise.

Räuberei, die. robbery.

Rauch, der, -(e)s. smoke.

rauchen, v. to smoke.

räuchern, v. to perfume, smoke.

rauh, adj. rough.

Raum, der, -(e)s. space, room.

recht, adj. and adv. right; very; rechts, to or at the right.

Recht, das, -(e)s. right, law.

rechtzeitig, adj. and adv. opportune; at the right time.

reden, v. to talk, to speak.

Regel, die. rule.

regelmäßig, adj. regular.

Regen, der, -s. rain.

Regenschirm, der, -s. umbrella.

regieren, v. to govern, to reign.

regnen, v. to rain.

Reh, das, -(e)s. roe.

reiben, irr. v. to rub.

reich, adj. rich.

Reichtum [Reichthum], der, -s. riches.

reif, adj. ripe.

Reim, der, -(e)s. rhyme.

rein, adj. clean, pure.

reinigen, v. to clean.

reinlich, adj. cleanly.

Reis, der, -es. rice.

reisen, v. to travel.

Reisende, der, -n, (participial adj. used as noun). traveller; ein Reisender, -en. a traveller.

reiten, irr. v. to ride (on horseback).

Remus, der. Remus.

rennen, irr. v. to run.

Republik, die. republic.

retten, v. to save.

Rhein, der, -s, pr. n. Rhine.

Richard, der, -s. Richard.

richtig, adj. correct.

Riese, der, -n. giant.

Rindfleisch, das, -es. beef.

Ring, der, -(e)s. ring.

Robert, der, -s. Robert.

Rock, der, -(e)s. coat.

Rohr, das, -(e)s. reed.

Rom, -s, pr. n. Rome.

Römer, ber, -8. Roman (man).
Romulus, ber. Romulus.
Rosa, bie, -8. Rosa.
Rose, bie. rose.
rot [roth], adj. red.
Rücken, ber, -8. back.
rufen, irr. v. to call, to cry.
Ruhe, bie. rest, quiet, calmness.
ruhig, adj. quiet; alone.
Ruhm, ber, -(e)8. glory, fame.
rühmen, v. glorify; refl. sich rühmen, to boast.
rühren, v. to stir; to touch.
rund, adj. and adv. round.
Russe, ber, -n. Russian (man).
Rußland, -8, pr. n. Russia.

Saal, ber, -(e)8. hall, salon, drawing-room.
Sachsen, -8, pr. n. Saxony.
Sack, ber, -(e)8. sack, bag.
Saft, ber, -(e)8. sap.
sagen, v. to say, tell.
Salat, ber, -(e)8. salad.
Salpeterstein, ber, -(e)8. saltpetre-stone.
Salz, bas, -e8. salt.
Samstag, ber, -(e)8. Saturday.
Sand, ber, -(e)8. sand.
Sandfläche, bie. sand-plain.
Sankt [Sanct] Helena, -8, pr. n. Saint-Helena.
Sarah, bie. Sarah.
satt, adj. satiated.
Sattler, ber, -8. saddler.
saufen, irr. v. to drink (of beasts).
Schachtel, bie. box.
Schaf, bas, -(e)8. sheep.
Schäfer, ber, -8. shepherd.
schaffen, irr. v. to create, to make; reg. to work.
schämen, v.; refl. to be ashamed.
schauen, v. to look.

Schauspiel, bas, -(e)8. play, drama.
scheinen, irr. v. to shine; to appear, seem.
scheitern, v. to be wrecked, to run aground.
schelten, irr. v. to scold.
Scheune, bie. barn.
schicken, v. to send; refl. es schickt sich, it is proper.
schießen, irr. v. to shoot.
Schiff, bas, -(e)8. ship.
Schinken, ber, -8. ham.
Schlacht, bie. battle; eine Schlacht liefern, to fight a battle.
Schlachtordnung, bie. battle-array.
schlafen, irr. v. to sleep.
schläfrig, adj. sleepy.
Schlafrock, ber, -(e)8. dressing-gown.
Schlafzimmer, bas, -8. sleeping-room.
schlagen, irr. v. to strike, beat.
schlecht, adj. bad.
schleichen, irr. v. to sneak, creep.
Schleier, ber, -8. veil.
schließen, irr. v. to lock.
Schloß, bas, -e8. lock; castle.
Schlüssel, ber, -8. key.
schmähen, v. to abuse.
schmelzen, irr. v. to melt.
Schmerz, ber, -e8. pain.
schmücken, v. to deck, adorn.
schmutzig, adj. dirty.
Schnee, ber, -8. snow.
schneiden, irr. v. to cut.
Schneider, ber, -8. tailor.
schneien, v. to snow.
schnell, adj. quick.
schon, adv. already.
schön, adj. beautiful, handsome, fine, nice.

Schokolade [Chocolade], die. chocolate.

Schrank, der, –(e)s. closet (movable), wardrobe, etc.

schreiben, irr. v. to write.

Schreibheft, das, –(e)s. copy-book, writing-book.

schreien, irr. v. to cry.

Schreiner, der, –s. joiner.

Schriftsteller, der, –s. writer, author.

Schublade, die. chest of drawers.

Schuh, der, –(e)s. shoe.

Schuhmacher, der, –s. shoemaker.

Schuld, die. debt; guilt.

Schule, die. school.

Schüler, der, –s. scholar, pupil; die Schülerin, scholar, etc. (fem.).

Schulter, die. shoulder.

Schürze, die. apron.

Schüssel, die. dish.

Schuster, der, –s. cobbler.

schütteln, v. to shake.

schwach, adj. weak, feeble.

schwarz, adj. black.

Schwarz, der, –ens. Schwartz, pr. n.

Schwede, der, –n. Swede (masc.); Schwedin, die, Swede (fem.).

Schweden, –s, pr. n. Sweden.

schweifen, v. to roam.

schweigen, irr. v. to be silent; Schweigen, das, –s. silence.

schweigsam, adj. silent.

Schwein, das, –(e)s. swine, pig, hog.

Schweinefleisch, das, –(e)s. pork.

Schweiz, die, pr. n. Switzerland.

Schweizer, der, –s. Swiss.

schwer, adj. heavy; difficult, hard.

Schwester, die. sister.

schwimmen, irr. v. to swim.

sechs, num. six; der, die, das sechste, the sixth.

sechsundzwanzig, num. twenty-six; der, die, das sechsundzwanzigste, the twenty-sixth.

sechzehn, num. sixteen; der, die, das sechzehnte, the sixteenth.

sechzig, num. sixty; der, die, das sechzigste, the sixtieth.

See, der, –s. lake.

See, die. sea.

Seele, die. soul.

segeln, v. to sail.

Seide, die. silk.

Seife, die. soap.

sein, seine, sein, poss. adj. his; her; its.

seiner, gen. of er and es. of him; of her; of it.

seiner, seine, seines, poss. pron. his; hers; its; der, die, das seine, his; hers; its; der, die, das seinige, his; hers; its.

seinerseits, adv. on his part, etc.

seit, prep. and conj. since.

Seite, die. side; page.

selber or selbst, pron. self; ich selbst, I myself, etc.

Seltenheit, die. curiosity.

Senf, der, –(e)s. mustard.

September, der, –s. September.

Serviette, die. napkin.

setzen, v. to set, place, put, seat; refl. to be seated, to sit down.

sich, refl. pron.; dat. and. acc. (to) himself; (to) herself; (to) itself; (to) themselves; (to) yourself; (to) yourselves; (to) one's self; each other.

sicher, adj. and adv. sure; surely.

sie, nom. and acc., fem. sing.; pers. pron. she, her; he, him; it.

ſie, *nom. and acc. plur.; pers. pron.* they, them.

Sie, *nom. and acc.; pers. pron.* you.

ſieben, *num.* seven; ber, bie, baß ſiebente, the seventh.

ſiebenunbzwanzig, *num.* twenty-seven; ber, bie, baß ſiebenunbzwanzigſte, the twenty-seventh.

ſiebzehn, *num.* seventeen; ber, bie, baß ſiebzehnte, the seventeenth.

ſieb(en)zig, *num.* seventy; ber, bie, baß ſiebzigſte, the seventieth.

Silber, baß, –ß. silver.

ſingen, *irr. v.* to sing.

ſinken, *irr. v.* to sink.

Sinn, ber, –(e)ß. sense; mind.

ſinnen, *irr. v.* to meditate.

Sitz, ber, –eß. seat.

ſitzen, *irr. v.* to sit.

Sflave [Sclave], ber, –n. slave.

ſo, *adv.* thus, so; ſo . . . alß, ſo . . . wie, so . . . as, as . . . as.

Sofa [Sopha], baß, –ß. sofa.

ſogar, *adv.* even.

Sohn, ber, –(e)ß. son.

ſolch, *adj.* such.

Solbat, ber, –en. soldier.

ſollen, *irr. v.* shall, to be to, ought; to be said to.

Sommer, ber, –ß. summer.

ſonbern, *conj.* but.

Sonnabenb, ber, –ß. Saturday.

Sonne, bie. sun.

Sonnenſchein, ber, –ß. sunshine.

Sonnenſchirm, ber, –ß. parasol.

Sonntag, ber, –ß. Sunday.

ſonſt, *adv.* formerly; else.

Sophie, bie, –nß. Sophia.

Spanien, –ß, *pr. n.* Spain.

Spanier, ber, –ß. Spaniard; bie Spanierin, Spanish woman.

ſpaniſch, *adj.* Spanish.

Sparren, ber, –ß. rafter.

Spaß, ber, –eß. fun.

ſpät, *adj. and adv.* late.

ſpazieren, *v.* or ſpazierengehen, *irr. v.; sep.* to take a walk.

ſpazierenfahren, *irr. v.; sep.* to take a drive.

Spaziergang ber, –ß. (pleasure-) walk.

Speicher, ber, –ß. granary, store-room.

Speiſe, bie. food.

Speiſeſchrank, ber, –ß. sideboard.

ſpeiſen, *v.* to dine.

Sperling, ber, –ß. sparrow.

Spiegel, ber, –ß. mirror, looking-glass.

Spiel, baß, –(e)ß. play, game.

ſpielen, *v.* to play.

Spieß, ber, –eß. spear.

Spital, baß, –(e)ß. hospital.

Sprache, bie. speech, language.

ſprechen, *irr. v.* to speak.

Spren, bie. chaff.

ſpringen, *irr. v.* to spring, jump.

Spule, bie. spool.

Staat, ber, –(e)ß. state.

Stabt, bie. city, town.

Stahl, ber, –(e)ß. steel.

Stahlfeber, bie. steel-pen.

Stall, ber, –(e)ß. stable.

Staubuhr, bie. time-piece.

ſtark, *adj.* strong; hard.

Stärke, bie. strength.

ſtatt *or* anſtatt, *prep.* instead.

Stecknabel, bie. pin.

ſtehen, *irr. v.* to stand.

ſtehlen, *irr. v.* to steal.

ſteigen, *irr. v.* to mount, climb.

Stein, ber, –(e)ß. stone.

ſteinern, *adj.* stone; of stone.

Steinkohle, die. hard coal.
Stelle, die. place, situation.
stellen, v. to place, to put; *refl.*
sich stellen, to pretend.
sterben, *irr. v.* to die.
Sterling, der, –(e)s. sterling.
Stern, der, –(e)s. star.
Stiefel, der, –s; *pl.* –n. boot.
Stiege, die. stairs.
Stift, der, –(e)s. pencil.
still, *adj.* still, quiet.
Stimme, die. voice.
Stirn, die. forehead.
Stock, der, –(e)s. stick, cane.
Stock(werk), das, –(e)s. floor,
story.
Storch, der, –(e)s. stork.
stoßen, *irr. v.* to thrust.
strafen, v. to punish.
Strahl, der, –(e)s; *pl.* –en. ray,
beam.
Straße, die. street, road.
strecken, v. to stretch.
streng, *adj.* strict, severe.
stricken, v. to knit.
Stroh, das, –(e)s. straw.
Strohhut, der, –(e)s. straw-
hat.
Strumpf, der, –(e)s. stocking,
sock.
Stück, das, –(e)s. piece.
Student, der, –en. student.
studieren [studiren], v. to study.
Studium, das, –s; *pl.* Studien.
study.
Stufe, die. step.
Stuhl, der, –(e)s. chair.
stumm, *adj.* dumb, mute.
Stunde, die. hour.
Stuttgart, –s, *pr. n.* Stuttgart.
suchen, v. to seek, look for.
Suppe, die. soup.
süß, *adj.* sweet.

tadeln, v. to blame.
Tadler, der, –s. fault-finder.
Tafel, die. table, board.
Tag, der, –(e)s. day.
täglich, *adj.* daily.
Talent, das, –(e)s. talent.
Tanne, die. fir.
Tante, die. aunt.
Tanz, der, –es. dance.
tapfer, *adj.* brave.
Tasche, die. pocket.
Taschenbuch, das, –(e)s. pocket-
book.
Taschentuch, das, –(e)s. handker-
chief.
Tasse, die. cup.
Tatze, die. paw.
Tau, das, –es. rope.
Taube, die. dove, pigeon.
taugen, v. to be of use, be good
for.
täuschen, v. to deceive.
tausend, *num.* thousand; **der,**
**die, das tausendste,** the thou-
sandth.
Teich, der, –(e)s. pond.
Teil [Theil], der, –(e)s. part.
teilen [theilen], v. to divide.
Teller, der, –s. plate.
Teppich, der, –(e)s. carpet.
teuer [theuer], *adj.* dear; expen-
sive.
Thal, das, –(e)s. valley.
That, die. deed.
Theater, das, –s. theatre.
Thee, der, –s. tea.
Thomas, der. Thomas.
Thor, das, –(e)s. gate.
Thron, der, –(e)s. throne.
thun, *irr. v.* to do.
Thüre, die. door.
tief, *adj.* deep.
Tier [Thier], das, –(e)s. animal.

Tiger, der, -s. tiger.

Tinte [Dinte], die. ink.

Tintenfaß [Dintenfaß], das, -es. inkstand.

Tisch, der, -(e)s. table.

Tischler, der, -s. joiner.

Tochter, die. daughter.

Tod, der, -(e)s. death.

todesmutig [todesmuthig], adj. death-defying.

tot [todt], adj. dead.

töten [tödten], v. to kill.

Ton, der, -(e)s. sound, tone.

träge, adj. idle.

tragen, irr. v. to carry, bear, take; to wear.

tränken, v. to water.

Traube, die. grape.

Traum, der, -(e)s. dream.

träumen, v. to dream.

traurig, adj. sad, sorry.

treffen, irr. v. to meet; to hit.

Treppe, die. stair-case.

treu, adj. faithful, true.

trinken, irr. v. to drink.

trotz, prep. in spite.

tüchtig, adj. able, good.

Tugend, die. virtue.

Türke, der, -n. Turk; Türkin, die, Turkish woman.

Türkei, die. Turkey.

Turm [Thurm], der, -(e)s. tower.

Übel [Uebel], das, -s. evil.

über, prep. over, above; on, about.

überall, adv. everywhere.

übergeben, irr. v. to hand over, deliver; to surrender.

überliefern, v. to deliver.

übermorgen, adv. day after to-morrow.

überraschen, v. to suprise.

übersetzen, v.; sep. to cross; to ferry over.

übersetzen, v. to translate.

Übersetzung [Uebersetzung], die. translation.

Übertreibung [Uebertreibung], die. exaggeration.

übertreten, irr. v.; sep. to step over, to go over.

übertreten, irr. v. to transgress, trespass, to infringe.

Übung [Uebung], die. exercise.

Uhr, die. clock, watch; wieviel [wie viel] Uhr? What o'clock?

Uhrmacher, der, -s. watchmaker.

Uhrschlüssel, der, -s. watch-key.

um, prep. around, about; um zu, in order to.

Umgang, der, -(e)s. intercourse.

umgänglich, adj. sociable.

Umgegend, die. environment.

umkommen, irr. v.; sep. to perish.

umsonst, adv. in vain.

Umstand, der, -(e)s. circumstance.

Umstandswort, das, -(e)s. adverb.

unartig, adj. ill-mannered, naughty.

unbestimmt, adj. indefinite.

und, conj. and.

Ungeduld, die. impatience.

ungefähr, adv. about.

ungeheuer, adj. immense.

ungerecht, adj. unjust.

ungeschicklich, adj. unskillful, awkward.

unglücklich, adj. unhappy, unfortunate.

unrecht, adj. wrong.

Unrecht, das, -(e)s. wrong.

unregelmäßig, adj. irregular.

unreif, adj. unripe.

uns, dat. and acc. of wir. (to) us.

unser, gen. of wir. of us.

unſer, unſ(e)re, unſer, *poss. adj.* our.

unſerer, unſ(e)re, unſ(e)res, *poss. pron.* ours; der, die, das unſ(e)re, ours, der, die, das unſrige, ours.

unter, *prep.* under, among.

unterdeſſen, *adv.* meanwhile.

untergehen, *irr. v.; sep.* to set.

unterhalten, *irr. v.* to entertain, amuse.

Unterhaltung, die. entertainment, amusement, conversation.

unterrichten, *v.* to instruct.

unterſuchen, *v.* to examine.

Unterſuchung, die. examination.

Untertaſſe, die. saucer.

Unübertrefflichkeit, die. sublimeness.

Unverſchämtheit, die. insolence.

unwohl, *adj.* unwell, indisposed.

unzufrieden, *adj.* discontented.

urteilen [urtheilen], *v.* to judge.

Vater, der, –s. father.

Vaterland, das, –(e)s. native country.

Veilchen, das, –s. violet.

verbergen, *irr. v.* to conceal.

verbeſſern, *v.* to improve; to correct.

verbieten, *irr. v.* to forbid.

verbinden, *irr. v.* to bind (up); to unite; to oblige.

Verbot, das, –(e)s. interdict, prohibition.

verderben, *irr. v.* to spoil.

verdienen, *v.* to deserve; to earn.

verfehlen, *v.* to miss.

verfließen, *irr. v.* to flow away; to pass away.

vergeblich, *adj.* vain; *adv.* in vain.

vergehen, *irr. v.* to pass away.

vergeſſen, *irr. v.* to forget.

Vergnügen, das, –s. pleasure.

vergrößern, *v.* to enlarge, increase.

verheiraten [verheirathen], *v.* to give in marriage; *refl.* to marry.

verirren, *v.; refl.* to go astray; lose one's way.

verkaufen, *v.* to sell.

Verkehr, der, –s. intercourse.

verklingen, *irr. v.* to die away (of sound).

verlangen, *v.* to demand, ask for.

verlaſſen, *irr. v.* to leave, abandon.

verlieren, *irr. v.* to lose.

vermehren, *v.* to increase.

vermiſchen, *v.* to mix (up).

vermieten [vermiethen], *v.* to let.

vermittelſt, *prep.* by means.

Vermögen, das, –s. faculty; property.

vermuten [vermuthen], *v.* to suppose.

vermutlich [vermuthlich], *adj.* probable.

Vernunft, die. reason.

verſchieden, *adj.* different.

verſchwinden, *irr. v.* to disappear.

verſichern, *v.* to assure.

verſorgen, *v.* to provide.

verſprechen, *irr. v.* to promise.

verſtehen, *irr. v.* to understand.

verſuchen, *v.* to try, attempt.

verteidigen [vertheidigen], *v.* to defend.

verwunden, *v.* to wound.

Verwünſchung, die. curse.

verzagen, *v.* to despair.

verzeihen, *irr. v.* to pardon.

Vetter, der, –s. cousin.

Vieh, das, –(e)s. beast, cattle.

viel, *adj.* much, a great deal;

viel(e), *pl.* many.

**vielleicht,** *adv.* perhaps.

**vier,** *num.* four; **der, die, das vierte,** the fourth.

**vierhundert** [**vier hundert**], *num.* four-hundred; **der, die, das vierhundertste,** the four-hundredth.

**Viertel,** das, –s. quarter.

**vierundzwanzig,** *num.* twenty-four; **der, die, das vierundzwanzigste,** the twenty-fourth.

**vierzehn,** *num.* fourteen; **der, die, das vierzehnte,** the fourteenth.

**vierzig,** *num.* forty; **der, die, das vierzigste,** the fortieth.

**Viktoria** *or* **Victoria,** die, –s. Victoria.

**Violine,** die. violin.

**Vogel,** der, –s. bird.

**Volk,** das, –(e)s. people, nation.

**voll,** *adj.* full.

**vollbringen,** *irr. v.* to accomplish.

**vom** *for* **von dem.**

**von,** *prep.* of, from, by; **von … an,** beginning with, since.

**vor,** *prep.* before, ago; of, from.

**voraussehen,** *irr. v.; sep.* to foresee; **vorausgesehen daß,** provided that.

**vorbei,** *adv.* over, past.

**vorgestern,** *adv.* day before yesterday.

**vorher,** *adv.* before.

**Vorhang,** der, –s. curtain.

**vorhersagen,** *v.; sep.* to foretell.

**vorig,** *adj.* previous.

**vorlesen,** *irr. v.; sep.* to read aloud.

**Vorstadt,** die. suburb.

**Vorstecknadel,** die. breast-pin.

**vorstellen,** *v.; sep.* to introduce.

**vortrefflich,** *adj.* excellent.

**vorübergehen,** *irr. v.; sep.* to pass.

**Vorwand,** der, –(e)s. pretence.

**Vorwort,** das, –(e)s. preposition.

**Wachs,** das, –es. wax.

**wachsam,** *adj.* watchful.

**wachsen,** *irr. v.* to grow.

**wagen,** *v.* to dare.

**Wagen,** der, –s. wagon, carriage.

**Wagner,** der, –s. wheelwright.

**Wahl,** die. choice; election.

**wählen,** *v.* to choose.

**wahr,** *adj.* true.

**während,** *prep. and conj.* during; while.

**Wahrheit,** die. truth.

**wahrscheinlich,** *adj.* probable.

**Waise,** die. orphan.

**Wald,** der, –(e)s. forest, woods.

**Wange,** die. cheek.

**wann,** *adv.* when.

**Wanne,** die. tub.

**warm,** *adj.* warm.

**warten,** *v.* to wait.

**warum,** *adv.* why.

**was,** *pron.* what; that which; **was für (ein),** what (a), what kind of.

**waschen,** *irr. v.* to wash.

**Wäsche,** die. clothes (linen).

**Wasser,** das, –s. water.

**wechseln,** *v.* to change.

**wecken,** *v.* to wake.

**weder,** *conj.* neither.

**Weg,** der, –(e)s. way, road.

**weg,** *adv.* away, off.

**wegen,** *prep.* on account.

**weggehen,** *irr. v.; sep.* to go away.

**Wegstunde,** die. one hour's walk.

**weh!** *interj.* woe!

**Weh,** das, –(e)s. woe, pain.

**weich,** *adj.* soft.

**weil,** *conj.* because.

**Wein,** ber, –(e)ß. wine.

**Weinberg,** ber, –(e)ß. vineyard.

**weinen,** v. to weep, to cry.

**Weintraube,** bie. grape.

**weise,** adj. wise.

**weiß,** adj. white.

**weiß,** 1st and 3d pers. sing. pres. indic. of **wissen.**

**weit,** adj. and adv. wide; far.

**Weizen,** ber, –ß. wheat.

**welcher, welche, welches,** rel. and interr. who, which, that, what.

**Welle,** bie. wave.

**Welt,** bie. world.

**Weltall,** baß, –ß. universe.

**wenig,** adj. and adv. little.

**wenigstens,** adv. at least.

**wenn,** conj. when, if; **wenn ... auch, wenn ... gleich, wenn ... schon,** although; **wenn ... nicht,** unless.

**wer,** pron. who; **wer ... auch,** whoever.

**werden,** irr. v. to become, to grow, to get; with infinitive, shall and will; with participle, to be.

**werfen,** irr. v. to throw, hurl.

**Werk,** baß, –(e)ß. work.

**wert [werth],** adj. worth(y).

**Wespe [Weßpe],** bie. wasp.

**Weste,** bie. vest, waist-coat.

**weswegen [weßwegen],** adv. wherefore.

**Wetter,** baß, –ß. weather.

**wider,** prep. against.

**widerstehen,** irr. v. to resist.

**wie,** adv. how, as; **wie ... auch,** however.

**wieder,** adv. again, back.

**wiegen,** irr. v. to weigh.

**Wien,** –ß, pr. n. Vienna.

**Wiese,** bie. meadow.

**wieviel [wie viel],** adj. how much?

**wieviel Uhr?** what o'clock? **ber, die, baß wieviel(f)te,** what day of the month? what number?

**wild,** adj. wild.

**Wilhelm,** ber, –ß. William.

**Wilhelmsstraße,** bie. William Street.

**Wille(n),** ber, –nß. will.

**Wind,** ber, –(e)ß. wind.

**Winter,** ber, –ß. winter.

**wir,** pron. we.

**wirklich,** adj. and adv. real; indeed.

**Wirtshaus [Wirthshaus],** baß, –eß. inn.

**wischen,** v. to wipe.

**wissen,** irr. v. to know.

**Wissenschaft,** bie. science.

**Witwe [Wittwe],** bie. widow.

**Witwer [Wittwer],** ber, –ß. widower.

**wo,** adv. where.

**wobei,** adv. at which or what.

**Woche,** bie. week.

**wodurch,** adv. by which or what.

**wofür,** adv. for which or what.

**woher,** adv. whence.

**wohin,** adv. whither.

**wohl [wol],** adj. and adv. well; probably.

**wohlbewaffnet,** adj. well-armed.

**wohlfeil,** adj. cheap.

**Wohlthäter,** ber, –ß. benefactor; **bie Wohlthäterin,** benefactress.

**wohnen,** v. to dwell, reside.

**Wohnung,** bie. residence.

**Wohnzimmer,** baß, –ß. sitting-room.

**Wolf,** ber, –(e)ß. wolf.

**wollen,** v. (to) will, to wish, want.

**womit,** adv. wherewith, with which or what.

woran, *adv.* at which *or* what.

worauf, *adv.* whereupon, upon *or* on which *or* what.

woraus, *adv.* from *or* out of which *or* what.

worin, *adv.* in which *or* what.

Wort, das, -(e)s. word.

Wörterbuch, das, -(e)s. dictionary.

worüber, *adv.* over which *or* what.

worunter, *adv.* among which *or* what.

wovon, *adv.* of, from which *or* what.

wozu, *adv.* to, for which *or* what.

Wunde, die. wound.

Wunder, das, -s. wonder, miracle.

wundern, *v.; refl.* to wonder; ich wundre mich *or* es wundert mich, I wonder.

wünschen, *v.* to wish, desire.

Wurm, der, -(e)s. worm.

Wurzel, die. root.

wußte, *imp. of* wissen.

Wüste, die. desert.

Xaver, der, -s. Xaver.

Zahl, die. number.

Zahlwort, das, -(e)s. numeral.

Zahn, der, -(e)s. tooth.

zanken, *v.* to quarrel, scold.

Zehe, die. toe.

zehn, *num.* ten; der, die, das zehnte, the tenth.

zehntausend [zehn Tausend], *num.* ten-thousand; der, die, das zehntausendste, the ten-thousandth.

zeichnen, *v.* to draw.

zeigen, *v.* to show.

Zeit, die. time.

Zeitung, die. newspaper.

Zeitwort, das, -(e)s. verb.

Zerlegung, die. dissection, dismemberment.

zerreißen, *irr. v.* to tear (to pieces).

zerrinnen, *irr. v.* to melt away.

zerstören, *v.* to destroy.

Ziege, die. goat.

ziehen, *irr. v.* to draw; to march, move.

Ziel, das, -(e)s. aim.

ziemlich, *adj. and adv.* considerable; pretty.

Zimmer, das, -s. room.

Zimmermann, der, -(e)s. carpenter.

Zoll, der, -(e)s. inch; custom, duty.

Zollhaus, das, -es. custom-house.

zu, *prep. and adv.* to, at; too.

zubringen, *irr. v.; sep.* to spend (time).

Zucker, der, -s. sugar.

zuerst, *adv.* at first.

zufrieden, *adj.* content(ed); satisfied.

Zug, der, -(e)s. draught; procession; train.

Zugvogel, der, -s. bird of passage.

zuhören, *v.; sep.* to listen.

Zukunft, die. future.

zukünftig, *adj.* future.

zuletzt, *adv.* last.

zumachen *v.; sep.* to shut.

Zunge, die. tongue.

zurück, *adv.* back.

zurückkehren, *v.; sep.* to return.

zurückkommen, *irr. v.; sep.* to come back.

zurücktragen, *irr. v.; sep.* to carry, bear back.

zusammen, *adv.* together.

zusammenkommen, *irr. v.; sep.* to meet.

zwanzig, *num.* twenty; der, die, das zwanzigste, the twentieth.

zwar, *adv.* indeed, it is true.

zwei, *num.* two; der, die, das zweite, the second.

Zweifel, der, –s. doubt.

zweihundert [zwei Hundert], *num.* two-hundred; der, die, das zweihundertste, the two-hundredth.

zweimal, *num.* twice.

zweiundzwanzig [zwei und zwanzig], *num.* twenty-two; der, die, das zweiundzwanzigste, the twenty-second.

zwingen, *irr. v.* to force.

zwischen, *prep.* between.

zwitschern, *v.* to twitter.

zwölf, *num.* twelve; der, die, das zwölfte, the twelfth.

# II. ENGLISH-GERMAN VOCABULARY.

a, an, *art.* ein, eine, ein.

abandon, *v.* verlassen, *irr.*

able, *adj.* fähig; **to be able,** können, *irr.*

about, *adv. and prep.* ungefähr; um, um . . . herum.

above, *adv. and prep.* oben, droben; oberhalb, über.

absent, *adj.* abwesend.

accept, *v.* annehmen, *irr.; sep.*

accomplish, *v.* vollbringen, *irr.*

accompany, *v.* begleiten.

according to, *prep.* nach.

account, *n.* Rechnung, die; **on account of,** wegen, *prep.*

accustom, *v.* gewöhnen.

across, *prep.* über.

act, *v.* handeln.

action, *n.* Handlung, die.

admiral, *n.* Admiral, der, –s.

admire, *v.* bewundern.

advise, *v.* raten [rathen], *irr.*

Africa, *pr. n.* Afrika, –s.

after, *prep.* nach; *conj.* nachdem.

after(wards), *adv.* nachher.

again, *adv.* wieder.

against, *prep.* gegen, wider.

ago, *prep.* vor.

agreeable, *adj.* angenehm.

aim, *n.* das Ziel, –(e)s.

air, *n.* Luft, die.

Albert, *pr. n.* Albert, der, –s.

alder, *n.* Erle, die.

Alexander, *pr. n.* Alexander, der, –s.

alive, *adv.* am Leben.

all, *adj.* all, aller, alle, alles; ganz; **not at all,** garnicht.

allow, *v.* erlauben; **to be allowed,** dürfen, *irr.*

almost, *adv.* fast.

alone, *adv.* allein.

aloud, *adv.* laut.

Alps, *pr. n.* Alpen, die, *pl.*

already, *adv.* schon.

also, *adv.* auch.

although, *conj.* obgleich, obschon, wenn gleich, wenn auch, wenn schon.

always, *adv.* immer.

ambassador, *n.* Gesandte, der, –n; *participial adj. used as noun;* **an ambassador,** ein Gesandter, –n.

Amelia, *pr. n.* Amalie, die, –ns.

America, *pr. n.* Amerika, –s.

American, *n.* Amerikaner, der, –s; Amerikanerin, die.

American, *adj.* amerikanisch.

amiable, *adj.* liebenswürdig.

among, *prep.* unter.

amount, *v.* betragen, *irr.*

amuse, *v.* unterhalten, *irr.*

amusement, *n.* Unterhaltung, die.

an, *art.; cf.* **a.**

angry, *adj.* zornig, böse.

animal, *v.* Tier [Thier], das, –(e)s.

Anna, *pr. n.* Anna, die, –s.

**annual,** *adj.* jährlich.

**answer,** *v.* antworten.

**answer,** *n.* Antwort, die.

**any,** *adj.* irgend ein, etc.; etwas; einiger, etc.; welcher, etc.; jeder, etc.

**anybody,** *pron.* jemand [Jemand].

**anything,** *pron.* etwas.

**apothecary,** *n.* Apotheker, der, –s.

**apple,** *n.* Apfel, der, –s.

**apple-tree,** *n.* Apfelbaum, der, –(e)s.

**April,** *pr. n.* April, der, –s.

**apron,** *n.* Schürze, die.

**Arab,** *pr. n.* Araber, der, –s.

**Arabia,** *pr. n.* Arabien, –s.

**arm,** *n.* Arm, der, –(e)s.

**around,** *adv. and prep.* herum; um . . . herum.

**arrival,** *n.* Ankunft, die.

**arrive,** *v.* ankommen; *irr.; sep.*

**art,** *n.* Kunst, die.

**article,** *n.* Bestimmungswort, das, –(e)s; Artikel, der, –s.

**as,** *adv. and conj.* als, wie, so; da, indem.

**ascend,** *v.* hinaufsteigen, *irr.; sep.*

**ashamed,** *adj.* beschämt; **to be ashamed,** sich schämen.

**ashes,** *n.* Asche, die, *sing.*

**Asia,** *pr. n.* Asien, –s.

**ask,** *v.* fragen; **to ask for,** verlangen, bitten, *irr.*

**ass,** *n.* Esel, der, –s.

**assist,** *v.* beistehen, *irr.; sep.*

**assistance,** *n.* Beistand der, –(e)s.

**assure,** *v.* versichern.

**astonishment,** *n.* Erstaunen, das, –s.

**at,** *prep.* an, zu, in; **at the house of,** bei; **at one o'clock,** um ein Uhr.

**Atlantic,** *adj.* atlantisch.

**attack,** *v.* angreifen, *irr.; sep.*

**attempt,** *v.* versuchen.

**attentive,** *adj.* aufmerksam.

**attract,** *v.* anziehen, *irr.; sep.*

**August,** *pr. n.* August, der, –s.

**aunt,** *n.* Tante, die.

**Austria,** *pr. n.* Österreich [Oesterreich], –s or Östreich, –s.

**author,** *n.* Schriftsteller, der, –s.

**autumn,** *n.* Herbst, der, –(e)s.

**avenge,** *v.* rächen.

**away,** *adv.* weg, fort.

**awkward,** *adj.* ungeschickt.

**back,** *n.* Rücken, der, –s.

**back,** *adv.* zurück.

**bad,** *adj.* schlecht.

**Baden,** *pr. n.* Baden, –s.

**bag,** *n.* Sack, der, –(e)s.

**bake,** *v.* backen, *irr.*

**baker,** *n.* Bäcker, der, –s.

**ball,** *n.* Ball, der, –(e)s.

**bank,** *n.* Ufer, das, –s; Bank, die.

**bare,** *adj.* bloß.

**barley,** *n.* Gerste, die.

**barn,** *n.* Scheune, die.

**baron** or **baronet,** *n.* Baron, der, –(e)s.

**basket,** *n.* Korb, der, –(e)s.

**bath,** *n.* Bad, das, –(e)s.

**bathe,** *v.* baden.

**battle,** *n.* Schlacht, die; **battle array,** Schlachtordnung, die.

**be,** *v.* sein, *irr.*; werden, *irr.*; **to be to,** sollen, *irr.*; müssen, *irr.*

**beam,** *n.* Strahl, der, –(e)s; Balken, der, –s, (wooden).

**bear,** *n.* Bär, der, –en.

**bear,** *v.* tragen, *irr.*; gebären, *irr.*

**beard,** *n.* Bart, der, –(e)s.

**beat,** *v.* schlagen, *irr.*

**beautiful,** *adj.* schön, prächtig.

**because,** *conj.* weil.

become, *v.* werden, *irr.*

bed, *n.* Bett, das, -es; *pl.* -en.

bed-room, *n.* Schlafzimmer, das,-s.

bee, *n.* Biene, die.

beef, *n.* Rindfleisch, das, -es.

beer, *n.* Bier, das, -(e)s.

befall, *v.* betreffen, *irr.*

before, *prep.* vor; *adv.* vorher; *conj.* bevor, ehe.

beg, *v.* bitten, *irr.*

begin, *v.* beginnen, *irr.*

behave, *v.* betragen, *irr.; refl.*

behind, *prep.* hinter; *adv.* hinten.

Belgium, *pr n.* Belgien, -s.

believe, *v.* glauben.

bell, *n.* Glocke, die; Klingel, die.

Bell, *pr. n.* Bell, -s.

belong, *v.* gehören.

below, *prep.* unter, unterhalb; *adv.* unten.

Belus, *pr. n.* Belus.

bench, *n.* Bank, die.

bend, *v.* biegen, *irr.*

benefactor, *n.* Wohlthäter, der, -s.

Berlin, *pr. n.* Berlin, -s.

beside(s), *prep.* neben; außer; *adv.* außerdem.

besiege, *v.* belagern.

best, *adj.; superl.* best; *adv.* am besten, am meisten, am liebsten.

better, *adj.; comp.* besser.

between, *prep.* zwischen.

bid, *v.* heißen, *irr.;* befehlen, *irr.*

big, *adj.* groß.

bill, *n.* Rechnung, die.

bind, *v.* binden, *irr.*

bird, *n.* Vogel, der, -s; bird of passage, Zugvogel, der, -s.

birthday, *n.* Geburtstag der, -(e)s.

bite, *v.* beißen, *irr.*

black, *adj.* schwarz.

Blair, *pr. n.* Blair, -s.

blame, *v.* tadeln.

blanket, Decke, die.

blind, *adj.* blind.

blood, *n.* Blut, das, -(e)s.

blow, *v.* blasen, *irr.*

blue, *adj.* blau.

board, *n.* Tafel, die.

boast, *v.* rühmen, *refl.*

boat, *n.* Boot, das, -(e)s; Schiff, das, -(e)s.

body, *n.* Körper, der, -s.

boil, *v.* kochen.

bonnet, *n.* Hut, der, -(e)s.

book, *n.* Buch, das, -(e)s; bookseller, Buchhändler, der, -s.

boot, *n.* Stiefel, der, -s; *pl.* -n.

borough, *n.* Flecken, der, -s.

borrow, *v.* borgen.

both, *adj.* beider, beide, beides; beide.

bottle, *n.* Flasche, die.

box, *n.* Schachtel, die; Kasten, der, -s.

boy, *n.* Knabe, der, -n.

bracelet, *n.* Armband, das, -(e)s.

brain, *n.* Gehirn, das, -(e)s.

branch, *n.* Ast, der, -(e)s.

bread, *n.* Brot [Brod], das, -(e)s.

break, *v.* brechen, *irr.;* break out, ausbrechen, *irr. sep.;* break to pieces, zerbrechen, *irr.*

breakfast, *v.* frühstücken.

breakfast, *n.* Frühstück, das, -(e)s.

breast, *n.* Brust, die.

breast-pin, *n.* Vorstecknadel, die.

breath, *n.* Atem [Athem], der, -s.

bridge, *n.* Brücke, die.

bright, *adj.* hell.

bring, *v.* bringen, *irr.*

broad, *adj.* breit.

brook, *n.* Bach, der, -(e)s.

brother, *n.* Bruder, der, -s.

brown, *adj.* braun.

**Brussels,** *pr. n.* Brüffel, -8.

**Brutus,** *pr. n.* Brutus, der.

**build,** *v.* bauen; **build up,** erbauen.

**building,** *n.* Gebäude, das, -8.

**bundle,** *n.* Bund, das, -(e)8, Bündel, das, -8.

**burn,** *v.* brennen, *irr.*

**bush,** *n.* Busch, der, -(e)8.

**business,** *n.* Geschäft, das, -(e).

**to busy,** *v.; refl.* sich beschäftigen, *refl.*

**but,** *conj.* aber, allein, sondern; **but for,** ohne.

**butcher,** *n.* Fleischer, der, -8.

**butter,** *n.* Butter, die.

**buy,** *v.* kaufen.

**by,** *prep.* von, durch, bei; *adv.* vorbei.

**cabbage,** *n.* Kraut, das, -(e)8 ; **cabbage-head,** Krautkopf, der,-8.

**Caesar,** *pr. n.* Cäfar, der, -8.

**cage,** *n.* Käfig, der, -8.

**cake,** *n.* Kuchen, der, -8.

**calf,** *n.* Kalb, das, -(e)8.

**call,** *v.* rufen, *irr.*

**calling,** *n.* Beruf, der, -(e)8.

**calm,** *adj.* still(e).

**calmness,** *n.* Stille, die.

**camel,** *n.* Kamel [Kameel], das, -8.

**can,** *v.* können, *irr.*

**candle,** *n.* Kerze, die, Licht, das, -(e)8; **candle-stick,** Leuchter, der, -8.

**cane,** *n.* Stock, der, -(e)8.

**cannon,** *n.* Kanone, die.

**cap,** *n.* Mütze, die, Kappe, die; Haube, die.

**capital,** *n.* Hauptstadt, die.

**captive,** *adj.* gefangen.

**capture,** *v.* fangen, *irr.; gefangen nehmen, *irr.*

**caravan,** *n.* Karawane [Karavane], die.

**card,** *n.* Karte, die; Billet, das, -(e)8.

**care,** *n.* Sorge, die, Acht, die; **to take care,** in acht [Acht] nehmen, *irr.*

**cargo,** *n.* Ladung, die.

**Caroline,** *pr. n.* Karoline [Caroline], die, -ns.

**carpenter,** *n.* Zimmermann, der, -(e)8.

**carpet,** *n.* Teppich, der, -(e)8.

**carriage,** *n.* Wagen, der, -8.

**carrion,** *n.* Aas, das, -e8.

**carrot,** *n.* Möhre, die, gelbe Rübe, die.

**carry,** *v.* tragen, *irr.*; **carry away,** forttragen, *irr.; sep.* fortreißen, *irr.; sep.*

**cart,** *n.* Karren, der, -8.

**Carthage,** *pr. n.* Karthago [Carthago], -8.

**Carthaginian,** *pr. n.* Karthager [Carthager], der, -8.

**case,** *n.* Fall, der, -(e)8; **in case,** falls, *conj.*

**Casino,** *n.* Kasino [Casino], das, -8.

**cast,** *v.* werfen, *irr.*

**castle,** *n.* Schloß, das, -e8.

**cat,** *n.* Katze, die.

**catch,** *v.* fangen, *irr.*

**cathedral,** *n.* Dom, der, -(e)8.

**Cato,** *pr. n.* Cato, der, -8.

**cattle,** *n.* Vieh, das, -(e)8.

**cave,** *n.* Höhle, die.

**cease,** *v.* aufhören, *sep.*

**cedar,** *n.* Ceder, die.

**ceiling,** *n.* Decke, die.

**celebrated,** *adj.* berühmt.

**cellar,** *n.* Keller, der, -8.

**certain,** *adj.* gewiß.

certificate, n. Certifikat [Certificat], das, –(e)s.

chaff, n. Spreu, die.

chain, n. Kette, die.

chair, n. Stuhl, der, –(e)s.

change, v. wechseln.

chapel, n. Kapelle [Capelle], die.

character, n. Charakter, der, –s.

charcoal-burner, n. Köhler, der, –s.

charitable, adj. mildthätig.

Charles, pr. n. Karl [Carl], der, –s.

chase, n. Jagd, die.

cheap, adj. billig, wohlfeil.

cheat, v. betrügen, irr.

cheek, n. Wange, die.

cheese, n. Käse, der, –s; pl. Käse.

chemise, n. Hemd, das, –(e)s; pl. –en.

chemistry, Chemie, die.

cherry, n. Kirsche, die.

chest (of drawers), n. Kommode [Commode], die, Schublade, die.

chicken, n. Hühnchen, das, –s.

child, n. Kind, das, –es.

childhood, n. Kindheit, die.

Chili, pr. n. Chili, –s.

chimney, n. Kamin, der, –(e)s.

chin, n. Kinn, das, –(e)s.

China, pr. n. China, –s.

chocolate, n. Schokolade [Chocolade], die.

choice, n. Wahl, die.

choose, v. wählen.

Christian, n. Christ, der, –en.

church, n. Kirche, die.

city, n. Stadt, die.

class, n. Klasse [Classe], die.

Claudius, pr. n. Claudius, der.

claw, n. Kralle, die.

clean, adj. rein.

cleanly, adj. reinlich.

clear, adj. klar.

climb, v. klettern.

cloak, n. Mantel, der, –s.

clock, n. Uhr, die; what o'clock? wieviel [wie viel] Uhr?

cloth, n. Tuch, das, –(e)s.

clothes, n. Kleider, die, pl.; Wäsche, die, sing. (linen).

clothing, n. Kleidung, die.

clover, n. Klee, der, –s.

coachman, n. Kutscher, der, –s.

coal, n. Kohle, die; hard-coal, Steinkohle, die.

coast, n. Küste, die.

coat, n. Rock, der, –(e)s.

cobbler, n. Schuster, der, –s.

cock, n. Hahn, der, –(e)s.

coffee, n. Kaffee [Caffee], der, –s.

cold, adj. kalt; to be cold, frieren, irr.; to take cold, sich erkälten, refl.

cold, n. Kälte, die.

colonel, n. Oberst, der, –en, Colonel, der, –s.

color, n. Farbe, die.

come, v. kommen, irr.; to come in, hereinkommen, irr.; sep.; to come back, zurückkommen, irr.; sep.

comet, n. Komet, der, –en.

command, v. befehlen, irr.

commence, v. beginnen, irr.

commerce, v. Handel, der, –s.

common, adj. gewöhnlich.

communicate, v. mitteilen [mittheilen], sep.

companion, n. Kamerad, der, –en.

compassion, n. Mitleid, das, –(e)s, Mitleiden, –s.

complain, v. beklagen, refl.

compliment, n. Kompliment [Compliment], das, –(e)s.

conceal, v. verbergen, irr.

conceive, v. begreifen, irr.

concern, v. betreffen, irr.

concert, n. Konzert [Concert], das, -(e)s.

confederation, n. Bund, der, -(e)s.

confess, v. gestehen, irr.

conjunction, n. Bindewort, das, -(e)s.

conquer, v. besiegen.

conscience, n. Gewissen, das, -s.

consider, v. halten, irr.; (as für).

content, v.; refl. begnügen, refl.

content(ed), adj. zufrieden.

contrary, n. Gegenteil [Gegentheil], das, -(e)s; on the contrary, im Gegenteil.

convenient, adj. passend.

conversation, n. Gespräch, das, -(e)s; Unterhaltung, die.

to cook, v. kochen.

cool, adj. kühl; kaltblütig.

copper, n. Kupfer, das, -s; coppersmith, Kesselschmied, der, -(e)s; Kupferschmied, der, -(e)s.

copy, v. abschreiben, irr.; sep.

copy-book, n. Schreibheft, das, -(e)s.

correct, v. verbessern.

correct, adj. richtig.

cost, v. kosten.

cottage, n. Hütte, die.

cotton, n. Baumwolle, die.

count, n. Graf, der, -en.

countess, n. Gräfin, die.

country, n. Land, das, -(e)s; in the country, auf dem Land; native country, Vaterland, das, -(e)s.

courage, n. Mut [Muth], der, -(e)s.

course, n. Lauf, der, -(e)s.

court, n. Hof, der, -(e)s.

cousin, n. Vetter, der, -s; Kousine [Cousine], die.

cover, v. bedecken.

cow, n. Kuh, die.

cravat, n. Halsbinde, die.

cream, n. Rahm, der, -(e)s.

create, v. schaffen, irr.

crew, n. Mannschaft, die.

cross, v. übersetzen, sep.

cry, v. schreien, irr.; rufen, irr.; weinen (weep).

Cuba, pr. n. Cuba, -s.

cup, n. Tasse, die.

cure, v. heilen.

curiosity, n. Neugierde, die; Seltenheit, die.

curtain, n. Vorhang, der, -(e)s.

custom, n. Gebrauch, der, -(e)s; Zoll, der, -(e)s; custom-house, Zollhaus, das, -es.

cut, v. schneiden, irr.

Cyprus, n. Cypern, -s.

damp, adj. feucht.

danger, n. Gefahr, die.

Darius, pr. n. Darius, der.

dark, adj. dunkel.

daily, adj. täglich.

date, n. Dattel, die, (fruit); Datum, das, -s, (day).

daughter, n. Tochter, die.

day, n. Tag, der, -(e)s; day after to-morrow, übermorgen, adv.; day before yesterday, vorgestern; one day, some day, einst, adv.

dead, adj. tot [todt].

deal, n. Teil [Theil]; a great deal, viel, sehr.

dear, adj. teuer [theuer], lieb.

death, n. Tod, der, -(e)s.

debt, n. Schuld, die.

deceive, v. täuschen.

December, n. Dezember [December], der, -s.

deed, n. That, die.

deep, adj. tief.

defend, v. verteidigen [vertheidigen].

definite, adj. bestimmt.

deliver, v. überliefern.

demand, v. verlangen.

depart, v. abreisen, sep.

describe, v. beschreiben, irr.

deserve, v. verdienen.

desire, v. wünschen.

desolate, adj. öde.

destroy, v. zerstören.

devour, v. (auf)fressen, irr.; sep.

diamond, n. Diamant, der, –en.

dictionary, n. Wörterbuch, das, –(e)s.

die, v. sterben, irr.

different, adj. verschieden.

difficult, adj. schwer.

dig, v. graben, irr.

diligent, fleißig.

dine, v. speisen.

dinner, n. Mittagsessen, das, –s, Essen, das, –s.

direct, adj. gerade; adv. gleich.

dirty, adj. schmutzig.

disappear, v. verschwinden, irr.

discontented, adj. unzufrieden.

discover, v. entdecken, erfinden, irr.

dish, n. Schüssel, die.

displease, v. mißfallen, irr.

dismemberment, n. Zerlegung, die.

dissection, n. Teilung [Theilung], Zerteilung, die, Zerlegung, die.

distinct, adj. deutlich.

distress, n. Not [Noth], die.

ditch, n. Graben, der, –s.

divide, v. teilen [theilen].

do, v. thun, irr., machen; sich befinden, irr.

dog, n. Hund, der, –(e)s.

done, adj. fertig.

donkey, n. Esel, der, –s.

door, n. Thür(e), die.

doubt, n. Zweifel, der, –s.

Douglas, pr. n. Douglas, der.

down, adv. herab, hinab, herunter, hinunter.

dozen, n. Dutzend, das, –s.

draught, n. Zug, der, –(e)s.

draw, v. ziehen, irr.; zeichnen.

dress, n. Kleid, das, –(e)s.

dress, v. ankleiden, sep.

dressing-gown, n. Schlafrock, der, –(e)s.

drink, v. trinken, irr.; (of beasts) saufen, irr.

drive, v. fahren, irr.

druggist, n. Apotheker, der, –s.

duke, n. Herzog, der, –s; duchess, Herzogin, die.

duck, n. Ente, die.

dumb, adj. stumm.

during, prep. während.

Dutch, adj. holländisch.

Dutchman, n. Holländer, der, –s.

duty, n. Pflicht, die.

dwell, v. wohnen.

each, adj. jeder, jede, jedes; each other, einander.

eagle, n. Adler, der, –s.

ear, n. Ohr, das, –(e)s; pl. –en.

early, adj. and adv. früh(e).

earn, v. verdienen.

earnest, adj. ernsthaft.

earth, n. Erde, die.

easy, adj. leicht.

eat, v. essen, irr.; (of beasts) fressen, irr.

edify, v. erbauen.

Edward, pr. n. Eduard, der, –s.

egg, n. Ei, das, –(e)s.

Egypt, pr. n. Ägypten [Aegypten], –s.

**eight,** *num.* acht; **the eighth,** der, die, das achte.

**eighteen,** *num.* achtzehn; **the eighteenth,** der, die, das achtzehnte.

**eighty,** *num.* achtzig; **the eightieth,** der, die, das achtzigste.

**either,** *conj.* entweder.

**eldest,** *adj.* ältest.

**elephant,** *n.* Elefant [Elephant], der, –en.

**eleven,** *num.* elf; **the eleventh,** der, die, das elfte.

**Eliza,** *pr. n.* Elise, die, –ns.

**Elizabeth,** *pr. n.* Elisabeth, die, –s.

**elsewhere,** *adv.* anderswo.

**Emma,** *pr. n.* Emma, die, –s.

**emperor,** *n.* Kaiser, der, –s.

**empire,** *n.* Kaiserreich das, –(e)s.

**empty,** *v.* leeren; sich ergießen, *irr.* (of rivers).

**endeavor,** *v.* sich bemühen.

**enemy,** *n.* Feind, der, –(e)s.

**England,** *pr. n.* England, –s.

**English,** *adj.* englisch.

**English(man),** *n.* Engländer, der, –s.

**English(woman),** *n.* Engländerin, die.

**enlarge,** *v.* vergrößern.

**enough,** *adv.* genug.

**enrich,** *v.* bereichern.

**entertain,** *v.* unterhalten, *irr.*

**entertainment,** *n.* Unterhaltung, die.

**entire,** *adj.* ganz.

**environment,** *n.* Umgegend, die.

**error,** *n.* Irrtum [Irrthum], der, –(e)s.

**escape,** *v.* entfliehen, *irr.*; entgehen, *irr.*

**especial,** *adj.* besonder; *adv.* besonders.

**espy,** *v.* erblicken.

**esteem,** *v.* achten.

**Europe,** *pr. n.* Europa, –s; **European,** *n.* Europäer, der, –s; Europäerin, die ; *adj.* europäisch.

**Eve,** *pr. n.* Eva, die, –s.

**even,** *adj. and adv.* eben; sogar, selbst.

**evening,** *n.* Abend, der, –s.

**ever,** *adv.* je(mals).

**every,** *adj.* jeder, jede, jedes; **everybody,** jedermann [Jedermann], –s; **everything,** alles [Alles].

**everywhere,** *adv.* überall.

**evil,** *n.* Übel [Uebel], das, –s, Böse, das, –en (*adj. used as noun*).

**exaggeration,** *n.* Übertreibung [Uebertreibung], die.

**examination,** *n.* Untersuchung, die.

**examine,** *v.* untersuchen.

**example,** *n.* Beispiel, das, –(e)s.

**excellent,** *adj.* vortrefflich.

**except,** *prep.* außer.

**exchange,** *n.* Börse, die.

**exclaim,** *v.* ausrufen, *irr.*; *sep.*

**exercise,** *n.* Aufgabe, die; Übung [Uebung], die.

**expect,** *v.* erwarten.

**expensive,** *adj.* teuer [theuer]; kostspielig.

**experience,** *n.* Erfahrung, die.

**extraordinary,** *adj.* außerordentlich.

**eye,** *n.* Auge, das, –s; *pl.* –n. **one-eyed,** einäugig, *adj.*

**face,** *n.* Gesicht, das, –(e)s.

**faculty,** *n.* Vermögen, das, –s; Fähigkeit, die.

**fail,** *v.* fehlschlagen, *irr.*; *sep.*

**fair,** *adj.* billig.

**faithful,** *adj.* treu.

**fall,** *v.* fallen, *irr.*; **to fall asleep,** einschlafen, *irr. sep.*

family, n. Familie, die.

fan, n. Fächer, der. -s.

Fanny, pr. n. Fanny, die, -s.

far, adv. weit; **as far as,** bis zu, prep.

farm, n. Bauerngut, das, -(e)s.

farmer, n. Bauer, der, -s or -n; pl. -n.

farrier, n. Hufschmied, der, -(e)s.

farthing, n. Pfennig, der, -s.

fast, adj. schnell.

fat, adj. fett.

father, n. Vater, der, -s.

fatten, v. mästen.

fault, n. Fehler, der, -s; **fault-finder,** Tadler, der, -s.

fear, v. fürchten.

February, pr. n. Februar, der, -s.

feeble, adj. schwach.

feel, v. fühlen; befühlen (by touching).

feign, v. heucheln.

fertile, adj. fruchtbar.

fetch, v. holen.

few, adj. wenig.

field, n. Feld, das, -(e)s; **ploughed field,** Acker, der, -s.

fifteen, num. fünfzehn; **the fifteenth,** der, die, das fünfzehnte.

fifty, num. fünfzig; **the fiftieth,** der, die, das fünfzigste.

fight, v. kämpfen; **to fight a battle,** eine Schlacht liefern.

fill, v. füllen.

find, v. finden, irr.

fine, adj. fein, schön, prächtig.

finger, n. Finger, der, -s.

finish, v. endigen.

fir, n. Tanne, die; Föhre, die.

fire, n. Feuer, das, -s.

first, adj. and adv. erst; **at first,** zuerst, adv.

fish, n. Fisch, der, -(e)s.

fishing-hook and rod, n. Angel, die.

fit, adj. passend.

five, num. fünf: **the fifth,** der, die, das fünfte.

five-hundred, num. fünfhundert [fünf Hundert]; **the five-hundreth,** der, die, das fünfhundertste.

flee, v. fliehen, irr.

flesh, n. Fleisch, das, -es.

flock, n. Herde [Heerde], die.

floor, n. Stock(werk), das, -(e)s.

florin, n. Gulden, der, -s.

flour, n. Mehl, das, -(e)s.

flow, v. fließen, irr.

flower, n. Blume, die.

fly, v. fliegen, irr.

fog, n. Nebel, der, -s.

follow, v. folgen.

food, n. Speise, die.

foot, n. Fuß, der, -es.

for, prep. für, um.

for, conj. denn.

forbid, v. verbieten, irr.

force, n. Gewalt, die.

force, v. zwingen, irr.

forehead, n. Stirn, die.

foreign, adj. fremd.

forest, n. Wald, der, -(e)s.

foretell, v. vorhersagen, sep.

forget, v. vergessen, irr.

fork, n. Gabel, die.

former, adj. früher; adv. sonst.

fortress, n. Festung, die.

fortune, n. Glück, das, -(e)s.

fortunate, adj. glücklich.

forty, num. vierzig; **the fourtieth,** der, die, das vierzigste.

fountain, n. Quelle, die; Brunnen, der, -s.

four, num. vier, **the fourth,** der, die, das vierte ; **four-in-hand.** vierspännig.

**fourteen,** *num.* vierzehn; **the fourteenth,** der, die, das vierzehnte.

**fox,** *n.* Fuchs, der, –es.

**franc,** *n.* (coin), Frank, der, –en.

**France,** *pr. n.* Frankreich, –s.

**Frankfort,** *pr. n.* Frankfurt, –s.

**Frederick,** *pr. n.* Friedrich, der, –s; **Frederick Street,** Friedrichstraße, die.

**free,** *adj.* frei.

**freedom,** *n.* Freiheit, die.

**freeze,** *v.* frieren, *irr.*

**French,** *adj.* französisch.

**French(man),** *n.* Franzose, der, –n; **French(woman),** Französin, die.

**fresh,** *adj.* frisch.

**Friday,** *n.* Freitag, der, –(e)s.

**friend,** *n.* Freund, der, –(e)s; *fem.* Freundin, die.

**friendship,** *n.* Freundschaft, die.

**frighten,** *v.; trans.* erschrecken; *intrans.* erschrecken, *irr.*

**from,** *prep.* von, aus.

**fruit,** *n.* Frucht, die, Obst, das, –es (*collectively*).

**fruitful,** *adj.* fruchtbar.

**full,** *adj.* voll.

**fun,** *n.* Spaß, der, –es.

**furnish,** *v.* liefern; möblieren [möbliren].

**furniture,** *n.* Möbel, die, *pl.*

**gain,** *n.* Gewinn, der, –(e)s.

**gain,** *v.* gewinnen, *irr.*

**game,** *n.* Spiel, das, –(e)s.

**garden,** *n.* Garten, der, –s.

**gardener,** *n.* Gärtner, der, –s; **gardner's wife,** Gärtnerin, die.

**garret,** *n.* Dachstube, die.

**gate,** *n.* Thor, das, –(e)s, Thür(e), die.

**general,** *n.* General, der, –(e)s.

**Geneva,** *pr. n.* Genf, –s.

**gentleman,** *n.* Herr, der, –n, *pl.* –eu; anständiger Mann.

**George,** *pr. n.* Georg, der, –s.

**German,** *adj.* deutsch; **German-(man),** Deutsche, der, –n (*adj. used as noun*); **German(woman),** Deutsche, die (*adj. used as noun*).

**Germany,** *pr. n.* Deutschland, –s.

**get,** *v.; intrans.* werden, *irr.; trans.* bekommen, *irr.;* holen.

**get up,** *v.* aufstehen, *irr.; sep.*

**gift,** *n.* Gabe, die, Geschenk, das, –(e)s.

**girl,** *n.* Mädchen, das, –s.

**give,** *v.* geben, *irr.;* es giebt [gibt], **there is, there are.**

**glad,** *adj.* froh; **I am glad,** es freut mich.

**glass,** *n.* Glas, das, –es.

**glove,** *n.* Handschuh, der, –(e)s.

**glow,** *v.* glühen.

**go,** *v.* gehen, *irr.;* fahren, *irr.* (in a vehicle); **go away,** fortgehen, *irr.; sep.;* **go out,** ausgehen, *irr.; sep.;* **go for,** holen.

**goat,** *n.* Ziege, die, –es.

**God,** *n.* Gott, der, –es.

**god-father,** *n.* Pate [Pathe], der, –n, Gevatter, der, –s; *pl.* –n.

**gold,** *n.* Gold, das, –(e)s; *adj.* golden.

**golden,** *adj.* golden.

**good,** *adj.* gut, artig.

**goodness,** *n.* Güte, die.

**goose,** *n.* Gans, die.

**govern,** *v.* regieren.

**grain,** *n.* Getreide, das, –es.

**grammar,** *n.* Grammatik, die.

**granary,** *n.* Speicher, der, –s.

granddaughter, n. Enkelin, die.

grandfather, n. Großvater, der, –s.

grandmother, n. Großmutter, die.

grandson, n. Enkel, der, –s.

grape, n. Weintraube, Traube, die.

grasp, v. greifen, irr.

grass, n. Gras, das, –es.

gray, adj. grau.

great, adj. groß.

Greece, pr. n. Griechenland, –s.

greediness, n. Gierigkeit, die, Naschhaftigkeit, die.

greedy, adj. gierig.

green, adj. grün.

ground, n. Boden, der, –s.

grow, v. werden, irr.; (in size); wachsen, irr.

guess, v. raten [rathen], irr.

guilt, n. Schuld, die.

gun, n. Gewehr, das, –(e)s, Flinte, die.

gun-powder, n. Schießpulver, das, –s.

hail, v. hageln.

hair, n. Haar, das, –(e)s.

half, adj. halb.

ham, n. Schinken, der, –s.

hand, n. Hand, die.

hand, v. händigen; to hand over, übergeben, irr.

handicraft, n. Handwerk, das, –(e)s.

handkerchief, n. Taschentuch, das, –(e)s.

handsome, adj. schön.

hang, v. hangen, irr.; hängen.

happen, v. geschehen, irr.

happy, adj. glücklich.

harbor, n. Hafen, der, –s.

hard, adj. hart; schwer; stark.

hare, n. Hase, der, –n.

harvest, n. Ernte, die.

hat, n. Hut, der, –(e)s.

hatred, n. Haß, der, –es.

have, v. haben, irr.

hay, n. Heu, das, –(e)s.

hazel-nut, n. Haselnuß, die.

he, pron. er; der, derjenige, etc.

head, n. Haupt, das, –(e)s, Kopf, der, –(e)s; head-ache, Kopfweh, das, –(e)s.

heal, v. heilen.

health, n. Gesundheit, die.

healthy, adj. gesund.

hear, v. hören; erhören (of prayers).

heart, n. Herz, das, –ens, pl. –en; by heart, auswendig, adv.

heat, n. Hitze, die.

heaven, n. Himmel, der, –s.

heavy, adj. schwer; stark.

heed, n. Acht, die; to give heed, achtgeben [Acht geben].

help, v. helfen, irr.

hen, n. Henne, die.

Henry, pr. n. Heinrich, der, –s.

her, dat. and acc. of she; pron. ihr; sie; of her, ihrer, gen.

her, poss. adj. ihr, ihre, ihr.

herd, n. Herde [Heerde], die.

here, adv. hier.

hers, poss. pron. ihrer, ihre, ihres; der, die, das ihre; der, die, das ihrige.

herself, refl. pron. sich.

herself, emphatic. selbst.

hide, v. verbergen, irr.

high, adj. hoch; comp. höher; superl. höchst; at the highest, höchstens, adv.

hill, n. Hügel, der, –s.

him, dat. and acc. of he; pron. ihm; ihn; of him, seiner, gen.

himself, refl. pron. sich.

himself, emphatic. selbst.

hire, v. mieten [miethen].

**his,** *poss. adj.* fein, feine, fein.

**his,** *poss. pron.* feiner, feine, fei-n(e)s, der, die, das feine, der, die, das feinige.

**history,** *n.* Geſchichte, die.

**hit,** *v.* treffen, *irr.*

**hither,** *adv.* hierher.

**hold,** *v.* halten, *irr.*

**hole,** *n.* Loch, das, –(e)s.

**holiday,** *n.* Feiertag, der, –(e)s.

**home,** *n.* Heimat [Heimath], die; **at home,** zu Hauſe; **home,** nach Hauſe.

**honest,** *adj.* ehrlich.

**honey,** *n.* Honig, der, –s.

**honor,** *n.* Ehre, die.

**hope,** *n.* Hoffnung, die.

**hope,** *v.* hoffen.

**horse,** *n.* Pferd, das, –(e)s; **on horse-back,** zu Pferd; **horse-shoe,** Hufeiſen, das, –s.

**hospital,** *n.* Spital, das, –(e)s.

**hot,** *adj.* heiß.

**hotel,** *n.* Hotel, das, –s.

**hour,** *n.* Stunde, die.

**house,** *n.* Haus, das, –es.

**how,** *adv.* wie; **however,** wie … auch; doch, jedoch, indeſſen.

**hundred,** *num.* hundert; **the hundredth,** der, die, das hundertſte.

**hung (with),** *participial adj.* behangen (mit).

**hungry,** *adj.* hungrig.

**hunting,** *n.* Jagd, die.

**hurl,** *v.* werfen, *irr.*

**husband,** *n.* Mann, der, –(e)s, Gemahl, der, –s, Gatte, der, –n.

**hut,** *n.* Hütte, die.

**I,** *pron.* ich.

**ice,** *n.* Eis, das, –es.

**idle,** *adj.* träge.

**if,** *conj.* wenn, ob.

**image,** *n.* Bild, das, –(e)s.

**immense,** *adj.* ungeheuer.

**immediately,** *adv.* (ſo)gleich.

**improve,** *v.* verbeſſern.

**in,** *prep. and adv.* in; drinnen, herein, hinein.

**increase,** *v.* vergrößern, vermehren.

**indeed,** *adv.* in der That, wirklich, ja, zwar.

**India,** *pr. n.* Indien, –s.

**infringe,** *v.* brechen, *irr.;* übertreten, *irr.*

**inhabit,** *v.* bewohnen.

**inhabitant,** *n.* Einwohner, der, –s.

**ink,** *n.* Tinte [Dinte], die; **ink-stand,** Tintenfaß [Dintenfaß], das, –es.

**inn,** *n.* Wirtshaus [Wirthshaus], das, –es.

**inside,** *prep. and adv.* innerhalb; drinnen.

**insolence,** *n.* Unverſchämtheit, die, Frechheit, die.

**instead,** *prep.* anſtatt, ſtatt.

**instruct,** *v.* unterrichten.

**insurrection,** *n.* Empörung, die.

**intercourse,** *n.* Verkehr, der, –(e)s, Umgang, der, –(e)s.

**interdict,** *n.* Verbot, das, –(e)s.

**into,** *prep.* in.

**introduce,** *v.* einführen, *sep.;* vorſtellen, *sep.*

**invent,** *v.* erfinden, *irr.*

**invention,** *n.* Erfindung, die.

**inventor,** *n.* Erfinder, der, –s.

**invite,** *v.* einladen, *irr.; sep.*

**Ireland,** *pr. n.* Irland, –s.

**iron,** *n.* Eiſen, das, –s; *adj.* eiſern.

**irregular,** *adj.* unregelmäßig.

**island,** *n.* Inſel, die.

**issue,** *v.* erlaſſen, *irr.*

**it,** *pron. nom.* er, ſie, eŝ; *acc.* ihn, ſie, eŝ; **of it,** ſeiner, ihrer, ſeiner; davou; **to it,** ihm, ihr, ihm; dazu.

**Italian,** *adj.* italieniſch; **Italian (man),** Italiener, der, -ŝ; **Italian (woman),** Italienerin, die.

**Italy,** *pr. n.* Italien, -ŝ.

**its,** *poss. adj.* ſein, ſeine, ſein, deſſen, deren.

**its,** *poss. pron.* ſeiner ſeine, ſein(e)ŝ, der, die, daŝ ſeine, der, die, daŝ ſeinige.

**jacket,** *n.* Jacke, die.

**James,** *pr. n.* Jakob [Jacob], der, -ŝ.

**January,** *pr. n.* Januar, der, -ŝ.

**Japan,** *pr. n.* Japan, -ŝ.

**Jew,** *n.* Jude, der, -n; **Jewess,** Jüdin, die.

**John,** *pr. n.* Johann, der, -ŝ.

**joiner,** *n.* Schreiner, der, -ŝ, Tiſchler, der, -ŝ.

**journal,** *n.* Blatt, daŝ, -eŝ; **daily journal,** Tageblatt, daŝ, -eŝ.

**judge,** *v.* urteilen [urtheilen].

**Juliet,** *pr. n.* Julie, die, -nŝ.

**Julius,** *pr. n.* Juliuŝ, der.

**July,** *pr. n.* Juli, der, -ŝ.

**jump,** *v.* ſpringen, *irr.*

**June,** *pr. n.* Juni, der, -ŝ.

**just,** *adj.* gerecht; *adv.* gerade.

**keep,** *v.* behalten, *irr.*

**kerchief,** *n.* Halstuch, daŝ, -(e)ŝ.

**kettle,** *n.* Keſſel, der, -ŝ.

**key,** *n.* Schlüſſel, der, -ŝ.

**kill,** *v.* töten [töbten].

**kilogram,** *n.* Kilogramm, daŝ, -(e)ŝ.

**kind,** *adj.* gütig.

**kindle,** *v.* anzünden, *sep.;* anmachen, *sep.*

**kindness,** *n.* Güte, die.

**king,** *n.* König, der, -(e)ŝ.

**kingdom,** *n.* Königreich, daŝ, -(e)ŝ.

**kitchen,** *n.* Küche, die.

**knee,** *n.* Knie, daŝ, -ŝ.

**knife,** *n.* Meſſer, daŝ, -ŝ.

**knit,** *v.* ſtricken.

**knock,** *v.* klopfen.

**know,** *v.* wiſſen, *irr.;* kennen, *irr.* (to be acquainted with).

**known,** *participial adj.* bekannt.

**labor,** *n.* Arbeit, die.

**laborer,** *n.* Arbeiter, der, -ŝ.

**ladder,** *n.* Leiter, die.

**lady,** *n.* Dame, die, Frau, die; **young lady,** Fräulein, daŝ, -ŝ.

**lake,** *n.* See, der, -ŝ.

**lament,** *v.* beklagen.

**land,** *n.* Land, daŝ, -(e)ŝ.

**land,** *v.* landen.

**language,** *n.* Sprache, die.

**large,** *adj.* groß.

**last,** *adj.* letzt; **at last,** zuletzt.

**late,** *adj.* ſpät; **lately,** neulich.

**laugh,** *v.* lachen.

**law,** *n.* Geſetz, daŝ, -eŝ.

**lawyer,** *n.* Advokat [Advocat], der, -en.

**lay,** *v.* legen.

**lazy,** *adj.* faul.

**lead,** *n.* Blei, daŝ, -(e)ŝ.

**lead,** *v.* führen.

**leader,** *n.* Führer, der, -ŝ.

**leaf,** *n.* Blatt, daŝ, -eŝ; Baumblatt, daŝ, -eŝ.

**leap,** *v.* hüpfen.

**learn,** *v.* lernen.

**learned,** *participial adj.* gelehrt.

**least,** *adj.* wenigſt, mindeſt; **at (the) least,** wenigſtenŝ, mindeſtenŝ, *adv.*

**leather,** *n.* Leder, daŝ, -ŝ.

**leathern,** *adj.* ledern.

**leave,** *v.* (ver)lassen, *irr.;* abgehen, *irr.; sep.;* abfahren, *irr.; sep.;* abreisen, *sep.*

**left,** *adj.* link; **to** *or* **on the left,** links, *adv.*

**leg,** *n.* Bein, das, -(e)s.

**lend,** *v.* leihen, *irr.*

**length,** *n.* Länge, die; **at length,** endlich, *adv.*

**lesson,** *n.* Lektion [Lection], die, Stunde, die.

**lest,** *conj.* damit nicht.

**let,** *v.* lassen, *irr.;* vermieten [vermiethen] *(houses, etc.).*

**letter,** *n.* Brief, der, -(e)s; **letter-carrier,** Briefträger, der, -s.

**Lewis,** *pr. n.* Ludwig, der, -s.

**liberty,** *n.* Freiheit, die.

**lie,** *n.* Lüge, die.

**lie,** *v.* lügen, *irr.* (to tell a falsehood).

**lie,** *v.* liegen, *irr.*

**life,** *n.* Leben, das, -s.

**lift,** *v.* heben, *irr.*

**light,** *n.* Licht, das, -(e)s.

**light,** *adj.* leicht; hell.

**lighten,** *v.* blitzen.

**ligneous,** *adj.* holzicht *or* holzig.

**like,** *adj.* gleich; **to be like,** gleichen, *ir.*

**like,** *v.* lieben, (gern) mögen, *irr.;* gern haben, *irr.;* **I like to sing,** ich singe gern.

**likeness,** *n.* Bild, das, -(e)s.

**lion,** *n.* Löwe, der, -n.

**lip,** *n.* Lippe, die.

**liquid,** *adj.* flüssig.

**listen,** *v.* zuhören, *sep.*

**little,** *adj.* klein; wenig.

**live,** *v.* leben; wohnen (dwell).

**load,** *n.* Ladung.

**load,** *v.* laden, *irr.*

**lock,** *n.* Schloß, das, -es.

**London,** *pr. n.* London, -s.

**long,** *adj. and adv.* lang.

**look,** *n.* schauen, sehen, *irr.;* (of appearance) aussehen, *irr.; sep.;* **to look at,** ansehen, *irr.; sep.,* betrachten ; **to look for,** suchen.

**looking-glass,** *n.* Spiegel, der, -s.

**Lord,** *n.* Herr, der, -n; *pl.* -en; Lord, der, s; *pl.* -s.

**lordly,** *adj.* herrlich.

**Lorely,** *pr. n.* Lorelei, die.

**lose,** *v.* verlieren, *irr.;* **to lose one's way,** sich verlieren.

**lot,** *n.* Los [Loos], das, -es.

**lottery,** *n.* Lotterie, die.

**loud,** *adj. and adv.* laut.

**Louis,** *pr. n.* Ludwig, der, -s.

**Louisa,** *pr. n.* Luise [Louise], die, -ns.

**love,** *v.* lieben.

**love,** *n.* Liebe, die.

**low,** *adj.* niedrig; leise.

**lung,** *n.* Lunge, die.

**Lutzen,** *pr. n.* Lützen, -s.

**Lyons,** *pr. n.* Lyon, -s.

**Madrid,** *pr. n.* Madrid, -s.

**magnificent,** *adj.* prächtig.

**mail,** *n.* Post, die.

**make,** *v.* machen, schaffen.

**malice,** *n.* Bosheit, die.

**mama,** *n.* Mama [Mamma], die.

**man,** *n.* Mensch, der, -en ; Mann, der, -(e)s.

**mankind,** *n.* Menschengeschlecht, das, -(e)s.

**manoeuvre,** *v.* manövrieren [manövriren].

**many,** *adj.* viele; **many a,** manch ein, etc.; mancher, etc.

**March,** *pr. n.* März, der, -es.

**march,** *v.* marschieren [marschiren].

**Margaret,** *pr. n.* Margarete [Margarethe], die.

mark, *n.* Mark, die (coin).

market, *n.* Markt, der, –(e)s.

marshal, *n.* Marschall, der, –s.

marry, *v.* heiraten [heirathen]; verheiraten [verheirathen], *refl.*

**Martin,** *pr. n.* Martin, der, –s.

**Mary,** *pr. n.* Marie, die, –(n)s.

mason, *n.* Maurer, der, –s.

mass, *n.* Masse, die.

mattress, *n.* Matratze, die.

master, *n.* Meister, der, –s; Lehrer, der, –s; Herr, der, –n.

**May,** *pr. n.* Mai, der, –s.

may, *v.* mögen, *irr.;* können, *irr.;* dürfen, *irr.*

me, *pron.* mir *(dat.)*, mich *(acc.);* of me, mein(er) *(gen.)*.

meadow, *n.* Wiese, die.

meal, *n.* Essen, das, –s, Mahl, das, –(e)s.

means, *n.* Mittel, das, –s; by means, vermittelst.

meanwhile, *adv.* unterdessen, indessen.

meat, *n.* Fleisch, das, –es.

medicine, *n.* Arznei, die.

meditate, *v.* sinnen, *irr.*

meet, *v.* treffen, *irr.;* begegnen; to go to meet, entgegengehen, *irr.; sep.*

melt, *v.* schmelzen, *irr.*

mention, *n.* Erwähnung, die.

merchant, *n.* Kaufmann, der, –(e)s.

metal, *n.* Metall, das, –(e)s.

metre, *n.* Meter, der, –s.

might, *n.* Macht, die.

mild, *adj.* mild.

milk, *n.* Milch, die.

mill, *n.* Mühle, die.

miller, *n.* Müller, der, –s.

millet, *n.* Hirse, der, –s.

mind, *n.* Sinn, der, –(e)s; to have a mind, Lust haben.

mine, *poss. pron.* meiner, meine, mein(e)s, der. die, das meine, der, die, das meinige.

minute, *n.* Minute, die.

miracle, *n.* Wunder, das, –s.

mirror, *n.* Spiegel, der, –s.

misery, *n.* Elend, das, –(e)s; Not, [Noth], die.

**Miss,** *n.* Fräulein, das, –s.

mist, *n.* Nebel, der, –s.

mistake, *n.* Fehler, der, –s.

mistaken, to be, *v.* sich irren.

mix (up), *v.* vermischen.

model, *n.* Muster, das, –s.

**Monday,** *n.* Montag, der, –(e)s.

money, *n.* Geld, das, –(e)s.

monkey, *n.* Affe, der, –n.

month, *n.* Monat, der, –(e)s.

monthly, *adj.* monatlich.

moon, *n.* Mond, der, –(e)s.

more, *adj. and adv.* mehr.

morning, *n.* Morgen, der, –s.

most, *adj.* meist; *adv.* am meisten; mostly, meistens.

mother, *n.* Mutter, die.

mount, *v.* steigen, *irr.*

mountain, *n.* Berg, der, –(e)s; Gebirge, das, –s (collectively).

mouse, *n.* Maus, die.

mouth, *n.* Mund, der, –(e)s.

**Mr.,** *n.* Herr, der, –n; *pl.* –en.

**Mrs.,** *n.* Frau, die, Madam(e), die.

much, *adj.* viel; *adv.* viel, sehr.

**Munich,** *pr. n.* München, –s.

music, *n.* Musik, die; music-book, Musikheft, das, –(e)s; music-lesson, Musikstunde, die; music-teacher, Musiklehrer, der, –s.

musket, *n.* Gewehr, das, –(e)s.

must, *v.* müssen, *irr.*

mutton, *n.* Hammelfleisch, das, –es.

my, *poss. adj.* mein, meine, mein,

**myself,** *refl. pron.* mir *or* mich.
**myself,** *emphatic.* ſelbſt.

**nail,** *n.* Nagel, der, –s.
**name,** *n.* Name(n), der, –ns.
**name,** *v.* nennen, *irr.*
**napkin,** *n.* Serviette, die.
**nation,** *n.* Nation, die.
**naughty,** *adj.* unartig.
**near,** *adj. and adv.* nahe.
**nearly,** *adv.* beinahe.
**neck,** *n.* Hals, der, –es; **necktie,**
  Halsbinde, die.
**need,** *v.* brauchen.
**need,** *n.* Not [Noth], die.
**needle,** *n.* Nadel, die.
**negligent,** *adj.* nachläſſig.
**neighbor,** *n.* Nachbar, der, –s *or*
  –n, *pl.* –n; *fem.* Nachbarin, die.
**neighborhood,** *n.* Nachbarſchaft,
  die.
**neither,** *conj.* weder.
**nephew,** *n.* Neffe, der, –n.
**nest,** *n.* Neſt, das, –(e)s.
**net,** *n.* Netz, das, –es.
**never,** *adv.* nie(mals).
**nevertheless,** *adv.* nichtsdeſtoweniger.
**new,** *adj.* neu.
**news,** *n.* Nachricht, die; Neues
  (*adj. used as neuter noun*).
**newspaper,** *n.* Zeitung, die.
**next,** *adj.* nächſt.
**nice,** *adj.* ſchön, hübſch.
**niece,** *n.* Nichte, die.
**night,** *n.* Nacht, die.
**nine,** *num.* neun; **the ninth,** der,
  die, das neunte.
**nineteen,** *num.* neunzehn; **the**
  **nineteenth,** der, die, das neunzehnte.
**ninety,** *num.* neunzig; **the nine-**
  **tieth,** der, die, das neunzigſte.

**no,** *adj.* kein, keine, kein; *adv.*
  nein; **no more,** nicht mehr.
**nobody,** *n.* niemand [Niemand],
  –(e)s.
**noise,** *n.* Lärm, der, –(e)s.
**none,** *pron.* keiner, keine, kein(e)s.
**nor,** *conj.* noch.
**north,** *n.* Nord(en), der, –ens.
**nose,** *n.* Naſe, die.
**not,** *adv.* nicht; **not at all,** garnicht.
**nothing,** *n.* nichts, *pron.*
**notice,** *v.* bemerken.
**November,** *n.* November, der, –s.
**now,** *adv.* nun, jetzt.
**nowhere,** *adv.* nirgends.
**number,** *n.* Zahl, die.
**nut,** *n.* Nuß, die.

**oats,** *n.* Hafer, der, –s.
**obedient,** *adj.* gehorſam.
**obey,** *v.* gehorchen.
**oblige,** *v.* verbinden, *irr.;* **to be**
  **obliged,** müſſen, *irr.*
**obtain,** *v.* erlangen.
**o'clock** *see* **clock.**
**occupy,** *v.* beſchäftigen.
**of,** *prep.* von, aus.
**off,** *adv.* ab, fort, weg.
**offer,** *v.* bieten, *irr.*
**offer,** *n.* Anerbieten, das, –s.
**officer,** *n.* Offizier [Officier], der,
  –s.
**often,** *adv.* oft.
**oil,** *n.* Öl [Oel], das, –(e)s.
**old,** *adj.* alt.
**omnibus,** *n.* Omnibus, der,
  –es.
**omnipotence,** *n.* Allmacht, die.
**on,** *prep.* auf; über; (sometimes),
  an; *adv.* an.
**once,** *adv.* einmal; einſt; **once**
  **more,** noch einmal.

one, *num.* ein,‾ eine, ein; *(without noun)*, einer, eine, ein(e)s; *indef. pron.* man.

only, *adj.* einzig; *adv.* nur, bloß, allein.

open, *adj.* offen.

open, *v.* öffnen, aufmachen, *sep.*

opportune, *adj.* gelegen, rechtzeitig.

opposite, *adj.* gegenüber, *prep.*

or, *conj.* ober.

order, *n.* Ordnung, die; Befehl, der, –(e)s, Verbot, das, –(e)s; **in order that,** damit; **in order to,** um ... zu.

order, *v.* befehlen, *irr.*

other, *adj.* anber.

ought, *v.* sollte.

our, *poss. adj.* unser, uns(e)re, unser.

ours, *poss. pron.* uns(e)rer, uns(e)re, uns(e)res, der, die, das uns(e)re, der, die, das unsrige.

out, *adv.* aus, heraus, hinaus.

out of, *prep.* aus.

outside, *prep. and adv.* außerhalb; braußen.

over, *prep. and adv.* über; vorbei.

ox, *n.* Ochse or Ochs, der, –en.

pack, *n.* Pack, das, –(e)s.

page, *n.* Seite, die.

pain, *n.* Schmerz, der, –es; *pl.* –en.

paint, *v.* malen.

painter, *n.* Maler, der, –s.

painting, *n.* Gemälde, das, –s.

pair, *n.* Paar, das, –(e)s.

palace, *n.* Palast, der, –(e)s.

pale, *adj.* bleich.

pan, *n.* Pfanne, die.

paper, *n.* Papier, das, –(e)s.

parasol, *n.* Sonnenschirm, der, –(e)s.

parcel, *n.* Päckchen, das, –s.

pardon, *v.* verzeihen, *irr.*

parents, *n.* Eltern, die.

Paris, *pr. n.* Paris.

park, *n.* Park, der, –(e)s.

parlor, *n.* Besuchszimmer, das, –s.

Parmenio, *pr. n.* Parmenio, der, –s.

part, *n.* Teil [Theil], der, –(e)s.

pass, *v.* vorübergehen, *irr.; sep.;* verfließen, *irr.*

past, *adj. and adv.* verflossen; vorbei, vorüber.

path, *n.* Pfad, der, –(e)s.

patience, *n.* Geduld, die.

pattern, *n.* Muster, das, –s.

pavement, *n.* Pflaster, das, –s.

paw, *n.* Tatze, die.

pay, *v.* bezahlen.

pea, *n.* Erbse, die.

peacock, *n.* Pfau, der, –(e)s.

pear, *n.* Birne, die.

pearl, *n.* Perle, die.

peasant, *n.* Bauer, der, –s or –n; *pl.* –n.

peck, *v.* picken.

pen, *n.* Feder, die.

pencil, *n.* Stift, der, –(e)s; **leadpencil,** Bleistift, der, –(e)s.

penknife, *n.* Federmesser, das, –s.

penny, *n.* Pfennig, der, –(e)s.

people, *n.* Volk, das, –(e)s (nation); Leute, die, (individuals); man, *(indef. pron.)*.

pepper, *n.* Pfeffer, der, –s.

perceive, *v.* bemerken.

perhaps, *adv.* vielleicht.

perish, *v.* umkommen, *irr.; sep.*

permission, *n.* Erlaubnis [Erlaubniß], die.

permit, *v.* erlauben; **to be permitted,** dürfen, *irr.*

**Persia,** *pr. n.* Perſien, –s.

**person,** *n.* Perſon, die.

**Peter,** *pr. n.* Peter, der, –s.

**Phenician,** *pr. n.* Phönizier [Phönicier], der, –s.

**philosopher,** *n.* Philoſoph, der, –en.

**philosophic,** *adj.* philoſophiſch.

**philosophy,** *n.* Philoſophie, die.

**physician,** *n.* Arzt, der, –es.

**piano(-forte),** *n.* Pianoforte, das, –s, Klavier [Clavier], das, –(e)s; **to perform upon the piano,** Klavier ſpielen.

**pick,** *v.* picken; pflücken; **pick up,** aufleſen, *irr.; sep.*

**picture,** *n.* Bild, das, –(e)s, Gemälde, das, –s.

**piece,** *n.* Stück, das, –(e)s.

**pig,** *n.* Schwein, das, –(e)s.

**pigeon,** *n.* Taube, die.

**pin,** *n.* Stecknadel, die.

**pistol,** *n.* Piſtole, die.

**place,** *n.* Platz, der, –es, Ort, der, -(e)s.

**place,** *v.* ſtellen, ſetzen, legen.

**plain,** *adj.* einfach.

**plain,** *n.* Fläche, die, Ebene, die.

**plant,** *n.* Pflanze, die.

**plate,** *n.* Teller, der, –s.

**play,** *n.* Spiel, das, –(e)s; Schauſpiel, das, –(e)s (drama).

**play,** *v.* ſpielen.

**pleasant,** *adj.* angenehm.

**please,** *v.* gefallen, *irr.;* belieben; **if you please,** gefälligſt, *adv.;* **as you please,** wie beliebt.

**pleasure,** *n.* Vergnügen, das, –s.

**plough** *or* **plow,** *n.* Pflug, der, –(e)s.

**pluck,** *v.* pflücken.

**plum,** *n.* Pflaume, die; **plumtree,** Pflaumenbaum, der, –s.

**pocket,** *n.* Taſche, die.

**pocketbook,** *n.* Taſchenbuch, das, –(e)s, Brieftaſche, die.

**poem,** *n.* Gedicht, das, –(e)s.

**poet,** *n.* Dichter, der, –s.

**point,** *n.* Punkt, der, –(e)s.

**Poland,** *pr. n.* Polen, –s.

**pole,** *n.* Pfahl, der, –(e)s.

**Polish,** *adj.* poliſch.

**polish,** *v.* polieren [poliren].

**polite,** *adj.* höflich.

**pond,** *n.* Teich, der, –(e)s.

**poor,** *adj.* arm.

**pork,** *n.* Schweinefleiſch, das, –(e)s.

**portfolio,** *n.* Brieftaſche, die.

**possible,** *adj.* möglich.

**post,** *n.* Pfahl, der, –(e)s.

**post(-office),** *n.* Poſt, die.

**potato,** *n.* Kartoffel, die.

**pound,** *n.* Pfund, das, –(e)s.

**powder,** *n.* Pulver, das, –s.

**power,** *n.* Kraft, die, Gewalt, die.

**praise,** *v.* loben.

**pray,** *v.* beten, bitten, *irr.;* **pray, (please),** bitte.

**prayer,** *n.* Gebet, das, –(e)s.

**precious,** *adj.* koſtbar.

**present,** *adj.* anweſend.

**present,** *n.* Geſchenk, das, –(e)s.

**pretend,** *v.* ſich ſtellen.

**pretty,** *adj. and adv.* hübſch; ziemlich.

**price,** *n.* Preis, der, –es.

**prince,** *n.* Fürſt, der, –en; Prinz, der, –en.

**prison,** *n.* Gefängnis [Gefängniß], das, –es.

**prisoner,** *n.* Gefangene, der, –en (*participial adj. used as noun*).

**prize,** *n.* Preis, der, –es; **the first prize,** das große Los [Loos].

**probable,** *adj.* wahrſcheinlich, vermutlich [vermuthlich].

product, *n.* Produkt [Product], das, -(e)8.
profession, *n.* Beruf, der, -(e)8.
professor, *n.* Profeffor, der, -8; *pl.* -en.
prohibition, *n.* Verbot, das, -(e)8.
promise, *v.* verfprechen, *irr.*
proof, *n.* Beweis, der, -es.
provided that, *conj.* vorausge= fehen daß, wenn nur.
provisions, *n.* Lebensmittel, die, *pl.*
Prussia, *pr. n.* Preußen, -8.
Prussian, *pr. n.* Preuße, der, -n (man); Preußin, die (woman).
Prussian, *adj.* preußifch.
punish, *v.* ftrafen.
pupil, *n.* Schüler, der,-8; Schülerin, die (*fem.*).
purse, *n.* Beutel, der, -8.
push, *v.* ftoßen, *irr.*
put, *v.* legen, fetzen, ftellen; to put (a weight) upon, laden auf; to put up, aufftellen, *sep.*; put on, *v.* anziehen, *irr.; sep.*

quarter, *n.* Viertel, das, -8.
quartz, *n.* Quarz, der, -es.
queen, *n.* Königin, die.
question, *n.* Frage, die.
quick, *adj.* fchnell.
quiet, *adj.* ruhig.
quite, *adv.* ganz.
quotation, *n.* Citat, das, -(e)8.

rafter, *n.* Sparren, der, -8.
railroad, *n.* Eifenbahn, die.
rain, *n.* Regen, der, -8.
rain, *v.* regnen.
rather, *adv.* lieber.
raven, *n.* Rabe, der, -ns.
ray, *n.* Strahl, der, -(e)8; *pl.* -en.
read, *v.* lefen, *irr.*
ready, *adj.* fertig, bereit.

real, *adj.* wirklich.
rebel, *n.* Empörer, der, -8.
rebellion, *n.* Empörung, die.
receive, *v.* empfangen, *irr.;* er= halten, *irr.*
receiver, *n.* Empfänger, der, -8.
reception, *n.* Empfang, der, -(e)8.
red, *adj.* rot [roth].
refresh, *v.* erquicken.
region, *n.* Gegend, die, Land, das, -(e)8.
regular, *adj.* regelmäßig.
reign, *v.* regieren.
rejoice, *v.* fich freuen.
relate, *v.* erzählen.
release, *v.* erlaffen, *irr.*
remain, *v.* bleiben, *irr.*
remember, *v.* fich erinnern.
remind, *v.* erinnern.
renowned, *adj.* berühmt.
repair, out of, baufällig.
reply, *v.* erwidern [erwiedern].
request, *v.* erfuchen, bitten, *irr.*
resemble, *v.* gleichen, *irr.*
reside, *v.* wohnen.
resist, *v.* widerftehen, *irr.*
resolve, *v.* fich entfchließen, *irr.*
return, *v.* zurückkehren, *sep.*
revolt, *n.* Empörung, die.
reward, *v.* belohnen.
reward, *n.* Belohnung, die.
Rhine, *pr. n.* Rhein, der, -(e)8.
ribbon, *n.* Band, das, -(e)8.
rich, *adj.* reich.
Richard, *pr. n.* Richard, der, -8.
riches, *n.* Reichtum [Reichthum], der, -8.
ride, *v.* reiten, *irr.* (on horse- back); fahren, *irr.* (in any vehicle).
ridiculous, *adj.* lächerlich.
rifle, *n.* Gewehr, das, -(e)8, Flinte, die.

**right,** *n.* Recht, das, –(e)s.

**right,** *adj.* recht; **to the right,** rechts, *adv.*

**ring,** *n.* Ring, der, –(e)s.

**ripe,** *adj.* reif.

**rise,** *v.* aufstehen, *irr.; sep.* (of persons); aufgehen, *irr.; sep.* (of sun, etc.).

·**river,** *n.* Fluß, der, –es.

**rhyme,** *n.* Reim, der, –(e)s.

**read,** *n.* Straße, die.

**roast,** *v.* braten, *irr.*

**roast,** *n.* Braten, der, –s.

**Robert,** *pr. n.* Robert, der, –s.

**Roman,** *pr. n.* Römer, der, –s.

**Rome,** *pr. n.* Rom, –s.

**rock,** *n.* Fels *or* Felsen, der, –ens.

**roe,** *n.* Reh, das, –(e)s.

**roof,** *n.* Dach, das, –(e)s.

**room,** *n.* Zimmer, das, –s; **drawing-room,** Saal, der, –(e)s; **sleeping-room,** Schlafzimmer, das, –s; **sitting-room,** Wohnzimmer, das, –s.

**root,** *n.* Wurzel, die.

**rose,** *n.* Rose, die.

**rough,** *adj.* rauh.

**round,** *adj.* rund; *prep.* um, um . . . herum.

**rule,** *n.* Regel, die.

**run,** *v.* laufen, *irr.;* rennen, *irr.;* **to run away,** weglaufen, *irr.; sep.,* fliehen, *irr.;* **to run aground,** scheitern; **to run after,** nachlaufen, *irr.; sep.*

**Russia,** *pr. n.* Rußland, –s.

**Russian,** *pr. n.* Russe, der, –n.

**rye,** *n.* Korn, das, –s.

**sack,** *n.* Sack, der, –(e)s.

**sad,** *adj.* traurig.

**saddler,** *n.* Sattler, der, –s.

**sail,** *v.* segeln.

**sailor,** *n.* Matrose, der, –n.

**salad,** *n.* Salat, der, –(e)s.

**salt,** *n.* Salz, das, –es.

**saltpeter-stone,** *n.* Salpeterstein, der, –(e)s.

**same, the,** *pron. and adj.* derselbe, dieselbe, dasselbe [dasselbe]; der, die, das nämliche.

**sand,** *n.* Sand, der, –(e)s.

**sap,** *n.* Saft, der, –(e)s.

**Sarah,** *pr. n.* Sarah, die, –s.

**satisfy,** *v.* befriedigen; **satisfied,** befriedigt, zufrieden.

**Saturday,** *n.* Sonnabend, der, –s, Samstag, der, –s.

**save,** *v.* retten, erretten.

**Saxony,** *pr. n.* Sachsen, –s.

**say,** *v.* sagen.

**scarcely,** *adv.* kaum.

**school,** *n.* Schule, die; **at school,** in der Schule.

**science,** *n.* Wissenschaft, die.

**scold,** *v.* schelten, *irr.;* auszanken, *sep.*

**sea,** *n.* Meer, das, –(e)s, See, die.

**seat,** *v.* setzen; **to be seated,** sich setzen.

**seat,** *n.* Sitz, der, –es, Platz, der, –es.

**second,** *adj.* zweite, der, die, das, –en.

**see,** *v.* sehen, *irr.*

**seek,** *v.* suchen.

**seem,** *v.* scheinen, *irr.*

**seize,** *v.* greifen, *irr.,* packen.

**sell,** *v.* verkaufen.

**send,** *v.* schicken, senden, *irr.*

**sense,** *n.* Sinn, der, –(e)s.

**September,** *pr. n.* September, der, –s.

**servant,** *n.* Diener, der, –s, Bediente, der, –n; *(fem.)* die Dienerin, die Magd, das Dienstmädchen, –s.

set, v. ſetzen, ſtellen; untergehen, *irr.; sep.*

seven, *num.* ſieben; **the seventh,** der, die, das ſiebente.

seventeen, *num.* ſiebzehn; **the seventeenth,** der, die, das ſiebzehnte.

seventy, *num.* ſiebzig; **the seventieth,** der, die, das ſiebzigſte.

several, *adj.* mehrere.

severe, *adj.* ſtreng.

shake, v. ſchütteln.

shall, v. ſollen, *irr.;* werden, *irr.* (*future tense*).

sharp, *adj.* ſcharf.

she, *pron.* er, ſie, es; derjenige, diejenige, dasjenige; der, die, das.

sheep, n. Schaf, das, –(e)s.

sheet, n. Betttuch, das, –(e)s.

shepherd, n. Hirt(e), der, –en.

shilling, n. Schilling, der, –s.

shine, v. ſcheinen, *irr.*

ship, n. Schiff, das, –(e)s.

shirt, n. Hemd, das, –(e)s; *pl.* –en.

shoe, n. Schuh, der, –(e)s.

shoe, v. beſchlagen, *irr.*

shoemaker, n. Schuhmacher, der, –s.

shoot, v. ſchießen, *irr.*

shop, n. Laden, der, –s.

short, *adj.* kurz.

shoulder, n. Schulter, die.

show, v. zeigen.

shut, v. zumachen.

shutter, n. Laden *or* Fenſterladen, der, –s.

sick, *adj.* krank.

side, n. Seite, die; **this side,** diesſeits, *adv. and prep.;* **that side,** jenſeits, *adv. and prep.*

side-board, n. Speiſeſchrank, der, –(e)s.

silence, n. Schweigen, das, –s.

silent, *adj.* ſchweigſam; **to be silent,** v. ſchweigen, *irr.*

silk, n. Seide, die; *adj.* ſeiden.

silver, n. Silber, das, –s; *adj.* ſilbern.

simple, *adj.* einfach.

since, *prep. and conj.* ſeit; *adv. and conj.* ſeitdem; *prep.* von ... an.

sing, v. ſingen, *irr.*

single, *adj.* einzig.

sink, v. ſinken, *irr.*

Sir, n. Herr, der, mein Herr, –n; *pl.* –en.

sister, n. Schweſter, die.

sit, v. ſitzen, *irr.;* **sit down,** ſich niederſetzen, *sep.*

situate(d), *adj.* gelegen.

situation, n. Lage, die; Stelle, die.

six, *num.* ſechs; **the sixth,** der, die, das ſechſte.

sixteen, *num.* ſechzehn; **the sixteenth,** der, die, das ſechzehnte.

sixty, *num.* ſechzig; **the sixtieth,** der, die, das ſechzigſte.

sky, Himmel, der, –s.

slave, n. Sklave [Sclave], der, –n.

slay, v. ermorden.

sleep, v. ſchlafen, *irr.*

sleeping-room, n. Schlafzimmer, das, –s.

sleepy, *adj.* ſchläfrig.

slipper, n. Pantoffel, der, –s.

slow, *adj.* langſam.

small, *adj.* klein.

smile, v. lächeln.

smoke, n. Rauch, der, –(e)s.

smoke, v. rauchen; räuchern.

snow, n. Schnee, der, –s.

snow, v. ſchneien.

snuffers, n. Lichtſchere [Lichtſcheere], die, Lichtputze, die.

so, *adv.* ſo, alſo.

soap, n. Seife, die.
sociable, adj. umgänglich.
society, n. Gesellschaft, die.
sock, n. Strumpf, der, -(e)s.
sofa, n. Sofa [Sopha], das, -s.
soft, adj. weich; leise.
soldier, n. Soldat, der, -en.
some, pron. and adj. welcher,
welche, welches, etwas; einiger,
einige, einiges.
somebody, pron. jemand [Jemand],
-es.
something, pron. etwas.
sometimes, adv. manchmal.
somewhere, adv. irgendwo.
son, n. Sohn, der, -(e)s.
song, n. Lied, das, -(e)s.
Sophia, pr. n. Sophie, die, -ns.
soon, adv. bald, frühe; sooner,
eher, früher.
sorry, adj. traurig; I am sorry,
es thut mir leid.
soul, n. Seele, die.
sound, n. Laut, der, -(e)s.
soup, n. Suppe, die.
Spain, pr. n. Spanien, -s.
Spaniard, pr. n. Spanier, der, -s.
Spanish, adj. spanisch; Spanish
woman, Spanierin, die.
sparrow, n. Sperling, der, -s.
speak, v. sprechen, irr.
spectacles (pair of), n. Brille,
die.
speech, n. Sprache, die.
spend, v. ausgeben, irr.; sep.
(money, etc.); zubringen, irr.;
sep. (time, etc.).
spite, n. Trotz, der, -es; in spite,
trotz, prep.
splendid, adj. prächtig.
spoil, v. verderben, irr.
spool, n. Spule, die.
spoon, n. Löffel, der, -s.

spot, n. Flecken, der, -s.
spring, v. springen, irr.
spring, n. Frühling, der, -s
(season); Quelle, die (water).
square, Platz, der, -es.
stable, n. Stall, der, -(e)s.
stag, n. Hirsch, der, -es.
staircase or stairs, n. Treppe, die;
up-stairs, oben, herauf, hinauf;
down-stairs, unten, herunter,
hinunter.
stake, n. Pfahl, der, -(e)s.
stand, v. stehen, irr.
star, n. Stern, der, -(e)s.
station, n. Bahnhof, der, -(e)s.
stay, v. bleiben, irr.
steal, v. stehlen, irr.
steel, n. Stahl, der, -(e)s.
steel-pen, n. Stahlfeder, die.
step, n. Stufe, die.
sterling, n. Sterling, der, -s.
stick, n. Stock, der, -(e)s.
still, adv. noch; dennoch, doch.
stocking, n. Strumpf, der, -(e)s.
stomach, n. Magen, der, -s.
stone, n. Stein, der, -(e)s.
stop, v. anhalten, irr.; sep.
store-room, n. Speicher, der, -s.
stork, n. Storch, der, -(e)s.
story, n. Geschichte, die (tale);
Stock, das, -(e)s (floor).
stove, n. Ofen, der, -s.
strange, adj. fremd.
stranger, n. Fremde, der, -n (adj.
used as noun).
straw, n. Stroh, das, -(e)s;
straw-hat, Strohhut, der, -(e)s.
stray, v. sich verirren.
street, n. Straße, die; main-
street, Hauptstraße, die.
strict, adj. streng.
strike, v. schlagen, irr.
strong, adv. stark.

structure, *n.* Bau, der, –s.

struggle, *v.* kämpfen.

student, *n.* Student, der, –en.

study, *n.* Studium, das, –s; *pl.* Studien.

**Stuttgart,** *pr. n.* Stuttgart, –s.

**sublimeness,** *n.* Unübertrefflich-keit, die.

suburb, *n.* Borstadt, die.

success, *n.* Erfolg, der, –(e)s.

such, *adj.* solch (ein), solcher, solche, solches.

suffer, *v.* leiden, *irr.*

sugar, *n.* Zucker, der, –s.

summer, *n.* Sommer, der, –s.

summon, *v.* laden, *irr.*

sun, *n.* Sonne, die.

**Sunday,** *n.* Sonntag, der, –(e)s.

superstition, *n.* Aberglauben, der, –s.

supper, *n.* Abendessen, das, –s, Abendbrot [Abendbrod], das, –(e)s.

suppose, *v.* vermuten [vermuthen].

sure, *adj.* sicher; to be sure, frei-lich, *adv.*

surprise, *v.* überraschen.

surrender, *v.* übergeben, *irr.;* er-geben, *irr.; refl.*

**Swede,** *pr. n.* Schwede, der, –n.

**Sweden,** *pr. n.* Schweden, –s.

sweet, *adj.* süß.

swim, *v.* schwimmen, *irr.*

swine, *n.* Schwein, das, –(e)s.

**Swiss,** *pr. n.* Schweizer, der, –s.

**Switzerland,** *pr. n.* Schweiz, die.

table, *n.* Tafel, die, Tisch, der, –(e)s.

tailor, *n.* Schneider, der, –s.

take, *v.* nehmen, *irr.*, tragen, *irr.;* fangen, *irr.;* to take a walk, spazieren gehen, *irr.*

talent, *n.* Talent, das, –(e)s.

talk, *v.* reden.

tall, *adj.* groß.

task, *n.* Aufgabe, die.

tavern, *n.* Gasthof, der, –(e)s.

tea, *n.* Thee, der, –s.

teach, *v.* lehren.

teacher, *n.* Lehrer, der, –s.

tear, *v.* zerreißen, *irr.*

tell, *v.* sagen, erzählen.

ten, *num.* zehn; the tenth, der, die, das zehnte.

ten-thousand, *num.* zehntausend; the ten-thousandth, der, die, das zehntausendste.

tepid, *adj.* lau.

than, *conj.* als.

thank, *v.* danken.

thanks, *n.* Dank, der, –(e)s.

thankful, *adj.* dankbar.

that, *pron.* jener, jene, jenes, der, die, das; *conj.* daß.

the, *art.* der, die, das; *adv.* je, desto.

theatre, *n.* Theater, das, –s.

thee, *pron.* dir (*dat.*), dich (*acc.*); of thee, deiner (*gen.*).

their, *poss. adj.* ihr, ihre, ihr.

theirs, *poss. pron.* ihrer, ihre, ihres, der, die, das ihre; der, die, das ihrige.

them, *pron.* ihnen (*dat.*), sie (*acc.*); of them, ihrer (*gen.*).

themselves, *pron. refl.* sich.

then, *adv.* dann, damals, da.

thence, *adv.* daher.

there, *adv.* da, dort; there is, there are, es ist, es sind; es giebt [gibt]; thereby, dabei; therefrom, davon; therein, da-rin; thereto, dazu; therewith, damit.

therefore, *adv.* darum, daher, also.

they, *pron.* fie.

thick, *adj.* bid.

thief, *n.* Dieb, der, –(e)s.

thimble, *n.* Fingerhut, der, –(e)s.

thine, *poss. pron.* deiner, deine, deines; der, die, das deine, der, die, das deinige.

thing, *n.* Ding, das, –(e)s.

think, *v.* denken, *irr.*, glauben.

third, *adj.* dritte, der, die, das, –en.

thirsty, *adj.* durstig.

thirteen, *num.* dreizehn; the thirteenth, der, die, das dreizehnte.

thirty, *num.* dreißig; the thirtieth, der, die, das dreißigste.

this, *pron.* dieser, diese, dieses, der, die, das, dies.

thither, *adv.* dahin, dorthin.

Thomas, *pr. n.* Thomas, der.

thou, *pron.* du.

though, *conj.* obgleich, obschon, wenn auch.

threaten, *v.* drohen.

three, *num.* drei; three times (thrice), dreimal [drei Mal]; three-hundred, dreihundert [drei Hundert].

throne, *n.* Thron, der, –(e)s.

through, *prep.* durch.

throw, *v.* werfen, *irr.*; to throw down, hinunterwerfen, *irr.; sep.*

thrust, *v.* stoßen, *irr.*

thunder, *v.* donnern.

Thursday, *n.* Donnerstag, der, –s.

thus, *adv.* so.

thy, *poss. adj.* dein, deine, dein.

thyself, *refl. pron.* dir, dich.

thyself, *emphatic.* selbst.

ticket, *n.* Billet, das, –(e)s; Karte, die.

tie, *v.* binden, *irr.*

tiger, *n.* Tiger, der, –s.

till, *prep. and conj.* bis; not till, erst, *adv.*

time, *n.* Zeit, die; Mal, das, –(e)s; three times, dreimal; in time, rechtzeitig, *adj. and adv.*

time-piece, *n.* Standuhr, die.

tired, *adj.* müde.

to, *prep.* zu, nach, an, in, auf, gegen.

to-day, *adv.* heute.

toe, *n.* Zehe, die.

together, *adv.* zusammen, beisammen.

to-morrow, *adv.* morgen; to-morrow morning, morgen früh; day after to-morrow, übermorgen.

tone, *n.* Ton, der, –(e)s.

tongue, *n.* Zunge, die.

too, *adv.* zu; auch.

tooth, *n.* Zahn, der, –(e)s.

torment, *n.* Qual, die.

touch, *v.* angreifen, *irr.; sep.*

towards, *prep.* gegen.

towel, *n.* Handtuch, das, –(e)s.

tower, *n.* Turm [Thurm], der, –(e)s.

town, *n.* Stadt, die.

trade, *n.* Handel, der, –s.

train, *n.* Zug, der, –(e)s.

transgress, *v.* übertreten, *irr.*

translate, *v.* übersetzen.

translation, *n.* Übersetzung [Uebersetzung], die.

travel, *v.* reisen.

traveller, *n.* Reisende, der, –n (*participial adj. used as noun*).

tree, *n.* Baum, der, –(e)s.

trespass, *v.* übertreten, *irr.*

trouble, *v.* bemühen.

trouble, *n.* Mühe, die, Not [Noth], die.

trowser, n. Hose, die.
true, adj. wahr.
trunk, n. Koffer, der, -s.
truth, n. Wahrheit, die.
try, v. versuchen, probieren [probiren].
tub, n. Butte, die, Wanne, die.
Tuesday, n. Dienstag, der, -s.
Turk, pr. n. Türke, der, -n.
Turkey, pr. n. Türkei, die.
turn, v. drehen.
twelve, num. zwölf; the twelfth, der, die, das zwölfte.
twenty, num. zwanzig; the twentieth, der, die, das zwanzigste.
twice, adv. zweimal [zwei Mal].
twirling-stick, n. Quirl, der, -s
twist, v. drehen.
two, num. zwei.

ugly, adj. häßlich.
umbrella, n. Regenschirm, der -(e)s.
uncle, n. Onkel, der, -s, Oheim der, -(e)s.
under, prep. unter.
understand, v. verstehen, irr.
undress, v. auskleiden, sep.
unfortunate, adj. unglücklich.
unhappy, adj. unglücklich.
united, adj. vereinigt, einig.
universe, n. Weltall, das, -s.
unjust, adj. ungerecht.
unless, conj. wenn nicht.
unripe, adj. unreif.
unskilful, adj. ungeschickt.
until, conj. bis.
unwell, adj. unwohl.
up, adv. auf, herauf, hinauf; up to, bis (zu), prep.
upon, prep. auf.
use, n. Gebrauch, der, -(e)s.
use, v. brauchen.

useful, adj. nützlich.
usual, adj. gebräuchlich, gewöhnlich.

vacation, n. Ferien, die, pl.
vain, adj. eitel; in vain, vergeblich, umsonst.
valley, n. Thal, das, -(e)s.
veal, n. Kalbfleisch, das, -es.
vegetables, n. Gemüse, das, -s.
veil, n. Schleier, der, -s.
verb, n. Zeitwort, das, -(e)s.
very, adv. sehr.
vest, n. Weste, die.
Vienna, pr. n. Wien, -s.
village, n. Dorf, das, -(e)s.
vinegar, n. Essig, der, -s.
vineyard, n. Weinberg, der, -(e)s.
violet, n. Veilchen, das, -s.
violin, n. Violine, die.
visit, v. besuchen.
visit, n. Besuch, der, -(e)s.
voice, n. Stimme, die.
volume, n. Band, der, -(e)s.

wagon, n. Wagen, der, -s.
waistcoat, n. Weste, die.
wait, v. warten.
wake, v. wecken.
walk, v. gehen, irr.
walk, n. Spaziergang, der, -(e)s; to take a walk, spazieren gehen; hour's walk, Wegstunde, die.
wall, n. Mauer, die; Wand, die (finished wall inside the house).
walnut, n. Wallnuß, die; walnut-tree, Wallnußbaum, der, -s.
want, v. brauchen, wünschen, wollen, irr.
war, n. Krieg, der, -(e)s.
wardrobe, n. Schrank, der, -(e)s.
warm, adj. warm.

**wash,** v. waſchen, *irr.*

**watch,** n. Uhr, die.

**watchmaker,** n. Uhrmacher, der, –8.

**water,** n. Waſſer, das, –8.

**water,** v. tränken.

**wave,** n. Welle, die.

**way,** n. Weg, der, –(e)8.

**we,** pron. wir.

**weak,** adj. ſchwach.

**wear,** v. tragen, *irr.*

**weather,** n. Wetter, das, –8.

**Wednesday,** n. Mittwoch, der, –8.

**week,** n. Woche, die.

**weep,** v. weinen.

**weigh,** v. wiegen, *irr.*

**well,** adj. and adv. wohl, gut; **well-mannered,** artig.

**well,** n. Brunnen, der, –8.

**wet,** adj. naß.

**what,** pron. was; adj. welcher, welche, welches; **what kind of (a),** was für ein, was für; **what is your name?** wie heißen S..?; *with prepositions* wo *or* wor (*before vowels*), *and the preposition attached:* **of what,** wovon, **in what,** worin, etc.

**wheat,** n. Weizen, der, –8.

**wheelwright,** n. Wagner, der, –8.

**when,** adv. and conj. wann; wenn, als.

**whence,** adv. woher.

**where,** adv. wo, wohin (whither).

**whether,** conj. ob.

**which,** pron. welcher, welche, welches, der, die, das; *referring to things and preceded by preposition often rendered by* wo *or* wor (*before vowels*), *and preposition annexed:* **for which,** wofür, **at which,** woran.

**while,** conj. während.

**whilst,** conj. indem.

**whistle,** v. pfeifen, *irr.*

**whistle,** n. Pfeife, die.

**white,** adj. weiß.

**who,** pron.; *rel.* welcher, welche, welches, der, die, das; wer (**he who**); *interr.* wer?

**why,** adv. warum.

**wide,** adj. weit, breit.

**widow,** n. Wiſve [Wittwe], die.

**widower,** n. Witwer [Wittwer], der, –8.

**wife,** n. Frau, die, Gattin, die, Gemahlin, die.

**wild,** adj. wild.

**will,** v. wollen, *irr.;* werden, *irr.* (*future tense*).

**will,** n. Wille(n), der, –ns.

**willingly,** adv. gern.

**William,** pr. n. Wilhelm, der, –8.

**win,** v. gewinnen, *irr.*

**wind,** n. Wind, der, –(e)8.

**window,** n. Fenſter, das, –8.

**wine,** n. Wein, der, –8.

**wing,** n. Flügel, der, –8.

**winter,** n. Winter, der, –8.

**wise,** adj. weiſe.

**wish,** v. wünſchen, wollen, *irr.*

**with,** prep. mit, bei.

**within,** prep. innerhalb; binnen.

**without,** prep. außerhalb; ohne.

**wolf,** n. Wolf, der, –(e)8.

**woman,** n. Frau, die.

**wonder,** n. Wunder, das, –8.

**wonder,** v. wundern; **I wonder,** ich wundre mich, es wundert mich.

**wood,** n. Holz, das, –es; Wald, der, –(e)8.

**wooden,** adj. hölzern.

**work,** n. Arbeit, die.

**work,** v. arbeiten.

**workman,** n. Arbeiter, der, –8.

**world,** *n.* Welt, die.

**worm,** *n.* Wurm, der, –(e)s.

**worth(y),** *adj.* wert [werth].

**wound,** *n.* Wunde, die.

**wound,** *v.* verwunden.

**wrecked, to get,** *v.* scheitern.

**write,** *v.* schreiben, *irr.*

**writer,** *n.* Schriftsteller, der, –s.

**writing-book,** *n.* Schreibheft, das, –(e)s.

**wrong,** *n.* Unrecht, das, –(e)s, Böses (*adj. used as noun*).

**wrong,** *adj.* unrecht.

**Xaver,** *pr. n.* Xaver, der, –s.

**yard,** *n.* Elle, die; Hof, der, –(e)s (court).

**year,** *n.* Jahr, das, –(e)s.

**yes,** *adv.* ja; **yes indeed,** jawohl; **oh yes,** ja doch.

**yesterday,** *adv.* gestern; **day before yesterday,** vorgestern, *adv.*

**yet,** *adv.* noch, doch, dennoch; **not yet,** noch nicht.

**yonder,** *adv.* dort.

**you,** *pron.* du, dir (*dat.*), dich (*acc.*); ihr, euch (*dat. and acc.*); Sie, Ihnen (*dat.*), Sie (*acc.*); man (*indef.*).

**young,** *adj.* jung.

**your,** *poss. adj.* dein, deine, dein; euer, euere, euer; Ihr, Ihre, Ihr.

**yours,** *poss. pron.* deiner, deine, deines, der, die, das deine, der, die, das deinige; eurer, eure, eures, der, die, das eure, der, die, das eurige; Ihrer, Ihre, Ihres, der, die, das Ihre, der, die, das Ihrige.

**yourself,** *refl. pron.* dir, dich, euch, sich; **you yourself,** du selbst; ihr selbst; Sie selbst.

**youth,** *n.* Jugend, die; Jüngling, der, –(e)s.

# GERMAN TEXT-BOOKS

PUBLISHED BY

# HENRY HOLT & CO., NEW YORK.

*These books are bound in cloth unless otherwise indicated.*

## Grammars and Exercise Books.

**Blackwell's German Prefixes and Suffixes.** By J. S. BLACKWELL, Professor in the University of Missouri. 16mo. 187 pp.

**Huss's Conversation in German.** By H. C. O. HUSS, Professor of Modern Languages in Princeton College. 12mo. 280 pp.

**Joynes-Otto First Book in German.** For young pupils. By EMIL OTTO. Revised by EDWARD S. JOYNES, Professor in the South Carolina College. 12mo. 116 pp. Boards.

**Joynes-Otto Introductory German Lessons, The.** New edition, with full vocabularies. By Prof. EDWARD S. JOYNES. 12mo. 252 pp.

**Keetels's Oral Method with German.** By JEAN GUSTAVE KEETELS. 12mo. 371 pp.

**Otis's Elementary German.** By CHARLES P. OTIS. 16mo. 832 pp.

☞ *There are two editions of this book: I. In German type; II. In Roman type, which edition will only be sent when specially ordered.*

**Otto's German Conversation Grammar.** By Dr. EMIL OTTO. New edition, revised, and in part re-written, by WM. COOK. 12mo. Half roan. 591 pp.

**Otto's Elementary German Grammar.** With a vocabulary by GEORGE MORITZ WAHL. 12mo. 315 pp.

**Otto's Translating English into German.** By Dr. EMIL OTTO. Edited by Prof. RHODES MASSIE and Prof. EDWARD S. JOYNES. 12mo. 167 pp.

**Spanhoofd's Deutsche Grammatik.** By A. W. SPANHOOFD, teacher in St. Paul's School, N. H. 16mo. 187 pp.

**Wenckebach und Schrakamp's Deutsche Grammatik für Amerikaner.** By CARLA WENCKEBACH, Professor in Wellesley College, and JOSEPHA SCHRAKAMP. 12mo. 291 pp.

**Whitney's Compendious German Grammar.** By WM. D. WHITNEY, Professor in Yale University. 12mo. 472 pp. Half roan.

**Whitney's Brief German Grammar**, based on the author's "Compendious German Grammar." By WM. D. WHITNEY. 16mo. 143 pp.

**Whitney-Klemm German by Practice.** By Dr. L. R. KLEMM. Edited by WILLIAM D. WHITNEY. 12mo. 305 pp.

## Natural Method and Conversation Books.

**Game of German Conversation.** By MME. F. JEFF TENSLER.

**Heness's Der neue Leitfaden.** Beim Unterricht in der deutschen Sprache. By GOTTLIEB HENESS. 12mo. 403 pp.

**Heness's Der Sprechlehrer unter seinen Schülern.** By GOTTLIEB HENESS. 12mo. 187 pp.

**Kaiser's Erstes Lehrbuch.** By H. C. KAISER, Ph.D. 12mo. 128 pp.

Schrakamp und Van Daell's Das Deutsche Buch.  By A. N. VAN DAELL
and JOSEPHA Schrakamp.  12mo.  144 pp.

Sprechen Sie Deutsch ?  18mo.  147 pp.  Boards.

Stern's Studien und Plaudereien.  First Series.  By SIGMON M. STERN,
Director of Stern's School of Languages.  12mo.  262 pp.

Stern's Studien und Plaudereien.  Second Series.  By SIGMON M.
STERN and MENCO STERN.  12mo.  380 pp.

Wenckebach's Deutscher Anschauungs-Unterricht.  By CARLA and
HELENE WENCKEBACH.  12mo.  451 pp.

Williams's German Conversation and Composition.  By ALONZO WIL-
LIAMS, A.M., Professor in Brown University.  12mo.  147 pp.

## Reading Books.

Fouqué's Undine.  With introduction, notes, and vocabulary, by H. C.
G. VON JAGEMANN, Professor in the Indiana University.  190 pp.

Hey's Fabeln für Kinder.  Illustrated by OTTO SPECKTER.  With
vocabulary.  (*In roman type.*)  12mo.  52 pp.  Boards.

Joynes-Otto Introductory German Reader.  By Dr. EMIL OTTO.
With notes and vocabulary by Prof. EDWARD S. JOYNES.  12mo.
282 pp.

Klemm's Lese- und Sprachbuecher.  In sieben Kreisen.  By Dr. L. R.
KLEMM.

Klemm's Abriss der Geschichte der deutschen Literatur.  Kreis VIII.
12mo.  385 pp.

Meissner's Aus meiner Welt.  Geschichten für Grosse und Kleine.
With vocabulary by CARLA WENCKEBACH.  12mo.  127 pp.

Otis's Grimm's Maerchen.  Selected and edited, with introduction,
notes, and vocabulary, by CHARLES P. OTTIS.  151 pp.

Otto's German Reader.  By Prof. E. P. EVANS.  12mo.  239 pp.
Half roan.

Schrakamp's Erzaehlungen aus der deutschen Geschichte.  By JOSEPHA
SCHRAKAMP.  12mo.  286 pp.

Simonson's German Ballad Book.  Prepared by Prof. L. SIMONSON, of
the Hartford (Ct.) High School.  12mo.  304 pp.

Storme's Easy German Reading.  By G. STORME.  16mo.  356 pp.

Wenckebach's deutsches Lesebuch.  By CARLA and HELENE WENCKE-
BACH.  12mo.  316 pp.

Wenckebach's Die schoensten deutschen Lieder.  By CARLA and
HELENE WENCKEBACH.  12mo.  363 pp.

Whitney's German Reader.  By WILLIAM D. WHITNEY, Professor in
Yale University.  12mo.  523 pp.  Half roan.

Whitney-Klemm Elementary German Reader.  By Dr. L. R. KLEMM.
Edited by Prof. W. D. WHITNEY.  12mo.  237 pp.

## Dictionary.

Whitney's Compendious German Dictionary.  (German-English and
English-German.)  By WILLIAM D. WHITNEY.  8vo.  900 pp.

*A complete catalogue and price-list of Henry Holt & Co.'s educa-
tional publications will be sent on application.*

## Whitney's German Texts.

Selected and annotated under the general editorship of Professor WILLIAM D. WHITNEY. 16mo. Cloth.

Goethe's Iphigenie auf Tauris. With an introduction and notes by FRANK-LIN CARTER, President of Williams College. 113 pp.

—— Faust. I. Theil. With an introduction and notes by WILLIAM COOK, late Professor in Harvard University. 290 pp.

Lessing's Minna von Barnhelm. With an introduction and notes by W. D. Whitney, Professor in Yale University. 188 pp.

—— Nathan der Weise. With an introduction and notes by H. C. G. BRANDT, Professor in Hamilton College. 158 pp.

Schiller's Wilhelm Tell. With an introduction and notes by A. SACHTLE-BEN, Professor in the College of Charleston, S. C. 199 pp.

——·Maria Stuart. With an introduction and notes by EDWARD S. JOYNES, Professor in South Carolina College. 222 pp.

## Seidensticker's German Scientific Monographs.

### With notes. 12mo. Paper.

No. I. Über Goethe's Naturwissenschaftliche Arbeiten. Von H. HELMHOLTZ. 53 pp.

No II. Über Bakterien, die Kleinsten lebenden Wesen. Von Dr. FERDINAND COHN. 55 pp.

## Student's Collection of Classic German Plays.

### 12mo. Paper.

Goethe's Hermann und Dorothea. With notes by CALVIN THOMAS. 104 pp.

—— Egmont. Edited by Professor WILLIAM STEFFEN. 118 pp.

Koerner's Zriny. With an introduction and notes by EDWARD R. RUGGLES, Professor in Dartmouth College. 126 pp.

Lessing's Emilia Galotti. With notes. 82 pp.

Schiller's Der Neffe als Onkel. With notes and a vocabulary by A. CLEMENT. 99 pp.

—— Jungfrau Von Orleans. Edited by Rev. A. B. NICHOLS, Instructor in German in Harvard University. 203 pp.

—— Wallenstein's Lager. With notes by E. C. F. KRAUSS. 60 pp.

—— Die Piccolomini. With notes by E. C. F. KRAUSS. 139 pp.

—— Wallenstein's Tod. With notes by E. C. F. KRAUSS. 210 pp.

—— Wallenstein, complete in one volume. Cloth.

## College Series of German Plays.

### 12mo. Paper.

Einer muss heiraten, by WILHELMI; and Eigensinn, by BENEDIX. With notes. 63 pp.

Three German Comedies. I. Er ist nicht eifersuechtig, by ELZ; II. Der Weiberfeind, by BENEDIX; III. Im Wartesalon erster Classe, by MUELLER. With notes. 24 pp.

Der Bibliothekar. By GUSTAV VON MOSER. With notes. 162 pp.

Die Journalisten. By GUSTAV FREYTAG. With notes. 178 pp.

Zopf und Schwert. By GUTZKOW. With notes. 173 pp.

Englisch. By GOERNER. With notes by A. H. EDGREN. 61 pp.

Badekuren. By PUTLITZ. With notes. 69 pp.

## Stern's Selected German Comedies.

Selected and Edited by Professor S. M. STERN. 12mo. Paper.

Ein Knopf. By JULIUS ROSEN. 41 pp.

Der Schimmel. By G. VON MOSER. 55 pp.

Sie hat ihr herz entdeckt. By W. MUELLER VON KOENIGSWINTER. 79 pp.

Simson und Delila. By EMIL CLAAR. 55 pp.

Er sucht einen Vetter. By JUNGMAN. 49 pp.

Er muss tanzen. By C. A. PAUL. 51 pp.

Gaenschen von Buchenau. By W. FRIEDRICH. 59 pp.

## German Plays for Children.

Kinder-Comoedien. By various authors. Edited and annotated in German by Professor TH. HENESS. Five plays in one volume 12mo. 141 pp.

## Unterhaltungs Bibliothek. (12mo. Paper.)

Andersen's Bilderbuch ohne Bilder. With notes and vocabulary by Professor L. SIMONSON of the Hartford (Ct.) High School. 104 pp.

Die Eisjungfrau u. andere Geschichten. With notes by E. C. F. KRAUSS. 150 pp.

Auerbach's Auf Wache; Roquette's Der gefrorene Kuss. The two in one volume. With notes. 126 pp.

Carove's Das Maerchen ohne Ende. With notes. 45 pp.

Ebers' eine Frage. With introduction and notes. 117 pp.

Eichendorff's Aus dem Leben eines Taugenichts. 132 pp.

Fouqué's Undine. With a glossary of the principal words and phrases. 137 pp. *See also Jagemann's edition under Reading Books.*

—— Sintram und seine Gefaehrten. 114 pp.

Grimm's Die Venus vor Milo; Rafael und Michel-Angelo. 139 pp.

Grimm's Kinder- und Hausmaerchen. With notes. 228 pp. *See also Otis's edition under Reading Books.*

Hauff's Das kalte Herz. 61 pp.

Heine's Die Harzreise. With introduction and notes. 97 pp.

Heyse's Anfang und Ende. 54 pp.

—— Die Einsamen. 44 pp.

Hillern's Hoeher als die Kirche. With notes and vocabulary. 46 pp.

Muegge's Riukan Voss. 55 pp.

—— Signa die Seterin. 71 pp.

Mueller's Deutsche Liebe. With English notes. 131 pp.

Nathusius' Tagebuch eines armen Fraeuleins. 163 pp.

Ploennies' Princessin Ilse. With notes by J. M. MERRICK. 45 pp.

Putlitz's Was sich der wald erzaehlt. 69 pp.

—— Vergissmeinnicht. With English notes. 44 pp.

Riehl's Der Fluch der Schoenheit. With introduction and notes by FRANCIS L. KENDALL. 77 pp.

Schiller's Das Lied von der Glocke. With introduction and notes by CHARLES P. OTIS, Ph.D. 70 pp.

Storm's Immensee. With notes. 34 pp.

Tieck's Die Elfen; Das Rothkaeppchen. With notes by Professor L. SIMONSON. 41 pp.

Vilmar and Richter's German Epic Tales. Told in prose. Die Nibe-

PUBLISHED BY

# HENRY HOLT & CO., New York.

*These books are bound in cloth unless otherwise indicated.*

————◆————

## Grammars and Exercise Books.

**Borel's Grammaire Française.** À l'usage des Anglais. Par Eugène Borel. Revised by E. B. Coe. 12mo. 450 pp. Half roan.

**Delille's Condensed French Instruction.** By C. J. Delille. 18mo. 148 pp.

**Eugène's Student's Comparative French Grammar.** To which are added French-English Exercises. Revised by L. H. Buckingham, Ph.D. 12mo. 284 pp.

**Eugène's Elementary French Lessons.** Revised and edited by L. H. Buckingham, Ph.D. 12mo. 126 pp.

**Gasc's The Translator.**—English into French. By Professors Gasc, L. Brun, and others. 12mo. 220 pp.

**Gibert's French Manual.** A French Pronouncing Grammar for Young Students. By M. Gibert. 12mo. 112 pp.

**Julien's Petites Leçons** de Conversation et de Grammaire. By F. Julien. Square 12mo. 222 pp.

**Otto's French Conversation Grammar.** Revised by Ferdinand Bôcher, Professor of Modern Languages in Harvard University. 12mo. 489 pp. Half roan.

**Pylodet's Beginning French.** Exercises in Pronouncing, Spelling, and Translating. By L. Pylodet. 16mo. 180 pp. Boards.

**Sadler's Translating English into French.** By P. Sadler. Revised and annotated by Prof. C. F. Gillette. 12mo. 285 pp.

**The Joynes-Otto Introductory French Lessons.** By Edward S. Joynes, Professor in University of South Carolina. 12mo. 275 pp.

**The Joynes-Otto First Book in French.** By Edward S. Joynes. 12mo. 116 pp. Boards.

**Whitney's French Grammar.** By William D. Whitney, Professor in Yale University. 12mo. 442 pp. Half roan.

**Whitney's Practical French.** Taken from the author's larger Grammar, and supplemented by conversations and idiomatic phrases. By Professor W. D. Whitney.

**Whitney's Brief French Grammar.** Systematically arranged, with exercises. By William D. Whitney. 16mo. 177 pp.

## Natural Method and Conversation Books.

**Alliot's Contes et Nouvelles.** Suivis de Conversations, d'Exercices de Grammaire. Par Madame L. Alliot. 12mo.

**Aubert's Colloquial French Drill.** By E. Aubert, Professor in the Normal College, New York City. Part I. 16mo. 66 pp. Part II. 118 pp.

**Le Jeu des Auteurs.** 96 Cards in a Box.

**Moutonnier's Les Premiers Pas dans l'Etude du Français** par la méthode naturelle. Par C. Moutonnier. 12mo. 197 pp. Illustrated.

**Pour Apprendre a Parler Français.** 12mo. 191 pp.

**Parlez-vous Français?** A pocket manual of French and English Conversation, with hints for pronunciation and a list of the irregular verbs. 18mo. 111 pp. Boards.

**Riodu's Lucie.** Familiar Conversations in French and English. By Mme. A. Riodu. 12mo. 128 pp.

**Stern & Méras' Étude Progressive** de la Langue Française. By SIGMON M. STERN and BAPTISTE MÉRAS. 12mo. 266 pp.

**Witcomb & Bellenger's French Conversation.** Dialogues on Familiar Subjects, to which is annexed the Summary of French Grammar, by DELILLE. 18mo. 259 pp.

## Reading Books.

**Æsop's Fables in French.** With vocabulary. 16mo. 337 pp.

**Alliot's Les Auteurs Contemporains.** Extraits choisis d'œuvres diverses, avec Notices Biographiques et Notes. By Mme. L. ALLIOT. 12mo. 371 pp.

**Aubert's Littérature Française.** Première Année. By E. AUBERT. 16mo. 338 pp.

**Bocher s Progressive French Reader.** With notes and vocabulary by F. BÔCHER, Professor in Harvard University. 12mo. 291 pp. Half roan.

**Fisher's Easy French Reading.** Historical tales and anecdotes, arranged with foot-notes, containing translations of the principal words. 16mo. 253 pp.

**Fleury's L'Histoire de France.** Racontée à la Jeunesse. Par M. LAMÉ FLEURY. 16mo. 372 pp.

**De Janon's Recueil de Poésies.** À l'usage de la Jeunesse Américaine. Par MLLE. CAMILLE DE JANON. 16mo. 186 pp.

**Joynes-Otto Introductory French Reader, The.** Edited, with notes and vocabulary, by EDWARD S. JOYNES. 12mo. 163 pp.

**Julien's Practical and Conversational Reader** in French and English. By F. JULIEN. Square 12mo. 182 pp.

**Lacombe's Petite Histoire du Peuple Français.** By PAUL LACOMBE. With Grammatical and Explanatory Notes by JULES BUÉ. 12mo. 212 pp.

**La Fontaine's Fables Choisies.** Edited, with notes, by LEON DELBOS. 12mo. 119 pp. Boards.

**Pylodet's Beginner French Reader.** With a complete vocabulary. Arranged by L. PYLODET. 16mo. 235 pp. Boards.

**Pylodet's Second French Reader.** With a complete French-English vocabulary. Compiled by L. PYLODET. Illustrated. 12mo. 277 pp.

**Pylodet's La Littérature Française Classique.** Tirées des Matinées Littéraires d' EDOUARD MENNECHET. 12mo. 393 pp.

**Pylodet's La Littérature Française Contemporaine.** Recueil en prose et en vers. 12mo. 310 pp.

**Pylodet's Gouttes de Rosée.** Petit Trésor poétique des Jeunes Personnes. 18mo. 188 pp.

**Pylodet's La Mère l'Oie.** Poésies, énigmes, chansons et rondes enfantines. Illustré. 8vo. 80 pp.

**Whitney's Short French Reader.** With notes and vocabulary. By W. D. WHITNEY. 16mo.

## Dictionaries.

**Bellow's French and English Dictionary** for the Pocket. 32mo. 600 pp.
———— The same. Larger print. 12mo. 600 pp. Half roan.

**Gasc's New Dictionary of the French and English Languages.** By FERDINAND E. A. GASC. 8vo. French-English part, 600 pp. English-French part, 586 pp. One volume.

**Gasc's Improved Modern Pocket Dictionary.** By F. A. E. GASC. 18mo. French-English part, 261 pp. English-French part, 387 pp. One volume.

## Students' Collection of Classic French Plays.

The first six with full notes by Prof. E. S. JOYNES. The last three with notes by LEON DELBOS, M.A. 12mo. Paper.

Le Cid. Par CORNEILLE. 110 pp.
Athalie. Par RACINE. 117 pp.
Le Misanthrope. Par MOLIERE. 130 pp. .
L'Avare. Par MOLIERE. 132 pp.
Esther. Par RACINE. 66 pp.
Cinna. Par CORNEILLE. 87 pp.
Le Bourgeois Gentilhomme. Par MOLIERE. 140 pp.
Horace. Par CORNEILLE. 78 pp.
Les Plaideurs. Par RACINE. 80 pp.

The foregoing in 3 vols., three plays in each, in the above order. 12mo. Cloth.

## Romantic French Drama. (12mo. Flexible covers.)

Ruy Blas. By VICTOR HUGO. With notes by RENA A. MICHAELS. 117 pp.

## College Series of Modern French Plays.

With English notes by Prof. FERDINAND BÔCHER. 12mo. Paper.

La Joie Fait Peur. Par Mme. DE GIRARDIN. 46 pp.
La Bataille de Dames. Par SCRIBE et LEGOUVÉ. 81 pp.
La Maison de Penarvan. Par JULES SANDEAU. 72 pp.
La Poudre aux Yeux. Par LABICHE et MARTIN. 59 pp.
Jean Baudry. Par AUGUSTE VACQUERIE. 72 pp.
Les Petits Oiseaux. Par LABICHE et DELACOUR. 70 pp.
Mademoiselle de la Seiglière. Par J. SANDEAU. 99 pp.
Le Roman d'un Jeune Homme Pauvre. Par O. FEUILLET. 100 pp.
Les Doigts de Fée. Par E. SCRIBE. 111 pp.

Above in 2 vols. Cloth. Vol I. containing the first five, Vol. II. the last four.

## Modern French Comedies. (12mo. Paper.)

Le Village. Par O. FEUILLET. 34 pp.
La Cagnotte. Par MM. EUGENE LABICHE et A. DELACOUR. 83 pp.
Les Femmes qui Pleurent. Par MM. SIRAUDIN et LAMBERT THIBOUST. 28 pp.
Les Petites Misères de la Vie Humaine. Par M. CLAIRVILLE. 35 pp.
Le Niaise de Saint Flour. Par BAYARD et LEMOINE. 38 pp.
Un Caprice. Par ALFRED DE MUSSET.
Trois Proverbes. Par TH. LECLERQ. 68 pp. With vocabulary.
Valerie. Par SCRIBE. 39 pp. With vocabulary.
Le Collier de Perles. Par MAZERES. 56 pp. With vocabulary.

## Selected French Comedies.

Original text, with a close English version on opposite pages.

En Wagon. Comédie en 1 acte. Par EUGENE VERCONSIN. 12mo. 44 pp.
C'était Gertrude. Comédie en 1 acte. Par EUGENE VERCONSIN. 12mo. 54 pp.

## French Plays for Children. (12mo. Paper.)

La Petite Maman, par Mme. DE M.; Le Bracelet, par Mme. DE GAULE. 38 pp.
La Vieille Cousine, par E. SOUVESTRE; Les Ricochets. 52 pp.
Le Testament de Madame Patural, par E. SOUVESTRE; La Demoiselle de St. Cyr, par DROHOYOWSKA. 54 pp.
La Loterie de Francfort, par E. SOUVESTRE. La Jeune Savante, par Mme. CURO. 47 pp.

## French Plays for Girls. (12mo. Paper.)

## Bibliotheque d'Instruction et de Recreation.

12mo volumes. Paper or Cloth.

Achard's Clos-Pommier, et Les Prisonniers du Caucase. Par XAVIER
DE MAISTRE. Cloth. 144 pp.

Achard's Clos-Pommier. Paper. 106 pp.

Bédollière's Mère Michel. With vocabulary. Cloth. 138 pp.
—— The same. Paper.

Biographies des Musiciens Célèbres. Cloth. 271 pp.
—— The same. Paper.

Carraud et Segur's Contes (Les Petites Filles Modèles, par Mme. DE SEGUR,
et Les Goûters de la Grand'mère, par Mme. Z. CARRAUD). With a list of
difficult phrases. Cloth. 193 pp.

Carraud's Les Gouters de la Grand'mère. With a list of difficult
phrases. Paper. 95 pp.

Choix de Contes Contemporains. With notes. By B. F. O'CONNOR. Cloth.
300 pp.
—— The same. Paper.

Erckmann-Chatrian's Conscrit de 1813. With notes. By Prof. F.
BÔCHER. Cloth. 286 pp.
—— The same. Paper.
—— Le Blocus. With notes. By Prof. F. BÔCHER. Cloth. 258 pp.
—— The same. Paper.
—— Madame Thérèse. With notes. By Prof. F. BÔCHER. Cloth. 216 pp.
—— The same. Paper.

Fallet's Princes de l'Art. Cloth. 334 pp.
—— The same. Paper.

Feuillet's Roman d'un Jeune Homme Pauvre. Cloth. 204 pp.
—— The same. Paper.

Féval's 'Chouans et Bleus.' With notes. Cloth. 188 pp.
—— The same. Paper.

Foa's Contes Biographiques. With vocabulary. Cloth. 189 pp.
—— The same. Paper.
—— Petit Robinson de Paris. With vocabulary. Cloth. 166 pp.
—— The same. Paper.

Macé's Bouchée de Pain. (L'Homme.) With vocabulary. Cloth. 260 pp.
—— The same. Paper.

De Maistre's Voyage Autour de ma Chambre. Paper. 117 pp.
—— Les Prisonniers du Caucase. Paper. 88 pp.

Merimée's Columba. Cloth. 179 pp.
—— The same. Paper.

Porchat's Trois Mois sous la Neige. Cloth. 160 pp.
—— The same. Paper.

Pressensé's Rosa. With vocabulary. By L. PYLODET. Cloth. 285.
—— The same. Paper.

Saint-Germain's Pour une Épingle. With vocabulary. Cloth. 174 pp.
—— The same. Paper.

Sand's Petite Fadette. Cloth. 205 pp.
—— The same. Paper.

Ségur et Carraud's Contes. (Petites Filles Modèles; Les Goûters de la
Grand'mère.) Cloth. 193 pp.

Ségur's Les Petites Filles Modèles. Paper. 98 pp.

Souvestre's Philosophe sous les Toits. Cloth. 137 pp.